DATE DUE

OCT 28 2015	

BRODART, CO. Cat. No. 23-221-003

To Form A More Perfect Union

A New Economic Interpretation
of the United States Constitution

ROBERT A. McGUIRE

OXFORD

UNIVERSITY PRESS

2003

OXFORD
UNIVERSITY PRESS

Oxford New York
Auckland Bangkok Buenos Aires Cape Town Chennai
Dar es Salaam Delhi Hong Kong Istanbul Karachi Kolkata
Kuala Lumpur Madrid Melbourne Mexico City Mumbai Nairobi
São Paulo Shanghai Taipei Tokyo Toronto

Published by Oxford University Press, Inc.
198 Madison Avenue, New York, New York 10016

www.oup.com

Oxford is a registered trademark of Oxford University Press

Library of Congress Cataloging-in-Publication Data
McGuire, Robert A. (Robert Allen), 1948–
    To form a more perfect union: a new economic interpretation of the United States Constitution /
by Robert A. McGuire
        p.   cm.
    Includes bibliographical references and index.
    ISBN 0-19-513970-4
    1. United States. Constitutional Convention (1787).   2. Constitutional history—United States.
3. Constitutional law—Economic aspects—United States.   4. United States—Economic conditions—
To 1865.   I. Title.
KF4520 .M393 2001
342.73′029—dc21   2001032185

9 8 7 6 5 4 3 2 1
Printed in the United States of America
on acid-free paper

To DAWN

Acknowledgments

The ideas and research involved in this examination of the formation of the Constitution are based upon a long collaboration with my former colleague, Robert L. Ohsfeldt, now with the University of Iowa. The collaboration started in 1983 while we were both faculty members in the economics department at Ball State University in Muncie, Indiana, and resulted in the publication of a number of articles on the Constitution. A preliminary analysis of the Constitution, in which the idea of a "new economic interpretation" first appeared in print, appeared in an article co-authored with Ohsfeldt in the *Journal of Economic History* (June 1984). Another article co-authored with Ohsfeldt, which serves as the basis of the findings presented in chapter 3, also appeared in the *Journal of Economic History* (March 1986). All econometric findings reported in chapter 3, though, are updated estimations of the issues previously discussed in print, employing new data corrected for a small number of errors discovered in the original data. Chapter 3 also includes many econometric findings based on new estimations conducted specifically for this book. The findings reported in chapters 4 and 5 have appeared, in altered form, in previously published articles. The findings reported in chapter 4 appeared in the *American Journal of Political Science* (May 1988) in an article published by myself. The findings reported in chapter 5 appeared in an article co-authored with Ohsfeldt in *Research in Law and Economics* (1997). The basis of the findings reported in chapter 6 is an article co-authored with Ohsfeldt in the *American Economic Review* (March 1989) and a chapter co-authored with Ohsfeldt in *The Federalist Papers and the New Institutionalism* (1989). All econometric findings presented in chapter 6, however, are updated estimations of the issues originally estimated and previously published, employing data corrected for a small number of errors found in the original data. In addition, chapter 6 includes many econometric findings based on new estimations conducted specifically for this book. All findings reported in chapter 7 are based on new estimations conducted specifically for this book; the genesis of the chapter, though, is an unpublished paper also co-authored with Ohsfeldt.

Over the years, many individuals have contributed to the research upon which the book is based. I thank the following individuals for their valuable comments and suggestions made years ago on earlier versions of parts of the research that appear in this book: John Antel, Richard D. Brown, Philip R. P. Coelho, Jere R. Daniell, Paul David, Lance Davis, Stanley L. Engerman, Richard A. Epstein, Albert Fishlow, Stephan F. Gohmann, Claudia Goldin, Bernard Grofman, Thomas Hazzlet, Robert Higgs, James H. Hutson, Calvin C. Jillson, Stanley Lebergott, Gary Libecap, Leonard P. Liggio, David E. Kaun, Jackson Turner Main, the late Paul McGouldrick, Gary Miller, Douglass C. North, Roger L. Ransom, William H. Riker, Hugh Rockoff, Eugene Silberburg, Robert Triest, John Joseph Wallis, Samuel Williamson, and Donald A. Wittman. In addition, I thank my former colleagues in the economics department at Ball State University for numerous conversations concerning the topic of this book.

I am grateful to the following individuals for their help in locating data: Trudi J. Abel, Project Archivist, New Jersey Historical Society; Jerry C. Cashion, Research Supervisor, North Carolina Division of Archives and History; Ruth Clayman, Senior Librarian, New York State Library; Elizabeth B. Corr, Lineage Research Chairman, Rhode Island State Society, Daughters of the American Revolution; Barbara E. Deibler, Rare Book Librarian, Pennsylvania State Library; Randy Goss, Senior Archivist, Delaware Bureau of Archives and Records Management; Patricia Hewitt, Reference Services, Massachusetts State Library; Owen S. Ireland, State University of New York at Brockport; Jane W. McWilliams, Senior Research Associate, Legislative History Project, Maryland State Archives; Zelda Moore, Reference Librarian, Bureau of Government Information Services, New Hampshire State Library; Jerome Nadelhaft, University of Maine; E. Lee Shepard, Archivist, Virginia Historical Society; Louis M. Waddell, Associate Historian, Division of History, Pennsylvania Historical and Museum Commission; and Wesley L. Wilson, Head, Maryland Department, Enoch Pratt Free Library, City of Baltimore.

I especially thank Norman K. Risjord, who many years ago provided the raw data from his study of politics in the Chesapeake and answered various questions about the data, and Forrest McDonald, who also many years ago answered questions concerning data contained in his 1958 study. Mathew Martin and Diego Vacaflores provided research assistance on the analysis in chapter 7. Jeanette Quinn, Sarah Snelting, and Sarah Thorley provided much appreciated assistance in typing portions of the book manuscript. I am particularly grateful to Price Fishback for encouraging me to write this book—without his urging, it would not have been undertaken. But the biggest debt still is to Robert L. Ohsfeldt, who contributed so much to this book yet was not part of the final product. I will forever be grateful to Ohsfeldt for his insight and diligence during our long collaboration, as well as for the real enjoyment I received from working with him over many years.

Akron, Ohio   Robert A. McGuire
2002

Contents

TO FORM A MORE PERFECT UNION

Prologue:
A New Economic Interpretation

> It has been frequently remarked that it seems to have been
> reserved to the people of this country, by their conduct and
> example, to decide the important question, whether societies of
> men are really capable or not of establishing good government
> from reflection and choice, or whether they are forever destined
> to depend for their political constitutions on accident and
> force.
>
> Alexander Hamilton, The Federalist No. 1

The Constitution of the United States replaced the Articles of
Confederation as the law of the land when on June 21, 1788, New
Hampshire became the ninth state to ratify the Constitution. Ratification
by only nine of the thirteen states was required to adopt the Constitution.
Congress subsequently declared it in effect March 4, 1789. Under the
Articles, the American political system consisted of a loose confederation
of largely independent states with a weak central government. Under the
Constitution, the Articles were replaced with a political system that
consisted of a strong central government with little state sovereignty. This
change in political institutions was to have a profound influence on the
history of the United States.

As Alexander Hamilton so aptly observed, "this country" *did* establish its
Constitution "from reflection and choice." This "reflection and choice" leads
to many important questions: What factors explain the constitutional
choices of George Washington, James Madison, Alexander Hamilton,
and the other Founding Fathers? Why did they include a prohibition on
state paper-money issues in the Constitution? Why did they decide to
allow for duties and imposts on imports but not on exports? Why did they
fail to adopt a clause requiring a two-thirds majority in the national legislature to establish laws concerning trade or a clause giving the national
government an absolute veto over state laws? What factors account for
the choices of the ratifiers to adopt the Constitution? Were the commercial activities or the slaveholdings of the ratifiers primary motivating
factors in the ratification process?

Since the mid nineteenth century, literally hundreds of scholars have
studied and debated the possible explanations for this important change
in the fundamental political institution of our nation. Many historians
have concluded that the Constitution was drafted and adopted as a result

of a consensus that the Articles were fatally flawed. Other scholars have argued that the limitations of the Articles could have been eliminated without fundamentally altering the balance of power between the states and the national government. Others have suggested that the adoption of the Constitution was the product of conflict between various economic interests and social classes within the nation.

Despite the often intense scholarly debate during the twentieth century regarding the motivation for the design and adoption of the Constitution, a prevailing scholarly interpretation began to emerge in the late 1950s. What emerged as the prevailing interpretation is that the making of the Constitution cannot be understood primarily in terms of the economic or financial interests involved. However, the prevailing view is not that economic interests did not matter at all, but rather that an economic interpretation of the Constitution should not be taken very seriously, because, as everyone knows, there were few if any alignments of specific economic or financial interests among the founders.

What is unknown to all but a small group of economic historians and other social scientists is that a critical reexamination of the behavior of the Founding Fathers regarding the Constitution has been underway since the mid 1980s. The reexamination, which employs formal economics and modern statistical techniques, involves the application of an economic model of the founders' voting behavior, as well as the collection and processing of large amounts of data on the economic interests and other characteristics of the men who drafted and ratified the Constitution. These findings, which challenge the prevailing scholarly interpretation of the Constitution, are relatively unknown because they have been confined to scholarly journals intended primarily for economists and others interested in what are often technical issues. Few if any general historians, nor many specifically interested in the Constitution, are likely to know of these findings. This book for the first time brings together the results of this reexamination, making them available to a much wider audience, and presents a wealth of new quantitative findings (more than half those reported in the book) about the behavior of our Founding Fathers.

Because this reexamination of the framing and adoption of the Constitution so seriously challenges the prevailing interpretation among scholars, a summary of the more important findings and conclusions is essential to understanding just how at odds they are with the prevailing view.

1. Despite the view among many constitutional and historical scholars that scholarship on the Constitution has been rightly exorcised of the ghost of Charles A. Beard, there is one unambiguous conclusion that can be drawn from the present study: There *is* a valid economic interpretation of the Constitution. The idea of self-interest can explain the design and adoption of the Constitution. This does not mean that either the framers or the ratifiers were motivated by a greedy desire to "line their own pockets" or by some dialectic concept of class or social interests. Nor does it mean that some conspiracy among the founders or some fatalistic

concept of "economic determinism" explains the Constitution. What it does mean is that the pursuit of one's interests both in a narrow financial (or pecuniary) sense and in a broader, nonpecuniary sense can help explain the drafting and ratification of the Constitution.

2. The Constitution was neither drafted nor ratified by a group of disinterested and nonpartisan demigods motivated only, or even primarily, by high-minded political principles to promote the nation's interest. The fifty-five delegates at the Philadelphia Constitutional Convention of 1787 who drafted the Constitution were motivated by self-interest, in a broad sense, in choosing its design. These framers of the Constitution can be viewed as rational individuals who were making choices in designing the fundamental rules of governance for the nation. In doing so, they rationally weighed the expected costs and benefits of each clause they considered. They included a particular provision in the Constitution only if they expected the benefits from its inclusion to exceed the costs. The more than 1,600 delegates at the thirteen state ratifying conventions can be viewed as rational individuals who were making the choice to adopt the set of rules embodied in the Constitution as drafted in Philadelphia. In doing so, they rationally weighed the expected costs and benefits of their decision to ratify. They voted to ratify only if the benefits they expected from adoption of the set of rules embodied in the Constitution exceeded the costs. If not, they voted against ratification.

3. Contrary to the prevailing view that the framers' specific economic or financial interests cannot be principally identified with one side or the other of an issue, the evidence presented here indicates that their economic interests can be so identified. When specific issues arose at the Philadelphia convention that had a direct impact on important economic interests of the framers, their economic interests, even narrowly defined, significantly influenced the specific design of the Constitution, and the magnitudes of the influences were often quite large. The framers' choices of specific issues were influenced by the types of economic interests likely to account for a substantial portion of their overall wealth or represent their primary livelihood.

4. Counter to the view popular among political scientists and legal scholars, and formalized by constitutional political economists, even when the framers were deciding on the general issue of the basic design of the Constitution to strengthen the national government, their economic and other interests significantly influenced them. In the terms of constitutional economics, even when the framers were making fundamental "constitutional" choices rather than more specific-interest "operational" choices, the modern evidence indicates the framers' choices were still consistent with self-interested and partisan behavior. In the terms of legal scholars, even when the framers were involved in the "higher lawmaking" of the constitutional founding, they were still self-interested and partisan. Partisan behavior thus explains even this "constitutional moment." The findings, however, do indicate that fewer economic or financial interests

mattered for the basic design of the Constitution than for its specific-interest aspects.

5. The strongest findings, by far, are for the ratifying conventions, in terms of both the number and the magnitude of the significant effects. Depending on the ratifying conventions examined and the particular interests involved, both broadly and narrowly defined economic interests had large significant influences on the ratification votes of the delegates. The findings for the ratifying conventions also indicate that the direction and magnitude of the influence of specific economic or other interests on the ratification votes are not identical across all thirteen conventions, suggesting that the characteristics and economic conditions of each state affected the expected impact of ratification on different interests across the thirteen states.

6. Contrary to the strongly held view that the founders' financial securities, especially their public securities holdings, had little or no influence on their behavior, or that delegates with such holdings were not generally aligned on common issues, their financial securities often had a significantly large influence, and the delegates with such holdings were often aligned with each other on the same issue. For a small number of the issues at the Philadelphia convention, the financial securities of the framers mattered. And during the ratification process, financial securities had a major influence. Delegates with private securities holdings (private creditors) or public securities holdings (public creditors), and especially delegates with large amounts of public securities holdings (generally, Revolutionary War debt), were influenced significantly to vote in favor of ratification.

This does not mean that all securities-holding delegates voted together at the constitutional conventions. It does mean that holdings of financial securities, controlling for other influences, significantly affected the probability of supporting some of the issues at the Philadelphia convention, particularly those issues that strengthened the central government. During ratification, it means that a delegate's financial securities, controlling for other influences, significantly increased his probability of voting for ratification at his state convention. An implication of these findings is that those delegates with financial securities who did *not* support strengthening the central government or did *not* vote for ratification were influenced to vote no by their other interests.

7. The view of many historical scholars is that slaveowning delegates and those who represented slave areas generally supported strengthening the central government as well as ratifying the Constitution. While this may be correct as far as it goes, the issue of the influence of slaveholdings on the behavior of the Founding Fathers, as with the influence of any factor, is actually more complex. The evidence presented here indicates that, although a majority of the slaveowners and a majority of the delegates from slave areas may have in fact voted for issues strengthening the central government or for ratification, the actual influence of slaveholdings or of representing slave areas per se was to significantly *decrease* a

delegate's likelihood of voting for strengthening the central government or for ratification.

As with the findings for financial securities, this does not mean that all slaveowning delegates or all delegates from slave areas voted together at the constitutional conventions. What it does mean is that slaveholdings, controlling for other influences, significantly *decreased* the probability of voting at the Philadelphia convention for issues that would have strengthened the central government and significantly *decreased* the probability of voting for ratification in the ratifying conventions. An implication of these findings is that these slaveowning delegates and the delegates from slave areas who *did* vote to strengthen the central government or *did* vote for ratification were influenced to vote yes by the effects of their other interests.

8. The findings confirm that the framers and ratifiers who were from the more commercial areas of their states were likely to have voted differently from individuals from the less commercial areas. Delegates who were from the more commercial areas were significantly more likely to vote for clauses in the Constitution that strengthened the central government and were significantly more likely to vote for ratification in the ratifying conventions. The framers and ratifiers who were from the more isolated, less commercial areas of their states were significantly less likely to support strengthening the central government and significantly less likely to vote for ratification.

But surprisingly, the findings for the ratification of the Constitution strongly conflict with the nearly unanimous scholarly view that the localism and parochialism of local or state officeholders were major factors in the opposition to the Constitution. The modern quantitative findings, in fact, indicate that there were no significant relationships whatsoever between any measure of local or state office holding and the ratification vote in any ratifying convention for which the data on officeholders were collected.

9. This study demonstrates the importance to historical outcomes of the specific actors involved in any historical process. In this case, it attests to the paramount importance of the specific political agents involved in the founding of the Constitution. The estimated magnitudes of the influences of many of the economic or other interests on the founders' behavior are large enough to suggest that the product of the constitutional founding most likely would have been dramatically different had men with dramatically different interests been involved. For example, had all the framers represented a state the size of the most populous state while possessing the average values of all other interests actually represented at the Philadelphia convention, the Constitution most certainly would have contained a clause giving the national government an absolute veto over all state laws. Or had all the framers represented a state with the heaviest concentration of slaves of all states while possessing the otherwise "average" interests actually represented, the Constitution likely would

have contained a clause requiring a two-thirds majority of the national legislature to enact any commercial laws.

With respect to ratification, the magnitudes of the influences of the economic and other interests on the ratification votes were even more considerable. The sizes of the estimated influences were considerable enough that the findings suggest the outcome of the ratification campaign almost certainly would have been different had men with different interests attended the ratifying conventions. For example, depending on the convention examined, had there been more debtors, more slaveowners, more individuals from the less commercial backcountry, or more individuals belonging to dissenting religions among the ratifiers, there would have been *no* ratification of the Constitution, at least not as it was actually written.

10. The overall findings of this study suggest that it is unlikely that *any* real-world constitution would ever be drafted or ratified through a disinterested and nonpartisan process. Because actual constitutional settings will always involve political actors who possess partisan interests and who likely will be able to predict the consequences of their decisions, partisan interests will influence constitutional choice. The findings of this reexamination of the design and adoption of the Constitution of the United States make it hard to envision *any* actual constitutional setting, including *any* setting to reform existing constitutions, in which self-interested and partisan behavior would not dominate. Constitutions *are* the products of the interests of those who frame and adopt them.

Many of the differences between the findings reported in this book and those found in the existing literature are a matter of the approach taken, as well as the questions asked, rather than a matter of arriving at fundamentally different answers to identical questions. Many studies in the existing literature question an economic interpretation of the Constitution because they question whether the Constitution is strictly an economic document designed solely to promote specific economic interests. Of course it was not designed only to promote economic interests. Many others question an economic interpretation because they question whether the founders were really attempting to solely, or even to principally, enhance their personal wealth or the wealth of those they represented as a result of creating the Constitution. Of course the founders were not. Others question an economic interpretation because they question whether the founders were really involved in a conspiracy to promote specific economic interests. Of course they were not. Still others question an economic interpretation because they question whether political principles, philosophies, and beliefs can be ignored in an attempt to understand the creation of the Constitution. Of course they cannot. In contrast, this reexamination of the Constitution does not take any of those positions.

Yet the conclusions drawn from the findings of this reexamination of the role of the economic, financial, and other interests of the founders *are* fundamentally different from the conclusions found in the existing literature. The primary reason is that the statistical technique employed in the reexamination yields estimates of the separate influence of a particular economic interest or factor on the founders' behavior (how they voted), taking into account and controlling for the influence of other interests and factors on their behavior. The existing literature nearly always draws conclusions about how the majority of the delegates with a particular interest—for example, how the majority of public securities–holding delegates—voted on a particular issue, *without* regard to the influence of other interests and factors on behavior and *without* any formal statistical analysis. Prior studies, consequently, do not control for the confounding influences of other factors when drawing conclusions about any particular factor. As a result, the present study and prior studies often reach different conclusions about the influence of the same economic or financial interest or other factor on the founders' behavior. The conclusions differ because in a sense the studies are asking different questions. The present study asks how a particular economic interest, for example, slaveowning, influenced the delegates' voting behavior taking into account all the influences of any other factors on those delegates' voting behavior. Prior studies more simply asked: How many of the founders with a particular economic interest, for example, how many slaveowning founders, voted the same on a particular issue?

The approach here to the making of the Constitution employs the methods of modern economic history, an explicit economic model and statistical techniques, to provide answers to historical questions that are of a fundamental legal and political nature. Individuals interested in constitutional history, constitutional law, and political science will share in this study's concern with the fundamental issues involved in the analysis. Individuals interested in the application of economic methodology to history will share interest in the method of analysis, which is based on rational choice and methodological individualism. But it may be asked by some: Has not the issue of an economic interpretation of the Constitution been settled long ago? Has not Charles A. Beard's economic interpretation been long ago refuted? From the perspective of the prevailing view, most scholars would believe the issues have been settled.

This reexamination argues otherwise: The issues have not been settled; Charles A. Beard's economic interpretation has not been refuted. The issues, in fact, have not been appropriately tested. Earlier historical studies did not have the benefit of modern economic methodology and systematic statistical analysis. As such, their conclusions cannot pass modern scientific scrutiny. Major advances in both economic thinking about political behavior and statistical techniques have taken place in the last thirty or so years. These modern advances allow for a systematic quantitative analysis of the voting behavior of the founders employing, among other data and evidence, the types of nonquantitative data about the founders that historians collected decades ago but never systematically analyzed, because the necessary statistical techniques did not exist and because they generally were not trained in quantitative analysis.

The findings in the pages that follow may be disquieting to readers of all political persuasions. They may be personally difficult for many to embrace. The evidence presented in this book suggests motivating factors and intent on the part of the Founding Fathers that may be distasteful to conservatives, moderates, and liberals alike. The methodology employed, rational choice and methodological individualism, will be acceptable to some readers but is likely to be troublesome to many others. Some may have difficulty because this economic approach to the creation of the Constitution appears too calculating, too deterministic, or too economic. What this study actually attempts is a dispassionate, almost antiseptic analysis of the founders: It does not offer a special approach to the behavior of the founders because of the unique position reserved for them in our nation's history. Rather, it treats them as it would any political actor. Yet many individuals tend to look at our Founding Fathers through rose-colored glasses. They often place the founders on a pedestal and treat them as demigods. Many contend that the founders were motivated primarily, if not solely, by high-minded political principles "To Form A More Perfect Union." This book takes a broader view.

The present study should not be viewed as indicating a particular position on the legitimacy of the Constitution. Nor should it be viewed as indicating a position on the proper contemporary role of the national or state governments. Though the results of this study may be objectionable or personally difficult for many to embrace, I hope an objective examination will show that it is an impartial, disinterested interpretation of the behavior of our Founding Fathers, employing what are today commonly accepted techniques of economic and statistical analysis.

Many important questions found in the constitutional and historical literature regarding the creation and adoption of the Constitution are addressed here: Were specific economic, financial, and other interests split over supporting the Constitution or supporting specific clauses in the Constitution? Did debtors tend to support or oppose the Constitution? Did slaveholdings significantly influence a delegate's stance on particular clauses in the Constitution? Did private and public securities holders (private and public creditors) tend to support or oppose the Constitution or particular clauses? Were regions of the country split over the Constitution based upon their commercial characteristics? Was support for the Constitution divided by religious beliefs or ethnicity? Were older delegates more likely to oppose the Constitution? Were delegates who served in the Revolutionary War or in the Continental Congress aligned one way or another? The chapters that follow attempt to answer these and other questions through the application of easily understood economic methodology and modern statistical rigor.

Chapter 1 discusses the evolution of the prevailing interpretation of the Constitution, traced from the nineteenth-century historical literature through the Progressive Era to Charles A. Beard's economic interpretation in 1913. The chapter reveals that the initial reception Beard received from within as well as outside the academy was very mixed. It then chronicles the rise and fall during the twentieth century of Beard's economic interpretation, including a critical examination of alternative views, revealing the immense influence Beard has had not only upon the historiography of the Constitution but also upon legal and political science scholarship.

Chapter 2 develops the modern economic approach to the Constitution. It explains how an economic way of thinking in general is relevant to understanding the drafting and ratification of the Constitution. The chapter then carefully outlines and systematically develops an economic methodology applied specifically to the behavior of the Founding Fathers. The chapter includes (1) a formal economic model of voting on the part of the delegates who attended the Philadelphia and the state ratifying conventions, (2) an empirical specification of the voting model, (3) a discussion of the statistical technique employed, and (4) the expected implications of the model. Appendix 2 contains a detailed description of the data, and their sources, employed to assess the voting behavior and to measure the economic interests and ideologies of the framers at Philadelphia, the delegates to the ratifying conventions, and the geographical areas the delegates represented.

Part I, consisting of chapters 3–5, concerns the drafting of the Constitution at the Philadelphia Constitutional Convention of 1787. The three chapters quantitatively examine the behavior of the men who designed the Constitution. The examination of the drafting of the Constitution is somewhat problematic, though, as no more than fifty-five men ever appeared at the Philadelphia convention and no more than forty or so were in attendance at the same time, yielding a very small database from which to quantitatively estimate voting behavior. There also are potential problems with the records of the votes cast at the Philadelphia convention, which were formally recorded for each state's delegation, not for individual delegates. The drafting of the Constitution at Philadelphia thus provides a somewhat problematic quantitative test of an economic interpretation of the Constitution.

Notwithstanding the potential problems, chapter 3 employs logistic regression to quantitatively examine the individual votes of the framers on specific issues considered at the Philadelphia convention. For example, the chapter quantitatively examines the framers' decisions on such key issues as whether the Constitution would include a national veto of state laws, a ban on export tariffs, and a ban on state paper money. It presents quantitative estimates, for each of the selected issues, of the effects of a framer's economic and financial interests and other characteristics on the probability of the framer having voted for the issue at the Philadelphia convention. The chapter includes an examination of the framers who attended the Philadelphia convention, a discussion of their economic interests and other characteristics, and a content analysis of the multitude of issues considered by the framers during the Philadelphia convention.

Chapter 4 offers a further look at the choice of the specific issues at the Philadelphia convention, presenting the results of an alternative approach to estimating voting behavior on the selected issues that may have more power to detect patterns in the votes. The alternative specification allows us to examine the influence on voting of substantially more measures of economic and other interests. The findings confirm most of the results presented in chapter 3. Chapter 4 also relates the quantitative findings for the selected issues from the Philadelphia convention point by point to the prevailing views found in the existing literature.

Chapter 5 examines the voting of the framers at the Philadelphia convention on the more general issue of the basic structural design of the Constitution. The chapter employs logistic regression to quantitatively examine the decision regarding whether the basic structure of the Constitution would be a decentralized confederation of essentially sovereign states, or a more consolidated, nationally oriented republic with little state sovereignty. Chapter 5 presents estimates of the effects of a framer's economic and financial interests and other characteristics on the probability of the framer having voted for an overall pro-national stance at the Philadelphia convention. The individual votes on the specific issues from Philadelphia examined in preceding chapters are combined into a single measure of a framer's overall pro-national stance at the convention. This overall pro-national vote provides more information about a framer's voting behavior. Thus, estimation of voting based on this pooled vote may have more power to detect the influence of the various economic and other interests than the estimations employed in chapters 3 and 4. Employing systematic hypothesis tests, chapter 5 also formally examines how well the theories of constitutional economics, theories that are based on a presumption of nonpartisan and disinterested behavior, can explain the basic structural design of the Constitution.

Part II, consisting of chapters 6 and 7, concerns the ratification process at the thirteen state conventions that met between 1787 and 1790 to consider adopting the Constitution. The two chapters examine the behavior of the men who ratified the Constitution. The examination of the ratification process provides a substantially larger database (observations on over 1,350 delegates) upon which to quantitatively estimate voting behavior than that available for the drafting of the Constitution. There also are no significant problems with the records of votes of the delegates at the thirteen ratifying conventions, as a record exists of each delegate's vote for all conventions. The ratification process thus provides a substantially better quantitative test of an economic interpretation of the Constitution than does its drafting.

Chapter 6 concerns the overall ratification process and employs logistic regression to quantitatively examine the voting of the men who attended the thirteen ratifying conventions grouped together in a pooled sample, as well as grouped into various pooled subsamples of the thirteen states. The chapter presents quantitative estimates of the effects of a delegate's economic and financial interests and other characteristics on the probability of the delegate having voted for ratification. The objective here is to present a quantitative picture of the overall ratification vote in the nation, and as it relates to various common characteristics among groups of states. Insufficient and limited data, or the lack of variance in the ratification vote, for six of the state conventions—Delaware, Georgia, Maryland, New Jersey, New York, and Rhode Island—require various pooled samples of the state conventions in order to understand the overall ratification process.

Chapter 7 employs logistic regression to quantitatively examine the voting behavior of delegates during the ratification vote within the individual state conventions for which sufficient data and a sufficient variance in the ratification vote are available. The vote on ratification is econometrically estimated separately for seven state conventions: Connecticut, Massachusetts, New Hampshire, North Carolina, Pennsylvania, South Carolina, and Virginia. The vote on ratification is then examined in further detail and econometrically reestimated separately for three of the seven state conventions—Massachusetts, North Carolina, and Virginia—for which additional data on the economic interests and other characteristics have been collected. The chapter presents quantitative estimates of the effects of a delegate's economic and financial interests and other characteristics on the probability of the delegate having voted for ratification at his state convention. The objective in chapter 7 is to determine how the ratification process differed across the individual ratifying conventions.

The epilogue considers the lessons learned from the reexamination of the creation and adoption of the Constitution. Among other issues, it discusses what would be the expected outcome of constitutional reform in the United States given the findings of this new economic interpretation of the Constitution. It also reflects on the implications for the expected outcome of an attempt to draft a new constitution, here or abroad, at any contemporary constitutional convention and for contemporary political voting behavior more generally.

ONE

The Evolution of the
Prevailing Interpretation

If the evidence presented here so thoroughly challenges and overturns the prevailing interpretation of the design and adoption of the Constitution, how could so many scholars be so wrong? Or are they? Do earlier studies merely approach and interpret the issues differently? Or are there some inherent biases in the earlier interpretations? A critical examination of the historiography of the making of the Constitution not only addresses these issues but also provides an essential introduction to a new economic interpretation.[1]

American historians in the first half of the nineteenth century appear to have lacked a strong view concerning the role of economic interests and the formation of the Constitution. The issue of the economic and financial interests of the founders does not appear to have been of considerable interest to them.[2] Some of the first scholarly treatments of the Constitution that involved economic motives are by the post-Civil War historians, who claimed that economic interests influenced the opponents of the Constitution, the Anti-federalists. But, the Founding Fathers, who wrote this "most wonderful work," were considered "to have risen to the heights of prophecy" and *not* motivated at all by economic interests.[3] Conversely, during the Progressive Era, the Constitution came under attack. According to Smith (1907), the Founding Fathers and their eighteenth-century supporters, the Federalists, were now considered to have foisted the Constitution on their democratic opponents. The Constitution was the product of the "conservative," "aristocratic" Federalists opposed by the "agrarian," "democratic" Anti-federalists. The Anti-federalists, not the Federalists, were now made to "seem embattled champions of the public good" (Hutson, 1981, p. 342).

Writing during the Progressive Era, Charles A. Beard (1913 [1935]) consolidated existing scholarly views of the Constitution and in the process offered what has become identified as "the" economic interpretation of the Constitution. Beard (pp. 16–18) argued that the formation of the Constitution was a conflict or struggle based upon competing economic interests—interests of both the proponents *and* opponents. Beard's view is that the framers in Philadelphia and the men that favored the Constitution during ratification—supporters of a strong, centralized government—were individuals whose primary economic interests were tied to personal property. Beard (pp. 31–51) claimed the Federalists, representing "personalty" interests, were mainly merchants, shippers, bankers, speculators, and private and public securities holders. The Anti-federalists—the opponents of the Constitution and supporters of a more decentralized government—were individuals whose primary economic interests were tied to real property. Beard (pp. 26–30) referred to this group as representing "realty" interests, consisting mainly of more isolated, less commercial farmers, who often were also debtors, and the northern manorial planters along the Hudson. Beard (pp. 29–30) argued, however, that many southern slaveowning planters, who held much of their wealth in personal property, had much in common with northern merchants and financiers and should be included as supporters of the Constitution.

According to Beard (pp. 31–51), support for his argument could be found in the economic conditions prevailing during the 1780s: By the conclusion of the Revolutionary War in 1783, the American economy faced serious problems. Shipping and trade activities had been disrupted seriously and continental currency became worthless because of wartime inflation. State governments were experiencing significant problems raising revenues and repaying those who held state financial securities. Prices had fallen rapidly from their wartime levels by the mid 1780s. States were under pressure to print paper money, increase land taxes, and declare debt moratoria. The federal government under the Articles of Confederation (a copy of which is contained in appendix 1) had no independent power to raise revenues and, thus, had trouble repaying its domestic and foreign debt. It also lacked the legal power to enforce uniform commercial or trade regulations—either at home or abroad—that might have been conducive to the development of a common trading area.

Beard (pp. 31–51) maintained that the primary beneficiaries under the Constitution would have been individuals with commercial and financial interests—particularly those with public securities holdings, who according to Beard had a clause included in the Constitution requiring the assumption of existing federal debt by the new national government. Commercial and financial interests also would benefit because of more certainty in the rules of commerce, trade, and credit markets under the Constitution. More isolated less commercial farmers, debtors, paper money advocates, and the northern planters along the Hudson would be the primary beneficiaries under the status quo. They would have had greater ability at the state level with decentralized government to avoid heavy land taxation—levied to pay off the public debt—and to promote paper money and debt moratorium issues. Consequently, they were likely opponents of the Constitution (pp. 26–30).

Although Beard's thesis eventually emerged as the standard historical interpretation and remained so until the late 1950s, it received a mixed reception when first published. The book was banned from high school libraries in Seattle, and Beard was labeled un-American (Blinkoff, 1936, p. 16). Former President William Howard Taft (1913) suggested that people are "used to muckraking in the case of living public men, but it is novel to impeach our institutions which have stood the test of more than a century, by similar methods with reference to their founders now long dead" (p. 3). Latané (1913) accused Beard of reducing "everything to a sordid basis of personal interest" (p. 700). Corwin (1920) suggested that Beard had "Socialistic sympathies" and had no basis for implying "that the Convention of 1787 was governed by unworthy motives" (pp. iv–v; also see Corwin, 1914). And Nicholas Murray Butler (1939), the president of Columbia University, where Beard held a professorship in 1913, declared: "It is a travesty to dignify so unscholarly an adventure by the title of an economic interpretation of history" (p. 96).

Many academic reviewers, however, looked favorably upon Beard's work. William E. Dodd suggested that Beard "has looked beneath the surface of things and brought to light many new facts, or old facts long overlooked" (1913, p. 163) and later concluded that Beard's book "is one of the most important works of recent times" (1916, p. 495). Another reviewer claimed that Beard made a "distinct contribution to knowledge of the financial circumstances and presumable motives of the leaders of 1787" (Levermore, 1914, p. 118). Still another added, "[N]one will deny that new light has been thrown upon this important question and that to a limited extent at least his position is unassailable" (Hall, 1913, p. 408). Faulkner (1924 [1960], p. 186) concluded that Beard's book was "the most authoritative study of the economic phases of the movement for the Constitution."[4]

Beard's thesis did not face serious scholarly challenges until the 1950s. Then, in the beginning of the cold war era, separate empirical examinations of the state ratification conventions in New Jersey, North Carolina, and Virginia contended that the voting at those conventions was almost antithetic to Beard's view.[5] The scholarly onslaught on Beard's interpretation had begun. Kenyon (1955) suggested that Beard misinterpreted the motives of the Anti-federalists, who she claimed were not as much concerned with a potential aristocracy as they were fearful of any government power that was not controlled at the local level. To her mind, the Anti-federalists were "Men of Little Faith" in the ability to design a republican government at a national level for the United States. Commager (1958) questioned the logical consistency of Beard's thesis, suggesting that the Constitution was not fundamentally an economic document as it had little if any influence on the economy. But the most detailed and influential challenges to Beard during the 1950s were those by Robert E. Brown

(1956) and Forrest McDonald (1958), who have had a lasting impact upon the study of the Constitution.[6]

Brown's (1956) critique dismisses an economic interpretation as utterly without merit, attacking Beard's conclusions in their entirety. Brown countered Beard's views that eighteenth-century America was not very democratic, that the wealthy were strong supporters of the Constitution, and that those without personal property generally opposed the Constitution. Brown examined the support for the Constitution among various economic and social classes, the democratic nature of the nation, and the franchise among the states in eighteenth-century America. He concluded that Beard was plain wrong, eighteenth-century America was democratic, the franchise was common, and there was widespread support for the Constitution. Brown, moreover, accused Beard of taking the Philadelphia debates out of context, inappropriately editing *The Federalist* No. 10 to support his case, and even misstating some facts. However, Brown (1956) offers no formal systematic analysis of whether any economic or financial interests influenced the behavior of any of the framers or those involved with ratification.

In contrast, McDonald's (1958) study empirically examines the wealth, economic interests, and votes of the framers at the Philadelphia convention and of the delegates to the thirteen state ratifying conventions. The study includes an accounting of several economic interests for about three-quarters (about 1,200) of all the founders, as well as evidence on the votes of the framers on key issues at the Philadelphia convention and the ratification vote of most delegates to the ratifying conventions. McDonald's primary interest was in testing Beard's thesis. Based on his evidence collected for the Philadelphia convention, McDonald concluded, "[A]nyone wishing to rewrite the history of those proceedings largely or exclusively in terms of the economic interests represented there would find the facts to be insurmountable obstacles" (p. 110). With respect to the ratification of the Constitution, he likewise concluded, "On all counts, then, Beard's thesis is entirely incompatible with the facts" (p. 357).

But McDonald, in contrast to Brown, did not argue that economic interests had *no* influence on the Constitution. He argued instead that the issue is too complex to put into Beard's dichotomy of "personalty" versus "realty" or into any other set of specific economic interests. McDonald's conclusion, more precisely, was that there is no measurable relationship between specific economic interests and voting at the Philadelphia convention or generally between specific economic interests and the ratification votes at most of the ratifying conventions. In particular, McDonald emphasized that public securities could not have been "the dynamic element within the dynamic element in the ratification," as Beard claimed, because there were as many public securities holders among the opponents of the Constitution as among its supporters (pp. 355–357). However, McDonald also offered no formal analysis of voting during the framing of the Constitution at Philadelphia or of the ratification votes at any of the thirteen ratifying conventions.

Although they offer no modern rigor, Brown and McDonald generally are credited to this day with delivering the fatal blows to Beard's economic interpretation of the Constitution.[7] Yet, despite the almost immediate acceptance of Brown and McDonald, both had their doubters from the outset. Benson (1960) suggested that neither Brown nor McDonald possessed a sufficient understanding of Beard's thesis to criticize it successfully, stating that Beard can more accurately be described as arguing that the economic interests of the citizens, not those of the framers and ratifiers, explain the movement toward the Constitution. According to Benson, evidence on the economic interests of the states and their citizens is necessary to resolve the issue of Beard's interpretation. Main (1960) and Schuyler (1961) held that parts of McDonald's data do not support some of his conclusions. Main (1960) also suggested that McDonald's data in some cases might be systematically biased against Beard. Whereas neither Benson (1960) nor Main (1960) offered any formal analysis of their own, both leaned toward an economic interpretation of the Constitution nonetheless.

In an empirically oriented study, Main (1961) argued there were voting patterns related to economic interests at the ratifying conventions. Although ambivalent toward an economic interpretation, Ferguson (1961), in an empirical study of public finance during the early national period, nonetheless maintained that there was widespread support among public creditors for the Constitution, contrary to the conclusions of McDonald.[8] Lynd (1967) argued that both studies by Brown and McDonald are flawed because both developed from a desire during the cold war era to refute Beard's so-called Marxist interpretation of the Constitution, and as a result neither addresses the validity of alternative economic interpretations.

But Lynd's conclusion concerning McDonald is misleading. McDonald (1958, chaps. 9–10) actually included lengthy discussion about whether an alternative economic interpretation of the Constitution is possible, and what it would take to test an alternative explanation. He maintained that the number of economic interest groups was substantially greater than Beard's simple classifications of "personalty" and "realty" interests— perhaps as many as seventy-five different subgroups of economic interests. As a result, McDonald suggested that what is needed is to place each delegate into a subgroup and then compare the votes for specific issues, or the ratification votes, across all subgroups. This was necessary because, as McDonald had previously concluded, "various interest groups operated under different conditions in the several states, and their attitudes toward the Constitution varied with the internal conditions in their states" (p. 357). Despite being ostensibly consistent with a modern economic approach, McDonald (pp. 411–414) firmly believed that neither any singular system of interpretation nor a priori hypotheses about individual behavior are likely to adequately explain any historical event. A methodology that eschews a priori hypotheses about behavior, however, appears counter to the assumption in economics of rational choice behavior.

As the debate over the Constitution continued throughout the 1960s, many historians were ambivalent toward the dispute over an economic interpretation, arguing that the issue was more complex.[9] And, although a few historians (see Main, 1961; Lynd, 1962; Rutland, 1966) still argued that the supporters and opponents of the Constitution represented distinctly different economic interests, an examination of economic interests was seldom the primary objective of most constitutional studies during the 1960s.

For example, Elkins and McKitrick (1961), who acknowledged the general importance of economic interests while also accepting the conclusions of McDonald (1958), examined the revolutionary nature of the Founding Fathers. They suggested that the leading Federalists, who were among the youngest of the founders, were more likely to have supported the Constitution because their initial public experiences were during the Revolution. As their experiences with the war and the Confederation government grew over time, these "Young Men of the Revolution" developed sympathies toward the requirements of a national government. In contrast, the leading Anti-federalists were among the older founders who had relatively little national experience with the war effort. They were more likely to have opposed a strong central government as a result of their much earlier public experiences with British colonial rule and the initial movement toward independence prior to 1776, and their more recent experiences defending the prerogatives of the state governments. The struggle over the Constitution thus was not fundamentally about economic interests, or ideology, or even nationalism. According to Elkins and McKitrick, "The key struggle was between inertia and energy" (p. 216). It was a struggle between the older and younger Founding Fathers.

Jensen (1964), in a continuation of more than two decades of scholarship on constitutional history and the Confederation period, concluded that many of the framers "who agreed on ultimate goals differed as to the means of achieving them, and they tended to reflect the interests of their states and their sections when those seemed in conflict with such goals" (pp. 44–45). He suggested that throughout the Philadelphia convention the framers expressed their common belief that men conducting public business must be restrained from using their influence to further their private interests (p. 106). Jensen's conclusion about the controversy over Beard is especially revealing, as he argued that the founders would have been bewildered because they "took for granted the existence of a direct relationship between the economic life of a state or nation and its government" (p. 127).

In a continuation of his earlier work, McDonald (1965) concluded with observations that are similar to those made in his 1958 study: Specific economic interests were not aligned on one side of an issue with other interests aligned on the other side. But he again does not dismiss a general economic interpretation. Nowhere does McDonald (1965) categorically consider economic interests to have been unimportant to the creation and adoption of the Constitution. In fact, he indicates that economic interests, of course, mattered to the founders, just not in a manner consistent with what he considered to be an "economic interpretation" of the Constitution.

In an influential study of the Philadelphia convention, Rossiter (1966) also argued that economic interests motivated the founders throughout their deliberations. In his view, the framers were "members of an elite adjusting the tensions of principle and interest within its own membership, and at the same time interacting with the publics to which it was ultimately accountable" (p. 15). Yet Rossiter contended that they were essentially "like-minded gentlemen" whose interests and political ideologies were similar (p. 15). And he openly rejected an economic interpretation during ratification, going so far as to claim that "Virginia ratified the Constitution . . . because of a whole series of accidents and incidents that *mock the crudely economic interpretation of the Great Happening* of 1787–1788" (p. 292, emphasis added). Furthermore, "[T]he evidence we now have leads most historians to conclude that no sharp economic or social line can be drawn on a nationwide basis" between the supporters and opponents of the Constitution (p. 295).

Similarly, in his widely acclaimed, and monumentally influential, study of the American founding, Wood (1969) concluded that it is nearly impossible to identify the supporters or opponents of the Constitution with specific economic interests from the historical record. To Wood, the founding can be better understood in terms of the fundamental social forces underlying the ideological positions of the founders, which influenced the decisions they made. The Constitution was founded upon these larger sociological and ideological forces. Wood, in fact, concluded, "The quarrel was fundamentally one between aristocracy and democracy" (p. 485). Yet nowhere does Wood categorically state that economic interests were unimportant to the founding. He apparently believes that, of course, they mattered but just not in any "fundamental" manner or consistent pattern. In later work, while emphasizing the importance of partisanship and self-interest, Wood (1987) also drew the conclusion that the founders could not have acted easily upon their own self-interests.

Although scholarship on the Constitution has continued over the years, most historical studies since the late 1960s have been highly skeptical of the importance of economic interests, contending that economic interests have been overemphasized and more important reasons for the adoption of the Constitution neglected. A possible reason for this is because, as Hofstader (1968) argued, "no historian today takes very seriously" the question of a conflict over economic interests in 1787 (p. 231). Later studies, as a result, investigated issues other than the influence of economic interests on the founders. For example, in an analysis of the founders

involved in the Declaration of Independence and the drafting the Constitution, Richard D. Brown (1976) has suggested that common ancestry was
an important factor, concluding that the shared political culture of those
founders of British ancestry was more important than other influences.
Others have examined such diverse issues as the maneuverings at the
constitutional conventions, the ideological leanings of the founders, the
democratic character of the constitutional founding, the capitalistic nature
of the Constitution, the historiography of its creation, and the role of
intellectual history in constitutional understanding.[10]

Rakove (1996) more recently examined the role of politics and ideas
in the Constitution's design and suggested that, in their explanations of
"why" the new government was approved, "many historians still view the
adoption of the Constitution largely in the context of a political struggle
between identifiable constituencies and interests." He maintained,
however, that "the terms used to describe these different coalitions have
changed over time" (p. 12). So, to Rakove, even "Gordon Wood's [1969]
monumental study" is still concerned with "a political struggle between
identifiable constituencies and interests" (p. 12). Acknowledging, then,
that both ideas *and* interests matter, the "true task" for Rakove is to find
the middle ground between the founders' interests and their higher
principles. But to accomplish this, he not only eschewed modern quantitative techniques but also apparently believed they have little value in
determining the middle ground. Such techniques treat the Philadelphia
convention just like "any legislative body" and the framers apparently
too much like ordinary politicians (p. 15).[11]

Much of the early political science literature on the founding era
generally accepted the relevance of the founders' economic interests in
understanding the creation and adoption of the Constitution. Then, starting
in the 1940s and 1950s, Douglass Adair made contributions concerning
the intellectual origins of the politics of the Founding Fathers that had
a profound impact on the political science literature. In attempting to
counter Beard's so-called "Marxian" view of *The Federalist*, Adair
traced the ideas found in the framers' political theory not only to the work
of the great political philosophers—Hobbes, Hume, Locke, and
Montesquieu, among others—but all the way back to classical antiquity.[12]
Similarly, Diamond (1959) questioned the predominant Beardian view
among political scientists that the Federalists were "anti-democratic."[13]
Roche (1961), likewise, contended that the framers were motivated to
reform the existing federal government, not corrupt it. According to
Roche, differences in their political principles rather than their economic
interests, better explain the Constitution. However, during the 1950s and
1960s, some political scientists still emphasized the anti-democratic incli-
nations contained in the Constitution (see Dahl, 1956; Burns, 1963).

By the beginning of the 1980s, a strong interest in applying modern
analysis to the Founding Fathers and the Constitution emerged among

political scientists. A common approach that developed is the application of rational choice models to identify voting coalitions, describe voting manipulation, and examine agenda setting during the founding of the Constitution. Modern political scientists generally emphasize the importance of political principles and ideologies among the delegates in Philadelphia and the ratifying conventions (and, often, partisan behavior among them) but downplay the importance of partisan *economic* interests in designing or adopting the Constitution. Even though this literature generally presumes individual rationality, it does not concentrate upon specific economic interests that may have influenced voting behavior during the drafting or ratification of the Constitution.

William H. Riker, who reputably has contributed much to understanding the Constitution among political scientists, placed little weight on the importance of economic interests per se despite an emphasis on rational choice theory. Riker (1979) proposed a general theory of constitutional formation within a rational choice framework to explain the formation of a centralized federal republic, arguing that a perception of a military threat or military opportunity to the status quo is necessary for a centralized government to be formed. Applying the theory to the Constitution, he concluded there were military threats to the status quo during the 1780s that explain its adoption. In a later study, Riker (1984) made use of the convention of 1787 to investigate a particular characteristic of constitution making—the dynamic manipulation of the delegates' choices of issues to consider (what he calls heresthetics)—which emphasizes the importance of political manipulation in designing the Constitution. Concluding that the framers were different from modern-day politicians, Riker (1987a) maintained that their achievements could not be duplicated today because "at no time were they constrained—in the way contemporaries often are—by the necessity of ardently representing opinions they believed to be foolish, simply in order to win the support of some marginal voters in their constituencies" (p. 11). Thus, according to Riker (1987a), there was near unanimity among the Philadelphia framers.[14] More recently, Fink and Riker (1989) have indicated the importance of strategic political maneuvering during the ratification campaigns, and Riker (1991) has emphasized the important influence on behavior of rhetorical argumentation, not interests, during ratification.

In contrast, Calvin C. Jillson argued for the importance of economic interests. Jillson (1981) has employed modern statistical techniques to describe the voting alignments among the states at the Philadelphia convention. The results indicated that most of the alignments long recognized by historians, for example, large state versus small state alignments, existed over those issues for which they were expected. Expanding on this approach, Jillson and Eubanks (1984) employed factor analysis to identify voting alignments among state delegations, concluding that issues of basic constitutional design were decided on the basis of principle, whereas votes involving more specific issues were decided by specific economic and political interests (p. 456). These studies are limited, however, because they do not use explicit data to measure specific economic or other interests. They employ the historical literature to categorize the economic and political interests of the states represented at the Philadelphia convention and then test whether the states voted together on particular issues, concluding that when they did, economic and political interests mattered.[15]

Many studies in the modern political science literature deemphasize economic interests, offering various political explanations for the adoption of the Constitution that underscore the importance of political alignments and coalitions, maneuvers, and rhetorical arguments.[16] A prominent exception, Eavey and Miller (1989) contended that economic interests within the states were important to the ratification of the Constitution. They hypothesized that because each state's constitution allocated power differently in the 1780s and because the national Constitution would have affected the state constitutions, economic groups would have been differently affected in different states, thus affecting the ratification votes across states. As with nearly all existing studies of the adoption of the Constitution, however, Eavey and Miller did not formally test their hypothesis.

The role of economic interests in the making of the Constitution among legal scholars is somewhat problematic. Although the issue of an economic interpretation is not typically a primary interest among legal theorists, many consider the founders to have been far from disinterested and nonpartisan. Many readily accept the premise that the framers and ratifiers were partisan and self-interested. Yet, even as legal scholars acknowledge the history of an economic interpretation of the Constitution, an economic interpretation is nearly always dismissed as either invalid or of little interest to constitutional understanding or theory. Moreover, the concept of self-interest in a broadly defined sense *and* the idea of an economic interpretation seldom are related to each other among constitutional theorists. Self-interest is typically viewed as the overall interests of the state or regions represented at the Philadelphia convention or of the local area represented at the ratifying conventions. If economic or financial interests are considered, their role is often framed in terms of a conspiracy among the founders to "line their own pockets" and then dismissed as unworthy of further consideration.

Legal scholarship usually blends both normative and positive analyses to explain the "true" meaning of the Constitution or the role of the founders, based on qualitative analysis of the historical record. To my knowledge, no quantitative or formal analysis of the founding era, or of the founders, exists within legal scholarship. The literature that is specifically concerned with the constitutional founding inevitably examines such philosophic issues as the legitimacy of the Constitution, its democratic or majoritarian nature, the republican aspects of the founding, the revolutionary character of the founders, or the countermajoritarian difficulty with judicial review. Legal scholars are often concerned with the role of the "people" during the founding, attempting to determine to what extent the founders acted in the name of the people, who are viewed in juristic approaches as the ultimate source of the authority embodied in a "democratic" constitution.

For example, Cass R. Sunstein, a republican revivalist and a majoritarian, maintains that the political theory contained in *The Federalist* emphasizes the deliberative nature of government representatives. As a result, the Constitution was designed with the Congress as the focal point for pursuing the interests of the community rather than private interests. Sunstein (1984) not only questioned the essential premise of an economic interpretation but also maintained that a pluralist constitution derived from competing interest-group politics is constitutionally prohibited. The American constitutional regime, in Sunstein's (1985, 1988–1989) view, was designed to advance the election of virtuous representatives who would govern according to their view of the "public interest."

Likewise, Ackerman (1991) attempted to recover the "true" revolutionary character of the founders and offered a "dualist" theory of the politics contained in *The Federalist*, arguing that the founders were "dualist democrats." Given political dualism, citizens behave differently during "constitutional politics" than during "normal politics." As a result, the founders, according to Ackerman, were able to suspend their self-interest during the framing, during our first "constitutional moment," and promote the "rights of citizens and the permanent interests of the community" (see chaps. 9 and 10).[17] Thus, Ackerman, who framed Beard's economic interpretation in stereotypical "counterrevolutionary" terms, dismissed Beard's "simple-minded story" while praising the "most un-Beardian seriousness" of the historians who in the 1950s and 1960s questioned it (p. 212). And, in heaping adulation on "Gordon Wood's great book of 1969," Ackerman proclaimed: "First, and most important, his book takes political culture seriously. His six-hundred page study does not contain a single statistical tabulation of the economistic kind" (p. 213). Quantitative and statistical evidence, as well as economic analysis, apparently are not to be considered "serious." [18]

In contrast, Klarman (1992), in an essay highly critical of Ackerman (1991), questioned the "portrayal of the Founders as dualist democrats" (p. 780) who "drafted the Constitution during one of those rare moments of suspended self-interest when the genuine voice of the People is heard" (p. 782). Klarman, in fact, emphasized "that particularistic interests dominated the agenda in Philadelphia" (p. 782). In support, he juxtaposed some issues debated at the Philadelphia convention and the different economic interests represented on each side (pp. 782–784). Although his evidence on the Philadelphia convention is consistent with the present economic view of the framing, Klarman, as most others, still succumbed to the view that Beard believed "the Framers were lining their own pockets" and that Beard's idea "has rightly been laid to rest" (p. 784, n.

150), citing, of course, the studies of Brown (1956) and McDonald (1958).[19]

In comparison to other constitutional theorists, in a rather insightful portrayal of an economic interpretation among legal scholars, Kahn (1992) recognized that Beard's (1913 [1935]) study of the Constitution was much more than merely about the Founding Fathers lining their own pockets. Kahn was concerned with the intellectual history of constitutional theory and in constitutional theory itself "to explain the conceptual possibility of constitutional self-government within the historical state" (p. x). To Kahn, Beard's work is truly relevant to understanding law and its evolution: Kahn recognizes that Beard's interest was in providing a general explanation of historical phenomena, with specific reference to the evolution of legal institutions and the Constitution, and as such, his work "rests at the intersection of history and law" (p. 118).

Many studies of the founding era also have concentrated on the ratification of the Constitution within individual ratifying conventions and the role that economic or financial interests played in the ratification in the individual states, often reaching quite different conclusions. This state-level ratification literature is best characterized by its lack of consensus concerning the division of economic and other interests in the contest over ratification of the Constitution. The studies generally examine voting patterns at a particular state ratifying convention, or voting patterns at several ratifying conventions, with each convention examined individually.[20] However, an absence of modern rigor and systematic analysis of the issues involved limits the usefulness of most existing studies of the state ratifying conventions.

Among the most detailed empirical studies are those that examine voting at ratifying conventions in states regarded as originally divided over the Constitution (New Hampshire, Massachusetts, Pennsylvania, and South Carolina). In the Pennsylvania ratifying convention, Brunhouse (1942) claimed, those delegates who owned public securities were more likely to have favored the Constitution; McDonald (1958) claimed they were more likely to have opposed the Constitution; and Main (1961) claimed they were divided on the Constitution. Main (1961) and Rutland (1966) argue that holders of public securities at the Massachusetts and New Hampshire conventions favored the Constitution. McDonald (1958) also maintained that the Massachusetts delegates who held public securities favored ratification and that the same might appear to be true for the very small number of securities holders in New Hampshire.[21] In the South Carolina ratifying convention, Nadelhaft (1981) concluded that voting for ratification is positively related to public securities holdings, but McDonald (1958) concluded that public securities holders in South Carolina opposed the Constitution.

In a critical review of McDonald (1958), Schuyler (1961, pp. 77–78) found that in the ten ratifying conventions with a division in their vote,

McDonald's own data indicate that nearly 70 percent of the holders of securities in excess of $1,000 in face value voted for ratification. McDonald's data on public securities holdings, as presented in Schuyler (1961), thus are in apparent conflict with McDonald's own conclusion that other than the Massachusetts and Connecticut conventions, "it is abundantly evident that there are no more grounds for considering the holding of public securities the dynamic element in the ratification than for considering this economic interest the dynamic element in the opposition" (McDonald, 1958, p. 357).

Delegates who owned private financial securities (private creditors) in Pennsylvania were more likely to have favored the Constitution according to Brunhouse (1942) and Main (1961) but more likely to have opposed it according to McDonald (1958). The historical literature on the Massachusetts ratifying convention generally concludes that delegates who were private creditors were important players at the convention and voted for the Constitution (see Main, 1961; McDonald, 1958; Rutland, 1966). Yet an account of the Massachusetts convention by Gillespie (1989) ignores the stance taken by either private or public securities holders, downplaying their importance. Daniell (1970) found that merchants and major landowners were among the supporters of the Constitution in New Hampshire, as did Main (1961) for South Carolina. In Pennsylvania, most merchants and those with extensive landholdings either voted for the Constitution according to Main (1961) or were divided on it according to McDonald (1958). Evidence concerning geographic patterns in the vote is quite mixed. Three studies found no geographic patterns in the vote at the ratifying conventions of Massachusetts, New Hampshire, or South Carolina. Five other studies found that delegates who were nearer navigable water or from coastal areas were more likely to have favored the Constitution than were delegates from more isolated inland areas in one or another of the three states.[22]

Much attention also has been given to the contest over ratification in states originally opposed to the Constitution (New York, North Carolina, Virginia, and Rhode Island). According to McDonald (1958), a majority of New York delegates who owned public securities voted against the Constitution, but Cochran (1932) claimed that support for the Constitution "was primarily a financial one. It was the desire of the security holders" (p. 181). Risjord (1978) argued that delegates in North Carolina who were creditors were more likely to have favored the Constitution. Main (1961) claimed that slaveowning delegates in North Carolina also favored the Constitution, while Pool (1950a,b) and McDonald (1958) argued that there was no relationship between slaveowning and voting for ratification among North Carolina convention delegates. McDonald (1958) concluded there was no relationship between voting and the creditor or debtor status of North Carolina delegates. Lienesch (1989) concluded that "the socio-economic divisions were blurred" at the North Carolina convention

(p. 348). For Rhode Island, Polishook (1961) indicated that paper money advocates generally opposed the Constitution, but McDonald (1958) argued that debtors and paper money advocates at the Rhode Island convention were more likely to have favored the Constitution. Bishop (1949), however, concluded that neither debtors nor paper money advocates were a source of division in Rhode Island.

The most thoroughly studied state is Virginia. Main (1961) argued that public securities holders at the Virginia convention favored the Constitution, while McDonald (1958) found no relationship between voting and public creditor status. Slaveowners in Virginia supported the Constitution according to Main (1961) and Risjord (1974), but according to Thomas (1953) and McDonald (1958) there was no relationship between slaveowning and voting. There is a similar lack of agreement concerning geographical voting patterns: McDonald (1958) found no geographic pattern in Virginia, while Main (1961) and Thomas (1953) claimed that delegates from coastal areas were more likely to have favored the Constitution than were delegates from more isolated, inland areas. In fact, McDonald (1958) concluded there was "no meaningful pattern whatever" between any interests and the ratification vote in Virginia (p. 268). Banning (1989) concluded that neither economic interests, nor military or political experience, nor any other private circumstance or attribute can explain the vote in Virginia. But he also claimed that the more commercial areas wanting navigation rights to the Mississippi voted for the Constitution while the less commercial areas voted against it.

With respect to states that generally favored the Constitution (Connecticut, Delaware, Georgia, Maryland, and New Jersey), there is comparably less analysis of the contest over ratification. Still, there is also a lack of consensus in the literature that does exist for these states. Delegates in Connecticut who owned public securities were overwhelmingly supporters of the Constitution according to Main (1961) and McDonald (1958). In New Jersey, Main (1961) and McCormick (1950) found that public creditors were more likely to have favored the Constitution, but McDonald (1958) suggested they were less likely to have favored it. In Delaware and Georgia, Main (1961) and McDonald (1958) argued that specific economic interests did not matter.[23] In Maryland, Crowl (1943, 1947) found that delegates who owned large numbers of slaves favored ratification and debtors and paper money advocates opposed it. But Main (1961) concluded that paper money advocates in Maryland were divided. McDonald (1958) found slaveowners divided over ratification in Maryland.

Studies of the ratification campaign also have drawn numerous conclusions about the impact of a delegate's personal characteristics on the ratification vote. Main (1961), for example, argued that the delegates of English ancestry, as opposed to Scottish or Irish ancestry, possessed an ideological sympathy for strong central governments because of their heritage. Main (1961) also suggested that younger delegates were more likely to have supported the Constitution because they lacked extensive experience with colonial rule and strong central governments. Jensen (1964) and Rutland (1966) argued that officers in the Revolutionary War were more likely to have supported ratification because they were the social elites in colonial America who preferred a British-style central government. Beard (1913 [1935]) also contended that the officers in the Society of the Cincinnati were strong supporters of the Constitution because they held many Confederation land warrants and public securities. Rutland (1966) argued that local and state officeholders at the time were ideologically inclined to have opposed the Constitution. Gillespie (1989) and Lienesch (1989) suggested that religion mattered, maintaining that Baptists and other dissenting sects were ideologically opposed to the Constitution whereas more conservative religions such as Congregationalist/Puritans ideologically favored ratification.

The inconsistencies across the ratification studies result at least in part because none employs formal economic methodology and systematic statistical techniques. It may be the case that scholars predisposed to find an absence of voting patterns related to economic interests conclude that any differences in the votes indicated by their data are "too small" to be important, while those otherwise predisposed conclude that almost any difference is important. This type of bias is always a potential danger when studies lack explicit hypotheses and hypothesis tests. Also important is the potential problem of interpretation when the ratification studies discuss the influence of a specific interest on the ratification vote nearly always in isolation from other interests; the studies thus do not account for the confounding influence on the ratification vote of other factors. But despite the considerable disagreement in the literature, it is easy to overstate the lack of consensus. Many scholars agree that economic factors played an important role in the ratification of the Constitution, but disagree about the specific divisions. A typical example is Hall (1972), who in his study of Massachusetts concluded that "the final vote on ratification, after all the speeches, pressure, compromises, and machinations, still reflected the basic socioeconomic divisions within the commonwealth" (p. 292). Yet different studies find different "basic socioeconomic divisions" in the vote on the Constitution because they lack any systematic hypothesis tests.[24]

The absence of modern rigor in the existing historical literature on the Constitution generally should not be surprising. At the time most histories of the Philadelphia convention or of the ratifying conventions were written, scholars in history and the social sciences were generally unfamiliar with statistical techniques other than simple comparisons of summary data. Moreover, conventional historical analysis is not oriented toward quantitative techniques and formal modeling in any event. And many multivariate statistical techniques have come into wide use only since the 1970s. The absence of quantitative techniques and formal modeling within modern legal scholarship should not be surprising either, as the use of such techniques is not standard methodology with the legal community. What is surprising, is that during the 1980s and 1990s the conclusions contained in the traditional historical literature generally have been accepted at face value by many scholars and have not been critically examined.

Most general discussions of the issue today argue that the Constitution came about because of a consensus to improve the general well-being of the country, not as a result of a conflict over economic interests.[25] And, even if economic interests are given a prominent role in the general discussions, the idea that specific economic interests can be aligned on one side of an issue and other economic interests on the other side is almost always dismissed.[26] Moreover, Brown (1956) and McDonald (1958) are nearly always emphasized, even among quantitative economic historians.[27]

Yet the findings of Brown and McDonald often are misinterpreted or misrepresented. They often are credited with providing the data that prove that economic interests were unrelated to the vote on the Constitution. But Brown provided no such data and McDonald provided no such analysis. They often are credited with concluding that economic interests and support for the Constitution were completely unrelated, but neither study actually made such a categorical claim. McDonald often is credited with suggesting a view of the Constitution that is almost antithetical to an economic interpretation, but his study suggests no such view. More precisely, many scholars uncritically make use of McDonald's conclusion that Beard significantly overstated the role of public securities in the founding, and the fact that public securities holders were both supporters and opponents of the Constitution, to dismiss Beard's economic interpretation of the Constitution.

Scholars often misrepresent Beard's central thesis as well. Beard's interpretation of the Constitution is often described as a "Marxist" analysis of conflict between dichotomous and homogeneous classes—his categories of "personalty" and "realty" interests—or as an indictment of the Founding Fathers for "lining their own pockets."[28] The editors of *The Intercollegiate Review* (1999) even included Beard's study on their list of "The Fifty Worst Books of the Century," concluding that he "reduces support for the U.S. Constitution to a conspiracy among the Founding Fathers to protect their economic interests" (p. 4).[29] Yet Beard (1913 [1935]) long ago rejected these accusations in his "Introduction to the 1935 Edition," in which he denied that his study was a "Marxist" view of the founders (pp. xii–xiii), referring readers to his *Economic Basis of Politics* (1922 [1934]), and denied that it was an assertion that the founders were " 'working merely for their own pockets' " (p. xvi), referring readers to the original text. In that text, he explicitly stated: "The purpose of such an inquiry is not, of course, to show that the Constitution was made for the personal benefit of the members of the Convention" (p. 73). The purpose is to answer the question: "Did they represent distinct groups whose economic interests they understood and felt in concrete, definite form through their own personal experiences with identical property rights, or were they working merely under the guidance of abstract principles of political science?" (p. 73).

An alternative interpretation suggests that Beard was claiming the Constitution was the product of the interplay of economic interests rather than the revelation of ultimate truth by disinterested patriots or the result of action by class or social interests. Beard likely was claiming merely that self-interest mattered, as he had maintained from the outset that an economic interpretation is not obviated, even if the opponents of the Constitution "benefited by the general improvement which resulted from its adoption." Even if they benefited, "it does not follow that the vague thing known as 'the advancement of the general welfare'" was the "guiding purpose" of the supporters (1913 [1935], p. 17). Any improvement in the general well-being, according to Beard, was coincidental to the pursuit of economic self-interest.

Moreover, Beard's economic interpretation was more general than only about the Founding Fathers; it was "designed to suggest new lines of historical research" (Beard, 1913 [1935], p. xix). Beard's interest was in a general explanation of historical phenomenon, with reference to the evolution of legal institutions and, in particular, to the American Constitution. An economic approach to American constitutional history was necessary both because "the economic interpretation of our history has been neglected" and because "the hypothesis that economic elements are the chief factors in the development of political institutions . . . has not been applied to the study of American history at large" (p. 6). Beard proposed a "scientific" study of the evolution of the Constitution because "the neglect [of economic factors] has been all the more pronounced in the field of private and public law" (p. 7). And, "In the absence of a critical analysis of legal evolution, all sorts of vague abstractions dominate most of the thinking that is done in the field of law" (p. 8), where there is a marked "absence of any consideration of the social and economic elements determining the thought of the thinkers themselves" (p. 9). As a result, the current "juristic theory of the origin and nature of the Constitution is marked by the same lack of analysis of determining forces which characterized older historical writing in general" (p. 10). Thus, according to Beard (pp. 1–14), a "scientific analysis" of the influence of economic interests is necessary to understand both our history and our law.

Scholars still disagree on the correct interpretation of Beard's work.[30] The disagreement is possibly because of the confusing nature of Beard's book. Beard uses terms imprecisely, continuously interchanging "economic interest" with "class interest," "class" with "group," and "economic interpretation" with "economic determinism." As a result, Beard is ambiguous enough to support a variety of interpretations, from the class analysis interpretation to an individualistic, self-interest view of the Founding Fathers.[31] Or possibly the disagreement is because, as Beard himself stated long ago: "Perhaps no other book on the Constitution has been more severely criticized, and so little read" (Beard, 1913 [1935],

p. vii). As a consequence, whatever reason may explain the disagreement, the pages that follow do not merely contain a resurrection of Charles A. Beard's economic interpretation; they contain what, in fact, is a new economic interpretation of the Constitution of the United States.

TWO

Economics and the Constitution

Economics is a way of thinking about the choices individuals make. It presumes that individuals are motivated by self-interest to maximize the satisfaction received from their choices, given their preferences and constraints. This is the concept of economic rationality. But neither self-interest nor rationality implies that individuals are concerned only with their financial or material well-being. Self-interest is applicable to choices over the entire range of human activities. More precisely, economics presumes that individuals take into account the benefits and the costs of their actions, making choices that are in their self-interest, broadly defined.

In the late 1780s, our nation's Founding Fathers—the framers of the Constitution and the delegates to the state ratifying conventions—faced many conflicting interests and forces as they pondered the choices to be made regarding what form of government to institute. Among the conflicting interests and forces were a new-found democratic ethos; the existing political ideologies of federalism and republicanism; the fundamental beliefs, ideologies, and aspirations of the citizens of their state or local area; and the citizens' economic interests. The founders also had their own fundamental beliefs, ideologies, and aspirations, as well as their own economic interests. Individuals who represented many different interests were present at the various constitutional conventions. Slaveowners, planters, merchants, financiers, and less commercial farmers, as well as men with other interests were present. Most of the founders represented more than one economic activity and owned more than one economic asset. A founder, for example, might have been a slaveowner, a financier, and an owner of western lands, as well as represented a state or local area with economic and other interests similar to his and other interests in conflict with his.

Because of these conflicting interests, the Founding Fathers had to make trade-offs. No framer or ratifier was in a position to satisfy all his conflicting interests with a single decision. Each had to make choices regarding whose interests and what forces he would satisfy and which ones he would trade off as he decided to support a particular issue at Philadelphia or to support or oppose ratification at his ratifying convention. There were no easy choices for the founders. In trying to do what was right, they had to weigh the likely ramifications in choosing a particular action. Taking a certain position might have directly benefited or harmed themselves or others. At other times, taking another position might have put them at odds with long-held beliefs and principles. Nonetheless, the founders had to make choices.[1]

Many scholars are critical of an economic interpretation without appearing to understand an important aspect of a modern economic approach to how the founders made their choices. These critics confuse the total and the partial effects of a particular choice. They confuse the partial effect of a particular choice because of a specific interest with the total of all the partial effects of that choice on a founder who has many conflicting interests. The critics fail to appreciate the fact that each founder represented multiple interests and could not satisfy all his interests with a single vote on any particular issue at Philadelphia or with a single ratification vote. Adoption of a particular issue at Philadelphia, or of ratification, could have had a partial effect on a founder with a specific interest such that the founder would have opposed that issue, or ratification, if he took into account only that partial effect. Yet the founder might have actually voted for the issue, or ratification, because the total of the partial effects of all his other interests outweighed the negative partial effect of the one specific interest.

Other critics view an economic interpretation as indicating that the Founding Fathers were involved in a concerted effort to impose their selfish interests upon the citizenry. Many view any economic interpretation as a direct attack upon the founders, an attack that questions the democratic foundations and legitimacy of the Constitution. But the use of formal economics to understand the behavior of the Founding Fathers is merely to treat their choices at the constitutional conventions as being made in a deliberate manner that took into account the consequences of their choices. An economic approach is not an argument against the legitimacy of the Constitution. The Constitution can be an economic document that was a product of its times, including having been based upon a property consciousness, and still be democratic and legitimate.

The Economic Model of the Founders' Voting Behavior

A good starting point to understand a modern economic analysis of political action is to describe the motivation of self-interested individuals in participating in political activities. A nonuniform, unequal distribution of the costs and benefits of government action across individuals, which is largely the result of a nonuniform, unequal distribution of the amounts and types of property individuals own, forms the basis for an individual's motivation to participate in political action. Given this nonuniformity in the outcomes of government activities, rational individuals take different positions on desired government actions because support for a specific action depends on the expected net benefits accruing to the individual as a result of that action.[2]

Because the decision-making costs of governing with a direct democracy increase as the size of the polity increases, citizens would rationally choose to select other citizens to represent them in the governing process to reduce the resource costs of governance. Individuals with a comparative cost advantage in providing representation services would choose to specialize in representing citizens. These specialists would become the representatives or politicians who offer their expertise to citizens and compete among each other for the citizens' votes. This representative form of government had emerged in what became the United States well before the Constitution was drafted. As a consequence, our nation's citizens did not have the opportunity to directly choose the content of the Constitution or to directly vote on ratifying the Constitution; their representatives, our Founding Fathers, made those choices for them.[3]

The voting behavior of political representatives is often analyzed in economics in the context of a simple principal-agent model.[4] The representative is the agent of the principals (the citizens or constituents) who elect and support him. Because the agent is subject to reelection and thus dependent upon future support, it is in the agent's self-interest to satisfy his constituents. The primary issue in this political agency literature concerns the relative role of various interests on the representatives' voting, especially whether politicians are perfectly faithful agents of their constituents or base their decisions on their own ideology.

In contrast, the property rights and public choice literature in economics suggests that political representatives are insulated enough from their constituents after elections that the representatives maximize their personal satisfaction.[5] Accordingly, political agents pursue economic rents (wealth) through their governmental decision-making authority, particularly because they face attenuated property rights to any residual from their governmental decisions. Because political agents have their own personal interests as well as face the interests of their constituents, this literature contends that personal rather than constituent interests better explain the behavior of politicians. Moreover, it is recognized that a politician's interests include not only economic interests narrowly defined (pecuniary interests) but also the politician's beliefs and ideologies (nonpecuniary interests) as well.[6]

If the costs of monitoring and policing the behavior of political agents were positive, constituent interests would not be the only determinant of political voting behavior. Costly monitoring and policing of political decision-makers suggest that the personal interests of political agents also would determine political voting behavior. Furthermore, not only are resources required, but also citizens have little incentive to monitor and police political actors because citizens cannot easily recognize or capture any net gains from efficient political decisions, as they are generally isolated from such decisions and do not have the rights to any potential gains.

Monitoring and policing costs in the late 1780s were high enough that the Founding Fathers had the opportunity to engage in personal self-interest voting. First, communication technology was relatively undeveloped. As Walton and Rockoff (1998) have observed, colonial America was "an age when bluff-bowed sailing ships typically took six weeks to cross the Atlantic and relaying news to the interior took additional weeks" (p. 73) because there were "rudimentary forms of communication and transportation at the time" (p. 76). This increased monitoring costs and consequently lessened constraints on the founders. Second, delegates to the Philadelphia convention were appointed, while delegates to the state ratifying conventions were elected, to attend one-time conventions and were not subject to reappointment or reelection to those conventions. Each state's credential to the Philadelphia convention, in addition, emphasized the independence of its delegates (Farrand, 1911, vol. 3, pp. 559–586). These factors increased policing costs and further lessened constraints on the founders' behavior.[7] Third, in the late eighteenth century there were few, if any, political institutions that constrained elected officials. There were, for example, no ethics or financial disclosure laws. According to Jensen (1964, pp. 127–130), during the 1780s educated men in fact commonly assumed that private economic interests influenced public choices.

Specifically, drawing on insights from both the political agency and the property rights/public choice literature, the economic model of the Founding Fathers' behavior presumes that they acted individually to maximize their personal satisfaction when voting during the various constitutional conventions. A founder would vote in favor of a particular issue at Philadelphia, or in favor of ratification, if he expected the net benefit he would receive to be greater if the issue, or the Constitution, were adopted. The benefit of voting to the founders was affected directly by the anticipated impact of their vote on their personal interests and indirectly by the anticipated impact of their vote on their constituent interests. A delegate's personal interests depended on his own economic interests and ideology; a delegate's constituent interests depended on his constituents' economic interests and ideologies. The interests of the delegates—both personal and constituent interests—may be purely economic (pecuniary interests, such as the ownership or value of specific economic assets) or ideological (nonpecuniary interests, such as beliefs about the moral correctness of particular forms of government). The potential effect of personal interests on a delegate's vote is straightforward; the delegate would have benefited or been harmed directly. The potential effect of constituent interests on a delegate's vote is through the impact of voting choices on the potential for maintaining the agency relationship (i.e., maintaining decision-making authority).[8]

On many issues a delegate's personal economic interests may have been in conflict with his constituents' economic interests, with his constituents' beliefs and ideologies, or with his personal beliefs and ideology. Conceptually, the partial effects of each of the economic interests and ideologies on voting are determined through their marginal impact on a delegate's expected benefit. But a single partial effect on the probability of voting does not predict a delegate's actual vote. The overall effect of a particular decision—the total of the partial effects of each interest—would have determined a delegate's actual vote. Because a delegate's interests most likely coincided often, as a practical matter, isolating the impact of personal interests from the impact of constituent interests on voting is an empirical question.

Defining a dichotomy between economic interests and ideology does not imply that it is contrary to self-interest to satisfy ideology—it is an economically rational endeavor, completely consistent with self-interest. The dichotomy is designed to separate pecuniary (economic) interests from nonpecuniary (ideological) interests. The inclusion of ideology as well as economic interests in the economic model explicitly models ideology as a systematic variable with an influence on voting independent of the influence of economic interests.

For the purposes at hand, ideology is defined as an individual's set of beliefs about social relations, including the individual's beliefs about how societies should be organized and what is considered good, bad, or neutral. An ideology tells an individual about the fundamental correctness of social relations and societies, and how to behave accordingly.[9] While it is recognized in theory that ideology affects behavior, practical difficulties may be encountered in a quantitative analysis. Ideologies and beliefs are unobservable and inherently difficult to measure. Yet they are essential for a complete examination of the Constitution's creation. While not revealing beliefs and ideology with perfect accuracy, a founder's personal attributes and characteristics such as ethnicity, religion, and political experiences are measurable and may serve as markers for his views concerning the fundamental correctness of different political systems.[10] To the extent these characteristics are correlated with such beliefs, they can serve as markers for ideological views toward the Constitution.[11] Similar markers also are measurable for the geographical areas the founders represented. Inclusion of these markers for ideology, at the minimum, allows the analysis to account for differences in factors other than pecuniary interests that may have affected voting behavior. Inclusion also recognizes that acting on one's beliefs is less costly in political, as opposed to economic, markets because personal wealth is often less directly involved in political decisions.[12]

The Formal Economic Model of the Founders' Voting Behavior

To clarify the founders' choice situation, the formal model of their voting behavior introduces a latent variable model of the choice situation facing each founder. The model clarifies the relationship among (1) a delegate's choice of the observed vote on a particular issue at Philadelphia or ratification, (2) a delegate's expected benefit from voting for the particular issue or ratification, and (3) a delegate's economic interests and ideology. Formally, define V_{ij} as the observed vote (yes or no) on a particular issue at Philadelphia or on ratification at a state ratifying convention of delegate i from state or local area j.[13] Let Y_{ij} represent a latent variable indicating the delegate's intensity of support for the issue or ratification. If Y_{ij} exceeds a critical value (Y_{ij}^{CV}), the delegate votes for the issue or ratification. The actual value of Y_{ij} is determined by (1) the ratio of the delegate's expected benefit if the issue or ratification is adopted (EB_i^A) to his expected benefit if the issue or ratification is not adopted (EB_i^N), (2) the ratio of his constituents' expected benefit if the issue or ratification is adopted (EB_j^A) to his constituents' expected benefit if the issue or ratification is not adopted (EB_j^N), and (3) a random error term (ε_{ij}). The formal model is

$$Y_{ij} = y[EB_i^A/EB_i^N, s(EB_j^A/EB_j^N)] + \varepsilon_{ij} \qquad (2.1)$$

where V_{ij} = Yes if $Y_{ij} > Y_{ij}^{CV}$, V_{ij} = No if $Y_{ij} \leq Y_{ij}^{CV}$, and where

$$EB_i^A/EB_i^N = f(PE_i, PI_i) \qquad (2.2)$$

and

$$EB_j^A/EB_j^N = g(CE_j, CI_j). \qquad (2.3)$$

Accordingly, the impact of a particular issue at Philadelphia or ratification on a delegate's expected benefit depends on the aggregate impact of any change in institutions resulting from its adoption on the level of expected benefit derived from his personal economic interests (PE_i) and personal ideological interests (PI_i). Also, the impact of any issue on a delegate's expected benefit depends on the aggregate impact of any consequent change in institutions on the level of his constituents' expected benefit derived from the constituents' economic interests (CE_j) and constituents' ideological interests (CI_j). As the political agent for his constituents, a delegate's vote was affected by the amount of future political support he expected to receive by voting to maximize his constituents' expected benefit or the amount of future political opposition he might have faced for failing to do so. The impact of constituent benefit on a delegate is conditional on the costs to constituents of monitoring and policing delegate behavior, which is indicated by the functional operator s.

The impact of a delegate's personal interests (PE_i and PI_i) on the likelihood of voting for a particular issue or ratification operates through the impact of the issue or ratification directly on the delegate's expected benefit. The impact of future political support on the likelihood of voting in a particular direction depends on the degree of divergence between a delegate's personal interests (PE_i and PI_i) and his constituents' interests (CE_j and CI_j), and the extent of slack in the political agency relationship. If the delegate's personal interests coincide with his constituents' interests, there is no source of conflict in the agency relationship. In this case, the benefit of potential future political support from voting consistent with his constituents' desires merely reinforces the impact of his personal interests. If, however, his personal and constituent interests do not coincide, future political considerations may constrain voting based on personal interests. The influence of constituent interests on a delegate's vote, of course, diminishes as the costs of detecting and punishing personal-interest voting increase.

The Empirical Estimation of the Founders' Voting Behavior

The Empirical Model

To test the economic model of voting behavior, the observed vote on a particular issue at Philadelphia or on ratification at the ratifying conventions is regressed on the measures of economic interests and ideologies of the founders and of their constituents. This procedure empirically determines the marginal impact of a specific variable on the probability of voting in favor of the given issue or ratification, *ceteris paribus*. To accomplish this, the following empirical counterpart to the formal model in equation 2.1 is estimated:

$$V_{ij} = f(PE_i, PI_i, CE_j, CI_j), \tag{2.4}$$

where V_{ij} is a dichotomous (dummy) variable for delegate i from state or local area j measuring his vote for (set equal to 1) or against (set equal to 0) a particular issue at Philadelphia or ratification; PE_i, a set of variables measuring the personal economic interests of each delegate; PI_i, a set of variables that serve as markers for the personal ideology of each delegate; CE_j, a set of variables measuring the economic interests of the constituents of each delegate; and CI_j, a set of variables that serve as markers for the ideology of the constituents of each delegate.

Data on the sets of variables have been collected for all delegates to the Philadelphia convention, for more that 1,350 delegates to the thirteen ratifying conventions, and for the state or local area that each delegate represented. A detailed description of the data and their sources and a discussion of the specific variables employed are contained in appendix 2.

The Statistical Technique

Because the dependent variable (V_{ij}) in equation 2.4 is limited—the delegate could only vote yes (equal to 1) or no (equal to 0)—estimates obtained by ordinary least squares (OLS) regression would be inefficient. Rigorous statistical inferences from the standard errors of coefficients estimated by OLS regression are not possible with dichotomous dependent variables (Maddala, 1977, p. 164). Alternative estimation procedures permit rigorous hypothesis testing in this case. The empirical voting model in equation 2.4 can be estimated employing limited dependent variable techniques that are well suited for the problem at hand. One such technique is logistic regression.

The advantages of logistic regression are well known.[14] The assumption that the error term in the OLS regression equation has a constant variance is untenable in the case of dichotomous dependent variables.[15] Because logistic regression does not require an assumption of a constant error variance, hypothesis testing is more precise than with OLS. Furthermore, the fact that the delegates' true probabilities of voting for a particular issue at Philadelphia or ratification must lie between 0 and 1 suggests a nonlinear relationship between the vote (V_{ij}) and the explanatory variables (PE_i, PI_i, CE_j, and CI_j). Specifically, empirical observation suggests that an S-shape function is more reasonable than a linear form. Logistic regression assumes this functional form.[16]

Estimation of multivariate logistic regression is analogous to estimation of OLS regression. A multivariate logistic model is designed to determine the marginal impact of each explanatory variable—the economic interests and ideologies of the delegates and of their constituents—on the dependent variable—the vote for or against a particular issue at Philadelphia or for or against ratification. A logit regression produces for each explanatory variable an estimated coefficient that captures that influence. The logistic coefficients can be transformed into a measure of the partial influence (its direction and magnitude) of the explanatory variable on the probability of a delegate voting for the issue being estimated, holding the influence of all other explanatory variables constant.[17] The benefit of this approach is that each potential factor, each explanatory variable, affecting the vote is examined separately from the influence of the other factors, while controlling for the influence of the other factors. This minimizes spurious relationships between any particular factor and voting behavior. For example, if the relationship between the vote on an issue and the slaveholdings of delegates is examined in isolation, a positive correlation may be indicated. But if other delegate and constituent interests are taken into account (e.g., the public securities holdings of the delegates), the correlation with slaveholdings could change and in fact be negative.[18]

The logistic regression coefficients can be expressed in the familiar partial derivative form of OLS regression. For a continuous explanatory variable (e.g., the value of a delegate's public securities holdings), the coefficient can be reported as the estimated marginal effect of a unit change in the explanatory variable on the probability of a yes vote, holding all other variables constant, calculated at the means of the explanatory variables. For example, if a one-unit increase in an explanatory variable caused an increase of one percentage point in the probability of voting for a particular issue, the marginal effect would be reported as .01. For a dichotomous explanatory variable (e.g., a delegate is classified as a merchant or not), the coefficient can be reported as the incremental effect of having the characteristic versus not having the characteristic on the probability of a yes vote, holding all other variables constant, calculated at the means of all other explanatory variables. For example, if the difference between the predicted probability of a yes vote for a delegate *with* a particular characteristic ($\hat{P}_1$) and the predicted probability *without* the characteristic ($\hat{P}_0$) is one percentage point, the incremental effect would be reported as .01. The predicted probability of voting ($\hat{P}$) for a particular issue at Philadelphia or ratification can be computed directly from the estimated logistic regression equation for a delegate with specific personal or constituent interests and characteristics. Comparisons of the predicted probabilities of voting in favor of the issue in question or ratification can then be made for a delegate with and without specific interests and characteristics, as well as for different values of the continuously measured interests and characteristics.[19]

Because there is no single, commonly used measure of the "goodness of fit" for logistic regression as there is for OLS, various alternative measures are found in the literature.[20] Pseudo $\bar{R}^2$ is a measure that is based on the model χ^2 statistic, the number of explanatory variables in the model, and the maximum of the likelihood function with only the constant in the model.[21] Current versions of statistical software programs also compute a generalized R^2 statistic for logistic regression and a Somers' D_{yx} statistic, which is based on the degree of concordance between the predicted probability of the vote and the observed vote for each observation.[22] The χ^2 statistic also can be reported for logistic regression to test the global hypothesis that all estimated coefficients in the model are zero. One or more of the four statistics are reported for various findings in the present study.

The Implications of the Economic Model of Voting

The implications of the economic model describe the expected effects of the specific economic interests and other characteristics on the probability of voting for the issue in question, controlling for the influence of all other interests and characteristics. The expected effects refer to the partial effect of each interest or characteristic on the probability of a yes vote, *ceteris paribus.* They do not refer to how the majority of delegates with a specific interest or characteristic voted. How any delegate with a specific interest voted depends not only on the partial effect of the specific interest but also on the total of all the partial effects of all other interests and characteristics of the delegate.

The implications of the voting model are based on the economic conditions during the 1780s. During the Confederation period, the economy faced severe problems.[23] The independence of the former colonies from the British Empire seriously disrupted foreign trade. Although trade was improving, it had not fully recovered. Individuals who held Confederation securities did not always receive interest when due and many feared a loss of principal. After the Revolutionary War, state debt moratorium measures and depreciation of the currency caused by state paper-money issues made hard-money advocates and creditors fearful. Governments had problems paying their debts and raising revenues, harming public securities holders. Although state and local interference in trade was not a major problem, many commercial interests apparently feared that local and state barriers to trade could develop in the future under the Articles of Confederation. Western landowners also were often impatient with the Confederation government because of its inability to establish order on the frontiers.

Under the Constitution, the power to tax, along with the authority to settle past federal debts, was firmly delegated to the central government, improving its financial future and thus capital markets. The assignment of the sole right to coin money and regulate its value to the central government as well as the prohibition on states from emitting paper money also might have been expected to improve capital markets. With respect to interstate trade, Walton and Shepherd (1979) suggest that "the possibility of such barriers [to interstate commerce] loomed as a threat until the Constitution specifically granted the regulation of interstate commerce to the federal government," concluding that the most important changes associated with the Constitution "were those changes that strengthened the framework for protection of private property and enforcement of contracts" (pp. 187–188). Such changes were most important because they increased the benefits of exchange (the cornerstone of a market economy), creating incentives for individuals to specialize in economic activities in which they had a particular advantage and engage in mutually advantageous exchange with individuals specializing in activities in which they had an advantage. The specific provisions in the Constitution which increased the benefits of exchange were those that prohibited the national and state governments from enacting ex post facto laws and prohibited the state governments from passing any "law impairing the obligation of contracts." These prohibitions promoted the development of a market economy because they constrained governments from interfering in economic exchange, making the returns to economic activity more secure.

Consequently, particular economic interests are expected, *ceteris paribus*, to *increase* the probability of voting for clauses in the Constitution that strengthened the central government or for ratification. Merchant and commercial interests increased support for the Constitution because it included tariff policy, trade regulation, and national security provisions that encouraged interstate and international trade through a decrease in the costs of commerce and trade activities (Wood, 1980, p. 8). Residing in or nearer coastal areas or nearer navigable water increased support for the Constitution because such areas generally represented more commercial interests (see Hutson, 1981; Libby, 1894; Main, 1961). Despite the possible obscuring effects of differences across states in the timeliness of payments of the public debt and assumption of portions of the federal debt by some states, ownership of private or public securities increased support for the Constitution, as did representing areas whose citizens held greater amounts of public securities. Support increased because the Constitution included a provision for the national government to assume federal credit obligations, a clause emphasizing the sanctity of private contracts, and a prohibition on ex post facto laws (McDonald, 1965, pp. 289, 321–325). Although treatment of western landowners varied across the states, western landholdings generally increased support because the Constitution included a stronger national government, authorized the central government to provide national security to western lands, and allowed for uniform rules for disposal of public land that encouraged settlement. Because earlier land ordinances had placed control of the Northwest Territories with the federal government, contemporary perceptions were that western land values would rise under the new national government (Hughes, 1983, pp. 94–101).

Other economic interests are expected, *ceteris paribus*, to *decrease* the probability of voting for clauses in the Constitution that strengthened the central government or for ratification. Financial liabilities (debt) decreased support for the Constitution because of the emphasis on the sanctity of contractual obligations and the ban on ex post facto laws, which debtors may have expected would make debt moratorium laws unconstitutional. Despite the possible obscuring effects of differences across states in the issuance of paper money, the Constitution's prohibition on state paper-money issues also generally decreased support among debtors (McDonald, 1965, pp. 289, 321–325). Local, less commercial farming interests decreased support for the Constitution because of a perception that its trade provisions strongly favored national interests at the expense of local interests, which could have been more fully satisfied at the state level (Wood, 1980, p. 8). Residing in more isolated inland areas, farther from the coast or navigable water, decreased support for the Constitution because such areas generally represented less commercial interests (Hutson, 1981; Libby, 1894; Main, 1961).[24]

The expected influence of slaveowning is somewhat tangled. Slaveowners feared a future northern majority would control the new national government and impose restrictions on the sovereignty of the states. They feared that a strong national government might impose restrictions on the slave trade and the expansion of slavery that would have adversely affected the value of slaves or the ability to produce slave-based products.[25] They also feared the imposition of trade restrictions that could have allowed northern merchants to monopolize the shipping of southern staples, charge monopoly rates, and reduce the value of southern exports.[26] On the other hand, some slaveowners (e.g., in Virginia) correctly perceived that they might benefit from a future ban on the international slave trade, as they were suppliers of slaves to other regions. Others also expected the value of their slaves to rise under a ban on the international slave trade. For some, a supposed vote trade over the three-fifths representation issue for slaves and the provision in the Northwest Ordinance prohibiting slavery might have muted their opposition to the Constitution.[27] The expected decrease in the costs of commerce under the new government also might have offset the concerns of slaveowners. The evidence from the debates at the Philadelphia convention and the ratifying conventions, however, suggests that slaveowners expected the direct costs of potential restrictions on slavery and oppressive trade restrictions to outweigh any general benefits of a decrease in the costs of commerce. Although slaveowners may have been more satisfied with the Constitution overall, the debates indicate they were still dismayed by the potential for negative restrictions on the use of slaves and burdensome trade laws. As a result, the implication is that, *ceteris paribus*, being a slaveowner or representing slaveowners *decreased* support for the Constitution.

Consistent with the claims of historians about the influence of personal attributes and other characteristics, older delegates may have developed a dislike for strong central governments because of their experiences with British colonial rule prior to 1776 and their early involvement in the movement toward independence. But younger delegates who fought in the Revolutionary War or experienced the Revolution as part of the Continental Congress may have been more sympathetic to a national government and thus more likely to support the Constitution (see Elkins and McKitrick, 1961; Main, 1961). Officers in the Revolutionary War may have been more likely to support the Constitution because they were considered the social elites who preferred a British–style central government (see Jensen, 1964; Rutland, 1966). Delegates of English ancestry, as well as those who represented areas with English descendents, as opposed to those of Scottish or Irish ancestry, may have been more likely to favor the Constitution because they were more sympathetic to strong central governments (Main, 1961). Delegates from more populous states may have been more likely to favor a stronger national government because they represented citizens who expected to dominate a new national government, and who possessed a more worldly view than citizens of less populous states (Jillson, 1981; Jillson and Eubanks, 1984). Individuals of conservative religions may have been more sympathetic to strong central governments while dissenting sects might not (Gillespie, 1989; Lienesch, 1989). To the extent that having children might proxy a conservative orientation, delegates with children may have been more likely to favor the Constitution.

Concerning the impact of the founders' interests on voting behavior more broadly, economic interests are more likely to account for more interest-specific aspects of the Constitution than to account for its more general aspects. Ideological interests are more likely to account for more general aspects, or the basic structure, of the Constitution than to account for its more interest-specific aspects.[28] Delegates whose economic interests were to support an issue were less likely to have done so if they anticipated that the issue would adversely affect their ideological interests. Delegates whose ideological interests were to support an issue were less likely to have done so if they anticipated the issue would adversely affect their economic interests.

PART I

The Philadelphia Convention
of 1787

THREE

The Choice of Specific Clauses in the Constitution

Despite the hundreds of studies on the formation of the Constitution and the importance of its specific design, none has formally and systematically analyzed the factors explaining the choices of specific clauses in the Constitution.[1] Accordingly, this chapter presents an economic analysis of voting on specific issues at the Philadelphia Constitutional Convention of 1787, concentrating on the choices the framers made in Philadelphia. The votes of the Philadelphia delegates on sixteen major issues proposed and debated at the convention are analyzed quantitatively and statistically related to the economic interests and ideologies of the delegates personally and of their constituents. The statistical findings provide evidence that suggests an economic interpretation of the behavior of our nation's Founding Fathers.[2]

The Philadelphia Convention

The story of the movement during the 1780s toward constitutional reform that led to the Philadelphia Constitutional Convention in 1787 has been told innumerable times.[3] The weaknesses of the Confederation government were obvious to many of America's leaders well before the end of the Revolutionary War. By the time of the peace treaty in 1783, there had already been some concessions among the states toward strengthening the federal Congress. By 1786, political leaders in many of the states were convinced that a broadly stronger central government was necessary. It was in that year in fact that Maryland asked Virginia to participate in a convention, along with Delaware and Pennsylvania, to consider commercial regulations among those states. At Virginia's suggestion, participation was extended to all thirteen states to consider interstate commercial regulations. In what became known as the unsuccessful Annapolis

Convention of 1786, only five states attended. But what the Annapolis convention accomplished was to recommend successfully that Congress call another convention of all states to meet in Philadelphia the following May to consider revising the Articles of Confederation more generally. That convention became the Philadelphia Constitutional Convention of 1787.

While there is still debate concerning the actual condition of the nation in the 1780s, what is evident from the historical record is that neither the economy nor the federal government could be said to be performing well during the Confederation period.[4] It also is evident from the record that the Congress, with the lead of several states, eventually felt it was necessary to call the Philadelphia convention to consider revisions to the Articles of Confederation. Whether there was a "real" crisis in the federal government or in the economy at the time of the Philadelphia convention is not as important as the fact that enough leaders in enough states perceived a crisis and were willing to convince others of one. And, even if they did not genuinely perceive a crisis, they were still willing to propagate the idea of a "crisis" to get a convention called. What is obvious from the historical record is that, whether real or imagined, economic and other problems were used to justify the Philadelphia convention.[5]

The Philadelphia convention was originally to begin May 14, but, unfortunately, not enough delegates were present, so the delegates who were assembled in Philadelphia adjourned from day to day until delegates from a sufficient number of states arrived. As a result, the convention did not actually begin until May 25, when twenty-nine delegates from nine of the thirteen states were finally in attendance. The officially authorized purpose of the convention from the Congress of the Confederation was to consider the amendment and revision of the Articles of Confederation to strengthen the central government's power over taxation, its authority to regulate interstate and international commerce, its ability to provide national defense, and its authority over a national judiciary. America's political leaders disagreed not so much over their desire for constitutional reform as over the magnitude of that reform.[6]

The convention generally operated as a committee of the whole, although it did organize itself into various committees from time to time. How it operated essentially allowed individuals the freedom to propose and discuss most any issue at the convention. Decisions on the issues and proposals at the convention were made through majority voting by state delegations, with the votes of each state decided by majority voting among that state's delegates. A scrutiny of the nearly four months of debates suggests that most of the important votes at the convention were either in favor of a strong, national form of government or in favor of a federal (confederation) form of government.[7] In fact, the major question at Philadelphia was whether there would be a strengthened, more powerful central government with state sovereignty or a strong, nationally oriented central government with little or no state sovereignty. Would there be a national system or a continued confederation? The answer came September 17, 1787, with the scrapping of the Articles of Confederation and completion of the strong, nationally oriented United States Constitution.[8]

The Framers

While seventy-four delegates were appointed to the convention by twelve states, only fifty-five of the appointees ever appeared in Philadelphia. Rhode Island, the thirteenth state, appointed no delegates to attend the convention. Of the fifty-five delegates who appeared, two departed the convention permanently within the first two weeks: William Churchill Houston (New Jersey) left after a week and George Wythe (Virginia) left during the middle of the second week. No more than eleven states were ever represented at any one time, no more than forty to forty-five of the framers were present at the same time, and probably well less than thirty framers were ever actively involved in the deliberation. Several framers, particularly those from or near Philadelphia, attended sporadically, and others arrived and departed throughout the summer (Farrand, 1911, vol. 3, pp. 586–590). While most of our nation's more prominent leaders were appointed, and attended the convention, some of our prominent leaders were absent from the proceedings. Some were in Europe (including John Adams and Thomas Jefferson), some were probably too opposed to be appointed (Samuel Adams being the most prominent) or too sick to attend (Henry Laurens being the most prominent), and others appointed choose not to attend (including Patrick Henry and Richard Henry Lee). An examination of the names of the delegates who were appointed and those who attended the Philadelphia convention, a list of which is provided in table 3.1, indicates that the convention still included a veritable "who's who" of early American politics.

What were the interests and experiences of the fifty-five framers who attended the convention? Although the framers were quite versatile and often participated in several occupations throughout their careers, they still can be generally classified, albeit with a fair amount of judgment involved, as having had a primary occupation. The forty-two framers listed as having one primary occupation or activity in table 3.1 included sixteen lawyers, seven politicians, six merchants, four planters, four judges, two less commercial farmers, two physicians (one retired), and one retired printer—Benjamin Franklin. The thirteen other framers listed—Nathaniel Gorham, Roger Sherman, Thomas Mifflin, John Francis Mercer, William Blount, William Richardson Davie, Richard Dobbs Spaight, Hugh Williamson, Pierce Butler, Charles Pinckney, Charles Coatsworth Pinckney, John Rutledge, and William Houstoun—are classified with two primary occupations or activities. As a result, in total there were twenty-two lawyers, fourteen politicians, thirteen planters, nine

Table 3.1. Delegates Appointed to the Philadelphia Constitutional Convention of 1787

State	Name	Primary Occupation or Activity
	Attended	
New Hampshire	Nicholas Gilman	Politician
	John Langdon, Jr.	Merchant
Massachusetts	Elbridge Gerry	Merchant
	Nathaniel Gorham	Merchant and politician
	Rufus King	Politician
	Caleb Strong	Lawyer
Connecticut	Oliver Ellsworth	Lawyer
	William Samuel Johnson	Lawyer
	Roger Sherman	Merchant and lawyer
New York	Alexander Hamilton	Lawyer
	John Lansing	Politician
	Robert Yates	Judge
New Jersey	David Brearley	Judge
	Jonathan Dayton	Lawyer
	William Churchill Houston	Lawyer
	William Livingston	Politician
	William Paterson	Lawyer
Pennsylvania	George Clymer	Merchant
	Thomas Fitzsimons	Merchant
	Benjamin Franklin	Printer (retired)
	Jared Ingersol	Lawyer
	Thomas Mifflin	Merchant and politician
	Gouverneur Morris	Lawyer
	Robert Morris	Merchant
	James Wilson	Lawyer
Delaware	Richard Bassett	Lawyer
	Gunning Bedford, Jr.	Lawyer
	Jacob Broom	Farmer
	John Dickinson	Lawyer
	George Read	Lawyer
Maryland	Daniel Carroll	Planter
	Daniel of St. Thomas Jenifer	Planter
	Luther Martin	Lawyer
	James McHenry	Physician (retired)
	John Francis Mercer	Planter and politician
Virginia	John Blair	Judge
	James Madison	Politician
	George Mason	Planter
	James McClurg	Physician
	Edmund Randolph	Politician
	George Washington	Planter
	George Wythe	Judge
North Carolina	William Blount	Planter and politician
	William Richardson Davie	Lawyer and planter
	Alexander Martin	Politician
	Richard Dobbs Spaight	Planter and politician
	Hugh Williamson	Physician and politician

Table 3.1. continued

State	Name	Primary Occupation or Activity
South Carolina	Pierce Butler	Planter and politician
	Charles Pinckney	Lawyer and planter
	Charles Coatsworth Pinckney	Lawyer and planter
	John Rutledge	Lawyer and planter
Georgia	Abraham Baldwin	Lawyer (former minister)
	William Few	Farmer
	William Houstoun	Lawyer and planter
	William Pierce	Merchant
	Never Attended	
New Hampshire	John Pickering	—
	Benjamin West	—
Massachusetts	Francis Dana	—
Connecticut	Erastus Wolcott	—
New Jersey	Abraham Clark	—
	John Neilson	—
Maryland	Charles Carroll	—
	Gabriel Duvall	—
	Robert Hanson Harrison	—
	Thomas Sim Lee	—
	Thomas Stone	—
Virginia	Patrick Henry	—
	Richard Henry Lee	—
	Thomas Nelson	—
North Carolina	Richard Caswell	—
	Willie Jones	—
South Carolina	Henry Laurens	—
Georgia	Nathaniel Pendleton	—
	George Walton	—

Note: A list of the delegates appointed to the Philadelphia convention and the attendance records are contained in Farrand (1911, vol. 3, appendix B). For a discussion of the various sources used for the determination of the primary occupation or activity of the Philadelphia framers, see appendix 2.

merchants, four judges, three physicians (one retired), two less commercial farmers, and one retired printer at Philadelphia.[9]

The historical record also indicates that three of the fifty-five framers who attended Philadelphia had served in the Stamp Act Congress, forty-two had served in the Congress of the United States (seven in the First Continental Congress), twenty-six had served in some military capacity during the Revolutionary War, eighteen had been officers during the war, twelve held western lands, and three were deeply in debt. Nearly all of the framers were from coastal areas, including the Chesapeake, and most were from major cities. All four South Carolina delegates, for example, had homes in Charleston, and all eight Pennsylvania delegates were from Philadelphia or the Philadelphia area.[10]

Although many of the fifty-five framers were prominent and wealthy, the available financial evidence indicates that by no means did they represent homogeneous economic interests. In fact, even though the record indicates that, on average, the framers' wealth holdings were substantially above that of an average freeman, it also indicates that many of them did not own any of the primary assets of the day. In terms of the framers' financial assets, thirty framers owned public securities (primarily Revolutionary War debt) with an average market value of nearly $2,200. Only twelve of the fifty-five framers owned private securities (bank stock and, in at least one case, a private loan) but with an average face value of almost $9,000. Nineteen framers owned slaves, with an average of a little more than ninety slaves each. The average market value of their slave-holdings was more than $16,700.[11] For these three assets alone, the average value, simply averaged over *all* fifty-five framers, is more than $8,900. This is in the range of four and a half to over eleven times more than estimated total physical wealth per free wealth holder in the late eighteenth century.[12]

The largest holders of public securities, and the market value of their holdings in 1787, were Elbridge Gerry ($10,000), James McClurg ($6,500), George Clymer ($6,350), Rufus King ($5,000), and Robert Morris ($4,500). All but Gerry owned private securities as well. Robert Morris also was a land speculator and had merchant interests, as did Clymer and Gerry. The market value of public securities holdings increased substantially from the late 1780s to the early 1790s, typically more than tripling by 1791. The largest holder of private securities, and the face value of the holdings in 1787, was Robert Morris ($52,000), followed by George Mason ($30,000), McClurg ($9,000), John Langdon, Jr. ($4,000), and King ($3,000). Langdon also had merchant interests as well as holdings of private and public securities. Five of the framers owned more than 100 slaves—George Mason (300 slaves), John Rutledge (243 slaves), Pierce Butler (143 slaves), Charles Pinckney (111 slaves), and Edmund Randolph (101 slaves).

Given that the framers of the Constitution were primarily lawyers, officeholders, merchants, financiers, and planters, it is obvious why historians have long argued that they were mainly persons of rank and distinction. But it is difficult to imagine any society that would choose individuals with no rank or distinction, or influence, to participate in constitutional reform. It is difficult to imagine that James Madison, who has been described as "a brilliant scholar and public servant," James Wilson, who was "an outstanding legal theorist of America in the latter eighteenth century," Gouverneur Morris, who had "marked ability as a statesman and public speaker," George Mason, who was "as influential and respected as a man can be in public affairs," or George Washington, who has been called "the greatest man in America—and, in the opinion of most Americans, the greatest in the world," would not have been appointed as a delegate to the Philadelphia convention.[13]

The Specific Issues Examined

The delegates who attended the Philadelphia convention voted on hundreds of issues and proposals. In fact, a scrutiny of the convention debates indicates that there were 569 recorded roll-call votes, as well as more than a couple hundred votes not recorded. But the recorded votes were by no means only on important issues. Many were on procedural and minor issues. Thus, only a sample of the roll-call votes on the major issues at the convention is examined here. McDonald's (1958) sixteen key votes at the Philadelphia convention are analyzed to determine if a formal examination of the votes employing modern statistical rigor leads to the same conclusion that McDonald reached from his informal examination: that there is no measurable relationship between specific economic interests and voting at Philadelphia.

Because each state had only one vote, determined by a simple majority within each delegation, and the votes were recorded only at the state level in the official journal of the convention, each delegate's vote had to be ascertained from other records as well as from the official journal. Existing evidence makes it possible to establish the probable votes of the Philadelphia delegates on the sixteen key issues from the historical records. The maximum number of votes employed for any of the issues, however, is fifty-three, because neither William Churchill Houston (New Jersey) nor George Wythe (Virginia) was present for any of the sixteen votes. These two delegates consequently are not included in any of the quantitative analysis of the Philadelphia votes.[14] The probable votes of the framers were determined from attendance records, votes and voting sentiments recorded in the diaries of individual delegates, and other available information.[15]

McDonald (1958, pp. 98–99) explains how the votes are determined, using as an example Roll Call 34, which was a motion to give absolute veto power over all state laws to the national legislature, considered on June 8. Because Massachusetts voted for the motion, its four delegates were all present, and Elbridge Gerry spoke strongly in opposition, McDonald concludes that Nathaniel Gorham, Rufus King, and Caleb Strong must have favored the motion. Because the three delegates from Connecticut were present, the state voted against the motion, and Oliver Ellsworth made a strong speech supporting a similar motion, William Samuel Johnson and Roger Sherman must have voted no. James Madison recorded Virginia's vote: George Mason and Edmund Randolph voted no; James McClurg, John Blair, and Madison voted yes; George Washington abstained; and George Wythe was absent. McDonald continues with this line of reasoning for each state delegation, indicating that at least on the sixteen key votes reliable information exists to assign votes to most delegates.[16]

According to McDonald (1958, pp. 99–100), the votes for the Pennsylvania delegates are an exception to the procedure, which is likely to be less successful for them because only two of the eight delegates, Gouverneur Morris and James Wilson, spoke much, and the Pennsylvania delegates were likely to have been occasionally absent because they lived in Philadelphia. But also because they lived in Philadelphia, it is difficult to determine whether they were absent for an extended period, as their absence was less likely to be recorded. The probable votes of the Pennsylvania delegates nevertheless can be deduced: (1) The economic interests of the Pennsylvania delegates, in Charles Beard's terms, were exclusively one of "personalty" interests; (2) the historical evidence suggests there was very little, if any, disagreement among the individual delegates; and (3) it is known how Pennsylvania as a state voted on each issue. While McDonald lists only the state's vote and does not deduce the individual votes of the Pennsylvania delegates, it can be inferred from the available information that their votes were nearly always the same on each issue. The probable votes thus are treated as unanimous on each issue for the Pennsylvania delegates who are listed as present for a vote.

The sixteen key issues, which are described in table 3.2, were chosen according to how well they represented the fundamental question at the convention. McDonald (1958) argues that the sixteen votes do represent the fundamental issue of whether to form a strong, nationally oriented government or to amend the existing confederation government, concluding that, "[i]n general, all sixteen questions bear directly upon Gouverneur Morris' classic statement of the 'great question' (September 17), 'shall there be a national Government or not?' "(p. 100).

The content of most of the issues indicates an obvious relationship to the fundamental question. The first issue, adding a requirement of judicial consent for exercising the presidential veto, constrains the power of the executive branch of the national government. It follows that a yes vote is pro-confederation. The second issue would grant the national legislature an absolute veto over all state laws and is obviously pro-national. The third issue, allowing national legislators to determine their own compensation instead of receiving fixed stipends, lessens constraints on the national legislators and is therefore pro-national.

The fourth issue, a vote to replace ratification of the Constitution by popularly chosen state conventions with ratification by existing state legislatures, and the fifth issue, disqualifying persons indebted to the national government (public debtors) from serving as national legislators, appear to be pro-confederation issues. The fourth issue gives more power to state governments, and the fifth constrains individuals who may have a stake in the national government. The sixth vote, which specifies the number of legislators at no less than a majority for a quorum, is difficult to interpret, but the debates suggest it is pro-confederation (Farrand, 1911, vol. 2, pp. 245–256).

The seventh issue, prohibiting the national government from imposing export tariffs, and the fourteenth issue, a vote to consider requiring two-thirds of the national legislature to enact navigation acts, are both

Table 3.2. Description of the Sixteen Votes at the Philadelphia Convention

Vote	Description of the Issue
Vote 1	To add a clause requiring a degree of national judicial consent for the use of the executive veto
Vote 2	To broaden the national legislature's veto power over states, giving it absolute veto power over all state laws
Vote 3	To adopt a clause allowing national legislators to determine their own compensation instead of adopting a clause specifying fixed stipends determined by the states
Vote 4	To strike a clause specifying direct election of delegates to state ratifying assemblies and replace it with a clause specifying ratification by state legislatures
Vote 5	To disqualify individuals indebted to the national government from serving as national legislators
Vote 6	To set the quorum of the national legislature at no less than a majority, preventing passage of laws by a minority
Vote 7	To prohibit the national legislature from enacting export tariffs
Vote 8	To give the national government the power to organize and arm state militias and to control the militias when they are called out at the national level
Vote 9	To prohibit states from issuing bills of credit
Vote 10	To prohibit states from enacting any bills of attainder or ex post facto (or retrospective) laws
Vote 11	To prohibit states from enacting trade embargoes
Vote 12	To strengthen a clause conditionally prohibiting state import tariffs, making it an absolute prohibition
Vote 13	To add a prohibition on state export tariffs to an existing clause prohibiting state import tariffs, so as to prohibit states from taxing either
Vote 14	To consider a clause requiring a two-thirds majority for the national legislature to enact any acts regulating commerce of the United States with foreign nations or among the states
Vote 15	To give the national government the responsibility for protecting each state from invasions and, at the request of the state government, for protecting each state from domestic violence
Vote 16	To strike a clause permitting the Constitution to be amended

Note: The descriptions are not verbatim transcripts of each roll-call vote but are interpretations of the essential questions involved in the votes. The actual sixteen votes are contained in Farrand (1911, vol. 1, pp. 130–147 [vote 30], 162–173 [vote 34], 369–382 [vote 74]; vol. 2, pp. 84–96 [vote 203], 116–128 [vote 230], 245–256 [vote 268], 352–365 [vote 336], 380–395 [vote 345], 434–440 [votes 387, 391, 392, 393, 394], 445–456 [vote 399], 457–470 [vote 415], and 621–640 [vote 559]).

Source: Reprinted from McGuire and Ohsfeldt, (1986, table 1, p. 92), with permission. Minor revisions have been made to some of the descriptions.

pro-confederation positions. The eight issue, giving the national legislature authority to organize and arm state militias and to govern them when employed by the national government, and the fifteenth issue, granting authority to the central government to provide both internal security and national defense, clearly represent pro-national positions. The ninth through thirteenth issues are prohibitions on specific acts by the states. They prohibit issuance of paper money and enactment of ex post facto laws, embargoes, and import and export tariffs by states. It follows that a yes vote on any of these represents a pro-national stance. The sixteenth vote was a motion to prohibit amendments to the Constitution. It is not obvious whether this motion should be considered pro-national or pro-confederation. But some in the convention seem to have viewed it as pro-confederation. For instance, George Mason (Virginia) "thought the plan of amending the Constitution exceptionable and dangerous" and apparently considered that a prohibition on amendments would prevent the national government from amending the Constitution to the detriment of minority states.[17]

The question arises of whether the sixteen votes represent the important issues at the convention. Six votes (the first, second, third, sixth, eight, and fifteenth) were about fundamental issues regarding whether sovereignty would remain with the states or with a new national government. Five votes (the ninth, tenth, eleventh, twelfth, and thirteenth) were prohibitions against the states, while three votes were on specific economic issues (the fifth, seventh, and fourteen). The two remaining votes appear to have been about important issues during the debates as well, the process of ratification of the Constitution (the fourth) and a prohibition on amending the Constitution (the sixteenth).[18]

Yet are the sixteen votes a representative sample of the 569 recorded votes? After a content analysis of the records of the Philadelphia debates, I would maintain that the sixteen votes are quite representative of the more important issues at Philadelphia.[19] The debates were examined to determine the number of important and minor votes at the convention. A vote was defined as important if it had a clear impact on the overall strength of the national or state governments, on specific economic interests, or on the basic structure of government. Minor votes consisted of issues about details of the day-to-day functioning and operations of the various branches of government, details of the operations of the convention itself, trivial editorial changes in clauses and motions, and other issues unimportant to the form of government.[20]

It was determined that 301 of the 569 recorded votes (52.9 percent) were votes on minor issues. The issues involved in another twenty of the 569 recorded votes (3.5 percent) were not noted in the convention records and could not be determined.[21] A small number of the minor votes, twenty-six out of the 301 (8.6 percent), consisted of motions for adjournment of the convention. Among the minor votes were a motion to form a committee to inspect the minutes of the convention's proceedings, a motion to strike out the age requirement for senators, several motions on how often to have a census, a motion to establish set meeting hours and disallow adjournments of the convention, and a motion to repeal the preceding motion and set new meeting hours for the convention.[22]

It was determined that 248 of the 569 recorded votes (43.6 percent) were on important issues. But the convention's journal contained no discussion of the debates for thirty-seven of the important votes (14.9 percent). The journal listed twenty-five of the important votes (10.1 percent) as determined unanimously. For these sixty-two votes, a determination of the framers' voting behavior is not likely because there is no record of voting sentiments or any variance in the vote. Because of repeat voting on the identical issue and different motions over essentially the same question, the remaining 186 important votes do not represent 186 separate issues. Probably no more than four or five dozen important recorded votes on separate issues existed and, with the likely exception of two of the votes, the sixteen votes included in the sample are on these issues.

The number of separate important issues in terms of general categories was surprisingly small. Several votes were associated with the composition of the legislature, the executive branch, and the national judiciary. In the case of the legislature, many votes were on the method of electing members and the apportionment of representatives. The method of selection of the executive and determination of the power of the executive versus the legislative branch accounted for numerous votes. Key votes also involved the structure of the judiciary and its power relative to the other two branches of government. In terms of the basic structure of the government, many votes consisted of motions about the powers of the central versus state governments and about prohibitions on the actions of the central versus the state governments. Among the more important issues were motions on requirements for implementing navigation acts, motions on the legality of import and export tariffs at both levels of government, and several motions on the authority and limits of different aspects of the military and police powers of the central and state governments.

The views of historians also support the conclusion that the sixteen votes were likely on the important issues of the convention. Jensen (1964) states unequivocally that "the bitterest fight in the whole Convention: [was] that between the North and the South over export duties, slavery, and navigation acts. So violent was it that both northerners and southerners threatened to break up the Convention by walking out" (p. 88). Others also contend that rules about implementing navigation acts and export duties were important.[23] Motions on navigation acts and export duties are both among the sixteen votes. Prohibitions on various aspects of states' rights, five of the sixteen votes, were also major issues at Philadelphia. Jensen (1964) concludes that, "[m]any of the delegates were probably more concerned with placing restraints upon the state legislatures, particularly in economic matters, than with the details of government" (p. 95). Moreover, most accounts of the convention conclude that how the proposed Constitution would be ratified and whether the proposed Constitution would be amendable were both major issues. Both are also among the sixteen votes. Furthermore, a comparison of the sixteen votes to the original Virginia Plan (a copy of which is contained in appendix 1), which was offered at Philadelphia as an outline for a new constitution, indicates that the issues contained in five of the sixteen votes are contained in the Virginia Plan. The issues contained in the first, second, third, fourth, and sixteenth votes are contained in the eighth, sixth, fourth and fifth, fifteenth, and thirteenth resolutions in the Virginia Plan, respectively.

The examination of the records of the debates also uncovered errors in McDonald's sample of votes. Inconsistencies were found at the state level between McDonald's votes and the records of the convention for three issues (the first, third, and fifth). It was not possible to determine if McDonald's recording of each delegate's votes was accurate for two of the three. An aggregation of the individual votes that McDonald (1958) recorded for each state for his first and third votes indicates that several states voted opposite the officially recorded state vote.[24] While the same problem existed for his fifth vote, it was determined that the actual vote for the issue should have been recorded as Roll Call 230 instead of Roll Call 228.[25] The correct vote (Roll Call 230) was included in the quantitative analysis for the fifth vote. Although the errors for the first and third votes may also be as minor as typographical errors, the correct votes could not be determined.[26]

The Estimation Procedure

The Empirical Model of the Philadelphia Convention

In estimating voting behavior, each vote is regressed on the economic interests and ideologies of the framers and of their constituents to determine the marginal (or incremental) impact of a specific variable on the probability of voting in favor of a given issue. The votes of the delegates to the Philadelphia convention on the sixteen issues are estimated with the following general empirical specification of the vote on issue i for delegate j from state k:

$$V_{i,jk} = g(PE_j, PI_j, CE_k, CI_k) \qquad (3.1)$$

where $V_{i,jk}$ is a dummy variable for a framer's vote on issue i, PE_j is the set of personal economic interest variables, PI_j is the set of markers for personal ideology, CE_k is the set of constituent economic interest variables, and CI_k is the set of markers for constituent ideology. Because a vote is limited to no (0) or yes (1), the estimation procedure is logistic regression.

The Specific Measures of the Economic and Ideological Interests

In the present chapter, the measures of the personal economic interests (PE_j) for each framer are the value of private securities owned, the value of public securities owned, the amount of slaves owned, the ownership of western lands, debtor status, and primary occupation. The markers for the personal ideology (PI_j) for each framer include his age, military rank in the Revolutionary War, and English ancestry. The measures of constituent economic interests (CE_k) for each state include estimates of state wealth, the number of slaves in the state, the distance of the framer's county of residence from navigable water, and the public funding credit per capita for the state. The markers for constituent ideology (CI_k) for each state include state population and the percentage of families of English ancestry in the state. A description of the specific measures of the economic interests and the markers for the ideologies of the framers and their constituents employed in the present chapter is contained in table 3.3. The sample means and standard deviations of the specific measures for the fifty-three framers who were in attendance past the second week are shown in table 3.4.[27]

Complexities in the Estimation Procedure

The task of estimating the votes of the framers on the sixteen issues is complicated by the multiplicity of proposals at Philadelphia and the corresponding prospect for strategic voting behavior—political maneuvering, agenda setting, compromise voting, and logrolling (vote trading). The rhetoric at the convention also may have affected the range of issues considered through its effect on the agenda considered. The presence of strategic voting and the dynamic nature of the choice process at the convention suggest that the individual votes may not have been independent of each other, or the only possible alternatives.

If a particular vote was a compromise, the framers must have originally preferred a different proposal. They also must have been unsuccessful at passing their preferred proposal. Voting patterns on a compromise vote would still exist to the extent the compromise issue was in the framers' or their constituents' interests. If the vote on a particular issue were a complete compromise among all the framers, then no voting patterns would exist. Although compromise voting cannot be explicitly accounted for in the economic model, only three of the sixteen votes analyzed appear to have involved compromise issues.[28]

If logrolling was present at the convention, that also creates potential problems. The lack of solutions offered by economic theory, however, prevents the determination of the extent and direction of logrolling on any specific issue.[29] A meaningful measurement of logrolling is nearly impossible. Without prior information, it is not possible to determine which

Table 3.3. Measures of the Votes and Personal and Constituent Interests of the Delegates at the Philadelphia Convention

Dependent Variable	
Vote	Equals 1 if the delegate to convention voted for a specific issue, 0 otherwise
Explanatory Variables	
Personal Economic Interests (PE_j)	
Western landowner	Equals 1 if the delegate owned western lands in 1787, 0 otherwise
Merchant	Equals 1 if the delegate's principal occupation was merchant engaged in interstate or international trade in 1787, 0 otherwise
Farmer	Equals 1 if the delegate's principal occupation was a farmer in 1787, 0 otherwise
Lawyer	Equals 1 if the delegate's principal occupation was a lawyer in 1787, 0 otherwise
Politician	Equals 1 if the delegate was primarily a politician in 1787, 0 otherwise
Debtor	Equals 1 if the delegate was in deep personal debt in 1787, 0 otherwise
Creditor	Equals 1 if the delegate owned any public or private securities in 1787, 0 otherwise
Value of public securities	Market value of public securities holdings in 1787, in $000s
Value of private securities	Face value of private securities holdings in 1787, in $000s
Slaveowner	Equals 1 if the delegate owned any slaves in 1790, 0 otherwise
Number of slaves	Number of slaves owned in 1790
Personal Ideology (PI_j)	
Age	The age of the delegate in 1787, in years
English ancestry	Equals 1 if the delegate was of English ancestry, 0 otherwise
Congress	Equals 1 if the delegate was a member of the Continental Congress, 0 otherwise
Officer	Equals 1 if the delegate was an officer in the Revolutionary War, 0 otherwise
Constituents' Economic Interests (CE_k)	
Slaves per 100 whites	Number of slaves per 100 whites in each delegate's state in 1790
Public funding credit per capita	Per capita amount due from the national government, or owed to it, subsequent to funding Revolutionary War expenditures in 1793 for each state, in $
Wealth	Net worth per probate-type wealth holder in 1774 for each state, in $
Distance	Miles from the center of a delegate's home county in 1787 to the nearest navigable water—a proxy for commercial activity
Constituents' Ideology (CI_k)	
Population in state	Total white population for each state in 1790, in 000s
English ancestry in state	Percentage of all families of English ancestry in each state in 1790

Note: For a discussion of the data, and their sources, that were used to measure each of the specific variables, see appendix 2.

Table 3.4. Means and Standard Deviations of the Personal and Constituent Interests for the Sample of Delegates at the Philadelphia Convention

Explanatory Variables	Sample Means	Sample Standard Deviations
Personal Interests		
Western landowner	.226	.4225
Merchant	.170	.3791
Farmer	.038	.1924
Lawyer	.396	.4938
Politician	.264	.4451
Debtor	.057	.2333
Creditor	.623	.4894
Value of private securities ($000s)	2.027	8.2167
Value of public securities ($000s)	1.229	2.1175
Slaveowner	.340	.4781
Number of slaves	32.358	61.3693
Age (years)	43.930	11.3998
English ancestry	.528	.5040
Congress	.755	.4344
Officer in war	.340	.4781
Constituents' Interests		
Slaves per 100 whites	28.060	27.7006
Public funding credit per capita ($)	−.791	5.1230
Wealth ($)	512.960	541.8633
Distance to navigable water (miles)	16.400	37.5665
Population in state (total white population, 000s)	257.132	139.4106
English ancestry in state (percent)	79.977	12.3318

Note: The number of observations is 53 because the data on William Churchill Houston (New Jersey) and George Wythe (Virginia) are not included in the sample means, as the two delegates are not included in any of the statistical analyses of the Philadelphia votes. The sample means for the dichotomous variables can be interpreted as the proportion of the 53 delegates classified as possessing the listed economic interest or characteristic.

votes among the hundreds of votes at the convention would have been exchanged in a vote trade, or which framers would have been involved. Without independent evidence on the existence of logrolling and its direction, even an estimated correlation among votes would not be sufficient support for the existence of vote trading.[30]

The mere possibility of logrolling does not mean it was a common occurrence. Many of the framers obviously possessed important and influential economic interests and strongly held ideologies that they were not willing to trade away. The convention's rules allowed repeat voting throughout—many votes did not lead to decisive actions.[31] Moreover, there is little evidence of vote trading. The literature on the history of the Philadelphia convention appears to discuss only one explicit vote trade. If logrolling were a common occurrence at Philadelphia, it seems that more than a single vote trade would be referred to in the large literature on the convention.[32]

Interestingly, Riker's (1984) study of the political maneuvering at the Philadelphia convention inadvertently offered support for a view that strategic behavior in general may not prevent self-interest voting. He showed that personal interests strongly influenced voting on the issue of the popular election of the president, indicating the strength of the "majority who found it distasteful." Riker's objective was to show the impact of political maneuvering on the range of alternatives brought before the convention. The art of political strategy, argues Riker, creates a situation of dynamic choice where new options are created, modified, discarded, and revived. Yet Riker demonstrated that despite the rhetoric, strategy, and numerous compromises, the issue of popular election lost five different times between June 2 and August 24 (pp. 6–12).

The existence of strategic behavior could obscure the effects of straightforward self-interest voting. Its existence could bias statistical tests against the hypothesis that economic and ideological interests influenced voting. Consequently, the extent to which the statistical results indicate voting patterns related to personal and constituent interests, in spite of the obscuring effects of possible strategic voting behavior, suggests the interests were likely to have had a strong influence on voting. But strategic behavior may not have been very common anyway. In an important study of roll-call voting in the United States Congress, covering every congressional roll call from 1789 to 1985, Poole and Rosenthal (1997, chap. 7) show that strategic voting among congressional legislators over the two centuries in fact was rare.

Another possible problem in the analysis is that there is an alternative to a yes or no vote on any issue: not voting. A potential selectivity bias could be introduced by excluding delegates who did not vote on a particular issue. Yet the votes for all the framers are not available for each issue.[33] Fortunately, Farrand (1911) includes information that offers a reasonable solution to the potential selectivity bias: a list of the framers, their attendance record, whether they signed the Constitution (only thirty-nine did), and, for thirteen of the sixteen nonsigning framers, whether the debates indicate if the framer favored or opposed the Constitution (vol. 3, pp. 586–590).[34] This information is used here to impute votes for the missing observations of the nonvoting delegates. A comparison of the actual voting frequencies with the adjusted voting frequencies (that include the actual votes and imputed votes), which are reported in table A3.1 in appendix 3, indicates that the percentage voting yes for both frequencies is very similar for all but the sixteenth vote. As a result, the findings reported here suggest that the magnitude of any potential selectivity bias is not large.[35]

Results of the Estimation of the Votes at the Philadelphia Convention

The Overall Results

The overall findings strongly suggest that economic interests and ideologies influenced the framers' votes at the Philadelphia constitutional convention during the spring and summer of 1787.[36] The findings indicate that the votes on some issues, however, were affected more than were others and some were affected differently. The economic model of voting was first estimated for each of the sixteen issues employing the full model specification described above in equation 3.1; it was then estimated for each issue employing a more parsimonious model specification. Given that the full model, whose findings are reported in table A3.2a,b, in appendix 3, consists of nineteen explanatory variables with only fifty-three observations (the number of delegates), estimation of the full model constrains the capacity of the data to say the least. Despite this, the estimated effects for the full model are briefly outlined to grasp a sense of the overall results before turning to a discussion of the findings for the more parsimonious model for several of the more important issues considered at Philadelphia.[37]

The overall results generally can be related to the fundamental question of support for a strong nationally oriented government or support for a confederation form of government. Delegates who represented areas nearer to navigable water or larger states were more likely to favor issues that increased the power of the national government relative to state governments. The results indicate a significant negative relationship between distance from navigable water and the probability of voting in favor of the pro-national issues contained in the second, eighth, ninth, tenth, thirteenth, and fifteenth votes. The findings also indicate a significant positive relationship between distance and voting for the pro-confederation issues contained in the fourth, fifth, sixth, seventh, fourteenth, and sixteenth votes. The results are not quite as strong for the population variable, though delegates from larger states still were significantly more likely to take a pro-national stance on nine of the votes without the known errors. If the finding for the first vote is included, larger states were more likely to take a pro-national stance on ten of the votes (see table A3.2a,b). But the findings for the first (and the third) vote are questionable because of the uncorrectable errors discovered in the records of the vote. In a small number of cases, delegates who represented slave states were less likely to vote in favor of issues strengthening the national government. The results for constituent slaveholdings indicate that delegates from states with heavier concentrations of slaves were significantly less likely to vote yes on one pro-national vote (the ninth) and significantly more likely to vote yes on two pro-confederation votes (the fifth and fourteenth).[38]

The influence of a delegate's personal interests on voting might not appear especially strong as there are few statistically significant results overall. Yet the estimates for the full model indicate that, for every vote, at least one of the personal economic interests of the delegates significantly influenced voting. Even such modest findings should be surprising given that a model specification with up to nineteen variables and only fifty-three observations was estimated. Moreover, for four different economic interests delegates voted unanimously on a total of eight different votes. Merchants voted unanimously against the fourteenth issue. The two less commercial farmers both voted against the second issue. Debtors voted unanimously in favor of the seventh issue and unanimously against the eleventh and twelfth issues. Delegates with private securities holdings voted unanimously in favor of the ninth issue and unanimously against the fourth and sixteenth issues (see table A3.2a,b). The unanimous votes alone indicate there were voting patterns for personal economic interests.

The markers for the personal ideology strongly mattered for at least one characteristic, as delegates who were officers in the Revolutionary War were significantly more likely to support a stronger national government in seven of the fourteen votes (the first and third votes being excluded). The results for Revolutionary War officer were not significant for all but one of the other seven votes. For experience in the Continental Congress, the findings were significant for six of the fourteen votes, with such delegates more likely to support a stronger national government in half the significant findings. But for the age and English ancestry of a delegate, the findings were significant for only three of the fourteen votes (the first and third excluded) for each characteristic.

The Detailed Results for Six Selected Votes

The economic model of voting was estimated for each of the sixteen issues for a more parsimonious specification of the model, whose estimates uncover several aspects of voting masked in the estimates of the full model and provide strong evidence for an economic interpretation of the drafting of the Constitution. The more parsimonious model contains only those explanatory variables generally considered to be more important during the drafting of the Constitution. The variables excluded either involved unanimous voting, were seldom significant in the full voting model, measure economic interests or characteristics that could be considered historically minor, or are variables likely to contain the most measurement error. The findings for six of the more important issues considered at the convention—the second, seventh, ninth, eleventh, thirteenth, and fourteenth—are discussed in detail below. The findings for all six votes are reported in table 3.5 and are expressed as the more intelligible marginal or incremental effect of a particular explanatory variable on the probability of a yes vote, with all other explanatory variables at their means.[39]

The Second Issue. On June 8, the Philadelphia convention considered whether the national legislature would be given an absolute veto over state laws, but the issue was defeated 19–24, with only 44.2 percent yes votes. The estimated model for the second issue indicates that a delegate to the convention with average values for all explanatory variables (the "average" framer) has a predicted probability of a yes vote of .379. The economic model thus predicts that, on average, the second issue had in essence a 38 percent probability of receiving a yes vote, which is a fairly accurate prediction of the actual voting outcome of 44.2 percent yes votes.[40] The findings also show that the two delegates who were less commercial farmers both opposed the second issue. Delegates who were from more isolated backcountry areas also were more likely to vote no, while delegates who represented large states were more likely to vote yes. Although not statistically significant at conventional levels, given the small sample size of the analysis of the Philadelphia votes, the estimated effect of a delegate's personal slaveholdings might, at best, hint at a negative impact on the probability of voting in favor of the second issue.[41]

The magnitudes of the marginal effects of two of the economic interests are quite small, however. If we consider the estimated effect of personal slaveholdings precise enough to not be the result of chance variation, it indicates that, for example, a 1 percent increase from the mean in the amount of a delegate's personal slaveholdings reduces the probability of a yes vote by just .203 percent, which means the response elasticity is –.203.[42] For distance from navigable water, the response elasticity is –.237. But the largest marginal effect on the vote is for the population of a delegate's state, with a response elasticity of 1.84. Delegates from more populous states apparently were much more likely to support a national veto over state laws, as a 1 percent increase in a state's population from the mean, for example, increases the probability of a yes vote by 1.84 percent.

Despite the two minor marginal effects, the predicted probabilities of voting in favor of the second issue are dramatically different for delegates with dramatically different interests and characteristics. Compare, for example, the various predicted probabilities of a yes vote reported in table 3.6 for different values of the significant variables, with mean values for all other variables. For different amounts of personal slaveholdings, the probabilities range from .459 to .039. This indicates that the likelihood of voting for the national veto over state laws for an otherwise average delegate who owned no slaves is essentially 46 percent, while the likelihood is essentially 4 percent if the delegate owned 300 slaves. A delegate with no slaves apparently was more than eleven times as likely to vote for the national veto than was a delegate with the most slaves of anyone. Findings for distance from navigable water indicate that the probability of voting yes for an otherwise average delegate from a coastal area is 47 percent, while it is less than 1 percent if the delegate was from the most isolated inland areas. Looking at the influence of a state's population, the probability of a yes vote for an otherwise average delegate from Virginia, the largest state, is about 84 percent, while it is only 5 percent for an otherwise average delegate from Delaware, the smallest state.

Table 3.5. Incremental and Marginal Effects of the Explanatory Variables in the Parsimonious Voting Model on the Probability of a Yes Vote on Selected Issues at the Philadelphia Convention

Explanatory Variables	Votes					
	Vote 2	Vote 7	Vote 9	Vote 11	Vote 13	Vote 14
Personal Economic Interests						
Western landowner	−.195	−.163	−.212	.144	.201	.396[d]
Merchant	−.169	.285[e]	.036	−.156	.011	U[No]
Farmer	U[No]	—	—	—	—	—
Debtor	—	U[Yes]	—	U[No]	—	—
Number of slaves owned	−.0024[e]	−.00009	.0036[c]	.0025[e]	−.0031	−.0019[d]
Value of private securities ($000s)	—	—	U[Yes]	—	—	—
Value of public securities ($000s)	−.0086	.0045	—	.079[c]	−.082[d]	−.033
Owner public securities	—	—	.193[d]	—	—	—
Personal Ideology						
Delegate-English ancestry	.069	−.037	−.133	−.021	−.132	.119
Officer	.067	−.230	.091	−.0069	.364[c]	−.270[c]
Constituents' Economic Interests						
Slaves per 100 whites	−.0015	.014[b]	−.0092[b]	−.00060	−.0076[d]	.013[a]
Distance to navigable water (miles)	−.0055[c]	.0019	−.0031[b]	.0041[c]	−.0052[b]	.0055[b]
Constituents' Ideology						
Population in state (000s)	.0027[a]	.00030	−.00018	−.0021[a]	.0019[b]	−.00087

[a] Statistically significant at the .01 level.

[b] Statistically significant at the .05 level.

[c] Statistically significant at the .10 level.

[d] P-value is less than .15. While not considered significant at conventional levels, the estimated effect may be precise enough to be treated as significant given the small sample size. See Leamer (1978, chap. 4, especially pp. 102–108, 114–117).

[e] P-value is between .15 and .30. While not significant, the estimated effect still may be suggestive of an influence on the vote given the small sample size.

Note: Number of observations for each specification is 53. The dependent variable for each selected issue is the observed vote for that issue, where a yes vote equals 1 and a no vote equals 0. Variables for which all delegates with the characteristic voted unanimously for a particular vote, marked with U[Yes] or U[No], were excluded from the estimation of that vote because the logit algorithm cannot converge with such variables included. Other variables were selected for exclusion because they were seldom significant in the full model, are generally considered historically minor variables, appear to be the least likely to affect voting on the issue in question, or are likely to contain the most measurement error. The incremental or marginal effect of each variable is calculated from the estimated logistic coefficients for the more parsimonious model specification for each vote reported in table A3.3a,b in appendix 3, with all other explanatory variables at their mean values.

It is not at all surprising that the economic model predicts that delegates from smaller states apparently were almost certain to vote against a national veto over state laws and that delegates from large states were almost as nearly certain to vote for it. The findings for a state's population, moreover, suggest just how different the Constitution might

Table 3.6. Predicted Probabilities of a Yes Vote on the Second Issue for a Delegate with Different Interests and Characteristics: Statistically Significant Variables

Economic Interests and Characteristics	Predicted Probability of a Yes on Vote 2
The "Average" Delegate	.379
Personal Slaveholdings (Number of Slaves)[a]	
0 (the least for any delegate)	.459
32.36 (the mean)	.379
50	.338
100	.236
150	.157
200	.101
300 (the most for any delegate)	.039
Distance from Navigable Water (Miles)	
0 (the nearest for any delegate)	.472
16.40 (the mean)	.379
50	.218
75	.135
100	.080
150	.026
200 (the farthest for any delegate)	.008
Population in State (Number of Whites)	
46,000 (the least populous)	.051
142,000	.140
209,000	.260
257,132 (the mean)	.379
314,000	.540
373,000	.698
442,000 (the most populous)	.837

[a] Not significant at conventional levels, but the estimated effect of the variable still may be precise enough to be suggestive of an influence on the vote.

Note: All predicted probabilities are calculated from the estimated logistic coefficients for Vote 2 reported in table A3.3a in appendix 3. The probability for the "average" delegate is calculated employing the mean values of all explanatory variables. For a dichotomous variable, the probability is calculated when the variable has a value of 1 and when the variable has a value of 0, with all other variables at their mean values. For a continuous variable, the probability is calculated for each value of the variable, with all other variables at their mean values. Because of rounding, the difference between the two predicted probabilities for a dichotomous variable may not be identical to its reported incremental effect. The populations listed are those for Delaware, New Hampshire, Maryland, the mean for all thirteen states, New York, Massachusetts, and Virginia—from the least to the most populous state.

have been had different delegates been in attendance. If, for example, more delegates from more populous states attended the Philadelphia convention, the Constitution might have included the national veto over state laws.

The findings for the second vote are quite plausible given the nature of state-level special-interest legislation that existed under the status quo.[43] Given the existence of debtor relief statutes in many states and the potential for debtor relief measures in other states, less commercial farmers, often with the potential for being deeply in debt, benefited from the status quo, according to McDonald (1965, pp. 321–332). As less commercial farmers had been among the primary beneficiaries of debtor relief measures at the state level, their opposition to a national veto over state laws is expected. Slaveowners feared that a national legislature, potentially dominated by northern states, might veto state laws concerning slavery.[44] Because citizens in large states might have expected to control the new national government, they might have had less to fear from a national veto of state laws.

In the convention, the debates on the issue on June 8 suggest that the delegates' sentiments reflected the estimated predictions of voting. Although he thought there should be some limits to the national negative, James Wilson (Pennsylvania), a nationalist with significant banking interests and no farming interests, argued that "the principal of it when viewed with a close & steady eye, is right."[45] One of the framers with the largest slaveholdings, Pierce Butler (South Carolina), remarked that he was "vehement agst. the Negative in the proposed extent, as cutting off all hope of equal justice to the distant States. The people there would not . . . give it a hearing" (Farrand, 1911, vol. 1, p. 168). And Gunning Bedford, Jr. (Delaware), could not have made the nature of the small states' apprehension of the issue more obvious at the convention: "Will not these large States crush the small ones whenever they stand in the way of their ambitions or interested views," asked Bedford, adding, "It seems as if Pa. & Va. by the conduct of their deputies wished to provide a system in which they would have an enormous & monstrous influence" (p. 167). But James Madison (Virginia), who in fact seconded the motion, supported the concept of an absolute national veto of state laws. He claimed his view "could not but regard an indefinite power to negative legislative acts of the States as absolutely necessary to a perfect system" and that experience showed that the states tended "to infringe the rights & interests of each other. . . . A negative was the mildest expedient that could be devised for preventing these mischiefs" (p. 164).

The Seventh Issue. Export tariffs by the national government were to be prohibited under the seventh vote, which was considered on August 21, and it barely passed with a vote of 23–22 or with just 51.1 percent yes votes. The estimated model indicates that the "average" delegate to the Philadelphia convention has a predicted probability of a yes vote of .560 on the seventh issue, an estimate that, again, is a reasonably accurate prediction of the actual voting outcome of 51.1 percent yes. The findings also show that the three delegates who were debtors unanimously opposed the seventh issue. Delegates who represented states with heavier concentrations of slaves were more likely to vote in favor of prohibiting export tariffs (see table 3.5). This finding is expected because well over half of the delegates from slave states obtained a major share of their livelihood from exports of rice and tobacco (McDonald, 1958, chap. 3). With the exception of merchants, the apparent indifference (lack of statistical significance) of delegates with other personal economic interests is expected as well. Because a majority of the delegates with merchant interests were involved in export trade, significant findings for the merchants were expected. And given the small sample size of the analysis of the Philadelphia votes, the estimated effect of merchant interests might hint at a positive impact on the probability of voting in favor of the tariff prohibition.[46]

If the estimated effect of the merchant variable is considered precise enough to suggest a significant impact, its magnitude can be observed directly from the incremental effect reported in table 3.5 for Vote 7. An otherwise average delegate who was a merchant has a predicted probability of a yes vote that is .285 greater than a delegate without merchant interests. Not a small impact! Compared to that, the magnitude of the marginal effect of constituent slave interests might appear rather modest. The response elasticity for constituent slaveholdings is .699. But this response elasticity does not tell the entire story. As with the second issue, delegates who represented widely divergent interests have widely divergent voting probabilities. Compare the various predicted probabilities of a yes vote, for otherwise average delegates, reported in table 3.7. As just noted, a delegate who was a merchant was 56 percent more likely to vote yes than was an otherwise average delegate who was not a merchant.[47] For different amounts of constituent slaveholdings, the predicted probabilities of the vote to prohibit national export tariffs range from .206 to

Table 3.7. Predicted Probabilities of a Yes Vote on the Seventh Issue for a Delegate with Different Interests and Characteristics: Statistically Significant Variables

Economic Interests and Characteristics	Predicted Probability of a Yes on Vote 7
The "Average" Delegate	.560
Merchant[a]	.790
Not a Merchant	.505
Constituent Slaveholdings (Slaves per 100 Whites)	
0 (the least for any state)	.206
15	.378
28.06 (the mean)	.560
40	.715
50	.816
60	.886
76 (the most for any state)	.951

[a] Not significant at conventional levels, but the estimated effect of the variable still may be precise enough to be suggestive of an influence on the vote.

Note: All predicted probabilities are calculated from the estimated logistic coefficients for Vote 7 reported in table A3.3a in appendix 3. All other details are as described in the note to table 3.6.

.951. An otherwise average delegate from a state with the heaviest concentration of slaves was nearly certain (95 percent) to favor prohibiting export tariffs, nearly five times more likely to do so than delegates from states with no slaves, indicating, without much doubt, that economic interests mattered strongly for this issue. This finding also suggests that had there been fewer delegates at the Philadelphia convention from slave states, the prohibition on export tariffs might not have passed. In the extreme, if all delegates, for example, had been from Massachusetts, a state with essentially no slaves per 100 whites, and had mean values for all other variables, the model predicts that the probability of voting for the tariff prohibition would have been less than 21 percent.

The findings for slave interests are more than supported by the record of the debates at Philadelphia. Indeed, it appears that nearly all southern slaveowning planters "sought to prevent taxes on exports" (McDonald, 1965, p. 289). Southerners certainly stated their opposition to national export tariffs during the debates. On August 21, Pierce Butler (South Carolina) made known that he "was strenuously opposed to a power over exports; as unjust and alarming to the staple States" (Farrand, 1911, vol. 2, p. 360). Gouverneur Morris (Pennsylvania), however, believed that "Tobacco, lumber, and live-stock are three objects belonging to different States, of which great advantage might be maed by a power to tax exports" (p. 360). Morris's fellow Pennsylvania delegate, James Wilson, also favored "the general power over exports" (p. 362). But George Mason (Virginia), the largest slaveowner among the delegates, argued that the southern states had legitimate reasons to suspect that national export tariffs would work to the advantage of northern interests at the expense of the South. As Mason argued, "The case of Exports was not the same with that of imports. The latter were the same throughout the States: the former very different. As to Tobacco other nations do raise it, and are capable of raising it as well as Virga. &c. The impolicy of taxing that article had been demonstrated by the experiment of Virginia" (p. 363). The very next day, responding to a wish of Gouverneur Morris (Pennsylvania) to reconsider, Pierce Butler (South Carolina) declared that he "never would agree to the power of taxing exports" (p. 374).

The Ninth Issue. A proposal made on August 28 to prohibit absolutely state paper money is the ninth vote, which passed overwhelmingly, 33–6, with 84.6 percent yes votes. The economic model indicates that the "average" delegate to the convention has a predicted probability of a yes vote of .859, nearly identical to the actual voting outcome of 84.6 percent yes. The findings, moreover, suggest that economic interests especially mattered on this issue (see table 3.5). The twelve delegates with private securities holdings voted unanimously in favor of it, and the public creditors (delegates who owned any amount of public securities) were essentially significantly more likely to favor the prohibition.[48] The solid support of the creditors is consistent with a belief among many delegates that state issuance of paper money was often irresponsible. It is consistent as well with the general perception that the new national government would be less likely to emit inflationary paper money than would the states (Walton and Shepherd, 1979, chap. 9). This may explain why delegates from the more isolated backcountry, possibly who represented economically distressed agrarian interests, were more likely to oppose the prohibition of state paper money.[49] Delegates from states with heavier concentrations of slaves also were more likely to oppose the prohibition, perhaps for similar reasons, but if a delegate personally owned slaves, the marginal effect was to increase the likelihood of voting in favor of prohibiting absolutely state paper money. The apparently conflicting effects of slave interests could be the result of the heterogeneous experiences of southern states over the issuance of paper money during the Confederation period.

The incremental effect for an otherwise average delegate who was a public creditor indicates that the predicted probability of a yes vote is .193 greater than that for a delegate with no public securities, a somewhat sizable effect on a delegate's vote. In contrast, the response elasticity for distance from navigable water is a mere −.050, a very trivial effect. For constituent slaveholdings, the response elasticity is larger but is still a very minor −.257.

As with the second and seventh votes, and despite the two minor marginal effects, delegates with substantially different interests had substantially different predicted probabilities on the ninth vote. Compare the various predicted probabilities of a yes vote reported in table 3.8. A delegate who was a public creditor was 26.5 percent more likely to vote yes than was an otherwise average delegate without any public securities. For different distances from navigable water, the probabilities range from .897 to .101, a huge range. A delegate from a coastal area has a 90 percent probability of voting to prohibit absolutely state paper money, while the probability of a yes vote is only 10 percent for a delegate from the most isolated inland area. Delegates from the most commercial areas (on the coast or navigable water) apparently were strongly aligned against state paper money, while those from the most isolated areas were nearly certain to vote against the prohibition. The predicted probabilities for different amounts of constituent slaveholdings indicate as well that an otherwise average delegate, for example, from Massachusetts, the state with the least concentration of slaves, was nearly certain (more than 97 percent likely) to vote to prohibit state paper money (see table 3.8).

The findings for the ninth vote also indicate just how different the outcome at Philadelphia would have been had different delegates been in attendance. In the extreme, if all delegates at Philadelphia had been from the most isolated inland areas with mean values for all other variables, the predicted probability of passing the prohibition on state paper money would be only 10 percent. If all the delegates at the constitutional convention had been from South Carolina, the state with the heaviest concentration of slaves, and had mean values for all other variables, the

Table 3.8. Predicted Probabilities of a Yes Vote on the Ninth Issue for a Delegate with Different Interests and Characteristics: Statistically Significant Variables

Economic Interests and Characteristics	Predicted Probability of a Yes on Vote 9
The "Average" Delegate	.859
Owner public securities	.922
No public securities	.729
Constituent Slaveholdings (Slaves per 100 Whites)	
0 (the least for any state)	.974
15	.934
28.06 (the mean)	.859
40	.737
50	.594
60	.433
76 (the most for any state)	.213
Distance from Navigable Water (Miles)	
0 (the nearest for any delegate)	.897
16.40 (the mean)	.859
50	.745
75	.630
100	.497
150	.251
200 (the farthest for any delegate)	.101

Note: All predicted probabilities are calculated from the estimated logistic coefficients for Vote 9 reported in table A3.3b in appendix 3. All other details are as described in the note to table 3.6.

predicted probability of a yes vote would be just 21 percent. In either case, the Constitution most likely would not have prohibited state paper money.

James Madison recorded very little discussion on this issue on August 28. Nathaniel Gorham (Massachusetts), a merchant and owner of western lands, was not sure about an absolute prohibition because another article "makes the consent of the Genl. Legislature necessary, and that in that mode, no opposition would be excited; whereas an absolute prohibition of paper money would rouse the most desperate opposition from its partisans" (Farrand, 1911, vol. 2, p. 439). The only other delegate to speak directly on the roll call, according to Madison, was Roger Sherman (Connecticut), one of the debtors at Philadelphia, who supported the absolute prohibition as a favorable means "for crushing paper money. If the consent of the Legislature could authorize emissions of it, the friends of paper money would make every exertion to get into the Legislature in order to license it" (p. 439). However, during the discussion of another roll call earlier in the debates on June 8, Elbridge Gerry (Massachusetts), a major financier at the convention, though opposed to a national negative on all state laws, did not have any "objection to authorize a negative to paper money and similar measures" (Farrand, 1911, vol. 1, p. 165).

The Eleventh Issue. States would have been prohibited from enacting trade embargoes under the eleventh issue, also considered on August 28 but strongly defeated, 13–29, with only 30.9 percent yes votes. The estimated model for the vote indicates that the "average" delegate to Philadelphia has a predicted probability of a yes vote of .333, a predicted vote that is nearly identical to the actual voting outcome of 30.9 percent yes. Yet interpreting the statistical findings for this issue could be complicated because the vote may have been part of a general compromise at the Philadelphia convention (along with the twelfth and thirteenth votes) to reach a consensus concerning state–level trade policy. Such a compromise could conceal voting related to the economic interests of the framers. Despite any obscuring effects of a possible compromise, the three debtors at the convention unanimously opposed the eleventh vote (see table 3.5). The findings indicate that public securities holdings and distance from navigable water (more isolated, less commercial areas) significantly increased the likelihood of favoring the prohibition on state trade embargoes. And, given the small sample size involved in the analysis, the estimated effect of personal slaveholdings might be considered precise enough to say that it also significantly increased the likelihood of voting for the prohibition.[50] Economic interests once again mattered for a vote on an important economic issue that arose at Philadelphia.

Coincidentally, three of the four significant marginal effects are quite similar in magnitude. The response elasticity for public securities holdings is .293; for distance from navigable water, .201; and for personal slaveholdings, .244. In all three cases, a 1 percent increase from the mean in the value of the variable, for example, causes a less than .3 percent increase in the predicted probability of voting to prohibit state trade embargoes. But for a state's population, the response elasticity is a much larger, −1.61. Despite the three extremely small marginal effects, the predicted probabilities of voting for the eleventh issue, as with the three previously discussed votes, are dramatically different for delegates with dramatically different interests and characteristics. Compare the various predicted probabilities of a yes vote reported in table 3.9 for the different values of the explanatory variables. For example, for different amounts of personal slaveholdings, the voting probabilities range from .257 to .911, indicating that the largest personal slaveholdings increase the likelihood of voting to prohibit state trade embargoes to close to certain. Also, for different values of public securities holdings, the probabilities range from .243 to .920, indicating that an increase in public securities holdings strongly increases the likelihood of voting in favor of the issue.

The findings indicate some potentially plausible voting patterns. The three debtors at the convention behaved consistently as states-rights advocates when on August 28 they unanimously opposed the prohibition on state trade embargoes. As one of them, Roger Sherman (Connecticut), argued, "the States ought to retain this power in order to prevent suffering & injury to their poor" (Farrand, 1911, vol. 2, p. 440). For the

Table 3.9. Predicted Probabilities of a Yes Vote on the Eleventh Issue for a Delegate with Different Interests and Characteristics: Statistically Significant Variables

Economic Interests and Characteristics	Predicted Probability of a Yes on Vote 11
The "Average" Delegate	.333
Personal Slaveholdings (Number of Slaves)[a]	
0 (the least for any delegate)	.257
32.36 (the mean)	.333
50	.379
100	.517
150	.654
200	.768
300 (the most for any delegate)	.911
Public Securities Holdings (Market Value)	
$ 0 (the least for any delegate)	.243
$ 1,229 (the mean)	.333
$ 2,500	.440
$ 3,500	.529
$ 5,000	.658
$ 7,500	.824
$10,000 (the most for any delegate)	.920
Distance from Navigable Water (Miles)	
0 (the nearest for any delegate)	.270
16.40 (the mean)	.333
50	.481
75	.595
100	.699
150	.854
200 (the farthest for any delegate)	.936
Population in State (Number of Whites)	
46,000 (the least populous)	.783
142,000	.595
209,000	.439
257,132 (the mean)	.333
314,000	.227
373,000	.144
442,000 (the most populous)	.081

[a] Not significant at conventional levels, but the estimated effect of the variable still may be precise enough to be suggestive of an influence on the vote.

Note: All predicted probabilities are calculated from the estimated logistic coefficients for Vote 11 reported in table A3.3b in appendix 3. All other details are as described in the note to table 3.6.

slaveowners, the majority of whom were involved in the export of rice and tobacco (McDonald, 1958, chap. 3), any desire to use trade embargoes for political purposes must have been outweighed by revenue concerns, as they were more likely to vote for the prohibition on embargoes. Yet George Mason (Virginia) could not have been more forceful in opposition to the prohibition, contending it "would be not only improper but dangerous, as the Genl. Legislature would not sit constantly and therefore could not interpose at the necessary moments;" the national legislature thus may not be able to respond to "the necessity of sudden embargoes during the war, to prevent exports, particularly in the case of a blockade" (Farrand, 1911, vol. 2, pp. 440–441). But James Madison (Virginia) believed "that such acts (by the States) would be unnecessary—impolitic—& unjust" (p. 440). And Gouverneur Morris (Pennsylvania) also found "the provision as unnecessary; the power of regulating trade between State & State, already vested in the Genl-Legislature, being sufficient" (p. 441).

Why delegates from the more isolated, inland areas (farther from navigable water) appear to have been nearly certain to vote in favor of the prohibition, however, is not obvious. Perhaps the findings for the distance from navigable water are a consequence of compromise voting on the issue in the attempt to reach a general compromise over export and import restrictions by states.

The Thirteenth Issue. Another issue taken up on August 28 was the thirteenth vote, which would have prohibited states from enacting export tariffs. The vote passed modestly, 25–17, with 59.5 percent yes votes. The economic model indicates that the "average" delegate to the convention has a predicted probability of .633 on the vote, an estimated prediction very close, again, to the actual voting outcome. It could be difficult to interpret the findings, however, because as noted for the eleventh vote, the proposal might have been part of the wider compromise involving both the eleventh and twelfth votes to reach a consensus concerning state–level trade restrictions. Yet despite the possible obscuring effects of compromise voting, the findings again include several significant results, indicating that economic interests mattered. Delegates who were officers in the Revolutionary War, who were from more commercial areas (nearer to navigable water), and who were from more populous states were statistically more likely to favor the prohibition on state export tariffs (see table 3.5). Given the small sample size, the estimates likewise suggest that the amount of a delegate's public securities holdings and the amount of constituent slaves in the state represented decrease the likelihood of support for the thirteenth issue.[51]

A discussion of the magnitudes of the effects is instructive. The incremental effect of being an officer is huge: An otherwise average delegate who was an officer has a predicted probability of a yes vote .364 greater than a delegate who was not an officer. The marginal effect on voting for a state's population is not small: Its response elasticity is a modest .786. In contrast, the response elasticity for a delegate's public securities holdings is a mere −.159; for constituent slaves, it is a more modest −.336; for distance from navigable water, it is a trivial −.134.

But despite the rather small marginal effects, the voting probabilities are still substantially different for substantially different interests. Compare, for example, the predicted probabilities reported in table 3.10

for different values of the variables. A delegate who was an officer was 75 percent more likely to vote yes than a delegate who was not an officer. Surprisingly, an otherwise average delegate who owned the largest amount of public securities has a probability of voting to prohibit state export tariffs of only .072, but if he owned no public securities the probability is .727, ten times as high! The estimates also indicate that delegates from the most commercial areas were highly likely to vote for the issue, while a delegate from the most isolated backcountry area (200 miles from navigable water) was nearly certain to oppose the issue. An otherwise average delegate who represented a state with the heaviest concentration of slaves was not very likely to vote to prohibit state export tariffs either (see table 3.10).

Why delegates with greater amounts of public securities would be less likely to vote to prohibit state export tariffs does not appear obvious. It might be especially difficult to comprehend considering that a delegate with the largest amount of public securities was not just less likely to vote in favor of the issue—he was nearly certain to vote against the prohibition (his probability of voting yes is barely 7 percent). This suggests that public creditors were opposed to a prohibition on state powers that arguably would have strengthened the national government. Perhaps they saw state export tariffs as a source of state revenues, which were viewed as necessary to ensure that public creditors received payment of their loans, perhaps to state governments. It also is possible that compromises involved in the issue of state import and export restrictions made this vote a compromise and thus obscured straightforward self-interest voting on the issue.

The economic reason why the delegates from slave states were likely to oppose the thirteenth vote also might not be obvious. But a possible explanation, given that state import tariffs had already been prohibited earlier in the convention, is that delegates from slaveholding states hoped to exploit through their state governments a degree of monopoly power in the export of slave-based products through export tariffs. States with export-based economies could potentially collect the bulk of revenues from interstate tariffs because of their monopoly position in tobacco and rice, while other states would be prevented from retaliating with import tariffs. The tariff–induced higher prices might not have had much impact on the amount of rice and tobacco sold because the importing states lacked viable alternatives—the importing states might have had relatively inelastic demands for rice and tobacco. As James Madison (Virginia) noted earlier in the debates when discussing *international* exports on August 16, tariffs on exports

"might with particular advantage be exercised with regard to articles in which America was not rivalled in foreign markets, as Tobo. &c. The contract between the French Farmers Genl. and Mr. Morris stipulating that if taxes sd. be laid in America on the export of Tobo. they sd. be paid by the

Table 3.10. Predicted Probabilities of a Yes Vote on the Thirteenth Issue for a
Delegate with Different Interests and Characteristics: Statistically Significant Variables

Economic Interests and Characteristics	Predicted Probability of a Yes on Vote 13
The "Average" Delegate	.633
Officer	.849
Not an officer	.485
Public Securities Holdings (Market Value)	
$ 0 (the least for any delegate)	.727
$ 1,229 (the mean)	.633
$ 2,500	.524
$ 3,500	.436
$ 5,000	.313
$ 7,500	.158
$10,000 (the most for any delegate)	.072
Constituent Slaveholdings (Slaves per 100 Whites)	
0 (the least for any state)	.812
15	.726
28.06 (the mean)	.633
40	.539
50	.457
60	.378
76 (the most for any state)	.265
Distance from Navigable Water (Miles)	
0 (the nearest for any delegate)	.713
16.40 (the mean)	.633
50	.450
75	.319
100	.211
150	.081
200 (the farthest for any delegate)	.028
Population in State (Number of Whites)	
46,000 (the least populous)	.229
142,000	.398
209,000	.536
257,132 (the mean)	.633
314,000	.735
373,000	.820
442,000 (the most populous)	.890

Note: All predicted probabilities are calculated from the estimated logistic coefficients for Vote 13 reported in table A3.3b in appendix 3. All other details are as described in the note to table 3.6.

Farmers, shewed that it was understood by them, that the price would be thereby raised in America, and consequently the taxes be paid by the European Consumer" (Farrand, 1911, vol. 2, p. 306).

The Fourteenth Issue. A requirement that a two-thirds majority of the national legislature would be necessary to enact any laws regulating trade would have been considered had the fourteenth vote passed at Philadelphia. But on August 29, it was soundly defeated 12–30, with only 28.6 percent yes votes. The estimated voting model indicates that the "average" delegate to Philadelphia has a predicted probability of a yes vote on the two-thirds requirement of only .206, an estimate that, again, is a reasonably close prediction of the actual voting outcome. An often-presumed vote trade might complicate interpreting the vote on the issue, however. John Rutledge (South Carolina) and other southern delegates are said to have agreed to vote against the two-thirds provision in exchange for support from Roger Sherman (Connecticut) and other New England delegates for an extension on the limitation of slave imports (see Jensen, 1964; compare to McDonald, 1965, chap. 6). Despite potential obscuring effects of the possible logrolling on the issue, the findings still show that the nine merchants were unanimous in their opposition while officers in the war were less likely to vote in favor of the issue, as well (see table 3.5). Delegates who represented slave states and those who represented more isolated backcountry areas were more likely to favor the proposal.[52]

The magnitudes of several of the effects are not trivial either. The incremental effect of being an officer is substantial: An otherwise average delegate who was an officer has a predicted probability of a yes vote .270 less than a delegate who was not an officer. The response elasticity for constituent slaveholdings is a fairly large 1.72. In contrast, for distance from navigable water, the elasticity is a modest .435.

As with the five previously discussed votes, the predicted probabilities for the fourteenth issue are considerably different for delegates with considerably different interests, as indicated by the predicted probabilities for different values of the explanatory variables reported in table 3.11. A delegate who was an officer was about 74 percent less likely to vote yes than an otherwise average delegate who was not an officer. For delegates who represented states with different constituent slaveholdings, the predicted probabilities range from .029 to .914. For different distances from navigable water, the probabilities range from .131 to .992. Both ranges are not only considerable but also indicate that, despite any supposed vote trade on the issue, economic interests once more mattered strongly for an important economic issue at the Philadelphia convention. For example, an otherwise average delegate from South Carolina, the state with the heaviest concentration of slaves, was over 91 percent likely to vote for the two-thirds provision. And a delegate from one of the most isolated, least commercial backcountry areas in North Carolina was virtually certain (99 percent likely) to vote for the two-thirds provision.

The results for the fourteenth issue also indicate just how different the outcome of the framing would have been had different delegates been present at Philadelphia. What if, in the extreme, all delegates in attendance at the Philadelphia convention had been from the most isolated inland areas or from the state with the heaviest concentration of slaves? The estimates of the predicted probabilities for distance and constituent slave-

Table 3.11. Predicted Probabilities of a Yes Vote on the Fourteenth Issue for a
Delegate with Different Interests and Characteristics: Statistically Significant Variables

Economic Interests and Characteristics	Predicted Probability of a Yes on Vote 14
The "Average" Delegate	.206
Officer	.066
Not officer	.336
Constituent Slaveholdings (Slaves per 100 Whites)	
0 (the least for any state)	.029
15	.086
28.06 (the mean)	.206
40	.396
50	.587
60	.755
76 (the most for any state)	.914
Distance from Navigable Water (Miles)	
0 (the nearest for any delegate)	.131
16.40 (the mean)	.206
50	.444
75	.648
100	.809
150	.958
200 (the farthest for any delegate)	.992

Note: All predicted probabilities are calculated from the estimated logistic coefficients for Vote 14 reported in table A3.3b in appendix 3. All other details are as described in the note to table 3.6.

holdings for otherwise average delegates in table 3.11 suggest that almost certainly the Constitution would have included a requirement of a two-thirds majority of the national legislature to enact any laws concerning trade.

In the debates on August 29, Charles Pinckney (South Carolina) proposed that the two-thirds requirement be considered because there were distinct commercial interests in the country and the "different interests would be a source of oppressive regulations if no check to a bare majority should be provided"; Pinckney further maintained that "[t]he power of regulating commerce was a pure concession on the part of the S. States" (Farrand, 1911, vol. 2, p. 449). His older cousin, Charles Coatsworth Pinckney (South Carolina), likewise argued that "it was the true interest of the S. States to have no regulations of commerce" but, citing the "liberal conduct toward the views of South Carolina" by the eastern states, conceded that "no fetters should be imposed on the power of making commercial regulations" (pp. 449–450). George Clymer (Pennsylvania) agreed there should be no "unnecessary restrictions. The Northern & middle States will be ruined, if not enabled to defend themselves against foreign regulations" (p. 450). And Gouverneur Morris (Pennsylvania), who also spoke against the issue, considered "the motion as highly injurious"

(p. 450). Yet Pierce Butler (South Carolina) "considered the interests of these [southern states] and of the Eastern States, to be as different as the interests of Russia and Turkey" (p. 451) but would vote against the provision in the spirit of reconciliation with the eastern states. Venting his frustration, George Mason (Virginia) emphatically maintained that "[t]he *Majority* will be governed by their interests. The Southern States are the *minority* in both Houses. Is it to be expected that they will deliver themselves bound hand & foot to the Eastern States, and enable them to exclaim, in the words of Cromwell on a certain occasion—'the lord hath delivered them into our hands'" (p. 451, emphasis in original).

About a week earlier in the debates on August 21, John Rutledge (South Carolina), former governor and a major slaveowner, expressed serious reservations about any union of northern and southern states because of the differences on trade issues. During a general discussion of trade issues, including discussion of a two-thirds requirement to enact export taxes, Luther Martin (Maryland) proposed a change that would allow a prohibition, or a tax, on the importation of slaves. Martin wanted to explicitly discourage the importation of slaves. In response, Rutledge, who did not believe the Constitution would encourage slave imports, maintained instead that "Religion & humanity had nothing to do with this question—Interest alone is the governing principle with Nations—The true question at present is whether the Southn. States shall or shall not be parties to the Union" (p. 364). Charles Pinckney (South Carolina) made it obvious during the August 21 debates that "South Carolina can never receive the plan [the Constitution] if it prohibits the slave trade" (p. 364). Much later on September 15, just two days before the convention finished the Constitution, still frustrated, George Mason (Virginia) argued that the failure to adopt a two-thirds requirement to enact trade regulations "would enable a few rich merchants in Philada, N. York & Boston, to monopolize the Staples of the Southern States & reduce their value perhaps 50 Per Ct" (p. 631).

The Results and Existing Historical Studies

The findings that economic interests were important at the Philadelphia convention are consistent with the views of some scholars who contend that economic interests mattered. Their studies, however, typically measure the impact of economic interests on the *overall* vote of delegates, drawing inferences from the frequency of votes of delegates with particular interests rather than estimating the partial effect of a specific interest on voting behavior. The studies nearly always draw conclusions about the influence of any interest—for example, slaveholdings or public securities holdings—on an issue based on the proportion of delegates with the interest who favored or opposed the issue, without controlling for the confounding influence of other interests (see, e.g., McDonald, 1958, pp. 349–357). As a result, it is not surprising that several studies conclude that slaveowners either favored the Constitution or were indifferent toward it.[53] Most of the delegates at Philadelphia who were slaveowners in fact often favored strengthening the central government and supported the Constitution. But it was not slaveholdings per se that influenced them to do so; it was the slaveowners' other interests. It also is not surprising that some studies conclude that public securities holders (public creditors) were split over the Constitution because delegates with public securities holdings in fact were both supporters and opponents on some issues at Philadelphia.[54] Yet it was not their public securities holdings per se that influenced them to vote differently; it was their other interests.

Because the conclusions found in the existing literature about slave-owners and public creditors typically consider each as a distinct group, it may be informative to ask how the economic interests and characteristics of slaveowners only and of public creditors only influenced their voting behavior. The effects of the various interests on the votes at Philadelphia can be calculated separately for those delegates who owned slaves and separately for those delegates who owned public securities. Such estimates might be more comparable to the conclusions in some existing studies. To accomplish this, the marginal or incremental effects of the explanatory variables for the six selected issues are calculated employing the means of the variables for the twenty-nine public creditors and the means of the variables for the eighteen slaveowners, respectively. The predicted probability of a yes vote for each issue likewise is calculated for the means of public creditors and slaveowners, respectively. Consequently, the effects of the various interests on the votes and the predicted voting probabilities are estimated for the "average" public securities owner (public creditor) and the "average" slaveowner to supplement the estimates already given for the "average" delegate.

The estimated effects for the "average" public creditor and the "average" slaveowner, reported in appendix 3, tables A3.4 and A3.5, respectively, provide even more support for the conclusions already drawn here, that economic interests mattered. Table A3.4 shows that the direction and magnitude of the estimated marginal or incremental effects of the various economic interests and characteristics for the "average" public creditor for all six issues, are essentially the same as those for a delegate who had average values for all economic interests and characteristics, the "average" delegate to Philadelphia.

The effects for the "average" slaveowner, reported in table A3.5, are qualitatively and quantitatively similar to those for the "average" delegate to Philadelphia for four of the six votes. For the second and seventh votes, however, the effects are qualitatively similar but quantitatively are one-half to two-thirds smaller for all variables except for the slave variable itself. These smaller marginal and incremental effects mean that the impact of a particular interest on the predicted probability of a yes vote (other than slaveownership itself) was much smaller for the "average" slaveowner than for the "average" delegate. The slave interests of the

Table 3.12. Predicted Probabilities of a Yes Vote on Selected Issues for the Average Delegate, the Average Public Creditor, and the Average Slaveowner

	Predicted Probability		
	Average Delegate	Average Public Creditor	Average Slaveowner
Vote 2	.379	.415	.236
Vote 7	.560	.524	.851
Vote 9	.859	.903	.746
Vote 11	.333	.331	.472
Vote 13	.633	.674	.224
Vote 14	.206	.159	.599
Number of Observations	53	29	18

Note: All predicted probabilities are calculated from the estimated logistic coefficients for the appropriate vote reported in table A3.3a,b in appendix 3. The predicted probabilities are calculated employing the mean values of all explanatory variables for all delegates (the "average" delegate), the mean values of all explanatory variables for the public creditor delegates only (the "average" public creditor), and the mean values of all explanatory variables for the slaveowning delegates only (the "average" slaveowner), respectively.

slaveowners apparently "swamped" the influence of their other interests, suggesting that slaveowners had especially strong interests involved in these two issues. Slaveowners apparently expected their slave interests to be especially affected by the second issue, which would give the national legislature absolute veto power over all state laws, and the seventh issue, which would prohibit the national legislature from enacting export tariffs. And those expectations on the part of slaveowners are perfectly consistent with an economic interpretation of the framers' voting behavior.

The predicted voting probabilities for public creditors and for slaveowners also yield important conclusions. Table 3.12 lists the estimated voting probabilities for the six selected issues for the "average" delegate, "average" public creditor, and "average" slaveowner at the Philadelphia convention. The predictions for the "average" delegate and the "average" public creditor for the six issues are not only similar, in one case (the eleventh issue) they are essentially identical. However, the estimated voting probabilities for the "average" delegate and the "average" slaveowner are quite different, and in two cases (the thirteenth and fourteenth issues) the voting probabilities are opposite each other. For the thirteenth vote, the voting predictions for the "average" delegate (.633) and "average" public creditor (.674) indicate a high likelihood of both voting for the prohibition on state export taxes. Yet, on average, slaveowners have only a .224 probability of voting for the prohibition. They were 65 percent less likely to support the issue than was the "average" delegate. For the fourteenth vote (the two-thirds requirement to enact trade laws), the estimates indicate that neither the "average" delegate nor the "average" public creditor was likely to vote for the issue. But, on average, slaveowners are estimated to have nearly a 60 percent probability of voting in favor of the requirement. They were over 190 percent more likely to support the issue than the "average" delegate!

The voting probabilities suggest that public creditors and the "average" delegate were likely to have voted the same at the convention, but that slaveowners were likely to have voted quite differently. An important implication is that if slaveowners had been the predominant delegates at the constitutional convention, the thirteenth issue prohibiting state export taxes likely would have failed and the fourteenth issue requiring a two-thirds majority to enact trade laws likely would have passed. That the fourteenth issue might have passed had slaveowners predominated may be one of the more important implications of this reexamination of the Philadelphia convention, because even if the two-thirds requirement to enact trade laws alone had been the only change in the Constitution, we would have had a fundamentally different constitution.[55]

The Predicted Votes for the Specific Delegates at the Philadelphia Convention

In addition to the analysis of the predicted voting probabilities for delegates with average values, or with various specific values, for the economic interests and characteristics, why not look at how the specific interests and characteristics of the actual delegates affected their predicted votes on the issues? How well does the economic model predict the voting behavior of specific delegates? The analysis employing the average or specific values for various characteristics and economic interests provides important evidence on the overall magnitude of the influence of each factor on the votes. But perhaps more historically interesting is to use the data collected on the specific delegates to predict their votes on each issue. Such an analysis will indicate how accurately the economic model predicts the votes of the fifty-three specific delegates to the Philadelphia convention. What percentage of the delegates' votes does the model predict correctly? Did certain individuals rise above their personal and constituent interests? Did others at Philadelphia tend to vote strictly their economic interests? Do James Madison's own economic interests and characteristics, for example, predict his votes well? Do the characteristics and economic interests of Alexander Hamilton or George Mason or George Washington predict their votes well? What about the predicted votes for the other Founding Fathers at Philadelphia?

The predicted votes for each of the fifty-three delegates for all sixteen issues are calculated using each delegate's own economic interests and characteristics and the estimated logistic coefficients for the more parsimonious model contained in table A3.3a,b. The predicted and actual votes for each delegate for each of the issues are reported in table 3.13a,b. To determine the accuracy of the model's predictions, a common method to

Delegate	State	Vote 1		Vote 2		Vote 3	
		Actual	Predicted	Actual	Predicted	Actual	Predicted
Nicholas Gilman	NH	0	.647	0	.404	0	.129
John Langdon, Jr.	NH	0	.761	0	.171	0	.611
Elbridge Gerry	MA	1	.473	0	.519	1	.773
Nathaniel Gorham	MA	0	.016	1	.614	0	.082
Rufus King	MA	0	.594	1	.875	1	.520
Caleb Strong	MA	0	.073	1	.521	1	.787
Oliver Ellsworth	CN	1	.443	1	.452	1	.580
William Samuel Johnson	CN	1	.529	0	.630	1	.321
Roger Sherman	CN	1	.290	0	.429	1	.199
Alexander Hamilton	NY	0	.288	1	.804	0	.034
John Lansing	NY	0	.077	0	.067	1	.972
Robert Yates	NY	0	.024	0	.213	1	.800
David Brearley	NJ	1	.714	0	.440	0	.096
Jonathan Dayton	NJ	0	.557	0	.236	0	.177
William Livingston	NJ	1	.634	0	.346	0	.143
William Paterson	NJ	1	.821	0	.372	1	.475
George Clymer	PA	0	.152	1	.881	0	.048
Thomas Fitzsimons	PA	0	.042	1	.714	0	.039
Benjamin Franklin	PA	0	.116	1	.847	0	.349
Jared Ingersol	PA	0	.095	1	.939	0	.105
Thomas Mifflin	PA	0	.020	1	.900	0	.007
Gouverneur Morris	PA	0	.095	1	.933	0	.105
Robert Morris	PA	0	.050	1	.708	0	.236
James Wilson	PA	0	.081	1	.823	0	.221
Richard Bassett	DE	1	.847	0	.127	0	.140
Gunning Bedford, Jr.	DE	1	.849	0	.149	0	.427
Jacob Broom	DE	1	.911	0	.099	0	.582
John Dickinson	DE	1	.868	1	.149	0	.116
George Read	DE	1	.925	1	.117	0	.533
Daniel Carroll	MD	0	.445	0	.217	0	.813
Daniel of St. Thomas Jenifer	MD	0	.348	0	.209	0	.727
Luther Martin	MD	1	.211	1	.460	1	.715
James McHenry	MD	0	.256	0	.414	0	.049
John Francis Mercer	MD	1	.514	1	.341	0	.285
John Blair	VA	0	.044	1	.855	0	.285
James Madison	VA	0	.010	1	.585	0	.264
George Mason	VA	0	.428	0	.180	0	.129
James McClurg	VA	0	.096	1	.879	0	.032
Edmund Randolph	VA	0	.030	0	.479	0	.631
George Washington	VA	0	.003	0	.747	0	.016
William Blount	NC	1	.080	1	.155	1	.892
William Richardson Davie	NC	0	.041	0	.424	1	.473
Alexander Martin	NC	0	.005	0	.015	1	.988
Richard Dobbs Spaight	NC	1	.551	0	.483	1	.775
Hugh Williamson	NC	0	.076	0	.390	1	.115
Pierce Butler	SC	1	.836	0	.059	1	.466
Charles Pinckney	SC	1	.578	1	.104	0	.093
Charles Coatsworth Pinckney	SC	1	.601	0	.138	1	.202
John Rutledge	SC	1	.980	0	.022	1	.466
Abraham Baldwin	GA	0	.574	0	.066	0	.183
William Few	GA	0	.294	0	.167	0	.008
William Houstoun	GA	0	.813	0	.063	1	.781
William Pierce	GA	0	.196	0	.064	0	.005
Percent Correct			79.25		83.02		75.47

Note: The actual vote for each delegate is the probable vote of the delegate at the Philadelphia convention as determined from Farrand (1911, vol. 1, pp. 130–147, 162–173, 369–382; vol. 2, pp. 84–96, 116–128, 245–256, 352–365, 380–395). A yes vote by a delegate equals 1, and a no vote equals 0. The predicted vote for each delegate is the estimated predicted probability of a yes vote for the delegate computed from the logistic estimates of the more parsimonious voting model specifications reported in table A3.3a in appendix 3. For the

Vote 4		Vote 5		Vote 6		Vote 7		Vote 8	
Actual	Predicted	Actual	Predicted	Actual	Predicted	Actual	Predicted	Actual	Predicted
0	.549	0	.050	0	.429	0	.088	1	.715
0	.841	0	.125	0	.111	0	.493	1	.379
1	.329	1	.503	1	.885	1	.418	0	.588
0	.099	0	.127	0	.000	1	.373	1	.839
0	.235	0	.059	1	.982	0	.256	1	.667
0	.525	0	.462	1	.885	1	.385	1	.353
1	.788	0	.220	0	.798	1	.262	0	.440
1	.350	0	.074	0	.395	1	.217	0	.610
1	.523	0	.029	0	.000	1	.510	0	.640
0	.004	0	.005	0	.002	1	.163	1	.958
1	.789	1	.987	1	.963	0	.406	0	.307
1	.365	1	.739	1	.607	0	.517	0	.222
0	.150	0	.019	0	.032	0	.141	1	.899
0	.377	0	.319	0	.087	0	.079	1	.891
0	.050	0	.035	0	.048	0	.157	1	.864
0	.273	1	.080	1	.213	0	.295	0	.720
0	.007	0	.003	0	.003	0	.349	1	.914
0	.010	0	.026	0	.000	0	.234	1	.974
0	.323	0	.356	0	.516	0	.154	1	.788
0	.031	0	.015	0	.015	0	.249	1	.844
0	.007	0	.001	0	.000	0	.327	1	.955
0	.031	0	.015	0	.015	0	.249	1	.844
0	.182	0	.179	0	.001	0	.407	1	.804
0	.045	0	.171	0	.002	0	.166	1	.929
1	.103	0	.060	1	.188	0	.228	1	.797
1	.906	0	.250	1	.938	0	.381	1	.354
1	.825	0	.226	1	.656	0	.431	1	.531
0	.092	0	.045	0	.160	0	.217	0	.821
1	.807	0	.179	1	.624	0	.416	1	.569
1	.530	0	.571	0	.060	1	.842	0	.726
0	.384	0	.680	0	.420	1	.823	0	.471
1	.668	1	.562	1	.291	1	.807	0	.633
0	.007	0	.030	0	.009	1	.826	0	.849
1	.177	1	.249	1	.540	1	.618	0	.776
0	.006	0	.096	0	.003	1	.945	1	.947
0	.007	1	.384	0	.008	0	.953	1	.708
0	.012	1	.691	1	.258	1	.872	0	.574
0	.000	0	.010	0	.245	1	.949	1	.933
0	.037	0	.653	1	.611	1	.960	1	.548
0	.005	0	.301	0	.000	0	.738	1	.964
1	.727	1	.983	0	.283	1	.583	1	.469
0	.088	1	.472	0	.028	1	.537	1	.770
0	.290	1	.994	0	.200	1	.811	0	.271
0	.154	1	.301	0	.028	1	.698	1	.821
0	.101	1	.358	0	.006	1	.568	1	.872
0	.061	0	.451	0	.228	1	.950	1	.627
0	.007	0	.153	0	.016	1	.883	1	.881
0	.030	0	.225	0	.160	1	.890	1	.880
0	.061	0	.451	0	.801	1	.949	1	.438
0	.221	1	.201	0	.268	1	.866	1	.586
0	.050	0	.035	0	.107	1	.650	1	.763
0	.754	1	.784	1	.875	0	.822	0	.338
0	.002	0	.008	0	.000	1	.888	1	.907
	83.02		81.13		86.79		81.13		71.70

interest of the reader, the estimated predicted probabilities for Votes 1 and 3 have been reported despite the uncorrectable errors discovered in their data. As a result of the errors, however, the findings for the two votes may be questionable. The percent correct is the percentage of the observed yes votes (= 1) with an estimated predicted value greater than .50 plus the percentage of the observed no votes (= 0) with an estimated predicted value less than .50.

Table 3.13b. The Vote and the Predicted Probability of a Yes Vote for the Delegates at the Philadelphia Constitutional Convention of 1787: The Ninth through Sixteenth Issues

Delegate	State	Vote 9		Vote 10		Vote 11	
		Actual	Predicted	Actual	Predicted	Actual	Predicted
Nicholas Gilman	NH	1	.984	1	.927	0	.367
John Langdon, Jr.	NH	1	.974	1	.455	0	.478
Elbridge Gerry	MA	1	.889	0	.515	1	.642
Nathaniel Gorham	MA	0	.650	1	.853	1	.047
Rufus King	MA	1	.958	1	.566	1	.260
Caleb Strong	MA	1	.786	1	.238	0	.376
Oliver Ellsworth	CN	1	.931	0	.495	0	.326
William Samuel Johnson	CN	1	.854	0	.684	0	.176
Roger Sherman	CN	1	.973	0	.640	0	.123
Alexander Hamilton	NY	1	.961	1	.980	0	.095
John Lansing	NY	0	.494	0	.335	1	.858
Robert Yates	NY	0	.221	0	.151	1	.458
David Brearley	NJ	1	.992	1	.973	0	.288
Jonathan Dayton	NJ	1	.971	1	.984	0	.518
William Livingston	NJ	1	.953	1	.962	0	.355
William Paterson	NJ	0	.929	0	.814	1	.294
George Clymer	PA	1	.985	1	.903	0	.133
Thomas Fitzsimons	PA	1	.981	1	.987	0	.096
Benjamin Franklin	PA	1	.848	1	.794	0	.176
Jared Ingersol	PA	1	.830	1	.767	0	.035
Thomas Mifflin	PA	1	.985	1	.958	0	.022
Gouverneur Morris	PA	1	.830	1	.767	0	.035
Robert Morris	PA	1	.885	1	.753	0	.132
James Wilson	PA	1	.792	1	.944	0	.068
Richard Bassett	DE	1	.931	1	.953	1	.591
Gunning Bedford, Jr.	DE	1	.911	1	.518	1	.571
Jacob Broom	DE	1	.963	1	.706	1	.600
John Dickinson	DE	1	.941	1	.960	1	.555
George Read	DE	1	.969	1	.740	1	.567
Daniel Carroll	MD	1	.904	0	.612	0	.398
Daniel of St. Thomas Jenifer	MD	1	.565	0	.355	0	.455
Luther Martin	MD	0	.580	0	.462	0	.286
James McHenry	MD	0	.448	0	.732	0	.205
John Francis Mercer	MD	0	.953	0	.834	1	.547
John Blair	VA	0	.680	0	.681	0	.092
James Madison	VA	0	.212	1	.260	1	.162
George Mason	VA	1	.967	0	.519	0	.598
James McClurg	VA	1	.468	1	.548	0	.221
Edmund Randolph	VA	1	.491	0	.131	0	.458
George Washington	VA	0	.560	1	.949	1	.104
William Blount	NC	1	.328	1	.504	0	.527
William Richardson Davie	NC	1	.533	1	.794	0	.298
Alexander Martin	NC	0	.150	0	.254	1	.893
Richard Dobbs Spaight	NC	1	.916	1	.759	0	.221
Hugh Williamson	NC	1	.635	1	.862	0	.235
Pierce Butler	SC	1	.849	1	.519	1	.696
Charles Pinckney	SC	1	.851	1	.908	1	.608
Charles Coatsworth Pinckney	SC	1	.900	1	.881	1	.705
John Rutledge	SC	1	.986	1	.444	1	.876
Abraham Baldwin	GA	1	.659	1	.525	0	.638
William Few	GA	1	.691	1	.856	0	.499
William Houstoun	GA	0	.625	0	.362	1	.711
William Pierce	GA	1	.678	1	.936	0	.327
Percent Correct			81.13		75.47		83.02

Note: The actual vote for each delegate is the probable vote of the delegate at the Philadelphia convention as determined from Farrand (1911, vol. 2, pp. 434–440, 445–456, 457–470, 621–640). A yes vote equals 1, and a no vote equals 0. The predicted vote for each delegate is the estimated predicted probability of a yes vote for the delegate computed from the logistic estimates of the more parsimonious voting model specifications reported in

Vote 12		Vote 13		Vote 14		Vote 15		Vote 16	
Actual	Predicted	Actual	Predicted	Actual	Predicted	Actual	Predicted	Actual	Predicted
1	.860	1	.903	0	.018	1	.802	0	.578
1	.242	1	.330	0	.061	1	.701	0	.358
0	.184	0	.501	0	.029	0	.407	0	.026
0	.110	1	.972	0	.178	1	.993	0	.040
1	.266	1	.685	0	.011	1	.622	0	.127
0	.591	1	.473	0	.253	1	.395	0	.559
0	.658	0	.606	0	.141	1	.556	0	.477
0	.515	0	.797	0	.066	1	.815	1	.314
0	.085	0	.743	0	.054	1	.970	1	.217
0	.373	1	.985	0	.005	1	.993	0	.180
1	.948	0	.382	1	.856	0	.096	1	.462
1	.763	0	.318	1	.784	0	.288	1	.784
1	.720	1	.953	0	.010	1	.963	1	.370
1	.939	1	.973	0	.056	1	.878	0	.170
1	.778	1	.932	0	.018	1	.941	1	.470
1	.570	0	.771	1	.069	0	.877	1	.308
0	.035	1	.930	0	.001	1	.986	0	.073
0	.124	1	.994	0	.006	1	.998	0	.025
0	.519	1	.942	0	.079	1	.790	0	.038
0	.137	1	.952	0	.023	1	.978	0	.114
0	.026	1	.989	0	.003	1	.999	0	.093
0	.137	1	.952	0	.023	1	.978	0	.114
0	.087	1	.917	0	.062	1	.960	0	.023
0	.423	1	.989	0	.073	1	.987	0	.035
1	.870	1	.802	0	.062	0	.817	1	.528
1	.788	1	.287	0	.414	0	.267	0	.471
1	.776	1	.403	0	.322	0	.552	0	.459
1	.853	1	.829	0	.049	1	.849	0	.480
1	.750	1	.443	0	.265	1	.602	0	.411
0	.256	0	.277	1	.592	1	.797	0	.137
0	.338	0	.126	1	.714	0	.463	0	.200
0	.203	0	.280	1	.700	0	.583	1	.096
0	.158	0	.542	1	.610	0	.912	0	.078
1	.437	0	.387	1	.104	0	.639	1	.155
0	.013	0	.549	1	.403	1	.971	0	.010
1	.047	1	.186	0	.855	1	.833	0	.061
0	.261	0	.098	1	.456	0	.634	0	.018
0	.014	1	.322	0	.311	1	.841	0	.007
0	.070	0	.048	1	.810	0	.359	0	.068
1	.162	1	.932	0	.572	1	.976	0	.008
1	.758	1	.423	1	.884	1	.382	0	.120
0	.504	1	.710	0	.262	1	.835	0	.343
1	.933	0	.117	1	.957	0	.182	1	.940
1	.172	1	.580	0	.131	1	.940	0	.096
1	.485	1	.875	1	.750	1	.899	0	.033
0	.233	0	.038	0	.773	1	.569	0	.092
0	.330	0	.268	1	.409	1	.860	0	.105
0	.314	0	.208	0	.403	1	.696	0	.080
0	.343	0	.010	0	.512	1	.369	0	.134
0	.519	0	.132	1	.913	1	.427	0	.244
0	.635	0	.465	1	.621	1	.602	0	.256
1	.580	0	.048	1	.823	0	.187	1	.269
0	.105	1	.624	0	.443	1	.986	0	.145
	75.47		71.70		84.91		81.13		79.25

table A3.3b in appendix 3. The percent correct is the percentage of the observed yes votes (= 1) with an estimated predicted value greater than .50 plus the percentage of the observed no votes (= 0) with an estimated predicted value less than .50.

determine a "correct" prediction is to score as correct all yes votes (equal to 1) whose predicted votes are greater than .50 and all no votes (equal to 0) whose predicted votes are less than .50. A predicted vote of exactly .50 would not be considered correct. The correct predictions using this scoring method for the fifty-three predicted votes for each issue are never less than 71.70 percent correct (for the eighth and thirteenth votes) and are as high as 86.79 percent correct (for the sixth vote). Overall, it appears that the economic model of voting predicts the votes of the fifty-three delegates with a fair degree of accuracy.

The predicted probabilities yield several insights. First, the economic model of voting predicted the votes of the New York and Pennsylvania delegates the most accurately. This suggests apparently strong partisanship on the part of the New York delegates—Alexander Hamilton, John Lansing, and Robert Yates—at the Philadelphia convention. Hamilton's and Lansing's own interests and characteristics predict their votes fifteen of sixteen times; Yates's votes are predicted correctly thirteen of sixteen times. The economic model predicts the votes of most of Pennsylvania's delegates sixteen of sixteen times, which is not surprising given their common interests and common voting behavior at Philadelphia. But it did miss on two of Benjamin Franklin's votes. Second, the model also predicts the votes of the four South Carolina delegates quite well. It predicts the total votes of the four delegates over all sixteen issues fifty-six of sixty-four times, with four of the incorrect predictions accounted for by just one delegate (John Rutledge). Third, the least accurate predictions are generally for delegates from the New England states. For example, the least accurate predictions for all the delegates from the three New England states (New Hampshire, Massachusetts, and Connecticut) represented at Philadelphia are the predicted votes for Caleb Strong (Massachusetts), whose votes are predicted correctly only eight of sixteen times. The findings thus indicate that Strong apparently rose above his own interests at Philadelphia at least on half of the sixteen votes. Fourth, the one delegate of all fifty-three whose votes apparently indicate the least partisanship because they were the least consistent with his own economic and other interests was William Patterson of New Jersey, whose votes are correctly predicted only five of sixteen times.

What about the votes of the prominent Virginia delegation, which included, among others, James Madison, George Mason, and George Washington? Were they primarily principled men whose votes at Philadelphia are not explained very well by their personal and constituent economic interests? Did they generally rise above their own economic and other interests at Philadelphia? The answer is, somewhat. The economic model correctly predicts the votes of James Madison only nine of sixteen times; the votes of George Mason and George Washington, ten of sixteen times. The findings provide some credence to the notion that "interests" may have influenced these individuals less than they did others at the convention.

The findings also may help explain why James Madison, for example, later in his political career switched to supporting states' rights over national powers. A close look at five of James Madison's votes (the seventh, eleventh, twelfth, thirteenth, and fourteenth votes in table 3.13a,b) shows that his own economic interests and characteristics predict voting probabilities dramatically different from his actual votes. Madison voted no on the seventh issue but his own characteristics and interests predict a voting probability of .953, indicating that Madison, who voted against it, should have voted with near certainty (95 percent) for it. Madison also voted no on the fourteenth issue, though his own characteristics and economic interests yield a predicted probability of a yes vote of .855. The records indicate that Madison voted yes on the eleventh, twelfth, and thirteenth votes while his own interests and characteristics predict a very low likelihood of voting for each issue—predicted probabilities of .162, .047, and .186, respectively. Madison's own interests indicate a less than 19 percent probability of favoring any one of the three, with a predicted probability of voting in favor of the twelfth issue of less than 5 percent. The findings thus suggest that the economic and other interests of James Madison, the "Father of the Constitution," can explain why he became less of a nationalist; it was in his interest!

A Summary of the Findings

This reexamination of the drafting of the Constitution at the Philadelphia convention reveals significant voting patterns related to the economic interests and ideologies of the delegates and of their constituents on several of the sixteen issues. The findings support the view that both personal and constituent interests played a role in determining specific provisions in the Constitution. The findings indicate voting patterns that can be said to generally support an economic interpretation of the Constitution because personal and constituent economic interests affected voting on particular issues primarily when those interests were more likely to be advanced by the outcome.

For issues with a direct, especially strong, economic impact, delegates who expected to benefit or expected their constituents to benefit because of their economic interests were more likely to support those issues. Delegates who expected to be adversely affected or expected their constituents to be adversely affected by the issues were more likely to oppose them. Few significant effects for economic interests are obtained for issues with little direct, or obscure, economic impact on individual delegates or their constituents.

The significant voting patterns make economic sense. For example, delegates with private securities holdings unanimously opposed state paper-money issues. Slaveowners, who represented the export interests of slave-based products, opposed national export tariffs. Both less commercial farmers opposed giving the national legislature the right to veto state laws while delegates with private securities holdings were more likely to support the issue. Delegates who were merchants involved in interstate and international commerce unanimously opposed requiring a two-thirds majority in the national legislature to enact laws concerning trade regulations. And delegates who represented more isolated, less commercial areas farther from navigable water were significantly more likely to vote for the two-thirds requirement.

The magnitude of the influence on the votes of many of the economic interests and characteristics of the delegates and of their constituents often was very large. The predicted probability of a yes vote on any given issue was considerably different for delegates with considerably different interests and characteristics. Moreover, the predicted voting probabilities for the specific individuals who attended Philadelphia provide even more support for the economic model of voting at the convention. The findings indicate, however, that certain delegates were less likely to have voted their specific interests than were other delegates. The predicted voting probabilities for different values of the explanatory variables across the selected issues confirm that the product of the convention almost certainly would have been different had the interests of those who attended Philadelphia been different. The estimated voting probabilities for the "average" slave-owning delegate also confirm that had slaveowners, for example, dominated the convention, we would have had a considerably different constitution.[56]

There are plausible reasons why the economic interests are not statistically significant across all the votes examined. In some cases the delegates were voting on issues of basic constitutional design, and in other cases they were voting on interest-specific issues. The lack of significant findings for the economic-interest variables on the basic design issues is not surprising given the general nature of the issues and their ambiguous or trivial impact on specific economic interests. Significant findings for the economic-interest variables are more likely when the Philadelphia delegates were voting on an issue with a specific economic content.

It is plausible, however, that the lack of significant findings for a large number of the economic and other interests results from the relatively weak data set for the Philadelphia convention. The overall sample size is relatively small, which may lead to imprecision in the estimated coefficients—there are never more than fifty-three delegates and as few as thirty-six when "not voting" delegates are excluded. It may be that considerable error is introduced into the estimating procedure because the dependent variables (the votes) are themselves based on an inference of a delegate's actual vote on each issue. Data problems with two of the issues (the first and third votes) exist. It is possible that other votes inferred for the delegates are in error. There is the supposed vote trade on one issue (the fourteenth vote), and three issues (the eleventh, twelfth, and thirteenth votes) appear to have involved attempts to develop an overall compromise on the issue of state-level trade regulation. If strategic behavior existed on other issues, that might obscure any voting patterns and weaken the statistical findings. The results are weaker for the votes that took place later in the convention because the delegates still in attendance decided most of the votes with larger majorities after many delegates departed. As a result, it is more difficult to detect voting patterns because of a smaller variance in the vote. Finally, with the exceptions of Jacob Broom (Delaware) and William Few (Georgia), there were no other farmers of only modest means in attendance at the Philadelphia convention, and there really were no delegates who were poor subsistence farmers in attendance. This lack of representation of individuals viewed as likely opponents of the Constitution makes it more difficult to detect statistical voting patterns and impossible in many cases to determine the statistical influence of less commercial, "small" farmers specifically.

FOUR

Another Look at the Choice of Specific Clauses

For some scholars, a potential difficulty with the estimation of voting behavior in chapter 3 might be that the personal interests of the framers were treated as primary motivating factors in the choices they made at the Philadelphia convention.[1] For some, the interests of the citizens (the framers' constituents) should have been paramount in explaining the choices made at Philadelphia. As the historiography on the Constitution indicates, the role of constituent interests versus personal interests in the creation of the Constitution can be viewed as an issue of competing hypotheses about the framers' behavior.[2] In an attempt to examine the implications of these potentially competing hypotheses for the conclusions about voting at Philadelphia, the present chapter contains a brief discussion of the findings of an alternative examination of the votes on the sixteen issues. The votes are estimated employing an alternative approach to that provided in chapter 3. The effects of a delegate's *personal* interests and ideologies on voting are estimated separately from the effects of a delegate's *constituent* interests and ideologies on voting. As the alternative estimation includes in the model specifications only one of the two sets of variables at a time, the estimation in the present chapter may have more power to detect patterns in the votes than did that of chapter 3.

Because the principal objective in chapter 3 was to determine whether an economic interpretation could explain the drafting of the Constitution, the findings reported for the votes at the Philadelphia convention were for only a primary set of the measures of the economic interests and markers for ideology. The sensitivity of the estimates to the specific measures and markers employed was not a primary concern. Accordingly, this chapter presents findings for the votes employing the various substitute measures that were collected for some of the variables. Also, because the effects on voting of *personal* interests and ideologies are estimated separately from the effects on voting of *constituent* interests and ideologies, estimation of the influence on voting of a substantially greater number of variables selected from each of the two sets of variables is feasible. The findings in the present chapter are then directly compared to the various hypotheses found in the existing historical literature.

An Alternative Empirical Model of the Philadelphia Convention

To determine voting behavior and estimate separately the effects of personal and constituent variables, the vote on issue i for delegate j from state k is estimated employing the following two general empirical specifications of the voting model:

$$V_{i,jk} = f(PE_j, PI_j) \tag{4.1}$$

and

$$V_{i,jk} = g(CE_k, CI_k), \tag{4.2}$$

where $V_{i,jk}$ is a dummy variable for a framer's vote on issue i, PE_j is the set of personal economic interest variables, PI_j is the set of markers for personal ideology, CE_k is the set of constituent economic interest variables, and CI_k is the set of markers for constituent ideology. As in chapter 3, because the vote is limited to a yes or a no, the estimation technique is logistic regression. The sixteen specific issues are estimated employing the data on the economic and ideological interests of the framers. A description of the specific measures of the economic interests and the specific markers for the ideologies of the framers and their constituents employed in the present chapter is contained in table 4.1. The sample means and standard deviations of the specific measures and markers for the fifty-three framers analyzed are shown in table 4.2.[3]

Results of the Alternative Estimation of the Votes at the Philadelphia Convention

General Voting Patterns

To determine the robustness of the estimates, alternative specifications of both economic models of voting were estimated for each of the sixteen issues. Table 4.3 summarizes the overall findings for the estimation of equation 4.1, and table 4.4 summarizes the overall findings for equation 4.2.[4] Several general observations can be made about the framers' voting behavior. First, the overall findings are quite similar to those given in chapter 3 and confirm the general conclusions already drawn—both personal *and* constituent economic interests *and* ideologies influenced voting on specific issues at Philadelphia. Second, the overall findings for the

Table 4.1. Measures of the Votes and Personal and Constituent Interests of the Delegates at the Philadelphia Convention

Dependent Variable

Vote — Equals 1 if the delegate to the convention voted for the specific issue, 0 otherwise

Explanatory Variables

Personal Economic Interests (PE_j):

Western landowner — Equals 1 if the delegate owned western lands in 1787, 0 otherwise

Merchant — Equals 1 if the delegate's principal occupation was merchant engaged in interstate or international trade in 1787, 0 otherwise

Farmer — Equals 1 if the delegate's principal occupation was farming in 1787, 0 otherwise

Lawyer — Equals 1 if the delegate's principal occupation was a lawyer in 1787, 0 otherwise

Politician — Equals 1 if the delegate was primarily a politician in 1787, 0 otherwise

Debtor — Equals 1 if the delegate was in deep personal debt in 1787, 0 otherwise

Public creditor — Equals 1 if the delegate owned any public securities in 1787, 0 otherwise

Private creditor — Equals 1 if the delegate owned any private securities in 1787, 0 otherwise

Public or private creditor — Equals 1 if the delegate owned any public or private securities in 1787, 0 otherwise

Slaveowner — Equals 1 if the delegate owned any slaves in 1790, 0 otherwise

Number of slaves — Number of slaves owned in 1790

Value of public securities — Market value of public securities holdings in 1787, in $

Value of private securities — Face value of private securities holdings in 1787, in $

Appreciation in public securities — Increase in the market value of the delegate's 1787 public securities holdings between 1787 and 1791, the time of the national government's assumption of the public debt, in $

Personal Ideology (PI_j):

Congress — Equals 1 if the delegate was a member of the Continental Congress, 0 otherwise

Military in war — Equals 1 if the delegate served in the military in the Revolutionary War, 0 otherwise

Officer in war — Equals 1 if the delegate had served as an officer in the Revolutionary War, 0 otherwise

96

English ancestry — Equals 1 if the delegate was of English ancestry, 0 otherwise

Scottish/Irish ancestry — Equals 1 if the delegate was of Scottish or Irish ancestry, 0 otherwise

Age — Age of the delegate in 1787, in years

Children — Number of children in the delegate's family in 1787

Constituents' Economic Interests (CE_k):

Slaves per 100 white persons — Number of slaves per 100 whites in each delegate's state in 1790

Slaves per slaveowning family — Number of slaves per slaveholding family in each delegate's state in 1790

Percentage of families with slaves — Percentage of all families with slaveholdings in each delegate's state in 1790

Public funding credit per capita — Per capita amount due from the national government, or owed to it, subsequent to funding Revolutionary War expenditures in 1793 for each state, in $

Wealth — Net worth per probate-type wealth holder in 1774 for each state, in $

Physical wealth — Total physical wealth per probate-type wealth holder in 1774 for each state, in $

Share of wealth in landholdings — Proportion of net worth in landholdings per probate-type wealth holder in 1774 for each state

Share of wealth in slaves — Proportion of net worth in slaves per probate-type wealth holder in 1774 for each state

Share of wealth in financial claims — Proportion of net worth in financial claims per probate-type wealth holder in 1774 for each state

Share of wealth in financial liabilities — Proportion of net worth in financial liabilities per probate-type wealth holder in 1774 for each state

Distance to navigable water — Distance from the center of a delegate's home county in 1787 to the nearest navigable water, in miles

Distance to Atlantic coast — Distance from the center of a delegate's home county in 1787 to the Atlantic coastline, in miles

Distance to major city — Distance from the center of a delegate's home county in 1787 to the nearest major city, in miles

Distance to Philadelphia — Distance from the center of a delegate's home county in 1787 to Philadelphia, in miles

Constituents' Ideology (CI_k):

Population — Total white population for each state in 1790, in 000s

English ancestry in state — Percentage of all families of English ancestry in each state in 1790

Scottish/Irish ancestry in state — Percentage of all families of Scottish and/or Irish ancestry in each state in 1790

Note: For a discussion of the data, and their sources, that were used to measure each of the specific variables, see appendix 2.

Table 4.2. Means and Standard Deviations of the Personal and Constituent Interests for the Sample of Fifty-Three Delegates at the Philadelphia Convention

Explanatory Variables	Sample Means	Sample Standard Deviations
Personal Interests		
Western landowner	.226	.4225
Merchant	.170	.3791
Farmer	.038	.1924
Lawyer	.396	.4938
Politician	.264	.4451
Debtor	.057	.2333
Private creditor	.226	.4225
Public creditor	.547	.5025
Public or private creditor	.623	.4894
Slaveowner	.340	.4781
Number of slaves	32.358	61.3693
Value of private securities ($)	2,026.890	8,216.7100
Value of public securities ($)	1,229.150	2,117.5400
Appreciation in public securities ($)	2,008.000	4,207.6000
Congress	.755	.4344
Military in war	.472	.5040
Officer in war	.340	.4781
English ancestry	.528	.5040
Scottish/Irish ancestry	.226	.4225
Age (years)	43.930	11.3998
Number of children	4.245	3.6946
Constitutents' Interests		
Slaves		
Slaves per 100 whites	28.060	27.7006
Slaves per slaveowning family	5.360	3.8994
Families with slaves (percent)	20.768	15.5634
Public securities status		
Public funding credit per capita ($)	−.791	5.1230
Wealth		
Wealth ($)	512.960	541.8633
Physical wealth ($)	513.980	542.0793
Share of wealth in landholdings (proportion)	.556	.2229
Share of wealth in slaves (proportion)	.195	.2002
Share of wealth in financial claims (proportion)	.158	.1251
Share of wealth in financial liabilities (proportion)	.210	.1022
Commercial activity		
Distance to navigable water (miles)	16.400	37.5660
Distance to Atlantic coast (miles)	54.940	49.5888
Distance to major city (miles)	54.400	50.7738
Distance to Philadelphia (miles)	209.792	194.2364
Population in state (total white population, 000s)	257.132	139.4106
English ancestry in state (percent)	79.977	12.3318
Scottish/Irish ancestry in state (percent)	9.881	3.8637

Note: The number of observations is 53 because the data on William Churchill Houston (New Jersey) and George Wythe (Virginia) are not included in the sample means, as the two delegates are not included in any of the statistical analysis of the Philadelphia votes. The sample means for the dichotomous variables can be interpreted as the proportion of the 53 delegates that are classified as possessing the listed economic interest or characteristic.

constituent-interest model might be considered slightly better than those for the personal-interest model because the proportion of the explanatory variables that are consistently significant is slightly greater for the constituent-interest model. The findings thus offer weak support for a conclusion that delegates might have responded more to their constituents' interests than to their personal interests.[5] Third, nearly all consistently significant variables have the expected signs. The economic interests and ideologies apparently affected the probability of a yes vote on most issues in a direction consistent with a rational choice view of the framers. Fourth, the overall findings for some of the sixteen votes are consistently not significant for most variables.[6]

Under what circumstances did personal economic interests significantly influence the framers' votes? The findings indicate that when the content of the issue suggests a direct impact on specific economic interests, the interests generally influenced voting. The findings in table 4.3 show several consistently significant variables for eight votes (the second, fifth, seventh, eleventh through fourteenth, and sixteenth). All but the sixteenth vote would appear to been directly affected by specific economic interests at the convention. The findings also indicate only one consistently significant economic variable, or unanimous voting for only one, for the fourth, sixth, ninth, and tenth votes and no consistently significant variables for the eighth and fifteenth. The content of all but the ninth vote (the prohibition on states from issuing bills of credit) suggests no apparent systematic relationship to any specific interest.[7] When the issue at Philadelphia did not directly affect economic interests there, the interests generally did not influence voting on the issue; but personal ideology may have (see the last six rows of table 4.3).

Under what circumstances did the constituent interests matter? The findings for all eight of the votes (the second, fifth, seventh, ninth, and eleventh through fourteenth) whose content indicates an apparent direct impact on particular interests at the convention indicate at least one or more consistently significant constituent interests. For the six votes (the fourth, sixth, eighth, tenth, fifteenth, and sixteenth) whose content suggests no apparent direct impact on any economic interest, nearly all consistently significant variables (eight of thirteen significant variables) are for the markers for constituent ideologies rather than economic interests. This may indicate that primarily ideological beliefs influenced voting when no specific economic interests were at stake.

Under what circumstances are the findings not significant for most of the explanatory variables for particular votes? In general, the model with only the personal-interest variables resulted in the fewest number of significant findings for particular votes, shown in table 4.3 for four votes (the fourth, eighth, ninth, and fifteenth). Interestingly, with the exception of the ninth vote, these are the votes expected to have had little or no direct impact on the specific interests represented at the Philadelphia convention.

Table 4.3. Summary of the Estimated Effects of the Explanatory Variables on the Probability of a Yes Vote at the Philadelphia Convention: Personal-Interest Model

Personal-Interest Variables	Summary of the Effects for Equation 4.1															
	Vote 1	Vote 2	Vote 3	Vote 4	Vote 5	Vote 6	Vote 7	Vote 8	Vote 9	Vote 10	Vote 11	Vote 12	Vote 13	Vote 14	Vote 15	Vote 16
Western landowner	—	—	—	—	Yes[b]	—	—	—	—	—	—	—	—	—	—	—
Merchant	—	U^{No}	—	—	—	—	—	—	—	—	—	No[c]	—	U^{No}	—	—
Farmer	—	—	—	—	—	—	—	—	—	—	U^{No}	U^{No}	—	—	—	—
Debtor	—	—	—	—	—	—	U^{Yes}	—	—	—	—	—	—	—	—	—
Slaveowner	—	—	—	—	Yes[c]	—	Yes[a]	—	—	No[c]	—	—	No[b]	Yes[a]	—	—
Number of slaves	—	—	—	—	—	—	Yes[b]	—	—	—	—	—	No[a]	—	—	—
Public securities	—	Yes[c]	—	—	—	Yes[b]	—	—	—	—	—	—	—	—	—	—
Private securities	U^{No}	—	—	U^{No}	—	—	—	—	U^{Yes}	—	—	—	—	—	—	U^{No}
Public/private creditor	—	Yes[b]	No[c]	—	—	—	—	—	—	—	No[c]	—	—	—	—	—
Appreciation in public securities	—	No[c]	—	—	—	—	—	—	—	—	—	—	—	—	—	No[c]
Age	Yes[b]	—	—	—	No[b]	No[c]	—	No[c]	—	No[c]	—	—	—	—	—	—
Children	Yes[b]	—	—	Yes[b]	—	Yes[c]	—	—	—	—	—	—	—	—	—	Yes[b]
Military in war	—	—	—	—	No[c]	No[b]	—	—	—	—	—	—	—	—	—	—
Congress	—	—	—	—	—	—	—	—	—	—	—	—	—	—	Yes[c]	—
English ancestry	—	—	—	—	—	—	—	—	—	—	—	—	—	—	—	—
Officer in war	—	—	No[b]	—	—	—	—	—	—	Yes[c]	—	—	—	—	—	No[c]

[a] Statistically significant at the .01 level.
[b] Statistically significant at the .05 level.
[c] Statistically significant at the .10 level.

Note: Each column is a summary of up to twenty-four estimated specifications of the voting model described in equation 4.1. Number of observations in each specification is 53. The dependent variable for each issue is the observed vote for that issue, where a yes vote equals 1 and a no vote equals 0. The symbols U^{Yes} and U^{No} indicate that the vote on the issue was unanimous, yes or no, respectively, for the voting delegates with the characteristic. Yes and No indicate that in all, or nearly all, model specifications, delegates with the characteristic were statistically more likely to have voted yes or no, respectively, on the issue at the significance level indicated by the footnote, ceteris paribus. No entry indicates the characteristic had neither a consistent sign nor a consistent statistically significant impact on voting. Despite the errors discovered in their data, the estimated effects are still summarized for Votes 1 and 3. As a result of the errors, however, the summaries for the two votes may be questionable.

100

Table 4.4. Summary of the Estimated Effects of the Explanatory Variables on the Probability of a Yes Vote at the Philadelphia Convention: Constituent-Interest Model

Constituent-Interest Variables	Summary of the Effects for Equation 4.2															
	Vote 1	Vote 2	Vote 3	Vote 4	Vote 5	Vote 6	Vote 7	Vote 8	Vote 9	Vote 10	Vote 11	Vote 12	Vote 13	Vote 14	Vote 15	Vote 16
Slaves[a]	No[c]	No[c]	No[b]	—	—	—	—	—	No[c]	No[b]	No[a]	—	—	Yes[a]	—	—
Public funding credit	—	—	—	No[c]	—	No[b]	—	—	—	—	—	—	—	—	—	—
Wealth[a]	—	—	No[b]	—	No[c]	—	—	—	—	—	Yes[b]	No[b]	—	—	—	—
Wealth in land	—	—	—	—	Yes[b]	—	—	No[b]	—	—	—	No[b]	No[c]	Yes[b]	—	—
Distance[a]	No[c]	Yes[b]	Yes[c]	—	—	—	—	Yes[c]	No[c]	No[c]	—	—	Yes[c]	—	—	No[c]
State population	—	—	—	—	—	—	Yes[b]	Yes[c]	Yes[c]	Yes[a]	—	—	Yes[c]	—	—	No[c]
English ancestry in state	—	—	Yes[b]	—	—	—	—	—	—	—	—	—	—	—	—	—
Scottish/Irish ancestry in state	—	—	—	No[c]	—	No[c]	—	Yes[b]	—	—	—	—	Yes[b]	—	Yes[c]	No[c]

[a] The row is a summary of the entire results for each vote for various estimated specifications that alternately employ each of the substitute measures of that economic interest.
[b] Statistically significant at the .05 level.
[c] Statistically significant at the .10 level.

Note: Each column is a summary of up to fifteen estimated specifications of the voting model described in equation 4.2. Number of observations in each specification is 53. The dependent variable for each issue is the observed vote for that issue, where a yes vote equals 1 and a no vote equals 0. Yes and No indicate that in all, or nearly all, model specifications delegates with the characteristic were statistically more likely to have voted yes or no, respectively, on the issue at the significance level indicated by the footnote, *ceteris paribus.* No entry indicates the characteristic had neither a consistent sign nor a consistent statistically significant impact on voting. Despite the errors discovered in their data, the estimated effects are still summarized for Votes 1 and 3. As a result of the errors, however, the summaries for the two votes may be questionable.

The Detailed Results for Selected Votes

Although many of the existing studies of the making of the Constitution do not concentrate on voting on individual issues, numerous hypotheses are offered about which interests primarily supported or opposed a strong national government. Conclusions thus can be drawn from the existing constitutional and historical literature about the stance of particular interests and characteristics on the individual votes based on whether the vote was an issue that would have strengthened or weakened the national government. How do the various hypotheses contained in the existing literature compare to the present analysis for individual votes? For example, how does Charles A. Beard's creditor hypothesis fare? Beard (1913 [1935], pp. 31–51) stressed the importance of the delegates' public securities holdings as an influence on voting in favor of a stronger national government. How does Jackson Turner Main's localism versus cosmopolitanism thesis fare? Main and other scholars have suggested that individuals from coastal areas or near navigable water (because they were more commercially oriented *and* cosmopolitan) supported the movement toward a stronger national government while individuals from more isolated inland areas (because they were less commercially oriented *and* localist) opposed the movement.[8]

How about Beard's hypotheses that merchants, western landowners, and slaveowners supported the strong central government embodied in the Constitution? Or his hypotheses that debtors and less commercial farmers opposed it? What about Main's (1961) argument that individuals of English ancestry, as opposed to descendants of other countries, were supporters of a strong national government? Richard D. Brown (1976) takes an even stronger position on the importance of ancestry when he maintains that "the shared British political culture of the Founding Fathers was more important than economic interest, occupation, or provincial origin" (p. 473). How well do these hypotheses explain the votes on the individual issues? The specific findings for five of the issues (the second, seventh, eleventh, thirteenth, and fourteenth votes) are reported in appendix 4, tables A4.1–A4.5.[9]

The Second Issue. The findings for the second issue, the vote on June 8 to give the national legislature an absolute veto over state laws, generally are as expected. As noted in chapter 3, for the delegates' personal interests, reported in the top half of table A4.1, the two delegates who were less commercial farmers both opposed the issue. Delegates with public securities holdings were significantly more likely to have voted yes. But delegates whose public securities holdings appreciated in value more than those of others were less likely to have voted yes (see the first three columns of the top half of table A4.1).[10] For constituent interests, the findings reported in the bottom half of table A4.1 indicate that the framers who represented slave areas generally were significantly less likely to have voted yes (see the first three columns), while delegates who represented wealthier constituents and delegates from more populous states were significantly more likely.

The results for the second vote appear consistent with an economic view of the framers, as the effects for most of the significant variables have the expected signs. Although not obvious, a plausible explanation exists for why the framers whose public securities holdings appreciated in value during the period were less likely to support the national veto. Some of the increase in the market value of public securities in the late 1780s was due to favorable state actions (see Ferguson, 1961, chap. 12). Those framers holding public securities may have expected favorable actions on the part of states in the future and accordingly opposed constraints—an absolute veto over state laws—on the future actions of states.

The findings offer support for two of Beard's hypotheses: that delegates holding public securities were more likely to favor a national veto over state laws and that less commercial farmers were less likely. The traditional historical view that large states favored a strong national government also is supported by the findings for the second vote. In what at first might appear to be contrary to Beard's views on the influence of slaveholdings, the results are *not* significant for personal slaveholdings and indicate that delegates who represented slave areas were *less* likely to vote for the national veto. Even though slaveowners feared adverse national legislation concerning slavery, Beard (1913 [1935], pp. 29–30) argues that slaveowners favored the Constitution because of their commercial and financial interests and their desires for a strong central government to quell possible slave revolts.

Recall, however, that when Beard and other scholars refer to the effect of a particular interest on voting, they are referring to the *overall* vote of someone with that interest based on how the majority of delegates with the particular interest voted. Yet the reference to the effect of a specific interest in this book is to the *partial* effect of that interest on the probability of a yes vote, holding all other interests constant. The partial effect tells us whether someone with a specific interest was more or less likely to vote yes, accounting for the confounding effects of all other interests on the vote. The partial effect of a particular interest does not tell us whether anyone with that interest voted yes. The *total* of all the partial effects of all of a delegate's interests determines his actual vote on any issue. Thus, Beard's overall conclusions about slaveowners favoring the Constitution and the findings here that the *partial* effect of slaveholdings per se *decreases* the likelihood of support for the strengthened central government in the Constitution can both be correct.

The Seventh Issue. The findings for the seventh issue, the motion considered on August 21 to prohibit the national legislature from enacting export tariffs, are reported in table A4.2. How do the various hypotheses about support for a strong national government fare regarding this attempt to prohibit national export tariffs? Regarding personal interests, delegates who were debtors unanimously favored the prohibition, and slaveowners also were significantly more likely to have favored the issue (see the top half of table A4.2). The results for constituent interests, reported in the bottom half of table A4.2, suggest that the only consistent influence on the vote was the English ancestry of the states: Delegates who represented states with a greater concentration of English descendants were significantly more likely to have voted in favor of the ban on national export tariffs.

The results for slaveowners are consistent with an economic interpretation, as it was in their self-interest to prohibit national export tariffs that would have increased the costs of export activities. The support of slaveowners on the seventh issue, again, appears to be in conflict with Beard's (1913 [1935], pp. 29–30) suggestion that slaveowners were interested in a stronger national government and consequently would have been likely to have opposed constraints on the future actions of the national government. But, again, Beard was stating his view of the *overall* position of plantation slaveowners based on all their economic interests, not merely their ownership of slaves.

There is a plausible explanation for the unanimous yes vote by the three debtors on the seventh issue. They may have expected that a future national export tariff would increase the costs of trade activity enough to put financiers, merchants, and others in a position to place pressure on debtors to pay their debts, and thus the debtors supported the ban on export tariffs. The apparent indifference (no significant findings) of the delegates who had, or who represented, other interests is expected. There are few evident reasons why the other specific interests would have been affected by passage of a prohibition on export tariffs.[11]

The Eleventh Issue.   The eleventh vote, the proposal on August 28 to prohibit states from enacting trade embargoes, was a prohibition on the actions of states. Do the findings confirm any of the existing hypotheses about support or opposition to a strong central government? Do they support any of the specific hypotheses based on an economic view of voting behavior? The findings for the personal interests that are reported in the top half of table A4.3 indicate that the debtors at the convention unanimously opposed the eleventh vote. Beard's debtors apparently were states' rights advocates, as he asserted. The effects for slaveholdings are always positive and statistically significant: Slaveowners were more likely to support the prohibition on state trade embargoes. Regarding constituent interests, whose findings are reported in the bottom half of table 4.3, delegates who represented wealthier citizens or citizens that owed the central government at the settlement of the Revolutionary War expenditures were significantly more likely to have voted yes on the issue. But delegates with more English descendants as constituents were only marginally more likely to have voted yes.[12]

The results suggest plausible voting patterns. Slaveowning delegates and delegates who represented wealthier states, states whose citizens were going to owe the central government after the war, or states with more English descendants all apparently wanted to prohibit states from enacting trade embargoes. The findings are consistent with an economic view of the Founding Fathers. As noted in chapter 3, the majority of slaveowning delegates were exporters of rice and tobacco, and their revenue concerns apparently outweighed any political concerns for the use of embargoes. If the net wealth variable captures involvement in commercial and trade activities (more commerce existed in wealthier states), it is straightforward why citizens of those states would have supported a prohibition on trade embargoes. Main's (1961) suggestion that citizens of English ancestry were more favorably disposed to support a strong central government while Scottish and Irish descendants were less disposed appears to be confirmed. In this case, English descendants were less concerned with states' rights while Scottish and Irish descendants apparently were strong states' rights advocates.

The Thirteenth Issue.   Also considered on August 28, the thirteenth issue was a vote to affix, to an existing clause prohibiting states from enacting import duties, a prohibition on states enacting export tariffs. How do the various hypotheses found in the existing literature fare? The estimates of the influence of personal interests on the vote reported in the top half of table A4.4 strongly suggest that slaveowners were more likely to have opposed the prohibition on state–level export tariffs. All four estimates for the variable measuring the number of slaves are negative and highly statistically significant. Delegates who were debtors or public securities holders also were less likely to have supported the issue, but the level of significance is somewhat marginal. The reason why slaveowners were less likely to have voted yes on the prohibition on state–level export tariffs, as already noted, is that they may have expected to use their state governments to exploit their monopoly power in the export of slave-based products through state export tariffs. Beard's public creditor hypothesis on the face of it may not appear to fare well. The findings indicate that delegates who owned public securities were significantly less likely to have voted for the prohibition on state export tariffs, suggesting that such delegates, at least on this vote, were not supporting a stronger central government. As argued in chapter 3, however, there are plausible reasons for this apparent anomaly. Public creditors might have viewed state export tariffs as a source of state revenues necessary for them to receive repayment of any prior loans to their state. Also noted in chapter 3, the compromises involved in the issue of state–level import and export restrictions could have obscured straightforward self-interest voting on this issue. The three debtors appear to have voted as Beard had asserted, as they were less likely to support the thirteenth vote.

Regarding constituent interests, whose findings are reported in the bottom half of table A4.4, delegates who represented more populous states, states with greater concentrations of Scottish and Irish descendants, or states owing the central government for Revolutionary War expenditures were significantly more likely to have supported the prohibition on export tariffs by states. Delegates who lived farther from the coast or navigable water were significantly less likely. The findings for delegates who represented large states and for delegates from backcountry areas are consistent with the literature. If citizens of more populous (and generally more urban) states possessed a more worldly view and expected to dominate the new national government, as Jillson and Eubanks (1984, pp. 443–445) claim, they may have possessed ideologies more willing to constrain state legislatures. Consistent with Libby's (1894) original argument about the geographical dispersion of the vote on the Constitution, the findings support this thesis because delegates who lived farther inland were less likely to have favored the prohibition on state–level export tariffs. Because delegates who represented states with more Scottish and Irish descendants were more likely to have voted yes, it appears that a strong anti-British ideology did not always correspond with support for states' rights issues.

The Fourteenth Issue.   If the fourteenth issue had passed on August 29, the convention would have considered a motion to require a two-thirds majority of the national legislature to enact trade laws. How well does an economic interpretation explain voting on the issue? For the personal interests, whose findings are reported in the top half of table A4.5, delegates who were merchants were unanimously opposed to the fourteenth vote. Delegates who served as officers in the Revolutionary War also were significantly less likely to have favored the issue. Slaveowners were significantly more likely to have voted yes, although the number of slaves owned does not appear to have been an important determinant of voting.[13] For the constituent interests, whose findings are reported in the bottom half of table A4.5, the results strongly indicate that delegates from slave areas and delegates farther from the coast or navigable water were more likely to have favored the two-thirds requirement. All estimated effects for the two variables are positive and highly significant.

The findings support several of the existing hypotheses and are consistent with an economic view of the behavior of the framers at Philadelphia. That merchants were unanimously opposed to the two-thirds requirement is consistent with McDonald's (1958, chap. 3) contention that a majority of the delegates with merchant interests was heavily involved in trade activities. They apparently expected the two-thirds requirement to have increased the costs of enacting favorable trade laws. But the finding strongly conflicts with McDonald's general ambivalence toward an economic interpretation of the Constitution. The result also supports Beard's contention that merchants were favorably disposed to support a strong central government. According to Main (1961) and Jensen (1964), delegates who were officers in the Revolutionary War possessed an elitist ideology and, as a result, were more sympathetic to strong central governments. These claims fare well, as the findings here indicate that officers were less likely to have supported the two-thirds requirement that would have placed a greater constraint on the national government. The findings strongly support contentions in the literature that citizens farther from the coast or navigable water were less commercially oriented, as the delegates from the more isolated, inland areas supported the two-thirds requirement to enact national trade laws.

A Summary of the Findings

When the effects of the personal-interest variables are estimated separately from the effects of the constituent-interest variables on the framers' votes, voting patterns for economic interests and ideologies are still present. Slaveowning delegates and delegates who represented slave states were more likely to favor the two-thirds requirement to enact trade laws in the national legislature, *ceteris paribus*. Slaveowners also were more likely to vote to prohibit export tariffs by the national government. The findings offer some, albeit weak, support for the argument that the framers were more responsive to the interests and ideologies of their constituents than to their personal interests and ideologies. Yet the findings still support the view that their personal economic interests played an important role at the Philadelphia convention. The findings also indicate that the estimated effects are fairly robust with respect to the specific measures and markers employed. The estimated effects when employing the various substitute measures for the variables for which substitute measures have been collected are often similar.

The findings in the present chapter, and those in chapter 3, that both the personal and constituent interests of the framers at Philadelphia mattered offer support for studies contending that economic interests in a broad sense mattered.[14] The findings in both chapters also support several specific hypotheses found in the literature. Main's (1961) localism versus cosmopolitanism hypothesis is well supported by the results for the distance variable. The traditional historical view that a split existed between large states and small states is confirmed. Main's (1961) suggestion that the English versus Scottish/Irish ancestry of the population is important in determining the framers' votes is supported in many cases. Beard's arguments that merchants favored a strong central government and that debtors opposed such a government also are supported. Some support is found for Beard's public creditor hypothesis. Other hypotheses do not fare as well, however. Little support is found for the various hypotheses in the existing literature about the influence of a delegate's age, Revolutionary War experience (but not officer status), political experience, or personal ancestry. Yet overall, the findings reported both here and in chapter 3 still are strongly at odds with any conclusion that there was *no* alignment between specific votes and specific economic interests during the drafting of the Constitution.

FIVE

The Choice of the Basic Design
of the Constitution

The examination of the Philadelphia convention presented so far offers an economic explanation for voting on interest-specific clauses considered for inclusion in the Constitution. The examination relied on the theory of self-interested, partisan behavior among constitutional actors. An alternative hypothesis in constitutional economics that has recently emerged suggests that disinterested, nonpartisan voting behavior may better explain the choice of the basic design of a constitution than a presumption of self-interested, partisan behavior. Yet the issue of disinterested, nonpartisan voting has not heretofore been formally analyzed.[1]

The analysis of voting behavior at the Philadelphia convention is now extended by a formal comparison of the economic theory of self-interested, partisan behavior to the economic theory of disinterested, non-partisan behavior.[2] A distinct aspect of the Philadelphia convention—the *general* issue of strengthening the national government (what will be referred to as supporting nationalism rather than confederation)—as an issue of basic constitutional design is examined. The extent to which partisan interests of the framers of the Constitution affected their support for, or opposition to, changing the basic structure of government—strengthening the national government relative to the state governments—is estimated.[3] Formal hypothesis tests are applied to the estimates to determine how well disinterested voting, compared to partisan voting, explains the vote on nationalism and basic constitutional design. The hypothesis tests formally determine the role of personal versus constituent interests, as well as the role of economic interests versus ideology, in the basic design of the Constitution.

The Issue of Basic Constitutional Design

Constitutional economics—the study of choice among alternative rules governing collective behavior—has become an important new field in economics in the last decade or so of the twentieth century. Its distinguishing characteristic, according to Buchanan (1990), is that it "directs analytical attention to the *choice among constraints*" (p. 3, emphasis in original). A key question in the constitutional economics literature is how rational actors make choices over the basic design of a constitution—the fundamental general rules contained in a constitution that are to be used for all future collective decisions. The conclusion is that a self-interested actor behaves differently during the constitutional stage of collective decision making than during any other stage—partisan interests do *not* influence the basic design of a constitution. This conclusion has a long history among economists interested in understanding the evolution of the fundamental rules of a society. In their pioneering contribution, Buchanan and Tullock (1962) argued that, because constitutional actors are behind a veil of uncertainty about their role in future collective decisions, "the purely selfish individual and the purely altruistic individual may be indistinguishable in their behavior" (p. 96). Both would choose the "best" constitution from the point of view of society because disinterested behavior would predominate behind the veil of uncertainty when choosing fundamental rules.[4]

An important task is to determine formally how well the presumption of disinterested behavior, as opposed to a presumption of partisan behavior, explains the adoption of the Constitution of the United States. The determination of whether nonpartisan, disinterested behavior or partisanship explains the basic design of the Constitution not only is of historical interest but also has important implications for understanding any future constitutional reform. As Mueller (1989) notes, "Despite its obvious importance to their theory, Buchanan and Tullock do not discuss the process by which the constitution gets written, or the procedure for selecting delegates to the constitutional convention to ensure that they all act in the disinterested manner. . . . [W]hether any group of delegates could abstract sufficiently from their own positions and ideologies . . . must remain an open question" (p. 433).

How well does constitutional economics explain the drafting of the Constitution? Did our Founding Fathers exhibit disinterested behavior when making choices of basic constitutional design? Or did they respond to partisan interests even when considering fundamental basic issues? Constitutional economists appear to accept the presumption that the Founding Fathers were disinterested. Buchanan and Vanberg (1989) pose the question, "How do we explain the behavior of James Madison in 1787, along with the behavior of those who followed his intellectual leadership?" (p. 15). They then explicitly model the behavior at the

Philadelphia convention as an actual example of constitutional economics, including the presumption of disinterested behavior. In another study of James Madison and the founding period, Dorn (1991) presumes that disinterested behavior apparently predominated in 1787. Lowenberg and Yu (1992, p. 61) argue that because a viable "exit" option existed for many of the parties at the Constitutional Convention—they claim that secession was feasible for several states—the convention delegates would have exhibited disinterested behavior. In an examination of how the Confederate States of America modified the Constitution of the United States, Holcombe (1992) appears to accept the presumption of disinterestedness when he suggests that the Confederate states made "the changes that were intended to correct perceived problems with the U.S. Constitution" (p. 763). These studies, however, provide little if any evidence for the conclusion that either the Philadelphia or the Confederate setting was a result of disinterested behavior. They simply presume a "constitutional" setting where disinterested behavior prevailed.

Constitutional Economics, Partisan Interests, and the Philadelphia Convention

Positive Theories of Constitutional Economics

In their original formulation of a theory of constitutional choice, Buchanan and Tullock (1962, chap. 6) describe two levels of collective decision making: the "constitutional" and the "operational" levels of public choice. They refer to the constitutional level as that level where individuals choose the set of general voting rules (decision-making rules) that are to be applied to all future collective choice—rules that contain no predictable outcome for specific interests. At this level, individuals are choosing the general rules based on their perceptions of the operation and general consequences of those rules. Buchanan and Tullock (1962) state that the rational individual at this higher level of constitution making "will not find it advantageous to vote for rules that may promote sectional, class, or group interests because, by presupposition, he is unable to predict the role that he will be playing in the actual collective decision-making process at any particular time in the future" (p. 78). Thus, voting at this level is not readily identifiable with specific interests because constitutional actors behave as if they are behind a veil of uncertainty. The discussion among the individuals will proceed without intense conflicts about the general effects or workings of rules because it "should not be unlike that of possible participants in a game. . . . Since no player can anticipate which specific rules might benefit him during a particular play of the game . . . [they] attempt to devise a set of rules . . . for the average or representative player" (pp. 79–80). Buchanan and Tullock then maintain that constitutional participants will likewise "take a position as 'a representative' or 'randomly distributed' participant," choosing "the best set of rules for the social group" (p. 96)—an efficient constitution. It follows that partisan interests do *not* matter for constitutional choice.

The operational level can be thought of as a lower level of collective choice. It is at this level that individuals make collective choices within certain agree-on rules. At the operational level, the individual calculus is similar to deciding on the allocation of resources within a well-defined time period where the individual knows his interests and position relative to others. This lower level of collective choice would correspond to choices over laws, regulations, and statutes, not over general decision-making rules. As Buchanan and Tullock (1962) note regarding the rational individual,

> he is assumed to be motivated by a desire to further his own interest, to max-
> imize his expected utility, narrowly or broadly defined. In this stage, which
> we have called and shall continue to call the *operational* as opposed to the
> *constitutional*, the individual's interest will be more readily identifiable and
> more sharply distinguishable from those of his fellows than was the case at
> the constitutional level of decision. (p. 120, emphasis in original)

It follows that partisan interests *matter* for operational issues.[5]

Under what conditions will this theory of constitutional choice not hold? Buchanan and Tullock (1962) contend that their analysis at the constitutional level is not applicable for societies with widely divergent economic or social groups. Accordingly, if there exists "a sharp cleavage of the population into distinguishable social classes or . . . groupings," individual members of a dominant interest group "would never rationally choose to adopt constitutional rules giving less fortunately situated individuals" equal standing (p. 80).[6] They contend that if the veil of uncertainty is not sufficiently thick, a "rational utility-maximizing individual will support the adoption of rules designed specifically to further partisan interests" and oppose the adoption of efficient constitutional rules (pp. 78–79). Buchanan and Tullock list six necessary conditions for rational utility-maximizing individuals to see through the veil and support rules that further partisan interests (pp. 72–79), suggesting that four of their conditions may be satisfied frequently: Individuals (1) can see through the veil if they are able to predict which issues will arise under alternative rules (efficient as well as inefficient alternatives), (2) can determine the outcomes of these issues, (3) prefer an outcome under an inefficient rule to all other outcomes under the efficient rule, and (4) all agree to the inefficient rule. But this last condition, unanimity of support for an inefficient rule, is not likely in a large-group setting. Thus, while Buchanan and Tullock contend that constitutional agreement is possible, explicit in their theory of constitutional choice also is unanimity of support for the efficient rule (the constitution).

Subsequent work goes beyond the highly stylized model of Buchanan and Tullock (1962) in an attempt to develop a more general model of constitutional contract. Buchanan (1975) argues that "allowance should be made for the existence of substantial differences among persons in the original . . . setting" (p. 54). Buchanan (chap. 4) then posits a positive theory of constitutional choice in which rational, self-interested individuals form a constitution from a state of anarchy: Behind a "veil of uncertainty," rational individuals are able to see that general decision-making rules, which promote the gains from direct production, specialization, and exchange, are in their self-interest. Yet, with substantial inequality, anarchy could be superior to direct production and exchange for self-interested individuals. In this case, constitutional agreement is still possible, but existing wealth differences must first be ameliorated through redistribution of wealth among the society's members. Brennan and Buchanan (1985) develop a positive constitutional theory that offers a self-interest explanation for choosing nonpartisan "rules of the game"— that is, for choosing a "just" constitution. But neither study addresses the question of whether constitutional theories explain actual constitutional choice in any real-world setting.

According to Buchanan and Vanberg (1989), the constitutional preferences of individuals, in fact, do contain an *interest* component, where preferences over alternative rules are formed by the outcome patterns of different rules; and a *theory* component, where preferences are formed by factual expectations, or theories, about the workings of alternative rules. Buchanan and Vanberg argue (pp. 16–17) that the lack of conflict over the expected workings of different rules (the theory component) in the traditional contractarian approach to constitutional choice either is an underlying assumption of the model, as in Buchanan and Tullock (1962), or is eliminated entirely by assuming that individuals are fully informed about the general effects of rules, as in Rawls (1971).[7]

In their application of constitutional economics to the Philadelphia constitutional convention, Buchanan and Vanberg (1989) present an explanation of the behavior of the delegates to the convention by presuming a lack of knowledge about the general effects of rules; individuals must invest resources to become better informed about the consequences and workings of alternative rules. Buchanan and Vanberg model "a constitutional convention, with a relatively large number of participants, charged with choosing among alternative sets of *general* rules for the political-legal-economic order" (p. 16, emphasis in original). Their model still presumes a veil of uncertainty that eliminates conflicts over partisan interests (the interest component) and leads to a "fair" constitution. They then concentrate on the information side of constitutional choice, arguing that it is rational for some individuals to defer to the expertise or leadership of others and for some individuals (James Madison) to invest resources to acquire that expertise. The equilibrium outcome is a constitution that contains both fair and quality rules—"fair" in terms of the distribution of the effects of rules and "quality" in terms of the effects of rules on the level of welfare—an efficient constitution. Buchanan and Vanberg conclude with the claim that while their model is not "*the* explanation of James Madison . . . [w]e have, we think, offered *an* explanation of this behavior" (p. 26, emphasis in original).

Buchanan (1991b) more recently has acknowledged the view starting to emerge in the rent-seeking literature that "identifiable and conflicting constitutional interests will prevent . . . [rational actors] from actually realizing the potential gains from constitutional cooperation" (p. 56) when they are placed in real-world settings. But he also suggests that instead of giving in to this skepticism, a better "approach should investigate the conditions under which . . . agreement may be facilitated in real, nonhypothetical choice situations" (p. 56). Although he is aware that the veil of uncertainty might be transparent in real-world contexts, he stresses that the characteristics of any actual constitutional setting, its institutional structure, determine the actual thickness of the veil. He also suggests that rational actors might recognize this "rent-seeking trap" and deliberately structure a constitutional setting so as to thicken the veil. Buchanan provides another factor—in addition to and independent of the veil of uncertainty—that can induce rational actors toward constitutional agreement: An individual's concern for stability will induce a preference for fair and impartial rules. There will be less compliance with rules that appear to be partial, more pressure to renegotiate, and less stability. This will induce greater preference for fair and impartial rules, and therefore constitutional agreement.[8]

Other constitutional economists also have begun to recognize that the theories of constitutional economics might not explain the United States Constitution that well. Holcome (1991) argues that it might be more appropriate for the Articles of Confederation to be viewed as our first constitution. The Articles, unlike the Constitution, did require the unanimous consent of the states for amendments. The Articles, however, contained no enforcement mechanisms (e.g., states could not be forced to pay taxes owed to the national government). As a result, it may be more accurate to view the Articles as a nonbinding agreement among the states, not a "constitution" in the sense meant in constitutional economics. Indeed, the Constitution was adopted by means contrary to the terms of the Articles; it was adopted with less than the unanimous consent of the states required to amend the Articles.[9]

Historical Context of the Philadelphia Convention

Following Buchanan's (1991b) recommended approach, this chapter examines the conditions and structure of a "real, nonhypothetical" constitutional setting to determine how well constitutional economics explains the drafting of an actual constitution.[10] The institutional structure of the Philadelphia convention, especially the rules governing the convention, suggests there probably was a fairly transparent veil of uncertainty. The rules of the convention allowed consideration of just about any type of proposal. Delegates were also allowed to reconsider and debate any previously defeated or tabled issue more or less at will. The framers also were concerned during their deliberations with how specific issues and proposals for the Constitution might affect particular interests they, their states, or their sections possessed.[11]

The personal interests and characteristics of the delegates to Philadelphia also suggest there was a fairly transparent veil of uncertainty. As already discussed, many of the Philadelphia framers had wealth positions that were well above average. In many cases, the wealth of the framers was concentrated in specific assets such as public or private securities, slaves, or western lands. And several framers would have been considered among the very wealthy in the 1780s. These concentrated yet diverse wealth holdings of the framers, as well as among their constituents, suggest the possibility that many of the framers could see through the veil of uncertainty because they could "reasonably" predict future issues. They could reasonably foresee (1) the range of future issues that would arise (e.g., the issue of slavery), (2) the outcome of the future issues under alternative decision-making rules (e.g., under nationalism vs. confederation), and (3) the expected gains and losses from the future issues under alternative rules (e.g., the value of slaves under nationalism vs. confederation).

Other important characteristics of the Philadelphia convention indicate that the historical setting was different from a pure constitutional setting. The number of convention delegates was very small—no more than fifty-five ever attended and only about two dozen or so actively participated. Yet a pure constitutional convention is a large-number setting—in the limit it should be all individuals who will be subject to the constitution. Second, the framers who attended Philadelphia were representatives (agents) of the states rather than individuals (principals) within the states. The convention can be more accurately described in a principal-agent framework than as a pure constitutional setting. Third, in addition to considering general decision-making rules, the Philadelphia convention considered and included numerous interest-specific rules. Rules concerning the use of import and export tariffs, regulation of interstate commerce, and prohibitions on the slave trade, for example, were all considered and debated in Philadelphia. Fourth, the historical record suggests that long-run stability was probably not the most important consideration among the Founding Fathers at the Philadelphia convention.[12]

Nationalism at the Convention

It follows that the Philadelphia convention does not fall neatly into a pure constitutional setting. Nor does the issue of nationalism—the general issue of strengthening the national government—fall neatly into the constitutional-level category. Given the historical context of the issue and

the circumstances of the choice, nationalism had some predictable consequences for specific categories of self-interest. Yet the issue of nationalism
is sufficiently broad that it does not fit neatly into the operational-level
category, either—or at least not as neatly as do more interest-specific issues
considered at Philadelphia. Among the multitude of issues were general
decision-making rules. The debates at Philadelphia indicate that many of
the important votes at the convention were either in favor of a strong,
national form of government or in favor of a confederation form of
government. Other issues were closer to the operational level of collective
choice. The extent to which nationalism is a constitutional or an operational issue thus is largely an empirical question.

To the extent that nationalism was a basic constitutional-design issue,
constitutional economics suggests that voting at Philadelphia on the issue
of nationalism would not have been related to partisan interests, and
would have differed from voting on more interest-specific issues. Specifically, to the extent that nationalism may be classified as an issue of basic
constitutional design, and to the extent that different ideological interests
represent differences in individuals' constitutional theories, ideological
interests would be expected to be important determinants of voting on
nationalism, while partisan economic interests would not. Economic interests would be unimportant because nationalism would now have less predictable consequences for any specific interest. It would be less costly to
act on one's ideologies (constitutional theories) when nationalism is more
"constitutional."

The Empirical Procedure

Voting on Nationalism or Basic Constitutional Design at the Philadelphia Convention

To understand voting on the basic design of the Constitution, we start
with the now familiar assumption that the framers acted individually to
maximize their personal satisfaction. Their votes were affected directly
by the expected impact on their personal interests and indirectly by
the expected impact on their constituents' interests. The potential effect
of personal interests on voting is straightforward. The effect of constituent
interests is through the impact of voting choices on the potential for
maintaining the agency relationship—maintaining their decision-making
authority. If the framers acted as perfectly faithful agents for their
constituents, then constituent interests, *not* personal interests, would
dominate in explaining voting. Because the costs of monitoring and
policing the actions of the framers were positive, however, personal and
not constituent interests may dominate voting behavior. This would be
evident if the framers voted to satisfy their own economic or ideological
interests when those interests were in conflict with their constituent
interests.

An Empirical Model of Voting on Nationalism

The empirical model of voting on nationalism is based on the following general empirical specification of the vote for delegate i representing state j at the Philadelphia convention:

$$P_{ij} = f(PE_i, PI_i, CE_j, CI_j), \qquad (5.1)$$

where P_{ij} is a measure of the frequency of a framer's votes in favor of a pro-national position (nationalism) during the drafting of the Constitution, PE_i is the set personal economic interest variables, PI_i is the set of markers for personal ideology, CE_j is the set of constituents' economic interest variables, and CI_j is the set of markers for constituents' ideology. The measure of the pro-national votes, P_{ij}, is the proportion of each delegate's votes in the sample of sixteen that favor a pro-national position:

$$P_{ij} = \left(\sum V_{ij,k} \right) / n, \qquad (5.2)$$

where $V_{ij,k}$ is 1 for a vote in favor of a pro-national position and 0 otherwise for issues $k = 1, \ldots n$.

To construct the measure of nationalism (P_{ij}), a delegate's overall pro-national position is measured as the proportion of the sixteen votes at the Philadelphia convention for which he voted in favor of clauses that were expected to strengthen the national government or weaken the state governments. The votes measured in this manner correspond more closely to the constitutional level of collective choice than to the operational level.

To determine if nationalism was a basic constitutional issue, the economic model of voting in equation 5.1 generally would be estimated. If no partisan interests (no explanatory variables) matter for voting on nationalism, then nationalism could be considered a basic constitutional design issue. However, with the low degrees of freedom in the economic model with all the partisan interests included, a hypothesis test that none of the coefficients is significantly different from zero would have very little power. Accordingly, estimation of the economic model in equation 5.1 only does not allow a formal determination of the role of the various partisan interests in voting on nationalism. As a result, the implications of constitutional economics (nonpartisan voting) versus political agency theory (partisan voting) are formally tested here employing a series of hypothesis tests regarding the model structure best supported by the data. Nonnested hypothesis tests are employed, as they appear to have more power in smaller samples.[13]

To test the implications of constitutional economics (nonpartisan voting) for the issue of nationalism with nonnested hypothesis tests, the following two general empirical specifications of rival voting models are estimated:

$$P_{ij} = g(PE_i, CE_j), \qquad (5.3)$$

$$P_{ij} = h(PI_i, CI_j), \tag{5.4}$$

where all variables are defined as above. Equation 5.3 represents the hypothesis that only economic (pecuniary) interests affected voting, while equation 5.4 represents the hypothesis that only ideological (nonpecuniary) interests mattered.[14] The latter is more consistent with the theory of constitutional economics for voting on issues of basic constitutional design, in that ideology may be viewed as a marker for differences in constitutional theories across delegates.

Nonnested hypothesis tests of the competing models are conducted by comparing the estimates derived from each model.[15] The hypothesis that the ideological-interest model is the true model can be tested to infer the degree to which nationalism, as measured in the model, was an issue of basic constitutional design. If the economic-interest model as the null hypothesis is rejected in favor of the alternative ideological-interest model, and the ideological-interest model as the null hypothesis cannot be rejected with the economic-interest model as the alternative, then only ideological interests mattered—a result consistent with nationalism being a basic constitutional design issue.

To test the implications of political agency theory (partisan voting) for the issue of nationalism with nonnested hypothesis tests, the following two general empirical specifications of rival voting models are estimated:

$$P_{ij} = g'(PE_i, PI_i), \tag{5.5}$$

and

$$P_{ij} = h'(CE_j, CI_j), \tag{5.6}$$

where all variables are defined as above. Estimation of the separate effects of the personal-interest model (eq. 5.5) and the constituent-interest model (eq. 5.6) on voting allows determination of the relative importance of each in predicting the probability of a pro-national stance. In the absence of voting for personal self-interest, the constituent-interest model is the correct model, but if the Philadelphia delegates were insulated from their constituents, the personal-interest model may be the appropriate model.[16]

The Specific Measures of the Votes and the Economic and Ideological Interests

Alternative measures of a pro-national position constructed from the sixteen votes from the Philadelphia convention, and the sixteen votes themselves, are described in table 5.1. As noted in chapters 3 and 4, each of the votes involved aspects of the Constitution that, to one degree or another, would have affected the balance of power between the state and national governments. The analysis of the impact of each of the issues on the strength of the central government indicates that a yes vote on the second, third, eighth through thirteenth, and fifteenth votes and a no vote

Table 5.1. Pro-national Position on Sixteen Votes at the Philadelphia Convention

Vote	P^A	P^B	Description of the Issue
Vote 1	No[NU]	No[NU]	To add a clause requiring a degree of national judicial consent for the use of the executive veto
Vote 2	Yes	Yes	To broaden the national legislature's veto power over states, giving it absolute veto power over all state laws
Vote 3[a]	Yes[NU]	No[NU]	To adopt a clause allowing national legislators to determine their own compensation instead of adopting a clause specifying fixed stipends determined by the states
Vote 4	No	No	To strike a clause specifying direct election of delegates to state ratifying assemblies and replace it with a clause specifying ratification by state legislatures
Vote 5	No	No	To disqualify individuals indebted to the national government from serving as national legislators
Vote 6	No	No	To set the quorum of the national legislature at no less than a majority, preventing passage of laws by a minority
Vote 7	No	No	To prohibit the national legislature from enacting export tariffs
Vote 8	Yes	Yes	To give the national government the power to organize and arm state militias and to control the militias when they are called out at the national level
Vote 9	Yes	Yes	To prohibit states from issuing bills of credit
Vote 10	Yes	Yes	To prohibit states from enacting any bills of attainder or ex post facto (or retrospective) laws
Vote 11[a]	Yes	No	To prohibit states from enacting trade embargoes
Vote 12[a]	Yes	No	To strengthen a clause conditionally prohibiting state import tariffs, making it an absolute prohibition
Vote 13	Yes	Yes	To add a prohibition on state export tariffs to an existing clause prohibiting state import tariffs, so as to prohibit states from taxing either
Vote 14	No[NU]	No	To consider a clause requiring a two-thirds majority for the national legislature to enact any navigation acts regulating commerce of the United States with foreign nations or among the states
Vote 15	Yes	Yes	To give the national government the responsibility for protecting each state from invasions and, at the request of the state government, for protecting each state from domestic violence
Vote 16[a]	NU	No	To strike a clause permitting the Constitution to be amended

[a] Votes for which my definition of the pro-nationalist position, P^A, differs from McDonald's (1958, pp. 101–108) definition of the pro-nationalist position, P^B.

Note: "Yes" indicates that a yes vote on the issue is a pro-national position. "No" indicates that a no vote on the issue is a pro-national position. "NU" indicates that the vote on the issue is not used in the measure of the pro-national position. For Vote 16, the pro-national position could not be determined with enough degree of certainty to include in P^A. The descriptions of each vote are the same as presented in table 3.3 and are interpretations of the essential questions involved in the actual votes (see the note to table 3.3).
Source: Reprinted from McGuire and Ohsfeldt (1997, table 1, p. 155), with permission. Minor revisions have been made to some of the descriptions.

on all others (the first, fourth through seventh, and fourteenth) except the sixteenth represent a pro-national position. Voting the opposite represents a pro-confederation stance. Because the impact of the sixteenth vote on the central government is not obvious, its pro-national position could not be determined.[17]

An alternative version of the pro-national position for all sixteen votes can be inferred from McDonald (1958, pp. 99–110).[18] It is similar to the measure offered in the present study, with the exception of four votes. McDonald implies that voting yes on the third, eleventh, twelfth, and sixteenth votes represents a pro-confederation position. The alternative version of nationalism is based on McDonald's presumption that the interests of the Pennsylvania delegates were, in Beard's terms, exclusively "personalty" interests. Accordingly, they were the most nationally oriented of all state delegations and consequently would have voted a straight pro-national position on all sixteen issues. McDonald's contention about the Pennsylvania delegates implies that their vote on each issue would determine the stance—pro-national or pro-confederation—on that vote.

In the empirical analysis in this chapter, the two alternative measures of nationalism are employed. The measure P^A includes the votes listed in table 5.1 with a Yes or No under the P^A column: Yes indicates that a yes vote is the pro-national position on the issue, No indicates a no vote is pro-national, and NU indicates the vote was not used. The second measure, P^B, includes the votes listed in table 5.1 with Yes or No under the P^B column and is the pro-national position on the votes inferred from McDonald (1958). The first and third votes are excluded from both P^A and P^B because of the known errors in the two votes. In addition, the fourteenth vote is omitted from my measure of nationalism, P^A, because of the often-cited possible vote trade, and the sixteenth vote is also omitted from P^A because of its ambiguous nature.[19] A description of the specific measures of the economic interests and the markers for the ideological interests of the delegates and their constituents employed in the present chapter is given in table 5.2.[20]

The Expectations of Voting on Nationalism

If partisan economic interests mattered at Philadelphia, the expected benefits and costs of nationalism versus pro-confederation to the different partisan interests would have determined each delegate's votes on the sixteen issues. If partisan interests mattered, creditors (public and private securities holders), western landowners, and merchants (interstate trade and commercial activities) are expected to have supported the formation of a stronger national government. They would have been in favor of the Constitution because of the expected net benefits to them. And debtors, farmers (less commercial, localized interests), and slaveowners are expected to have opposed the formation of a stronger national government, and the Constitution, because of the expected net costs to them.

Table 5.2. Measures of the Personal and Constituent Interests of the Delegates at the Philadelphia Convention

Personal Economic Interests (PE_i)

Western landowner	Equals 1 if the delegate owned western land, 0 otherwise
Merchant	Equals 1 if the delegate's principal occupation was merchant, 0 otherwise
Farmer	Equals 1 if the delegate's principal occupation was farmer, 0 otherwise
Debtor	Equals 1 if the delegate was in deep personal debt, 0 otherwise
Private securities owner	Equals 1 if the delegate owned any private securities, 0 otherwise
Public securities owner	Equals 1 if the delegate owned any private securities, 0 otherwise
Slaveowner	Equals 1 if the delegate owned any slaves, 0 otherwise

Personal Ideology (PI_i)

Age	Age of the delegate
English ancestry	Equals 1 if the delegate was of English ancestry, 0 otherwise
Officer in war	Equals 1 if the delegate was an officer in the Revolutionary War, 0 otherwise

Constitutents' Economic Interests (CE_j)

Slaves per 100 whites	Slaves per 100 of the white population in each state
Distance to navigable water	Distance from the center of each delegate's home county to the nearest navigable water, in miles

Constitutents' Ideological Interests (CI_j)

Population	Total white population for each state, in 000s
English ancestry in state	Percentage of all families of English ancestry in each state

Note: The sample means and standard deviations for each of the variables are those presented in table 4.2 in chapter 4. For a discussion of the data, and their sources, that were used to measure each of the specific variables, see appendix 2.

Source: Reprinted from McGuire and Ohsfeldt (1997, table 2, p. 156), with permission. Minor revisions have been made to the table.

With respect to the ideological interests (nonpecuniary factors) that affected attitudes toward the issue of nationalism, older delegates, those with Revolutionary War experiences, and those with experience in the Continental Congress are expected to have opposed strengthening the central government. Individuals of English ancestry (especially relative to those of Scottish and Irish ancestry), individuals nearer to navigable water (more commercial), and individuals from more populous states are expected to have supported a stronger national government.

The Estimation Strategy

Because the measure of nationalism (P_{ij}) is based on a set of votes, each limited to a yes or a no, the economic model of voting is estimated employing logistic regression for grouped data. The framers' votes on the various issues are treated as "repeated trials" for determining their positions on the issue of nationalism, where votes in favor of pro-national issues represent "successes." Although the unit of observation is the delegate (the number of observations equals fifty-three), the estimation procedure takes into account the number of trials (votes) on which the measure of the pro-national position for each delegate is based. This method is statistically more efficient than ordinary least squares (OLS) regression.[21]

The grouped procedure, however, is based on the assumption that all the votes are essentially identical. An alternative estimation technique is to treat each vote as a separate issue. This is the technique employed in chapters 3 and 4. But this technique ignores the similarity in the various votes concerning nationalism. Furthermore, the results obtained in chapters 3 and 4 do not permit hypotheses to be addressed formally concerning voting behavior on the issue of nationalism.[22] Finally because many delegates who left the Philadelphia convention early were likely to be pro-confederation, excluding them from an analysis that employs the pooled votes might introduce sample selection bias; thus, each delegate's missing votes also are replaced with the imputed votes, as done in chapters 3 and 4.

Results of the Estimation of Voting on Nationalism at the Philadelphia Convention

The estimates of the alternative economic models of voting on nationalism employing my measure of a pro-nationalist stance (P^A) are presented in table 5.3. The explanatory variables included characterizes the alternative model specifications. Specification 1 includes both personal-interest and constituent-interest variables, specification 2 includes only personal-interest variables, and specification 3 includes only constituent-interest variables. The purpose of the alternative model specifications is to formally examine the various hypotheses about the roles of constituent and personal interests in voting. Given the relatively small sample of delegates, a model with as many as fourteen explanatory variables strains the capacity of the data. To improve the precision of the estimates, some of the explanatory variables that are not statistically significant in specifications 1–3 are excluded in alternative specifications reported in the remaining columns of table 5.3.[23]

The findings indicate that delegates who were deeply in debt were more likely than others to be pro-confederation (the first column). For a hypothetical delegate who was in debt, with average values of all other interests, the predicted value of P^A is .33, which is 49 percent less than the predicted value of .62 for an otherwise average delegate without deep personal debt. The framers who were officers during the Revolutionary War were more pro-national than those who were not officers. The predicted value of P^A for an otherwise average officer is .71, which is 18 percent

Table 5.3. Incremental and Marginal Effects of Personal and Constituent Interests on the Probability of a Yes Vote on Nationalism at the Philadelphia Convention: Dependent Variable P^A

Explanatory Variables	Alternative Model Specifications					
	1	2	3	4	5	6
Personal Interests						
Western landowner	.004	.022	—	—	—	—
Merchant	.067	.079	—	—	—	—
Farmer	−.088	−.059	—	−.113	−.093	—
Private securities owner	−.019	.060	—	.012	.082	—
Public securities owner	−.003	−.007	—	—	—	—
Slaveowner	−.114[d]	−.116[b]	—	−.107[d]	−.127[b]	—
Debtor	−.287[b]	−.291[b]	—	−.252[b]	−.248[b]	—
Age	−.0012	−.0004	—	—	—	—
Officer in war	.112[b]	.129[b]	—	.120[b]	.137[a]	—
English ancestry	−.020	−.470	—	—	—	—
Constitutents' Interests						
Slaves per 100 whites	.0003	—	−.0015[c]	.00008	—	−.0015[c]
Distance to navigable water (miles)	−.0018[b]	—	−.0018[a]	−.0018[a]	—	−.0019[a]
English ancestry in state	−.0045[c]	—	.0065	−.0045[c]	—	−.0069[a]
Population in state (000s)	.0001	—	.0000	—	—	—
Pseudo $\bar{R}^2$	.204	.123	.195	.309	.227	.213

[a] Statistically significant at the .01 level.
[b] Statistically significant at the .05 level.
[c] Statistically significant at the .10 level.
[d] P-value is less than .20. While not considered significant at conventional levels, the coefficient may be precise enough to be treated as significant given the small sample size. See Leamer (1978, chap. 4, especially pp. 102–108, 114–117).

Note: Number of observations for each specification is 53. The dependent variable, P^A, is my measure of nationalism and is the proportion of a delegate's votes at Philadelphia, out of the selected votes, that were in favor of a pro-national position. The incremental or marginal effect of each variable is calculated with all other explanatory variables at their mean values. Pseudo $\bar{R}^2$ is calculated as $\bar{R}^2 = [(\chi^2 - 2k)/(-2L_R)]$, where χ^2 is the model χ^2 statistic, k is the number of explanatory variables in the model, and L_R is the maximum of the likelihood function restricted with only the constant in the model. It is a measure of the goodness of fit of the estimated model.

Source: Reprinted from McGuire and Ohsfeldt (1997, table 3, p. 160), with permission.

greater than the predicted value of .60 for those who were not officers. If constituent-interest variables are excluded from the model, the framers with personal slaveholdings appear to have been less pro-national than were other delegates (specification 2). No other personal interest variables are statistically significant.

Regarding the constituent-interest variables, delegates who represented areas nearer navigable water were more pro-national than were others. The predicted value of P^A for a delegate who lived 10 miles from navigable water is 5 percent higher than that for a delegate who lived 25 miles from navigable water. The English ancestry of a delegate's constituents is associated with lower levels of measured nationalism (P^A), contrary to the hypothesis of historians. Constituent slave interests are negative and significant, but only if the framers' personal interests are excluded from the model (specifications 3 and 6). The state's population, as a marker for the ideological interests of constituents, is not statistically significant in any of the model specifications.

The findings employing the alternative measure of the pro-national position (P^B) inferred from McDonald (1958) generally produce similar (but somewhat less precise) results, as shown in table 5.4. The predicted value of the pro-national position for the framers who had been officers in the Revolutionary War is about 30 percent higher than that for delegates who had not been officers. Distance from navigable water is strongly

Table 5.4. Incremental and Marginal Effects of Personal and Constituent Interests on the Probability of a Yes Vote on Nationalism at the Philadelphia Convention: Dependent Variable P^B

Explanatory Variables	Alternative Model Specifications					
	1	2	3	4	5	6
Personal Interests						
Western landowner	−.126[c]	−.071	—	—	—	—
Merchant	.118	1.240[d]	—	—	—	—
Farmer	−.041	−.084	—	−.109[d]	−.085	—
Private securities owner	.096[d]	.122[b]	—	1.270[c]	.145[b]	—
Public securities owner	.033	.046	—	—	—	—
Slaveowner	−.074	−.204	—	−.054	−.061[d]	—
Debtor	−.195[d]	−.190[c]	—	−.136[d]	−.120	—
Age	−.001	−.0003	—	—	—	—
Officer in war	.151[a]	.134[a]	—	.131[a]	.139[a]	—
English ancestry	−.045	−.051	—	—	—	—
Constituents' Interests						
Slaves per 100 whites	.0004	—	−.0011	.0002	—	−.0009
Distance to navigable water (miles)	−.0027[a]	—	−.0028[a]	−.0024	—	−.0025[a]
English ancestry in state	−.0023	—	−.0042[d]	−.0013	—	−.0037[d]
Population in state (000s)	.0006[b]	—	.0002[d]	—	—	—
Pseudo $\bar{R}^2$	.110	.012	.113	.184	.136	.092

[a] Statistically significant at the .01 level.

[b] Statistically significant at the .05 level.

[c] Statistically significant at the .10 level.

[d] P value is less than .20. While not considered significant at conventional levels, the coefficient may be precise enough to be treated as significant given the small sample size. See Leamer (1978, chap. 4, especially pp. 102–108, 114–117).

Note: Number of observations for each specification is 53. The dependent variable, P^B, is McDonald's (1958, pp. 101–108) measure of nationalism and is the proportion of a delegate's votes at Philadelphia, out of the selected votes, that were in favor of a pro-national position, according to McDonald. All other details are as described in the note to table 5.3.

Source: Reprinted from McGuire and Ohsfeldt (1997, table 4, p. 161), with permission.

and negatively associated with pro-national voting. In contrast to the results using P^A, the tendency for those with private securities interests to be more pro-national than other framers is statistically significant employing P^B. The size of a state's population also is positive and statistically significant in some specifications. Overall, the measures of goodness of fit for the specifications employing P^B are lower than for the same specifications employing P^A.[24]

The findings reported in the present chapter are reasonably consistent with the implications of the estimates of voting on each issue individually. Chapters 3 and 4 include informal assessments of the relationship between particular interests and voting to strengthen the national government across votes, with each vote estimated individually. The informal assessments of patterns across the various individual votes suggest that the Founding Fathers who owned slaves or were from slave areas were less pro-national, and the founders who had been officers in the Revolutionary War or who were closer to navigable water were more pro-national. Less obvious patterns for the personal debt and farming interests of the founders were also indicated in the individual-vote results. For the issues identified as *more* operational, the effects of the personal-interest and constituent-interest variables were more consistently significant statistically and larger in magnitude than those for the issues identified as *less* operational.

Nonnested Hypothesis Tests

Although the individual-vote analysis appears consistent with the theories of constitutional economics (partisan interests matter more for *more* operational issues), analyzing votes individually does not permit the overall role of economic and ideological interests on voting on a pro-national position to be assessed formally. With the pooled measure of a pro-national position, the issues are formally addressed through a series of nonnested hypothesis tests concerning the alternative models. The results of hypothesis tests employing the more limited set of explanatory variables are reported in table 5.5.[25]

The first hypothesis test (table 5.5, row 1) is a test of the null hypothesis that the personal-interest variables were the only factors that affected voting; the alternative hypothesis is that only the constituent-interest variables affected voting—the framers acted as perfectly faithful agents of their constituents. The null hypothesis is rejected at the 1 percent level of significance. The second test (row 2) reverses the hypotheses: The null hypothesis is now that only constituent-interest variables affected voting, and the alternative hypothesis is that only personal-interest variables mattered. The null hypothesis is again rejected at the 1 percent level of significance. Together, the results suggest that neither null hypothesis is acceptable—both constituent-interest and personal-interest variables influenced voting. It appears that voting on the basis of personal interests

Table 5.5. Nonnested Tests of Rival Models of Voting on Nationalism at the Philadelphia Convention

Interests Affecting Voting	Null Hypothesis	Alternative Hypothesis	Likelihood Ratio Test[a]
1. Personal	$P^A = f$ (PE, PI)	$P^A = f$ (CE, CI)	9.64
2. Constitutent	$P^A = f$ (CE, CI)	$P^A = f$ (PE, PI)	9.98
3. Economic	$P^A = f$ (PE, CE)	$P^A = f$ (PI, CI)	9.37
4. Ideological	$P^A = f$ (PI, CI)	$P^A = f$ (PE, CE)	11.29
5. Personal economic	$P^A = f$ (PE)	$P^A = f$ (PI), $P^A = f$ (CE), $P^A = f$ (CI)	11.87
6. Personal ideological	$P^A = f$ (PI)	$P^A = f$ (PE), $P^A = f$ (CE), $P^A = f$ (CI)	13.02
7. Constituent economic	$P^A = f$ (CE)	$P^A = f$ (PE), $P^A = f$ (PI), $P^A = f$ (CI)	11.50
8. Constituent ideological	$P^A = f$ (CI)	$P^A = f$ (PE), $P^A = f$ (PI), $P^A = f$ (CE)	24.20

[a] P-value (χ^2 with df = 1) is <.01 in all cases.

Note: The null hypotheses are that the only interests that affect voting are these listed in the first column. All tests above are for the limited model specifications. The null hypotheses in all of the nonnested tests are rejected.
Source: Reprinted from McGuire and Ohsfeldt (1997, table 5, p. 163), with permission.

occurred in the Philadelphia convention even on the general issue of basic constitutional design—the issue of nationalism.[26]

Similarly, the third and fourth tests (table 5.5, rows 3 and 4) concern the role of economic interests versus ideology. The null hypothesis that only economic interests affected voting is rejected at the 1 percent level, but the null hypothesis that only ideology affected voting is also rejected. Again, the results suggest that both types of interests (economic as well as ideological) affected the voting behavior of the framers. It is possible that the measures of economic interests are correlated with unmeasured, inherent ideological preferences for a stronger national government, but there is no particular reason to presume this is the case. It appears that economic interests influenced voting for a reasonably basic element of constitutional design (the relative strength of the national government). The finding is at odds with the notion that, as a basic constitutional design issue, partisan economic interests should not affect voting on nationalism.

The remaining hypothesis tests concern the roles of the various general elements of personal and constituent interests: The fifth test (table 5.5, row 5) concerns the role of personal economic interests versus all others; the sixth test (row 6), personal ideology versus all others; the seventh test (row 7), constituent economic interests versus all others; the eighth test (row 8), constituent ideology versus all others.[27] Each null hypothesis is rejected, suggesting that all interests played a role in influencing voting even on the basic design of the Constitution at the Philadelphia convention.[28]

A Summary of the Findings

The theories espoused in constitutional economics assert that partisan economic interests do *not* influence constitutional choices. Such theories have been applied to explain the behavior of the men who drafted the Constitution in 1787. The statistical analysis here of voting patterns on the issue of nationalism generally refutes these explanations: Both partisan *personal* interests and partisan *constituent* interests influenced voting on nationalism at the Philadelphia convention. Moreover, both partisan *economic* (pecuniary) interests and partisan *ideological* (nonpecuniary) interests appear to have influenced voting on nationalism at Philadelphia. Every null hypothesis in which the true model of voting behavior included only one specific type of partisan interest is rejected by the nonnested hypothesis tests, suggesting that each type mattered. Despite the very general nature of nationalism and the limited ability of the framers to predict the future implications of a more powerful national government with certainty, the findings indicate voting patterns for each type of partisan interest.

Because actual constitutional settings will always involve political agents who possess partisan interests, and because actual constitutional rules are likely to have predictable consequences for at least some interests, partisan interests will influence actual constitutional choice. Although *fewer* interests mattered when nationalism was the issue at the Philadelphia convention compared to when the specific issues were considered individually in chapters 3 and 4, *many* partisan interests still mattered significantly for nationalism. Given the overall findings of the reexamination of the framing of the Constitution at the Philadelphia convention, which has now been completed, it is hard to envision any written constitution or actual constitutional setting in which partisan self-interest would not matter.

PART II

The Ratification of the Constitution, 1787–1790

SIX

The Overall Ratification Vote in the Nation

The present chapter offers a test of an economic interpretation of the Constitution employing a statistical analysis of the overall ratification vote in the nation, an examination that employs a sample of 1,212 delegates from the thirteen state ratifying conventions.[1] There are several good reasons to argue that the contest over ratification represents the ultimate test of an economic interpretation of the Constitution. First, representatives from all thirteen states were given an opportunity to voice not only their support for the Constitution but also their opposition to it. Second, the eligible citizens of the thirteen states directly elected delegates to represent them at their state ratifying conventions. As a result, the delegates to the ratifying conventions explicitly represented, and were thus constrained by, constituents. Third, there were a greater number of delegates involved in the ratification process, yielding a very large sample, which allows a much stronger statistical test of the factors influencing voting than does the analysis of the drafting of the Constitution.[2] Fourth, because of the greater number of delegates involved, a wider variance for the economic and other interests represented at the state ratifying conventions exists. An analysis of the ratification vote, accordingly, might have more power to detect any patterns in the vote related to the economic and other interests. Fifth, no inferences are required to determine the votes of the delegates to the ratifying conventions because they were officially recorded for each of the thirteen ratifying conventions. Sixth, because voting at the ratifying conventions was a straight up or down vote on an essentially fixed issue—the Constitution as drafted—many of the empirical problems related to strategic voting behavior inherent in the analysis of the individual issues are avoided. While some elements of strategic behavior were present at the ratifying conventions, examples of such behavior are relatively few compared to the possible strategic behavior at the Philadelphia convention.[3]

The Ratification of the Constitution

The Philadelphia convention finished its business on September 17, 1787; the Constitution was complete, and it was to be delivered to the Congress of the United States in New York for its consent to forward the Constitution on to the thirteen states for their ratification. Within a week the Constitution had been delivered to Congress, along with resolutions of the Philadelphia convention to the Congress recommending that the method of ratification should be by state conventions chosen by the people of each state and that the consent of nine states should be required for ratification. (See appendix 1 for copies of the convention's letter and resolutions to Congress.) With little fanfare, a resolution was proposed in Congress on September 26, 1787, to submit the Constitution to the states. On September 28, Congress had voted to transmit the Constitution, with neither its approval nor its disapproval, to the state legislatures so that each of them could submit it to state conventions of delegates chosen by the people of their respective states. The Constitution would then go into effect among the states so acting upon the ratification of the conventions of nine states, as declared in Article VII of the Constitution.

During the next two and one-half years, the legislatures of the thirteen states provided for special elections for the purpose of electing delegates, who represented particular counties or townships within their state, to ratifying conventions in the respective states.[4] The campaign for ratification took place within states as well as across the nation. It was at once one campaign for ratification, as well as thirteen separate campaigns each with its own uniqueness. From the early unanimous decision of Delaware's thirty delegates to ratify on December 7, 1787, to the begrudging decision of Rhode Island to, at last, ratify the Constitution by two votes on May 29, 1790, the battle lines were drawn among the supporters and opponents of the Constitution. The state-by-state ratification votes listed in table 6.1 indicate just how little of a contest there was in some states and yet how contested ratification was in others.

The supporters, many of whom were nationalists but called themselves Federalists, argued that there was a crisis in the country, that action was needed quickly, and that the Constitution was a well-constructed "federal" solution to the weaknesses inherent in the Articles of Confederation.[5] The opponents, most of whom were for a "federal" form of government (they generally supported a confederation among the states) but who became labeled Anti-federalists, countered that the Federalists were intimidating the country into immediate action. Anti-federalists contended that the Constitution was an unknown system which set up a consolidated national government that would destroy state sovereignty. In their view, the proposed national government was a movement toward a monarchy. As a result, the people, they argued, required a bill of rights in the Constitution.[6] The objective of the supporters was fairly straightforward—ratifying the Constitution as soon as possible. The objective of the opponents

Table 6.1. The Ratification Vote and Date of Ratification
at the Thirteen State Ratifying Conventions

Order	State	Vote	Date
1	Delaware	30–0	12/07/1787
2	Pennsylvania	46–23	12/12/1787
3	New Jersey	38–0	12/18/1787
4	Georgia	26–0	01/02/1788
5	Connecticut	128–40	01/09/1788
6	Massachusetts	187–168	02/06/1788
7	Maryland	63–11	04/26/1788
8	South Carolina	149–73	05/23/1788
9	New Hampshire[a]	57–47	06/21/1788
10	Virginia	89–79	06/25/1788
11	New York	30–27	07/26/1788
12	North Carolina[b]	194–77	11/21/1789
13	Rhode Island[c]	34–32	05/29/1790

[a] Second convention. First convention adjourned without a vote.
[b] Second convention. First convention voted 84–184 against ratification on August 1, 1788.
[c] Call for a convention defeated seven times. The Constitution was finally ratified after the national government under the Constitution had been in effect fifteen months and Providence had seceded from Rhode Island to protest the state's continued opposition to the Constitution.

Source: Reprinted from McGuire and Ohsfeldt (1989b, table 12.2, p. 193), with permission. Minor revisions have been made to the appearance of the table.

was equally straightforward—stop ratification of the Constitution as drafted.[7]

An examination of the behavior of the "Founding Fathers" during the ratification of the Constitution is an examination of the behavior of the founders who lost as well as the founders who won; it is an examination of the behavior of the Anti-federalists as well as the Federalists. And during the ratification campaign there was substantial Anti-federalist opposition to the Constitution. The ratification vote in four of the state conventions in fact was so close that small changes in their votes would have defeated the Constitution.[8] In Massachusetts, the vote was 187–168, in New Hampshire it was 57–47, in New York it was 30–27, and in Virginia it was 89–79. If ten supporters in Massachusetts, six supporters in New Hampshire, two supporters in New York, and six supporters in Virginia had changed, the Constitution would have been defeated. A change of 24 votes out of a total of 684 votes cast in these four ratifying conventions—less than 4 percent of the votes cast—would have changed the outcome of ratification. Without Massachusetts, New Hampshire, New York, and Virginia, or even two or three of these states, there would have been no union, at least not under the terms of the Constitution as drafted.

The question here is how well an economic model of the voting behavior of the founders, the Anti-federalists as well as the Federalists, explains the ratification votes in the thirteen state conventions. Were there clear divisions of economic interests over ratification? Did specific economic interests align on one side of the ratification issue while other interests aligned on the other side? The answers to these questions may represent the ultimate test of an economic interpretation of the Constitution.

The Estimation Procedure

The Empirical Model of the Overall Ratification Vote

To determine the role of each factor in the overall ratification process, the following general empirical specification is estimated:

$$V_{ij} = f(PE_i, CE_j, CI_j, TO_j), \tag{6.1}$$

where V_{ij} is a dummy variable for delegate i from county or township j measuring his vote for or against ratification, PE_i is the set of personal economic interest variables, CE_j is the set of the constituents' economic interest variables, CI_j is the set of markers for the constituents' ideology, and TO_j is a set of variables intended to capture the impact of the timing of the ratifying convention and other factors unique to state j on the overall ratification process. Because of a lack of data for the delegates from all thirteen ratifying conventions, markers for a delegate's ideology are not included in the empirical estimation of the overall ratification process.[9] Although the formal model of voting behavior developed includes a delegate's ideology as an explanatory variable, its exclusion should not cause severe problems if the omitted variables are not strongly correlated with the included variables.[10] Logistic regression is once again employed to estimate voting patterns, as the dependent variable is limited to a yes or no vote on the ratification of the Constitution.

The Estimation Strategy

To understand the relationship between the personal and constituent interests of the delegates and voting on the ratification of the Constitution, all state ratifying conventions should be considered in the empirical analysis. Ideally, voting patterns within each state convention should be estimated separately. The available data, however, do not permit this estimation strategy to be pursued completely. The delegates at three of the state ratifying conventions (Delaware, Georgia, and New Jersey) ratified the Constitution unanimously—no within-state variation in the vote exists for the three states. Logistic regression, or any other type of statistical technique designed to estimate the relationship between a choice variable and the factors determining the choice, is not possible with zero variance in the dependent variable (the vote). Data limitations related to insufficient sample size or insufficient variation in the vote prevent the vote on ratification from being estimated separately for three additional states (Maryland, New York, and Rhode Island). The sample limitation or the lack of variation in the dependent variable would lead to inefficient estimation (or imprecise estimates of the coefficients) for the three states. Sufficient data exist for all but the markers for a delegate's ideology to permit the ratification vote to be estimated separately for each of the remaining seven conventions (Connecticut, Massachusetts, New Hampshire, North Carolina, Pennsylvania, South Carolina, and Virginia). But the amount of data available varies across the seven states and is limited for the constituent-interest variables, because several can only be measured at the state level, making the data requirements for the separate estimation somewhat problematic. Because of these limitations, estimation of the ratification vote for the seven conventions separately is postponed until chapter 7.[11]

In an attempt to develop a general understanding of voting patterns in the overall ratification process, given the limitations of the data, a variegated estimation strategy will be pursued here. The economic model of voting is first estimated for the thirteen conventions pooled together. An advantage of pooling all the conventions together is that it facilitates generalizations regarding the impact of personal-interest and constituent-interest variables on voting in the ratification process. Pooling the conventions together not only allows the use of data from all states but also allows the use of more constituent-interest variables: Measures of constituent interests that are available only at the state level can be included in the pooled model of voting.[12] But pooling the data from different ratifying conventions imposes restrictions on the nature of the voting patterns determined by the empirical analysis. In the overall pooled sample, for example, the estimated marginal effect of each explanatory variable on the probability of a vote for ratification of the Constitution is restricted to be the same across states. The impact on voting of institutional and other factors unique to each state can be captured only through variables contained in TO_j. Specifically, the impact is captured through the use of regional and other dummy variables, which reflect the approximate overall strength of the support for the Constitution across states. Likewise, the effect of timing considerations can only be captured through the use of dummy variables contained in TO_j. The use of the timing dummy variables restricts the marginal effects of the personal-interest and constituent-interest variables to be constant over time.

The rules under which the conventions voted on the Constitution declared that the Constitution would be considered adopted when nine of the thirteen ratifying conventions had, by a majority vote of the convention delegates, ratified the Constitution. Given this decision rule, the outcome in a particular ratifying convention may have affected the vote in subsequent conventions. The impact of timing considerations complicates an analysis of voting across different conventions employing the overall pooled sample.[13]

Although no concrete evidence of any vote trading among delegates at different ratifying conventions exists, elements of compromise were important in the voting for ratification in several states. The most important compromise was to allow recommended or suggested "bill of rights" amendments to be open for debate and subject to vote in many of the conventions. Accordingly, instead of rejecting the Constitution, ratification with recommended or suggested amendments took place in several states. Riker (1987a) argues that this compromise was essential to the Federalists in attaining the momentum needed for a successful ratification campaign. The ratification vote, consequently, is not as straightforward as it may appear. Yet because the effects of the different interests on voting for ratification are estimated within the given structure of the voting rules selected, the bill of rights issue does not effect the essential expectations of an economic model of voting on ratification. The bill of rights issue also is accounted for with variables contained in TO_j.

As an alternative method to capture state-specific institutional and other factors unique to each state that might have affected the ratification vote, a state fixed-effects model is estimated. A state dummy variable (a 1 or a 0) for each state is included in various specifications of the estimated model for the sample pooled over all thirteen conventions. The inclusion of a dummy variable for each state allows the natural probability of voting for the Constitution to vary across the ratifying conventions (reflected in different coefficients of the state dummy variables—the state fixed effects). But it restricts the marginal relationship between the probability of a yes vote and the economic and other interests to be constant across the thirteen conventions.

Alternative specifications of the economic model of voting that relax some of the restrictions implied by pooling over all thirteen conventions also are employed. This is accomplished by estimating the economic model of voting for various other samples of ratifying conventions (grouped by common geographical or institutional characteristics). The results from the alternative specifications of the economic model for the various samples are compared to each other and to the results from the entire pooled sample to determine the severity of the restrictions implied by pooling the data from all thirteen conventions. The procedure also illustrates the robustness of the findings with respect to changes in the specification of the empirical model.

The Specific Measures of the Economic and Ideological Interests and the State-Specific and Timing Factors

The specific measures of the personal and constituent economic interests and markers for the constituents' ideology are the primary measures employed in earlier chapters, as well as several supplementary measures: ownership of public securities in excess of $1,000, share of wealth in public securities, a public securities instrumental variable, value of slaves owned, share of wealth in slaves, and a slave instrumental variable. The supplementary measures are employed to help determine the exact influence of slaveholdings and public securities holdings on the ratification vote. As noted in appendix 2, it may be that a threshold amount of public securities or the share of total wealth held in slaves or public securities influenced voting behavior. Descriptions of the specific measures of the personal and constituent economic interests, the markers for the constituents' ideological interests, and the state-specific and timing factors employed in the present chapter are given in table 6.2. And the sample means and standard deviations of the specific measures employed in the present chapter for the sample of delegates analyzed are shown in table 6.3.[14]

A dichotomous (dummy) variable for states that issued paper money during the Confederation period is included in the thirteen-state sample to account for the possible influence of direct experience with paper money among the delegates within a state's ratifying convention. The political history of paper money may have intensified creditor versus debtor conflicts in the ratification process in states where paper money had been issued as a means of debtor relief. States that had issued paper money were often accused of abusing their authority. Delegates in states that had actually abused their authority, or in which the delegates had come to believe they had, may be expected to have been more likely to oppose the Constitution. In these cases, a state's adoption of paper money proxies support for debtor relief and a strong pro-confederation sentiment within the state. The effect of the dummy variable is expected to be negative.[15]

Two dummy variables are included in selected specifications for the thirteen-state sample to incorporate differences across states in the nature of the ratification of the Constitution. Several states ratified the Constitution with various nonbinding declarations of constitutional interpretation and recommendations for amendments (see Elliot, 1836 [1888], vol. 1, pp. 318–338). Two subsets of states are defined according to the strength of their nonbinding conditions of ratification—states that included only recommendations for amendments (the first dummy variable) and states that included stronger declarations of constitutional interpretation and recommendations for amendments (the second dummy variable), implying more conditional ratification. Because both represented compromise proposals, the effects of both dummy variables are expected to be positive. A delegate was more likely to have voted for ratification if the vote represented a compromise between supporters and opponents of ratification.

Two dummy variables are included in the estimated model for the sample pooled over all thirteen conventions and for selected subsets of the overall sample to account for the influence of timing considerations on the delegates' voting behavior. The first dummy variable measures the order of each state's ratifying vote in the overall ratification process. The

Table 6.2. Measures of the Ratification Vote and Personal and Constituent Interests of the Delegates at the Thirteen State Ratifying Conventions

Dependent Variable	
Ratification vote	Equals 1 if the delegate to the state ratifying convention voted to ratify the Constitution (0 otherwise)
Explanatory Variables	
Measures of Personal Economic Interests (PE_i)	
Merchant	Equals 1 if the delegate's principal occupation was a merchant (0 otherwise)
Western landowner	Equals 1 if the delegate owned western lands (0 otherwise)
Farmer	Equals 1 if the delegate's principal occupation was a farmer (0 otherwise)
Debtor	Equals 1 if the delegate was in deep personal debt (0 otherwise)
Private creditor	Equals 1 if the delegate owned any private securities (0 otherwise)
Slaveowner	Equals 1 if the delegate owned any slaves in 1790 (0 otherwise)
Number of staves owned	Number of slaves owned by the delegate in 1790
Value of slaves	Market value of slaves owned by the delegate in 1790 ($000s)
Slave share	Value of the delegate's slaves as a share of the value of the delegate's total assets
Slave instrument	Instrumental variable for the slave share variable
Owner public securities	Equals 1 if the delegate owned any public securities (0 otherwise)
Owner of more than $1,000 in public securities	Equals 1 if the delegate owned more than $1,000 in public securities (0 otherwise)
Value of public securities	Market value of the delegate's public securities holdings ($000s)
Public securities share	Value of the delegate's public securities holdings as a share of the value of the delegate's total assets
Public securities instrument	Instrumental variable for the public securities share variable
Measures of Constituents' Economic Interests (CE_i)	
Slaves per 100 Whites	Slaves per 100 of the white population in the delegate's home county in 1790
Public funding credit	Per capita amount due from the national government, or owed to it, subsequent to funding the Revolutionary War expenditures in 1793 for each state ($)
Distance to navigable water	Distance from the center of the delegate's home county to nearest navigable water (miles)

138

Measures of Constituents' Ideology (CI)

Population — Total white population in the delegate's state in 1790 (000s)

English ancestry of citizens — Percentage of all families in the delegate's home county or township of English ancestry in 1790

Measures of Timing and Other Factors (TO$_i$)

Order — Order of each state's ratifying convention in the ratification process

Moot — Equals 1 if the state ratifying convention voted on the Constitution after nine states had already approved the Constitution (0 otherwise)

New England states — Equals 1 if the delegate was from one of the New England ratifying conventions of Connecticut, Massachusetts, New Hampshire, or Rhode Island (0 otherwise)

Middle Atlantic states — Equals 1 if the delegate was from one of the Middle Atlantic ratifying conventions of New York, New Jersey, Pennsylvania, or Delaware (0 otherwise)

Southern states — Equals 1 if the delegate was from one of the southern ratifying conventions of Georgia, North Carolina, South Carolina, Virginia, or Maryland (0 otherwise)

State — Equals 1 if the delegate was from this state ratifying convention (0 otherwise)

Paper money — Equals 1 if the state issued paper money during the Confederation period (0 otherwise)

Recommended amendments — Equals 1 if the state convention ratified the Constitution with recommended amendments (0 otherwise)

Recommended amendments and declarations — Equals if the state convention ratified the Constitution with declarations of interpretation and recommended amendments, implying even more conditional ratification (0 otherwise)

Note: For a discussion of the data, and their sources, that were used to measure each of the specific variables, see appendix 2.

Table 6.3. Means and Standard Deviations of the Ratification Vote and Personal and Constituent Interests for the Sample of Delegates at All Thirteen Ratifying Conventions

Variables	Sample Means	Sample Standard Deviations
Ratification Vote	.606	.4890
Personal Economic Interests (PE$_i$)		
Merchant	.106	.3075
Western landowner	.128	.3341
Farmer	.263	.4405
Debtor	.025	.1554
Private creditor	.041	.1990
Substitute Measures of Slave Interests		
Slaveowner	.456	.4983
Number of slaves owned	15.746	41.8733
Value of slaves owned ($000s)	2.913	7.7466
Share of total assets in slaves (proportion)	.137	.1929
Instrumental variable for slave share	1.707	.8422
Substitute Measures of Public Securities Interests		
Owner public securities	.352	.4779
Owner of more than $1,000 in public securities	.158	.3645
Value of public securities owned ($000s)	1.507	6.5856
Share of total assets in public securities (proportion)	.062	.1496
Instrumental variable for public securities share	1.603	.8612
Value of total assets owned ($000s)	15.876	34.0786
Constituents' Economic Interests (CE$_j$)		
Slaves per 100 whites	68.552	161.1548
Public funding credit per capita ($)	1.304	4.3233
Distance to navigable water (miles)	40.375	48.5225
Constituents' Ideology (CI$_j$)		
Population (total white population, in 000s)	271.519	121.0783
English ancestry of citizens (percent)	85.734	11.9722
Timing and Other Factors (TO$_j$)		
Order	8.059	3.2047
Moot	.389	.4876
New England states	.348	.4766
Middle Atlantic states	.134	.3404
Southern states	.518	.4999
Paper money	.493	.5002
Recommended amendments	.227	.4190
Recommended amendments and declarations	.529	.4994

Note: Number of observations is 1,212. The sample means for the dichotomous variables can be interpreted as the proportion of the sample of delegates who are classified as possessing the listed economic interest or characteristic.

second dummy variable measures whether the issue of ratification was moot for each state—that is, whether the Constitution had been ratified previously by the required nine states. Delegates in ratifying conventions held later in the ratification process are expected to have been more likely to vote no, while delegates in conventions held after adoption by nine states, are expected to have been less likely to vote no. The traditional argument is that the Anti-federalists (opponents of the Constitution) were not well organized and thus adopted delaying tactics. Their tactics worked best in states where opposition to the Constitution was naturally strong. Ratifying conventions later in the campaign therefore had more Anti-federalists. After adoption by nine states, delaying tactics could no longer stop the Constitution. If delegates did not want to be left out of the Union entirely, they would have been less likely to vote no after adoption than before.[16]

Two regional dummy variables, one for the New England states and one for the southern states, are employed in an attempt to capture the impact on voting of factors common to each region, reflecting the approximate overall strength of support for ratification among the states in each region relative to states in the Middle Atlantic region (the excluded category). As noted, an alternative variable is employed in the estimation to capture state-specific factors unique to each state—a state dummy variable for each state is included in a state fixed-effects model for the sample pooled over the thirteen conventions.

Results of the Estimation of the Overall Ratification Process

Estimates Employing the Overall Pooled Sample

Overall Pooled Estimates. How accurately does the economic model of voting predict the actual voting outcome for the thirteen conventions examined? As shown in table 6.1, the total vote in the thirteen ratifying conventions examined was 961–684 (or 58.4 percent yes) counting the first North Carolina convention that rejected ratification, the convention examined here. (If the second North Carolina convention is counted instead, the vote was 1071–577 or 65 percent yes.) The estimated model for the overall pooled sample, whose findings are reported in table 6.4, indicates that the predicted probability of a yes vote for the "average" ratifier (a delegate with average values for all explanatory variables) is .695 under specification 1. The economic model thus predicts that, on average, the issue of ratification had a 69.5 percent probability of receiving a yes vote, which is a reasonable prediction of the actual voting outcome for the thirteen conventions examined.[17]

Consistent sources of controversy in the historical literature on the ratification of the Constitution concern the role of merchants, creditors (especially those with public securities holdings), debtors, and the commercial orientation and geographical location of the areas represented.

The findings for the overall pooled sample provide strong evidence to address these issues. Delegates with merchant interests and public or private securities holdings were more likely to have voted to ratify the Constitution than were others. Delegates who were in deep personal debt were less likely to have ratified, other factors constant. The estimated effect of merchant interests is positive and statistically significant in all specifications in table 6.4. The estimated effect of the ownership of private securities is

Table 6.4. Incremental and Marginal Effects of the Explanatory Variables on the Probability of a Yes Vote on Ratification: All Ratifying Conventions Pooled

Explanatory Variables	Alternative Model Specifications		
	1	2	3
Personal Economic Interests			
Merchant	.142[a]	.127[b]	.118[b]
Western landowner	.097[b]	.091[b]	.094[b]
Private creditor	.206[a]	.204[a]	.193[a]
Debtor	−.200[c]	−.208[b]	−.211[b]
Farmer	.054[d]	.063[c]	.073[b]
Slaveowner	−.246[a]	−.243[a]	—
Value of slaves ($000s)	—	—	−.00082
Owner public securities	.054[d]	—	—
Owner more than $1,000 public securities	—	.140[a]	—
Value of public securities ($000s)	—	—	.022[a]
Constituents' Economic Interests			
Slaves per 100 whites	.00019[d]	.00019[d]	.00017
Public funding credit per capita ($)	−.035	−.034	−.040[c]
Distance to navigable water (miles)	−.0040[a]	−.0040[a]	−.0039[a]
Constituents' Ideology			
Population (000s)	−.0027[b]	−.0027[b]	−.0027[b]
English ancestry of citizens (percent)	.0014	.0018	.00085
Timing and Other Factors			
Order	−.213[b]	−.217[b]	−.216[b]
Moot	.648[c]	.667[b]	.632[b]
New England states	.013	.0094	.123
Southern state	.446[b]	.468[b]	.320[c]
Paper money	−.077	−.074	−.083
Recommended amendments	.276	.283	.272
Recommended amendments and declarations	.167	.163	.250

[a] Significant at .01 level.
[b] Significant at .05 level.
[c] Significant at .10 level.
[d] P-value is less than .12. While not significant at conventional levels given the sample size, the estimated effect may be precise enough to be suggestive of an influence on the ratification vote.

Note: Number of observations for each specification is 1,212. The dependent variable in each specification is the observed vote on the ratification of the Constitution for all thirteen ratifying conventions, where a yes vote equals 1 and a no vote equals 0. The incremental or marginal effect of each variable on the ratification vote is calculated from the logistic coefficients estimated for model specifications 5–7, respectively, in table A6.1 in appendix 6, with all other explanatory variables at their mean values.

positive and highly statistically significant in all specifications, as is the ownership of western land. The effect of debtor interests is negative and statistically significant in all specifications.

Delegates who were farmers also were more likely to have voted to ratify the Constitution than were others. The estimated effect is positive and statistically significant, or marginally significant, in all estimated specifications. The finding for farmers, though different from the Philadelphia convention, does not really conflict with the finding that the Philadelphia delegates who were farmers of only modest means were less likely to support strengthening the central government. Recall that only two Philadelphia delegates, Jacob Broom (Delaware) and William Few (Georgia), were classified as farmers of, at most, only modest means. For the thirteen ratifying conventions, the number of delegates who were farmers is much larger (more than 26 percent of the delegates, as shown in table 6.3) and includes all those earning a living from the land with three or fewer slaves. Consequently, the measure of farming interests for the ratifying conventions is a broader measure than being only a "poor subsistence farmer." It should not be surprising that such delegates would have been more likely to vote in favor of ratification.[18]

In terms of the magnitude of the effects, a comparison of the predicted probabilities of a yes vote on ratification for an otherwise average delegate with different economic interests and characteristics, which are reported in table 6.5, indicates nontrivial differences for most interests. With all other explanatory variables at their sample means, owning any private securities *increases* the predicted probability of a yes vote 30 percent, while being in personal debt *decreases* the predicted probability of a yes vote 29 percent. Being a merchant increases the predicted probability 19 percent; owning western lands increases it 14 percent; while being a farmer increases it only 8 percent.[19]

The findings also indicate that delegates who held relatively large amounts of public securities were more likely to have voted for the Constitution than were those without public securities. The estimated effect for ownership of any public securities is positive but marginally statistically significant at best.[20] But the impact of public securities holdings is much stronger when the interests are measured either as the market value of the public securities held or as the ownership of public securities holdings with a market value in excess of $1,000.[21] The estimated effect of the market value of public securities is positive and highly statistically significant, as is the incremental effect of ownership of public securities in excess of $1,000. The magnitude of the effect is much different between the two variables, however. The response elasticity of the market value of the holdings is a trivial .0469, indicating that, for example, a 1 percent increase in the value of public securities holdings increases the predicted probability of a yes vote by a trivial .047 percent.[22] Yet the predicted probability of a yes vote for a delegate with public securities holdings in excess of $1,000 is 21 percent greater than for a delegate without either those

Table 6.5. Predicted Probabilities of the Ratification Vote for a Delegate with Different Interests and Characteristics: Significant Variables for the Overall Pooled Sample

Economic Interests and Characteristics	Predicted Probability of a Yes Vote
The "Average" Delegate	.695
Merchant	.819
Not a merchant	.687
Owner western land	.779
No western land	.681
Owner private securities	.889
No private securities	.683
Debtor	.500
Not a debtor	.699
Farmer[a]	.735
Not a farmer	.680
Slaveowner	.548
Not a slaveowner	.795
Owner public securities[a]	.730
No public securities	.675
Owner more than $1,000 public securities	.815
Owner less than $1,000 public securities	.675
Public Securities Holdings (Market Value)	
$ 0 (the least for any delegate)	.669
$ 500	.680
$ 1,000	.691
$ 1,506.57 (the mean)	.703
$ 5,000	.773
$ 10,000	.852
$ 20,000	.942
$ 30,000	.979
$108,859 (the most for any delegate)	.999
Constituent Slaveholdings (Slaves per 100 Whites)[a]	
0 (the least in any area)	.682
30	.687
68.55 (the mean)	.695
100	.701
300	.738
600	.788
900	.830
1,200	.866
1,482.40 (the most in any area)	.893
Distance from Navigable Water (Miles)	
0 (the nearest for any delegate)	.831
20	.771
40.37 (the mean)	.695
60	.610
80	.517
100	.422

Table 6.5. continued

Economic Interests and Characteristics	Predicted Probability of a Yes Vote
150	.219
200	.100
255 (the farthest for any delegate)	.036
Population in State (Number of Whites)	
46,000 (the least populous)	.975
140,000	.923
170,000	.891
233,000	.787
271,519 (the mean)	.695
288,000	.649
314,000	.572
373,000	.388
442,000 (the most populous)	.210
Moot	.965
Not moot	.317

[a] Not significant at conventional levels, but the estimated effect of the variable may be precise enough to be suggestive of an influence on the ratification vote.

Note: All predicted probabilities are calculated from the estimated logistic coefficients for specification 5 reported in table A6.1 in appendix 6, except for the variables measuring the ownership of more than $1,000 public securities and the value of public securities which are calculated from the logistic coefficients for specifications 6 and 7, respectively, in table A6.1. The variable measuring the order of ratification, although significant, is not listed because interpreting the magnitudes of its effect is problematic as it is not strictly a continuous variable. The predicted probability for the "average" delegate is calculated employing the mean values of all explanatory variables. For a dichotomous variable, a predicted probability is calculated when the variable has a value of 1 and when the variable has a value of 0, with all other explanatory variables at their mean values. For a continuous variable, the predicted probabilities are calculated for each value of the variable, with all other explanatory variables at their mean values. Because of rounding, the difference between the two predicted probabilities for a dichotomous variable may not be identical to its reported incremental effect. Because different specifications are used for the public securities variables, the two predicted probabilities for no securities holdings may not equal each other. The populations listed are those for Delaware, South Carolina, New Jersey, Connecticut, the mean for all thirteen states, North Carolina, New York, Massachusetts, and Virginia, from the least to the most populous state.

holdings or any public securities holdings. Despite the trivial marginal effect of the market value of public securities holdings, however, the predicted probability of a yes vote for an otherwise average delegate with widely different market values differs widely; it ranges from .669 with no public securities to .999 with the most public securities holdings, essentially a 100 percent likelihood of voting yes (see table 6.5). These are not unimportant differences.[23]

The findings for public securities confirm the contentions of Main (1961) and Schuyler (1961) but run counter to McDonald's (1958, pp. 355–357) assertion that no general voting patterns related to public securities holdings were present during the ratification campaign. McDonald, however, does acknowledge voting patterns related to public securities holdings in two of the ratifying conventions (Connecticut and Massachusetts). The findings here also challenge more general treatments of the subject that conclude that the modern evidence is inconsistent with Beard's (1913 [1935]) contention that public securities holders were among the most important delegates behind ratification.[24]

The ratification debates indicate that the benefits under the Constitution to individuals with public securities holdings were hotly debated. In the Virginia convention, James Madison in fact argued, "We must make effectual provision for the payment of the interest of our public debts" (Elliot, 1836 [1888], vol. 3, p. 308). George Mason, who considered the clause requiring the assumption of the depreciated Continental debt a dubious aspect of the Constitution, complained that "we must pay it shilling for shilling. . . . The nominal value must . . . be paid" (p. 472).[25] Concerned whether Mason and other delegates believed that individuals with public securities holdings should be treated differently under the new government, James Madison retorted, "Do gentlemen wish the public creditors should be put in a worse situation? . . . There cannot be a majority of the people of America that would wish to defraud their public creditors" (p. 473). This did not satisfy Patrick Henry, as he had "heard there were vast quantities of that money packed up in barrels: those formable millions are deposited in the Northern States" and they "acquired it for the most inconsiderable trifle" (p. 475). In the New York press, Marcus was straightforward about the benefits to public securities holdings, proudly proclaiming during the campaign in New York, "It [the Constitution] is in the Interest of all Public Creditors, because they will see the credit of the States rise, and their Securities appreciate" (Bailyn, 1993, pt. 1, p. 127).

The findings for the impact of personal slaveholdings on the probability of voting to ratify the Constitution offer even more support for an economic interpretation of the ratification of the Constitution. While the value of slaveholdings does not have a statistically significant effect, the incremental effect of the ownership of any slaves is negative, statistically significant, and sizable in magnitude. A delegate who owned slaves was 31 percent less likely to have voted for the Constitution than one who owned no slaves, other things equal (see table 6.5). The findings suggest that, while the value of personal slaveholdings did not significantly affect voting, the *ownership* of slaves had a substantial negative influence on the likelihood of voting for ratification, a conclusion different from that found in many existing studies.[26]

And the sentiments expressed during the ratification debates suggest that slave ownership per se would have decreased the probability of a slaveowner voting for ratification. Although the Constitution did not directly restrict the operation of slavery, and actually prohibited any national ban on the international slave trade for twenty years, many delegates still believed that the slave trade clause in fact would negatively restrict slavery. James Wilson (Pennsylvania) was just one among many northerners who believed slavery was restricted in the Constitution. As Wilson declared during the debates in Pennsylvania, "I consider this as laying the foundation for banishing slavery out of this country" and besides, "an immediate advantage is also obtained; for a tax or duty may be imposed on such importation" that "operates as a partial prohibition," and Wilson was even hopeful that "it will be prohibited altogether" in a few years (Elliot, 1836 [1888], vol. 2, p. 452). Among southern slave-owners, the sentiments were even stronger. Although a supporter of an immediate ban on the international slave trade, during the Virginia debates, George Mason still believed that "we have no security for the property of the kind which we have already" because the national government "may lay such a tax as will amount to manumission" (vol. 3, p. 452). And in the North Carolina convention, James Galloway concurred with these sentiments: "With respect to the abolition of slavery, it requires the utmost consideration. The property of the Southern States consists principally of slaves. If they [the framers] mean to do away slavery altogether, this property will be destroyed. I apprehend it [the slave trade clause] means to bring forward manumission" (vol. 4, p. 101).

Although the predicted probabilities of voting for ratification shown in table 6.5 are not less than 50 percent for an otherwise average delegate with any one of the personal economic interests listed, that is not the case for a delegate who might have had more than one of the statistically significant interests. For example, the predicted probability for an otherwise average delegate who was a debtor *and* a slaveowner is .347. And, if that otherwise average slaveowning debtor also was neither a merchant nor had any financial securities holdings, the predicted probability of a yes vote is only .300. An important implication that can be drawn from these predicted probabilities is that ratification of the Constitution likely would have failed had more debtors and slaveowners, and fewer merchants and private and public securities holders, been present at the state ratifying conventions.

Turning to the effects of constituent interests, they generally are weaker than for the personal interests of the ratifiers (see table A6.1). The fairly weak results, however, more likely result from the limitations of the constituent-interest variables than from their true effects on voting. With respect to the effect on the vote of constituent slaveholdings, it is positive in all specifications but not statistically significant in any.[27] The impact of constituent public securities holdings is negative in all specifications but not consistently significant. There was no statistical pattern in the vote related to the ancestry of constituents. And in what may seem contrary to their interest, delegates in the less populous states were *more* likely to vote for ratification, as indicated by the highly statistically significant negative coefficients for the population variable in all specifications. The statistically significant negative effect of a state's population on the ratification vote perhaps can be explained by the compromise during the drafting that accorded states equal representation in the Senate. The compromise on representation might have reduced the expected political costs to the less populous states under the Constitution. Because the compromise in the Constitution reduced the loss of power for small states, it would have increased the likelihood that a small-state delegate would vote for ratification.

The strongest finding for any of the constituent interests, by far, is for the distance variable. Delegates from the more commercial areas (nearer navigable water) were more likely to have favored the Constitution than were those who represented less commercial, backcountry counties, as indicated by the negative and strongly significant effects of the distance variable in all specifications.[28] This finding confirms many of the conclusions in the historical literature regarding the geographical distribution of the ratification vote, providing strong evidence that those from the more isolated, less commercial areas of the country were in fact opposed to the Constitution. As a result, the finding is strongly in conflict with McDonald's (1958, 1963) conclusions that the vote was *not* systematically related to the geographical location of the delegates.

Yet the magnitudes of the marginal effects of the constituent interests shown in table 6.4 are quite small. If the estimated effect of constituent slaveholdings is considered precise enough to not be the result of chance variation, its marginal effect is a miniscule .00019. And its estimated response elasticity is only .0192, indicating that, for example, a 1 percent increase in the amount of a constituent slaveholdings from its mean increases the probability of voting yes a trivial .0192 percent. For distance from navigable water, its marginal effect is −.00405, with a response elasticity of −.235. For the population of a delegate's state, its marginal effect is only −.00267, but its response elasticity is a more sizable −1.043, indicating that a 1 percent decrease in a state's population from its mean, for example, increases the probability of a yes vote slightly more than 1 percent.

In spite of the very small marginal effects, the predicted probability of voting yes on ratification for the two statistically significant constituent variables are quite different for delegates with quite different values of the variables, similar to the findings for nearly all of the marginal effects for the Philadelphia convention. Compare, for example, the various predicted probabilities of a yes vote reported in table 6.5 for an otherwise average delegate with different values of the significant constituent-interest variables. For the distance variable, the probabilities range from slightly over 83 percent for a delegate from a coastal area (zero miles from navigable water) to well less than 4 percent if the delegate was from the most isolated inland area (255 miles from navigable water). The range also is quite substantial for the population variable. The predicted probability of voting yes is about 21 percent if an otherwise average delegate represented a state with, for example, a population the size of Virginia, and it is well over 97 percent if he represented a state with, for example, a population the size of Delaware. Again, an important implication that can be drawn from the findings is that the Constitution likely would not have been ratified had more delegates who represented more isolated inland areas been present at the ratifying conventions.

The effects on the vote of the two variables that capture the effects of timing considerations are as expected and are sizable magnitudes. Delegates from states later in the ratification process were less likely to have voted for ratification (the statistically significant negative signs on the order variable). And the estimated marginal effect of the variable actually is not that small, because as a practical matter when the order of ratification is increased from its mean by one (which strictly speaking is more than a "marginal" increase), the predicted probability of a yes vote decreases from .695 for the "average" delegate to .455 for an otherwise average delegate (see specification 1 in table 6.4). But after nine states had ratified and the issue of ratification was moot, delegates were more likely to have voted for ratification (the significantly positive signs on the moot variable), as they could no longer prevent adoption of the Constitution. The incremental effect of the moot variable, .648, is substantial to say the least. For an otherwise average delegate from one of first nine states to ratify, the predicted probability of voting for ratification is just .317; but after the issue of the Constitution was moot, the predicted probability is nearly certain, .965. As with the effect of any of the variables, however, care must be taken when interpreting this incremental effect. It is the partial effect on the ratification vote of the Constitution having already been adopted when an otherwise average delegate votes for ratification, holding all other factors constant. Yet, as a discerning reader will recognize, many of the delegates in the last four ratifying conventions (e.g., in the North Carolina convention) were *not* otherwise "average" delegates.

Alexander Hamilton's (New York) speculations at the beginning of the ratification campaign on who would support the proposed Constitution are entirely consistent with the findings for the overall ratification vote. As Hamilton maintained,

> The new constitution has in favour of its success these circumstances—a very great weight of influence of the persons who framed it . . . the goodwill of the commercial interests throughout the states which will give all its efforts to the establishment of a government capable of regulating protecting and extending commerce of the Union—the goodwill of most men of property in the several states who wish a government of the union able to protect them against domestic violence and the depredations which the democratic spirit is apt to make on property . . . the hopes of the Creditors of the United States that a general government possessing the means of doing it will pay the debt of the Union. (Bailyn, 1993, pt. 1, pp. 9–11)

Against this support was the opposition of two or three important delegates at the Philadelphia convention and the state office holders, according to Hamilton, who further argued: "[A]dd to these causes the disinclination of the people to taxes and of course to a strong government—the opposition of all men much in debt who will not wish to see a government established one object of which is to restrain this means of cheating Creditors" (Bailyn, 1993, pt. 1, pp. 9–11).

Overall Pooled Estimates for the State Fixed-Effects Model.   As an alternative, a state fixed-effects model for the overall pooled vote is estimated to control for state-specific differences that could have affected the ratification vote across the thirteen ratifying conventions. The state fixed-effects model includes state dummy variables for each state in place of the timing and other variables contained in TO_j, and in place of other variables measured at the state-level of aggregation. The state dummies are intended to capture the influence of all factors unique to each state. In addition to including state dummy variables, one specification of the state fixed-effects model is reported with the asset share variables, and another specification is reported with the instrumental variables, as substitutes for each other, for a delegate's slaveholdings and public securities holdings. This helps determine whether a delegate's share of total assets in either slaves or public securities was an important influence on the ratification vote, rather than merely ownership of an asset or the absolute amount of the asset owned.[29]

The findings for the state fixed-effects model, which are reported as the logistic coefficients for the alternative model specifications in appendix 6 (table A6.2), are nearly identical to the overall ratification findings reported above.[30] The estimates for merchants, ownership of western land, and ownership of private securities are all positive and significant, or highly significant, in all four reported specifications, indicating that delegates with these characteristics were more likely to support ratification. Delegates who were in personal debt were less likely to favor the Constitution: The effect of debtor status is negative and mildly significant in the four specifications. Delegates who were farmers were apparently more likely to favor the Constitution. The effect of farmer interests is positive and significant in two of the specifications and is suggestive of a relationship in the other two specifications. Delegates from more commercial areas were more likely to favor ratification than were those from the less commercial backcountry, as indicated by the negative and highly significant distance variable in all four specifications. Not surprisingly, the findings also indicate state-specific differences among the ratifying conventions, as most of the state dummy variables are statistically significant.

With respect to the impact of slaveholdings on the probability of voting for ratification, the findings for the state fixed-effects model indicate that *ownership* of slaves is negative and significant. But the value of a delegate's slaveholdings is not significant, the same result found above. The lack of statistical significance for the value of slaves, however, may be explained by the large variance in the value of total assets owned by slaveowners. As a result, when the value of a delegate's slaveholdings is converted to the value of slaveholdings as a share of the value of total assets, a negative coefficient is obtained that is suggestive of a relationship (see specification 3 in table A6.2).[31] When the share variable for a delegate's slaveholdings is converted to an instrumental variable for the slave share, a negative and significant coefficient is obtained (see specification 4 in table A6.2). These findings mean that delegates with relatively large shares of their total assets (their portfolio) in the form of slaves apparently were less likely to ratify the Constitution than were those who owned no slaves. That the "portfolio effect" of slaveholdings matters when simple owner-ship or the market value of slaves does not is entirely plausible. And, once more, the conclusion that slaveowners were less likely to ratify appears to conflict with the conclusions found in much of the existing literature. But recall, again, that the existing literature is nearly always, if not always, referring to the *overall* vote for ratification of the majority of slavehold-ers, not to the *partial* effect of slaveholdings per se on the probability of favoring ratification.

The state fixed-effects findings for public securities holdings also are similar to those reported earlier for public securities. The finding for del-egates who held public securities suggests that they might have been more likely to vote for the Constitution than those without public securities.[32] And the impact of public securities holdings is much stronger when mea-sured as the value of the public securities held; when the relative value of a delegate's public securities holdings are taken into account, the results are even stronger. To determine the "portfolio effect" of public securities holdings, the model is estimated with the value of a delegate's public secu-rities holdings as a share of his total assets, and with the instrumental vari-able for the public securities share as an alternative. The estimated effect of both is positive and highly significant (see specifications 3 and 4 in table A6.2). These state fixed-effects estimates provide still more support for the role of public securities holdings in the ratification of the Constitution while also controlling across the ratifying conventions for any state-specific factors unique to each state.

Estimates Employing the Less Restricted Pooled Models

Estimates by Region.   To examine the robustness of the findings, voting patterns at the state ratifying conventions are estimated employing data from states pooled by geographic region (the South, Middle Atlantic, and New England).[33] The procedure allows the empirical model to identify dif-ferential regional influences on the ratification vote, perhaps owing to differences between regions in economic conditions and institutional structures, in a manner not possible by estimating voting patterns with the data pooled for all thirteen states. A summary of the estimated effects of the economic and other interests on the ratification vote for various alter-native specifications of each regional model is reported in table 6.6.[34]

As in the overall pooled results, the effect of slaveholdings is negative and nearly always significant in both the South and Middle Atlantic

Table 6.6. Summary of the Estimated Effects of the Explanatory Variables on the Probability of a Yes Vote at the State Ratifying Conventions: Selected Samples by Region

Explanatory Variables	South	Middle Atlantic	New England
Merchant	—	—	Yes
Western landowner	Yes	—	Yes
Private creditor	—	—	Yes
Debtor	No	—	—
Farmer	—	Yes	Yes
Substitute Measures of Slave Interests			
Slaveowner	No	No	—[a]
Value of slaves owned	—	No?	—[a]
Slave share	No?	—	—[a]
Slave instrument	No	No	—[a]
Substitute Measures of Public Securities Interests			
Owner public securities	—	—	Yes
Owner more than $1,000 public securities	Yes	—	Yes
Value of public securities	Yes	Yes?	Yes
Public securities share	Yes	Yes?	Yes
Public securities instrument	—	—	Yes
Slaves per 100 whites	Yes?	—	—[a]
Public funding credit per capita	No?	—[a]	—
Distance to navigable water	No	No	No
Population	—	—[a]	—
English ancestry of citizens	No?	Yes	Yes?
Order	No	No	No
Number of Observations	628	162	422

[a] The model cannot be estimated with this variable included.

Note: The dependent variable in each sample is the observed vote for ratification of the Constitution, where a yes vote equals 1 and a no vote equals 0. A "Yes" (or "No") indicates that delegates with this characteristic had a statistically significant greater probability of a yes (or no) vote on the Constitution in all specifications estimated. A "Yes?" (or "No?") indicates that delegates with this characteristic had a statistically significant, or marginally significant, greater probability of voting in favor (or against) the Constitution in most specifications estimated. No entry indicates there was no consistent statistically significant pattern in voting related to the characteristic.

regions, the two regions for which personal slaveholdings are included in the voting model.[35] Other findings are somewhat sensitive to the region included in the model, however. The results for public securities holdings across regions are similar to the estimates based on the overall pooled sample, but they are not quite as robust across regions as are the findings for slaveholdings. The effect of the ownership of any public securities is positive and significant in New England, but not significant elsewhere. The estimated effect of all the other measures of public securities holdings is positive and significant in New England, and most are positive and significant in the South, but only two of the measures are marginally significant in the Middle Atlantic. These findings, in part, confirm McDonald's (1958) conclusion that support for the Constitution among delegates with public securities tended to be concentrated in the New England states of Connecticut, Massachusetts, and New Hampshire. But this overlooks the finding for the value of the delegates' public securities holdings in the South. When a state fixed-effects model is estimated, the share variable for the value of public securities holdings has a positive and marginally significant effect in the Middle Atlantic and remains highly significant and positive in the other regions.[36] The state fixed-effects findings offer some support for the conclusions of Brunhouse (1942) and McCormick (1950), who suggest that delegates in the Middle Atlantic region with public securities holdings were more likely to vote to ratify.

The effect of merchant interests is positive and highly significant in the New England states, but is not statistically significant in the South or the Middle Atlantic. The findings may be explained in part if personal merchant interests of delegates are correlated with unmeasured constituent merchant interests to a greater degree in New England than in other regions. Given the heavy involvement of New England merchants not only in the coastal trade but also in international trade, it is not surprising that they would be strong supporters of ratification. New England merchants apparently expected a strong, nationalist government to lower the costs of commercial activities through strengthening trade relations. As a result, merchants were more likely to have voted to ratify the Constitution.

Among the other findings of note, the effect of western landholdings is positive and statistically significant in the South and New England, as expected, but is not significant in the Middle Atlantic. The findings for the Middle Atlantic may be explained in part by the fact that there were generally few western landholdings among the delegates and the citizens of that region. The effect of private securities holdings is positive and statistically significant in New England, where such interests may have been more heavily concentrated. The effect of farming interests is positive and significant in all specifications in the Middle Atlantic and New England regions. As a result, delegates who were farmers in these two regions were more likely to support ratification than were otherwise identical delegates, consistent with the overall pooled findings. For the constituent interests, the regional results are rather mixed. The only exceptionally strong results are for the distance and the timing variables. The estimated effects of distance from navigable water and the order of ratification are consistently negative and highly significant in all estimated models for all three regions, which is consistent with the findings for the overall pooled sample.

Estimates by the Nature of Ratification. One of the limitations of the overall pooled model relates to the impact of a compromise on voting in the ratification process—a compromise over ratification with recommended amendments. Although "conditional" ratification, strictly speaking, may not have been permitted for the ratification of the Constitution, many borderline Anti-federalists were persuaded to vote for adoption when recommendations for amendments were offered (Riker, 1987a). Sam Adams (Massachusetts) was one of those with doubts and reservations, who admitted, after John Hancock, president of the Massachusetts convention, proposed recommended amendments, that "the proposition submitted will have a tendency to remove such doubts" (Elliot, 1836 [1888], vol. 2, p. 123). Several states even declared their interpretations of the meaning of the Constitution in their letters of ratification. Completely unconditional ratification with no declarations of interpretation or recommendations for amendments took place in six states—Connecticut, Delaware, Georgia, Maryland, New Jersey, and Pennsylvania. Ratification with only recommendations for amendments took place in two states— Massachusetts and New Hampshire. More conditional ratification that included not only recommendations for amendments but also declarations of constitutional interpretation took place in five states—New York, North Carolina, Rhode Island, South Carolina, and Virginia. Even if conditional ratification, strictly speaking, was not allowed, these five states, in fact, ratified "conditionally."[37]

In the samples of ratifying conventions grouped by the nature of ratification, delegates who were slaveowners were less likely to have supported ratification, other things constant, as were delegates who represented the more isolated backcountry. Constituent slave interests had no statistically significant effect on the vote in any of the three samples in which the variable is included. The results for the other personal or constituent interests appear to vary across the samples. Table 6.7 summarizes the findings for several alternative model specifications for each sample of conventions grouped by the nature of ratification.[38]

The findings for the samples of conventions that ratified with some form of condition are more often significant and more consistent with each other than they are with the findings from the conventions that ratified unconditionally (see table 6.7). For example, private securities and public securities holders were more likely to have favored ratification relative to delegates without such securities holdings in conventions where the Constitution was adopted with qualifications or conditions concerning amendments. But there were no significant findings related to private or public securities holdings when the conventions that ratified unconditionally were grouped together (Connecticut, Delaware, Georgia, Maryland, New Jersey, and Pennsylvania). These results may reflect, in part, a greater degree of consensus on the Constitution among the delegates of the unconditionally ratifying states than among those of the conditionally ratifying states, hence fewer statistically significant voting patterns are observed for the unconditional states. Economic and other interests mattered less to delegates from those states. The findings for the conditional states generally have the same sign and significance as the overall pooled sample, which suggests that, although the bill of rights issue may have been essential for ratification, as Riker (1987a, pp. 28–31) contends, the

Table 6.7. Summary of the Estimated Effects of the Explanatory Variables on the Probability of a Yes Vote at the State Ratifying Conventions: Selected Samples by Nature of Ratification

Explanatory Variables	Unconditional Ratification	With Recommendations Only	With Declarations and Recommendations	With Declarations or Recommendations
Merchant	—	Yes	—	Yes
Western landowner	—	—	Yes?	Yes
Private creditor	No	Yes	Yes?	Yes
Debtor	No	—	—	No
Farmer	Yes	Yes?	—	Yes?
Substitute Measures of Slave Interests				
Slaveowner	No	—[a]	No	No
Value of slaves owned	—	—[a]	—	—
Substitute Measures of Public Securities Interests				
Owner public securities	—	Yes	Yes	—
Owner more than $1,000 public securities	—	Yes	Yes	Yes
Value of public securities	—	—	Yes	Yes
Slaves per 100 whites	—	—[a]	—	—
Public funding credit per capita	No	No	No	No
Distance to navigable water	No	—[a]	No	No
Population	No	—[a]	Yes?	—
English ancestry of citizens	—	Yes	—	—
Order	—[a]	—[a]	—[a]	—[a]
Number of Observations	296	275	641	916

[a] The model cannot be estimated with this variable included.

Note: See the note to table 6.6.

compromise over it did not weaken the influence of economic or other interests on the ratification vote—an economic interpretation of the ratification of the Constitution is still valid.

Estimates by the Chronological Order of Ratification.   Because of the rules under which the Constitution was considered by the states, the outcome of a particular ratifying convention in some cases affected the voting outcome at a subsequent ratifying convention (e.g., Virginia's outcome affected New York). Accordingly, it might be the case that conventions that ratified earlier in the overall process should not be grouped with those later in the process. Table 6.8 summarizes the findings for a number of alternative model specifications for each sample of conventions grouped by their order in the ratification process.[39]

Most of the findings in table 6.8 for the three different samples containing combinations of the first nine ratifying conventions are the same as the findings for the overall pooled sample. Merchants, western landowners, and delegates with public securities holdings were more likely to have voted for ratification than were others. Delegates who were personal debtors were less likely. Delegates who represented more isolated

Table 6.8. Summary of the Estimated Effects of the Explanatory Variables on the Probability of a Yes Vote at the State Ratifying Conventions: Selected Samples by Order of Ratification

Explanatory Variables	First Nine States	First Nine (unanimous excluded)	Fifth through Ninth	Tenth through Thirteenth
Merchant	Yes	Yes	Yes	—
Western landowner	Yes	Yes	Yes	—
Private creditor	Yes?	Yes?	—	Yes?
Debtor	No	No	No	—
Farmer	—	—	—	—
Substitute Measures of Slave Interests				
Slaveowner	No	—	—	No?
Value of slaves owned	—	—	—	—
Substitute Measures of Public Securities Interests				
Owner public securities	Yes	Yes	Yes	—
Owner more than $1,000 public securities	Yes	Yes	Yes	Yes
Value of public securities	Yes	Yes	Yes	—
Slaves per 100 whites	Yes	Yes	Yes	No
Public funding credit per capita	No	No	No	—
Distance to navigable water	No	No	No	No
Population	No	—	—	Yes
English ancestry of citizens	—	—	—	—
Number of Observations	741	662	600	471

Note: See the note to table 6.6.

backcountry areas also were less likely to have ratified the Constitution than were those who represented areas closer to navigable water.

However, the patterns in the ratification vote in the last four ratifying conventions (those voting after the adoption of the Constitution was moot) are weaker. Many interests showed no patterns related to the ratification vote, as indicated by few statistically significant results. Two of the explanatory variables also have signs different from the three other samples. Overall, the findings for the last four conventions curiously still are consistent with an economic interpretation of the Constitution—economic interests matter less when their value has diminished: If a delegate in one of the last four state conventions voted against his personal interests in supporting the Constitution or not, that decision would have had less impact on the delegate than before the Constitution was adopted.

Estimates by Presence or Absence of State Paper Money. Historians long have argued that abuses by states in the issuance of paper money during the Confederation period at least partly fueled the movement to the Constitution. Voting patterns in ratifying conventions in states that had issued paper money during the 1780s may differ from voting patterns in states with no paper money issued during that time. To examine this hypothesis, the model is estimated for two samples of states grouped by the presence or absence of paper money issues during the 1780s. The paper money states are Georgia, New Jersey, New York, North Carolina, Pennsylvania, Rhode Island, and South Carolina. The states not issuing paper money are Connecticut, Delaware, Maryland, Massachusetts, New Hampshire, and Virginia. Table 6.9 summarizes the findings for various alternative model specifications for the two samples of conventions.[40]

In several cases, the findings are similar for both samples. The delegates who were slaveowners or who represented more isolated backcountry areas were less likely to favor ratification, other things equal. The variable measuring the order of ratification also produced a negative and significant finding. The alternative measures of public securities holdings indicate that delegates who were public creditors generally were more likely to have supported ratification, in both samples, with one important exception: Delegates who owned any amount of public securities were *less* likely to vote for ratification in states *with* paper money. Yet the effect of private securities holdings on the probability of a yes vote is positive and statistically significant but only for delegates in states *without* paper money. Similarly, the effect of the debtor status of a delegate is negative and statistically significant only for states *without* paper money.

Overall, there were many fewer significant findings for the states *with* paper money, indicating that economic interests apparently were *less* important in those states. The results for the paper money states, and the apparently perverse finding for owners of public securities, may appear to be inconsistent with the argument that state issuance of paper money was an important economic factor in fueling the movement for the

Table 6.9. Summary of the Estimated Effects of the Explanatory Variables on the Probability of a Yes Vote at the State Ratifying Conventions: Selected Samples by Presence of Paper Money

Explanatory Variables	States with Paper Money	States without Paper Money
Merchant	Yes?	Yes
Western landowner	—	Yes
Private creditor	—	Yes
Debtor	—	No
Farmer	Yes?	—
Substitute Measures of Slave Interests		
Slaveowner	No	No
Value of slaves owned	—	—
Slave share	—	—
Slave instrument	No	No
Substitute Measures of Public Securities Interests		
Owner public securities	No	Yes
Owner more than $1,000 public securities	—	Yes
Value of public securities	Yes	Yes
Public securities share	Yes	Yes
Public securities instrument	—	Yes
Slaves per 100 whites	Yes	No?
Public funding credit per capita	No	No
Distance to navigable water	No	No
Population	No?	—
English ancestry of citizens	Yes	—
Order	No	No
Number of Observations	598	614

Note: See the note to table 6.6.

Constitution. But the lack of significant findings may be evidence of the heterogeneous experiences with paper money across the individual states that issued paper during the Confederation period. Common voting patterns, and thus significant findings, related to specific economic interests from a pooled sample of state conventions of delegates with heterogeneous experiences would be less likely.[41] A plausible reason that delegates who owned private financial securities were significantly more likely to vote for ratification, and those who were debtors significantly less likely, for only the states without paper money may be that these states had more homogeneous experiences. It also may be that knowledge of the experiences of the paper money states, if they in fact abused their issuance of paper money, adversely affected the expectations of the delegates from the states without paper money.

In an attempt to distinguish among the different experiences of individual paper money states, voting patterns also are estimated employing a state fixed-effects model, which uses state dummy variables to capture state-specific factors unique to each state, for the states with and without paper money. The state fixed-effects findings also are accounted for in the summary of findings in table 6.9. (The actual logistic estimates for the state fixed-effects model are reported in appendix 6, tables A6.19 and A6.20.) Again, the results for the states *with* paper money contain many fewer significant findings than do those for the states *without* paper money and, in a few cases, are different from the findings for most other samples reported in this chapter. Only in a few cases are the results similar for both samples: The effect of distance from navigable water is negative and highly significant in all specifications for both samples. Delegates who were slave-owners were also significantly less likely to vote for ratification in both samples. The other findings for the states *with* paper money either are not significant or, at best, are marginally significant for only a small number of variables in some specifications reported in tables A6.19 and A6.20.

However, for the states *without* paper money, delegates who were merchants, owned western land, owned private securities, or owned public securities were all more likely to favor ratification, as indicated by the positive and significant coefficients for each of the variables in all estimated model specifications. Delegates who were debtors or who owned slaves were significantly less likely to vote for ratification. As a result, the findings for states *without* paper money attest to the robustness of the estimates of the economic model of voting, as they are similar to those reported throughout this chapter for the overall pooled sample and most other samples with significant results. Overall, the estimates of the state fixed-effects model for the two samples of ratifying conventions provide even more evidence of the likely heterogeneous experiences of the individual states that issued paper money during the Confederation period.

A Summary of the Findings

Significant voting patterns for many economic interests are found in the overall ratification process. To a degree, the nature of the impact of economic factors on the ratification vote differs by region and other factors that are common among different sets of states. While some results are altered across the various samples, several general conclusions regarding the division of interests in the ratification vote appear to be supported by the entire empirical analysis of the ratification process. First, delegates who were merchants or farmers, or who owned western lands or private or public securities generally were significantly more likely to have supported ratification than other delegates, *ceteris paribus*. Second, delegates who were in personal debt, owned slaves, or represented more isolated back-country areas generally were significantly less likely to have ratified than were other delegates, *ceteris paribus*. Third, the most robust results across all samples and specifications and the strongest results in terms of the magnitude of the effects are obtained for delegates who were merchants, western landowners, or private creditors; who owned large amounts of public securities or slaves; or who represented more isolated backcountry areas. Fourth, the least consistent patterns in the ratification vote are indicated for delegates who represented more populous states, areas with heavier concentrations of slaves, or areas with heavier concentrations of English descendants. Fifth, the magnitudes of the effects of economic interests are large enough that had different interests been represented at the state ratifying conventions, there likely would have been no ratification of the Constitution as drafted.

The findings of the overall ratification process strongly support an economic interpretation of the adoption of the Constitution. The results also confirm many of the conclusions contained in one of the more comprehensive but informal empirical studies of the ratification process—Jackson Main's 1961 study. While the findings are likewise consistent with some of the conclusions contained in Forrest McDonald's 1958 study, they overwhelmingly conflict with McDonald's principal conclusions concerning *no* relationship between the ratification vote in many states and specific economic and sectional interests in those states. The findings likewise overwhelmingly conflict with Clinton Rossiter's (1966) overall conclusion about ratification "that the evidence we now have leads most historians to conclude that no sharp economic or social line can be drawn on a nationwide basis between these two camps [the supporters and opponents]" (p. 295).

The differences in the findings across the four less-restricted pooled models are plausible. First, many of the differences across the regions can be attributable to the rather imprecise estimates for the Middle Atlantic region, whose delegates were overwhelmingly Federalist, making estimation of voting alignments more difficult. The data regarding the personal-interest variables for this region are among the poorest and its sample size the smallest; not surprisingly, most of the personal-interest variables are not significant for the Middle Atlantic. Second, the few significant findings for the sample of conventions that ratified unconditionally, the sample of the last four conventions to ratify, and the sample of the conventions from states that issued paper money during the period are all plausible given the particular aspects of ratification in the first two sets of conventions, and the likely heterogeneous experiences with paper money in the last set. Third, the data necessary to measure constituent interests are limited, and the few constituent-interest variables that are included in the estimation are very rough approximations of actual constituent interests. Fourth, many of the personal-interest variables of the delegates may act as proxies for similar but unmeasured constituent interests. The degree of correlation between the observed personal-interest variables and the unobserved constituent-interest variables may vary across states, contributing to differences across the less-restricted pooled models in the estimates for the personal-interest variables. However, this need not be true. Fifth, differences in economic conditions and institutions across states, *not* accounted for in the various pooled models, could have generated differences in the ratification vote, as indicated by the many significant state dummy variables in the estimated state fixed-effects models. As a result, the ratification process can be even better understood if the ratification vote is estimated separately for each state convention, the task to which chapter 7 turns for seven of the ratifying conventions.

SEVEN

The Ratification Vote within
Individual State Conventions

In an attempt to provide a test of the relationship between economic interests and the contest over the ratification of the Constitution, chapter 6 examined the voting of the delegates during the overall ratification process. Because of the sparseness of the data for several states and because some constituent-interest variables are available at the state level only, the data for delegates from all thirteen state conventions were pooled together, and different combinations of state conventions also were pooled into various subsamples. Yet the ratification process was essentially thirteen separate contests.[1] And pooling the data from different state conventions into a single sample could have been formally rejected as an appropriate sampling procedure for the overall pooled sample.[2] Pooling the data from different state conventions also can place unnecessary restrictions on the statistical analysis.[3] The impact on voting of a delegate's personal ideology was not estimated as well because the data employed as markers for personal ideology were not readily available. As a result, no formal tests of the role of economic (pecuniary) interests versus ideological (nonpecuniary) interests in explaining voting were included in chapter 6. Consequently, the conclusions concerning the role of economic interests in explaining the vote to ratify the Constitution may not be completely warranted.[4]

Accordingly, the vote among the delegates within individual ratifying conventions is examined in the present chapter. Estimating the ratification vote within an individual convention separate from the other conventions allows better estimation of the voting behavior and avoids the econometric restrictions encountered with the pooled samples employed in chapter 6. Sufficient data exist to permit the ratification vote to be estimated separately for each of seven state conventions: Connecticut, Massachusetts, New Hampshire, North Carolina, Pennsylvania, South Carolina, and

Virginia. But the amount of data available varies across the seven conventions. Data are also quite limited for the constituent-interest variables because two of the previously employed measures, the net public funding credit per capita and population in each state, are state-level variables. And state-level variables cannot be employed for a within-state examination of voting because the data would be identical for each delegate within the same convention. The data for the seven states, moreover, is so limited for the markers for each delegate's ideology that they cannot be employed for all seven conventions. As a result, estimation of the ratification vote separately for the individual conventions will be in two steps.

In the first step, to develop a general understanding of how voting patterns differ across individual conventions for as many conventions as possible, employing the limited data, the ratification vote is estimated separately for each of the seven conventions. Discussion of the findings for this preliminary estimation will facilitate generalizations regarding the uniqueness of each state's ratification for as many states as possible.

In the second step, the ratification vote is reestimated separately for three of the ratifying conventions—Massachusetts, North Carolina, and Virginia—employing additional data collected on the personal characteristics and political experiences of the delegates. These ratifying conventions are reexamined for several reasons. First, the three were among the largest ratifying conventions—yielding a sample of 735 delegates in total. Second, Massachusetts was a key New England state in the contest over ratification, and Virginia was a key state in the South. Historians regard both as crucial to union. Third, North Carolina was the only state convention to explicitly reject the Constitution.[5] The additional personal and political data collected for these three conventions serve as markers for the personal ideology of the delegates to the three conventions and allow a determination of the impact of a delegate's ideology on the ratification vote. They also allow a formal test of whether voting based on economic interests or voting based on ideological interests best explains the ratification process for these three conventions.

The Estimation Procedure for the Ratification Vote within the Seven Conventions

To determine the role of each interest in the ratification vote for each of the seven conventions separately, the following empirical model is estimated with logistic regression:

$$V_{ij} = f(PE_i, CE_j, CI_j), \tag{7.1}$$

where V_{ij} is a dummy variable for delegate i from county or township j measuring his vote for or against ratification, PE_i is the set of variables measuring personal economic interests, CE_j is the set of variables measuring constituents' economic interests, and CI_j is the set of variables that serve as the markers for constituents' ideology. The markers for each delegate's personal ideology (PI_i) are not included in the estimation for the seven conventions because data on the personal characteristics and political experiences are not readily available for the delegates from all seven states. The specific measures of the economic interests of the delegates and their constituents and the markers for the constituents' ideological interests for the seven ratifying conventions are described in table 7.1.[6]

Given the paucity of the data for several of the variables for the seven ratifying conventions, it might be appropriate to question whether there are enough differences in the characteristics and interests represented across the seven conventions to justify estimating the voting model for each convention separately. It turns out that there are substantial differences across the samples of delegates for the conventions. This is readily apparent from a comparison of the sample means of each variable for the delegate samples for the seven conventions, which are shown in table 7.2 along with their standard deviations.

For example, in table 7.2 the sample means indicate that the proportion of merchants in the delegate samples for the seven conventions ranges from a high of 26 percent in Connecticut to less than 3 percent in North Carolina. The proportion of public creditors (delegates who owned any public securities) in the delegate samples ranges from a high of 62 percent in South Carolina to well less than 2 percent in the North Carolina sample. And the number of slaveowners is quite different as well, ranging from 92 percent of the delegate sample in South Carolina to no slaveowners in both the Connecticut and New Hampshire samples. With respect to the constituent-interest variables, note that the mean percentage of citizens of English ancestry in a delegate's local area ranges from less than 58 percent in Pennsylvania to more than 96 percent in Connecticut. For constituent slaveholdings in a delegate's home county, the sample means range from a high of 313 slaves per 100 whites in South Carolina to barely more than one-tenth slave per 100 whites in New Hampshire and zero slaves per 100 whites in Massachusetts!

Results of the Estimation of the Ratification Vote in the Seven Conventions

For the most part, the findings for the ratification vote for the seven conventions—Connecticut, Massachusetts, New Hampshire, North Carolina, Pennsylvania, South Carolina, and Virginia—are consistent with the implications of the economic model of voting on ratification. For the statistically significant effects, delegates with personal or constituent interests that were expected to benefit from the Constitution generally were more likely than other delegates to have voted for ratification, while those with interests expected to lose from ratification generally were more likely to have voted against it. In addition, the magnitudes of the effects are often

Table 7.1. Measures of the Ratification Vote and Personal and Constituent Interests for Seven of the Ratifying Conventions

Dependent Variable	
Ratification vote	Equals 1 if the delegate to the state ratifying convention voted to ratify the Constitution (0 otherwise)
Explanatory Variables	
Personal Economic Interests (PE$_j$)	
Merchant	Equals 1 if the delegate's principal occupation was a merchant (0 otherwise)
Western landowner	Equals 1 if the delegate owned western lands (0 otherwise)
Farmer	Equals 1 if the delegate's principal occupation was a farmer (0 otherwise)
Debtor	Equals 1 if the delegate was in deep personal debt (0 otherwise)
Private creditor	Equals 1 if the delegate owned any private securities (0 otherwise)
Slaveowner	Equals 1 if the delegate owned any slaves in 1790 (0 otherwise)
Value of slaves	Market value of slaves owned in 1790 ($000s)
Owner public securities	Equals 1 if the delegate owned any public securities (0 otherwise)
Owner more than $1,000 public securities	Equals 1 if the delegate owned more than $1,000 in public securities (0 otherwise)
Value of public securities owned	Market value of a delegate's public securities holdings ($000s)
Constituents' Economic Interests (CE$_j$)	
Slaves per 100 whites	Slaves per 100 of the white population in the delegate's home county in 1790
Distance to navigable water	Distance from the center of the delegate's home county to nearest navigable water (miles)
Constituents' Ideology (CI$_j$)	
English ancestry of citizens	Percentage of all families in the delegate's home county or township of English ancestry in 1790

Note: The seven ratifying conventions are Connecticut, Massachusetts, New Hampshire, North Carolina, Pennsylvania, South Carolina, and Virginia. For a discussion of the data, and their sources, that were used to measure each of the specific variables, see appendix 2.

Table 7.2. Means and Standard Deviations of the Ratification Votes and the Personal and Constituent Interests for the Sample of Delegates to Seven of the Ratifying Conventions

	Sample Means						
Variables	CN	MA	NH	NC	PA	SC	VA
Ratification vote	.837	.602	.559	.359	.645	.618	.539
	(.3714)	(.4906)	(.5007)	(.4808)	(.4824)	(.4874)	(.5001)
Personal Economic Interests (PE_i)							
Merchant	.261	.157	.102	.027	.0645	.094	.032
	(.4415)	(.3650)	(.3048)	(.1632)	(.2477)	(.2928)	(.1778)
Western landowner	.098	.005	.119	.136	.242	.106	.214
	(.2987)	(.0680)	(.3261)	(.3440)	(.4317)	(.3086)	(.4117)
Farmer	.239	.181	.356	.141	.306	.276	.532
	(.4289)	(.3855)	(.4829)	(.3487)	(.4648)	(.4486)	(.5006)
Debtor	.022	.009	.000	.0045	.048	.041	.0065
	(.1466)	(.0960)	—	(.0674)	(.2163)	(.1993)	(.0806)
Private creditor	.022	.065	.034	.009	.113	.012	.026
	(.1466)	(.2468)	(.1825)	(.0951)	(.3191)	(.1081)	(.1596)
Slaveowner	.000	.005	.000	.854	.226	.918	.857
	—	(.0680)	—	(.3534)	(.4215)	(.2757)	(.3511)
Value of slaves ($000s)	.000	.00171	.000	3.0416	.0806	10.6081	3.8730
	—	(.02518)	—	(4.2862)	(.1942)	(15.5956)	(5.7626)

Owner public securities	.554	.292	.136	.018	.597	.618	.429
	(.4998)	(.4556)	(.3453)	(.1340)	(.4945)	(.4874)	(.4965)
Owner more than $1,000 public securities	.261	.153	.085	.009	.323	.2765	.149
	(.4415)	(.3606)	(.2809)	(.0951)	(.4713)	(.4486)	(.3576)
Value of public securities ($000s)	1.9832	1.9333	1.0663	.1078	2.0400	3.4992	.6690
	(4.9503)	(8.0584)	(4.5755)	(1.2322)	(4.2430)	(12.1710)	(1.9567)
Constituents' Economic Interests (CE$_j$)							
Slaves per 100 whites	1.106	.000	.136	42.461	.723	316.086	81.753
	(1.0198)	—	(.2435)	(29.6442)	(.5088)	(319.5306)	(52.2359)
Distance to navigable water (miles)	26.870	20.861	39.966	78.582	77.823	29.141	49.948
	(14.1439)	(24.0310)	(27.0676)	(68.6711)	(64.8177)	(30.0745)	(44.1651)
Constituents' Ideology (CI$_j$)							
English ancestry of citizens (percent)	96.208	94.760	94.261	85.008	57.766	80.938	85.838
	(.5532)	(1.1014)	(1.3962)	(7.3049)	(13.9898)	(3.1437)	(7.4281)
Number of Observations	92	216	59	220	62	170	154

Note: The seven ratifying conventions are Connecticut, Massachusetts, New Hampshire, North Carolina, Pennsylvania, South Carolina, and Virginia. The sample standard deviations are in parentheses. The sample means for the dichotomous variables can be interpreted as the proportion of the delegate sample to the respective ratifying convention that is classified as possessing the listed economic interest or characteristic.

quite large. While several of the variables had no apparent effect on the vote in many states, few of the statistically significant results are contrary to the implications of the economic model.[7]

As noted throughout this book, a consistent source of controversy in the literature concerns the role of creditor interests (particularly the role of public securities) in the adoption of the Constitution. The findings for all seven conventions, which are reported in tables 7.3–7.5, indicate the important influence of creditor interests on the ratification votes.[8] For the Connecticut convention, the estimated effect of owning any amount of public securities, despite not being statistically significant at conventional levels, may be precise enough to suggest that it was not the result of chance variation.[9] And, if the estimate is considered precise enough, owning any public securities increases the predicted probability of a yes vote for an otherwise average delegate from .792 to .916 (or about 16 percent). Delegates with large holdings of public securities in Connecticut apparently were even stronger supporters of the Constitution. The twenty-four delegates with more than $1,000 of public securities voted unanimously in favor of ratification, as did the two delegates with private securities interests. In Massachusetts, owning any public securities increases the predicted probability of a yes vote from .567 to .812 (or 43 percent). Owning more than $1,000 of public securities increases the predicted probability from .599 to .872 (or almost 46 percent). And the fourteen delegates in Massachusetts with private securities interests voted unanimously in favor of ratification.[10]

In Virginia, among the alternative measures of public securities interests, only delegates with holdings of public securities in excess of $1,000 were significantly more likely to have supported ratification. For an otherwise average delegate, owning more than $1,000 of public securities increases the predicted probability from .512 to .822 (or 60 percent).[11] In South Carolina, only the value of public securities holdings had a significant impact on voting, the estimated response elasticity is .174, which indicates that a 1 percent increase in the value of public securities holdings from its sample mean, for example, would increase the voting probability by .174 percent.[12] For the remaining states, no statistical patterns in the vote related to public securities interests are indicated.

The findings in at least four of the ratifying conventions provide support for the view that delegates with personal holdings of private or public securities were more likely to have voted for ratification than were others.[13] This is consistent with Main's (1961) and McDonald's (1958) conclusions concerning delegates in Connecticut and Massachusetts who owned public securities. With respect to South Carolina, the findings confirm the conclusions of Nadelhaft (1981) but contradict McDonald (1958). Main (1961) and McDonald (1958) conclude that public securities holdings had, at most, a minor effect on voting in the Virginia ratifying convention. But, as noted, an otherwise average Virginia delegate with large public securities holdings (more than $1,000) was 60 percent more

Table 7.3. Incremental and Marginal Effects of the Explanatory Variables on the Probability of a Yes Vote on Ratification at the Seven Ratifying Conventions, 1787–1788: Specification One

Explanatory Variables	State Ratifying Convention						
	CN	MA	NH	NC	PA	SC	VA
Merchant	.103	.311[a]	.356	Yes[e]	-.292	.248[c]	-.391[d]
Western landowner	Yes[e]	—	.224	-.098	-.035	.352[b]	.086
Private creditor	Yes[f]	Yes[e]	-.412	-.124	.290[c]	-.418	.170
Debtor	No[f]	-.076	—	—	.179	-.657[a]	—
Farmer	.048	.065	.100	.169[d]	.289[c]	-.147[d]	-.168[c]
Slaveowner	—	—	—	-.166	-.529[b]	-.326[b]	-.332[b]
Public securities owner	.124[d]	.245[a]	.043	.162	-.097	-.039	.073
Slaves per 100 whites	—	—	—	-.0036[b]	-.455[b]	.00033[b]	-.0024[b]
Distance to navigable water (miles)	.0023	-.0068[a]	-.0064[c]	-.0059[a]	-.0033[b]	-.0041[a]	-.0037[a]
English ancestry of citizens (percent)	.073	.036	.155[b]	.0011	.014[b]	.020[d]	-.0083
Predicted Probability of a Yes Vote the "Average" Delegate	.872	.650	.574	.265	.758	.683	.560
Number of Observations	92	216	59	220	62	170	154

[a] Statistically significant at the .01 level.
[b] Statistically significant at the .05 level.
[c] Statistically significant at the .10 level.
[d] P-value is less than .15.
[e] The delegates in the sample with this characteristic voted unanimously (Yes or No).
[f] The two delegates in the sample with this characteristic voted unanimously (Yes or No).

Note: The dependent variable for each convention is the observed ratification vote at the convention, where a yes vote equals 1 and a no vote equals 0. A variable excluded (–) for any convention has insufficient variance to be included in the voting model. The predicted probability of a yes vote for the "average" delegate at each convention is calculate employing the mean values of all explanatory variables in the model specification. The incremental or marginal effect of each variable is calculated from the logistic estimates of the model specification of the ratification vote for each convention reported in table A7.1 in appendix 7, with all other explanatory variables at their mean values.

Table 7.4. Incremental and Marginal Effects of the Explanatory Variables on the Probability of a Yes Vote on Ratification at the Seven Ratifying Conventions, 1787–1788: Specification Two

Explanatory Variables	State Ratifying Convention						
	CN	MA	NH	NC	PA	SC	VA
Merchant	.117	.294[b]	.365	Yes[e]	-.251	.233[d]	-.343
Western landowner	Yes[e]	—	.218	-.097	.00023	.352[b]	.060
Private creditor	Yes[f]	Yes[e]	-.412	-.125	.276[d]	-.426	.223
Debtor	No[f]	-.089	—	—	.207	-.670[a]	—
Farmer	.094	.064	.099	.171[d]	.278[c]	-.132	-.156[c]
Slaveowner	—	—	—	-.169	-.539[b]	-.323[b]	-.334[b]
Owner >$1,000 public securities	Yes[e]	.273[b]	.016	.535	-.186	.091	.309[b]
Slaves per 100 whites	—	—	—	-.0034[b]	-.465[b]	.00034[b]	-.0021[b]
Distance to navigable water (miles)	.0026	-.0072[a]	-.0065[c]	-.0059[a]	-.0037[a]	-.0041[a]	-.0037[a]
English ancestry of citizens (percent)	.109[d]	.038	.156[b]	.00078	.015[b]	.021[d]	-.0060
Predicted Probability of a Yes Vote The "Average" Delegate	.862	.653	.575	.267	.758	.685	.567
Number of Observations	92	216	59	220	62	170	154

[a] Statistically significant at the .01 level.
[b] Statistically significant at the .05 level.
[c] Statistically significant at the .10 level.
[d] P-value is less than .15.
[e] The delegates in the sample with this characteristic voted unanimously (Yes or No).
[f] The two delegates in the sample with this characteristic voted unanimously (Yes or No).

Note: The incremental and marginal effects are calculated from the logistic estimates for each convention for the model specification reported in table A7.2 in appendix 7. All other details are as described in the note to table 7.3.

Table 7.5. Incremental and Marginal Effects of the Explanatory Variables on the Probability of a Yes Vote on Ratification at the Seven Ratifying Conventions, 1787–1788: Specification Three

Explanatory Variables	State Ratifying Convention						
	CN	MA	NH	NC	PA	SC	VA
Merchant	.0034	.288[b]	.238	Yes[e]	-.150	.151	-.424[c]
Western landowner	Yes[e]	—	.219	-.119	-.028	.277[b]	.094
Private creditor	Yes[f]	Yes[e]	-.602	-.208	.241	-.377	.376
Debtor	No[f]	-.100	.092	—	.196	-.728[a]	—
Farmer	.0031	.063	—	.282[b]	.260[c]	-.054	-.205[b]
Value of slaveholdings ($000s)	—	—	—	.022[b]	-.264	-.0025	-.022[b]
Value of public securities holdings ($000s)	.0081	.027	.050	.129	.0063	.038[b]	.058[d]
Slaves per 100 whites	—	—	—	-.0038[b]	-.540[b]	.00032[b]	-.0028[b]
Distance to navigable water (miles)	.00008	-.0073[a]	-.0061[c]	-.0056[a]	-.0031[a]	-.0034[a]	-.0048[a]
English ancestry of citizens (percent)	.0018[d]	.040	.144[b]	.0014	.015[b]	.015[d]	-.0072
Predicted Probability of a Yes Vote The "Average" Delegate	.996	.667	.589	.277	.753	.764	.558
Number of Observations	92	216	59	220	62	170	154

[a] Statistically significant at the .01 level.
[b] Statistically significant at the .05 level.
[c] Statistically significant at the .10 level.
[d] P-value is less than .15.
[e] The delegates in the sample with this characteristic voted unanimously (Yes or No).
[f] The two delegates in the sample with this characteristic voted unanimously (Yes or No).

Note: The incremental and marginal effects are calculated from the logistic estimates for each convention for the model specification reported in table A7.3 in appendix 7. All other details are as described in the note to table 7.3.

likely to have favored ratification than were other average Virginia delegates with no such holdings—not a small effect at all.

Several other inferences about voting on ratification also can be drawn from the findings. Merchants were more likely to have supported or unanimously supported ratification in Massachusetts, North Carolina, and South Carolina. There is no statistically consistent pattern in the vote related to merchant interests in the remaining four states. Western landowners were more likely to have supported or unanimously supported ratification in Connecticut and South Carolina, and delegates in deep personal debt were more likely to have opposed or unanimously opposed ratification in Connecticut and South Carolina as well.

The findings reported so far for the individual conventions generally are consistent with sentiments expressed during the ratification debates. Amos Singletary, an opponent in the Massachusetts convention, expressed the fears of many that the Constitution was designed to promote the interests of

> [t]hese lawyers, and men of learning, and moneyed men, that talk so finely and gloss over matters so smoothly, to make us poor illiterate people swallow down the pill, expect to get into Congress themselves; they expect to be the managers of this Constitution and get all the power and all the money into their own hands, and then they will swallow up all us little folks, like the great *Leviathan*, Mr. President; yes, just as the whale swallowed up *Jonah*. (Elliot, 1836 [1888], vol. 2, p. 102, emphasis in original)

Rawlins Lowndes, an opponent in the South Carolina convention, exhibited a common belief that the Constitution was designed to promote northern commercial interests because "the Eastern States . . . [were] so guarded in what they had conceded to gain the regulation of our commerce, which threw into their hands the carrying trade." Moreover, Lowndes maintained that the eastern states would then have the "power to lay us under payment of whatever freightage they thought proper to impose" (Elliot, 1836 [1888], vol. 2, vol. 4, p. 288). Yet merchants in the South Carolina (and the North Carolina) ratifying convention were *more* likely to have supported ratification. What is unknown is whether they agreed with Lowndes but were supporters of the Constitution nonetheless because they expected commercial interests to benefit overall from ratification, or because they still expected to personally benefit, or whether they merely disagreed with Lowndes' expectations.

What is more, in Pennsylvania, and in two of the three southern conventions examined (South Carolina and Virginia), delegates who personally owned slaves were *less* likely to have voted for ratification than were others.[14] In Pennsylvania, owning slaves is estimated to reduce the probability of voting for ratification for an otherwise average delegate from .845 to .316 (or about 63 percent); in South Carolina, from .960 to .634 (or 34 percent); and in Virginia, from .835 to .503 (or 40 percent). Differences of these magnitudes are by no means small and, along with

the direction of the effects, appear to be at odds with studies of the ratification process, which conclude that slaveholding delegates were more
likely to have favored ratification or that no patterns in the ratification
vote were related to personal slaveholdings.[15] The value of personal slaveholdings, however, had a statistically significant negative effect only for
the Virginia convention.[16]

Consistent with expectations, constituent slave interests reduce a
delegate's probability of voting for ratification in three of the four states
that include the slave variables. In response elasticity terms, it is estimated
from the specification in table 7.3 that a 1 percent increase in constituent
slaveholdings from the sample mean, for example, reduces the predicted
probability of a yes vote the most in North Carolina (.585 percent)
and Pennsylvania (.424 percent). For Virginia, a 1 percent increase in
constituent slaveholdings from the sample mean is estimated to decrease
the predicted probability .351 percent. These findings contradict several
studies, which conclude that constituent slave interests in these states
increased support for ratification (e.g., Main, 1961; Risjord, 1978) or had
no effect on the vote (e.g., McDonald, 1958; Thomas, 1953). For South
Carolina, however, constituent slave interests are estimated to *increase* the
probability of a yes vote. The result, while contrary to the expectations
offered here, confirms the conclusion in Nadelhaft's (1981) study of South
Carolina. The finding here for South Carolina suggests that perhaps delegates to the South Carolina convention who represented slave areas were
less concerned with the potential negative impact of a future national government on slavery than were those from ratifying conventions in other
slave states. Perhaps the South Carolina delegates were more concerned
about possible slave revolts or concerns about the maintenance of slavery
that a stronger national government might have better addressed.

The strongest finding overall for the seven conventions is for distance
from navigable water. Delegates who represented constituents from more
isolated, less commercial areas (farther from navigable water) were highly
significantly less likely to have voted for ratification than were other delegates in all model specifications for six of the seven ratifying conventions.
As indicated in tables 7.3–7.5, the magnitude of the impact in absolute
terms is most pronounced in the Massachusetts and New Hampshire
conventions. In response elasticity terms, however, the distance elasticity
is largest for North Carolina, it is −1.739. For the other five conventions,
the elasticity is one-fourth, or less, of the North Carolina elasticity. For
New Hampshire, it is −.443; for Pennsylvania, −.339; for Virginia, −.332;
for Massachusetts, −.218; and for South Carolina, −.177. Despite the very
small marginal effects for five of the conventions, the predicted probability of a yes vote still is dramatically different for delegates representing
dramatically different areas of a state, similar to the findings throughout
this book. As a result, the predicted probability of voting in favor of
ratification for a delegate who represented the most commercial areas
of a state (nearest to navigable water) is between .730 and .927 for the six

ratifying conventions; for a delegate who represented the least commercial areas of a state (farthest from navigable water), it is between .002 and .357 for the six conventions. Thus, there in fact is a dramatically wide range for each convention.

Delegates who represented counties with relatively large concentrations of families of English ancestry were significantly more likely to have favored ratification in New Hampshire and Pennsylvania, and, possibly marginally so, in South Carolina (see tables 7.3–7.5).[17] The apparent impact of English ancestry on the vote is quite dramatic in New Hampshire, where an increase of 1 percentage point in the percent of families of English ancestry in a delegate's home county increases the predicted probability of a yes vote by more than 25 percent. The variation in the English ancestry variable in New Hampshire, however, is quite limited. It ranges only from 91.5 to 95.6 percent across counties in New Hampshire, with a coefficient of variation of only .0148.[18] Because of such small variation, the results for New Hampshire should be interpreted cautiously. For Pennsylvania and South Carolina, the estimated magnitude of the impact of English ancestry on the vote is less dramatic, but perhaps more plausible. In South Carolina, an increase of 1 percentage point in English ancestry increases the predicted probability by 2.37 percent, and in Pennsylvania by 1.09 percent. The findings for English ancestry confirm Main's (1961) argument concerning the impact of ancestry on the ratification vote and suggest that Brown's (1976) view about the importance of the shared British political culture among the framers of the Constitution might have carried over to the issue of ratification.

The estimates of the effects of the various economic interests on the ratification vote in the seven conventions yield interesting and important generalizations across the individual conventions. Generally, voting behavior does not appear to be radically different from one convention to the next, though there are exceptions. The estimates for the seven conventions, however, are based on a set of delegates far from complete, and on a limited model specification and data; the estimated model does not include any markers for a delegate's personal ideology. Consequently, the estimates may not accurately indicate the true effects of the economic interests on the vote. The estimated model also precludes formal tests of the role of economic (pecuniary) versus ideological (nonpecuniary) interests in the ratification vote.

A Reexaminination of the Massachusetts, North Carolina, and Virginia Ratifying Conventions

The additional data collected on the personal characteristics and several economic interests of the delegates to the Massachusetts, North Carolina, and Virginia conventions allow more precise estimation of the true effects of the various interests on the ratification vote in each convention. The additional data also allow for a formal test of the role of economic (pecuniary) versus ideological (nonpecuniary) interests in the ratification vote in the three conventions.

The Empirical Model for the Three Ratifying Conventions

In reexamining the ratification vote for the Massachusetts, North Carolina, and Virginia ratifying conventions, the following empirical model is estimated with logistic regression separately for each of the three conventions to determine the role of each interest in voting for ratification:

$$V_{ij} = f(PE_i, PI_i, CE_j, CI_j), \qquad (7.2)$$

where V_{ij}, PE_i, CE_j, and CI_j are defined above. PI_i is the set of additional variables that are the markers for each delegate's personal ideology, which were not available for the estimations above. Estimation of equation 7.2 alone, however, does not allow for a formal determination of the role of each *set* of interests. The relative magnitude of the influence of each group of interests on voting is formally determined employing a series of nonnested hypothesis tests regarding the model structure that is best supported by the data.

The Estimation Procedure for the Three
Ratifying Conventions

The influence of ideology versus economic interests on the ratification vote for the three conventions is examined by estimating two rival empirical voting models:

$$V_{ij} = g(PI_i, CI_j) \qquad (7.3)$$

and

$$V_{ij} = g^*(PE_i, CE_j). \qquad (7.4)$$

Equation 7.3 represents the hypothesis that only ideological (nonpecuniary) interests affected voting, and equation 7.4, that only economic (pecuniary) interests affected voting. The former is more consistent with the theories of constitutional economics (nonpartisan behavior); the latter is more consistent with the theories of political agency (partisan behavior).

Nonnested hypothesis tests of the rival models are conducted by comparing the logistic estimates derived from each model, which allows for an inference about the role of ideology versus economic interests in the ratification vote. The hypothesis tests are conducted by first selecting the null hypothesis that the ideological-interest model is the true model and a corresponding alternative hypothesis that the economic-interest model is the true model, then selecting the economic-interest model as the null hypothesis and the ideological-interest model as the alternative hypothesis. If the ideological-interest model as the null cannot be rejected in favor of the alternative economic-interest model, and if the economic-interest model as the null is rejected with the ideological-interest model as the alternative, this suggests that only ideological interests affected the ratification vote. If, on the other hand, the economic-interest model as the null cannot be rejected in favor of the alternative ideological-interest model, and if the ideological-interest model as the null is rejected with the economic-interest model as the alternative, this suggests that only economic interests affected the ratification vote.[19]

The Specific Measures of the Economic and Ideological Interests for the Three Ratifying Conventions

The supplementary data collected on the personal attributes and political experiences of the delegates to the three ratifying conventions serve as markers for the delegates' ideological interests. The personal attributes include a delegate's age, ancestry (ethnicity), religion, and Revolutionary War experience and whether he was an officer in the war. The political experiences include whether a delegate held any positions in local government before or after ratification, held any positions in state government before or after ratification, served in the Continental Congress before ratification, or held any positions in the new national government after ratification. More data also were collected for several economic interest variables for many of the delegates to the three ratifying conventions. A greater number of delegates were identified as merchants, private creditors, private debtors, and western landowners, especially for Massachusetts and North Carolina, where the data were initially so limited that in several cases the variable could not be included in the model specifications reported in tables 7.3–7.5. For Massachusetts, data were collected for ninety-three more delegates (43 percent more) than before. For North Carolina, data were collected for forty-one more delegates (about 19 percent more) than before. For Virginia, data were collected for eleven more delegates (7 percent more) than before.[20]

The specific measures of the economic interests and the markers for the ideological interests for the Massachusetts, North Carolina, and Virginia delegates and their constituents are described in table 7.6.[21] The measures of the constituents' economic interests and ideological markers are still quite limited. Data for the religious affiliation, age structure, or occupations of the populations of the three states at the county or township level are not available. One cost of analyzing the state ratifying conventions separately is that constituent characteristics that are measurable only at the state level of aggregation must be excluded from the analysis. An analysis of the ratification vote at individual ratifying conventions requires the data to be measured at the county or township level, the delegate's area of representation at the state conventions.

Because the reexamination now involves only three ratifying conventions, the question again might be whether there are many differences in the economic and ideological interests across the three states and among

Table 7.6. Measures of the Ratification Vote and Personal and Constituent Interests for the Reexamination of the Massachusetts, North Carolina, and Virginia Ratifying Conventions

Dependent Variable

Ratification vote
Equals 1 if the delegate to the state ratifying convention voted to ratify the Constitution (0 otherwise)

Explanatory Variables

Measures of Personal Economic Interests (PE_i)

Merchant
Equals 1 if the delegate's principal occupation was a merchant (0 otherwise)

Western landowner
Equals 1 if the delegate owned western lands (0 otherwise)

Farmer
Equals 1 if the delegate's principal occupation was a farmer (0 otherwise)

Debtor
Equals 1 if the delegate was in deep personal debt (0 otherwise)

Private creditor
Equals 1 if the delegate owned any private securities (0 otherwise)

Slaveowner
Equals 1 if the delegate owned any slaves in 1790 (0 otherwise)

Value of slaves
Market value of slaves owned in 1790 ($)

Owner public securities
Equals 1 if the delegate owned any public securities (0 otherwise)

Owner more than $1,000 public securities
Equals 1 if the delegate owned more than $1,000 in public securities (0 otherwise)

Value of public securities owned
Market value of a delegate's public securities holdings ($)

Markers for Personal Ideology (PI_i)

Local officeholder before convention
Equals 1 if the delegate was a local officeholder prior to the ratifying convention (0 otherwise)

State officeholder before convention
Equals 1 if the delegate was a state officeholder prior to the ratifying convention (0 otherwise)

Member of the Continental Congress
Equals 1 if the delegate was a member of the Continental Congress prior to the ratifying convention (0 otherwise)

continued

Table 7.6. continued

Markers for Personal Ideology (PI$_j$) continued	
Local officeholder after convention	Equals 1 if the delegate was a local officeholder after the ratifying convention (0 otherwise)
State officeholder after convention	Equals 1 if the delegate was a state officeholder after the ratifying convention (0 otherwise)
National officeholder after convention	Equals 1 if the delegate was a national officeholder or an appointee to a national position after the ratifying convention (0 otherwise)
Officer in Revolutionary War	Equals 1 if the delegate was an officer in the Revolutionary War (0 otherwise)
Age in years	Age of the delegate at the time of the ratifying convention, in years
Congregational/puritan	Equals 1 if the delegate's religion was Congregational/Puritan (0 otherwise)
Baptist	Equals 1 if the delegate's religion was Baptist (0 otherwise)
Episcopalian/anglican	Equals 1 if the delegate's religion was Episcopalian/Anglican (0 otherwise)
Presbyterian	Equals 1 if the delegate's religion was Presbyterian (0 otherwise)
English ancestry	Equals 1 if the delegate's ancestry was English (0 otherwise)
Scottish/Irish ancestry	Equals 1 if the delegate's ancestry was Scottish or Irish (0 otherwise)
Measures of Constituents' Economic Interests (CE$_j$)	
Slaves per 100 whites	Slaves per 100 of the white population in the delegate's home county in 1790
Distance to navigable water	Distance from the center of the delegate's home county to nearest navigable water (miles)
Distance to Atlantic coast	Distance from the center of the delegate's home county to the Atlantic coast (miles)
Markers for Constituents' Ideology (CI$_j$)	
English ancestry of citizens	Percentage of all families in the delegate's home county or township of English ancestry in 1790
Scottish/Irish ancestry of citizens	Percentage of all families in the delegate's home county or township of Scottish or Irish ancestry in 1790

Note: For a discussion of the data, and their sources, that were used to measure each of the specific variables, see appendix 2.

the delegates within each convention. The greater the number of differences, the more likely different voting patterns will be observed. There are,
in fact, substantial differences among the delegate samples for the three
conventions, as shown by the sample means of the variables for each convention in table 7.7. Slightly more than 17 percent of the Massachusetts
delegates in the sample, for example, are merchants while in North
Carolina and Virginia they are only 5.4 percent or fewer. At the Virginia
convention, 40 percent of the delegates in the sample possess public securities, in Massachusetts, 20.4 percent; and in North Carolina, 1.5 percent.
And slaveholdings are quite different as well. In the Virginia convention,
84.2 percent of the delegates in the sample are slaveowners; in North
Carolina, 80.5 percent; and in Massachusetts, less than 2 percent. There
are substantial differences across the three conventions in the measures of
the constituent interests and ideologies as well. Note, for example, the difference across the three conventions in the mean distance from navigable
water for a delegate—86.2 miles for the North Carolina convention,
61.8 miles for the Virginia convention, and only 22.4 miles for the
Massachusetts convention.

Results of the Reestimation of the Vote in the Massachusetts, North Carolina, and Virginia Ratifying Conventions

A common hypothesis about the ratifying process is that state officeholders were opponents of the new government. As Alexander Hamilton long
ago stated, "Among the most formidable of the obstacles which the
new Constitution will have to encounter may readily be distinguished
the obvious interest of a certain class of men in every State to resist all
changes which may hazard a diminution of the power, emolument, and
consequence of the offices they hold under the State establishments" (*The
Federalist*, 1937 [1788], Paper No. 1). More generally, prior political
experience, in particular political offices held *before* a ratifying convention, is viewed as an important determinant of attitudes toward the new
government. Likewise, the economic model suggests that the ambitions of
a delegate for future political office also would have been an important
determinant of voting for the Constitution because such ambitions would
have constrained a delegate to satisfy the interests of his present, and
potentially future, constituents. While far from an ideal measure, political offices held *after* a delegate's ratifying convention might capture some
aspect of a delegate's ambitions for future political office *at the time* the
convention met.[22]

Surprisingly, however, one of the major findings of the reexamination
of the ratification votes is that neither a delegate's prior political experience (experience *before* the ratifying convention) nor future political experience (experience *after* the convention) matters for the ratification votes
in Massachusetts, North Carolina, or Virginia. The findings indicate that,
except in one case, no matter what variable is employed to measure prior

Table 7.7. Means and Standard Deviations of the Vote and the Explanatory Variables for the Reexamination of the Massachusetts, North Carolina, and Virginia Ratifying Conventions

Variables	Massachusetts		North Carolina		Virginia	
	Sample Means	Sample Standard Deviations	Sample Means	Sample Standard Deviations	Sample Means	Sample Standard Deviations
Ratification Vote	.557	.4976	.310	.4635	.533	.5004
Personal Economic Interests						
Merchant	.172	.3776	.046	.2098	.054	.2278
Western landowner	.026	.1591	.119	.3241	.230	.4223
Private creditor	.094	.2921	.054	.2257	.079	.2702
Farmer	.311	.4635	.184	.3881	.509	.5014
Debtor	.032	.1772	.061	.2403	.079	.2702
Slaveowner	.019	.1382	.805	.3973	.842	.3654
Number of slaves owned	.026	.1957	14.552	21.8441	21.139	31.5620
Value of slaveholdings ($)	4.790	36.2000	2,692.070	4,041.1500	3,910.790	5,838.9600
Owner public securities	.204	.4035	.015	.1231	.400	.4914
Owner more than $1,000 public securities	.107	.3093	.008	.0874	.139	.3474
Value of public securities holdings ($)	1,351.430	6,791.0900	90.831	1,131.5600	624.430	1,897.2900
Personal Ideology						
Local officeholder before convention	.356	.4796	.015	.1231	.036	.1878
State officeholder before convention	.408	.4922	.601	.4905	.697	.4610
Member continental congress before convention	.036	.1856	.027	.1619	.073	.2605

	Mean	S.D.	Mean	S.D.	Mean	S.D.
Local officeholder after convention	.197	.3987	0	0	.006	.0778
State officeholder after convention	.340	.4744	.475	.5003	.473	.5008
National officeholder/appointee after convention	.052	.2219	.084	.2784	.164	.3711
Officer in Revolutionary War	.307	.4622	.172	.3785	.406	.4926
Age of delegate (years)	49.600	10.0150	41.760	6.5430	42.430	8.9450
Congregational/Puritan	.699	.3751	0	0	0	0
Baptist	.087	.2309	.269	.1403	0	0
Episcopalian/Anglican	.019	.1128	.385	.1538	.804	.2101
Presbyterian	.058	.1915	.312	.1359	.087	.1492
English ancestry of delegate	.838	.3421	.371	.1773	.537	.3482
Scottish/Irish ancestry of delegate	.139	.3216	.629	.1773	.362	.3358
Constituents' Economic Interests						
Slaves per 100 whites	0	0	39.357	29.7695	81.463	52.0093
Distance to navigable water (miles)	22.392	24.4337	86.184	69.1025	61.766	79.5522
Distance to Atlantic coast (miles)	27.437	33.4101	122.329	96.8040	145.560	110.0187
Constituents' Ideology						
English ancestry of citizens (percent)	94.715	1.1529	84.557	7.2499	85.795	7.0227
Scottish/Irish ancestry of citizens (percent)	4.828	.9554	13.053	6.2594	9.167	1.8216
Number of Observations	309		261		165	

Note: The sample means for the dichotomous explanatory variables can be interpreted as the proportion of the delegate sample to the respective ratifying convention that is classified as possessing the listed economic interest or characteristic.

political experience or to capture political ambition for future office, the results are never statistically significant in any specification for any convention. In addition, neither the inclusion nor exclusion of any of the political-experience variables in any specification materially affects the signs or the magnitudes of the coefficients of the other explanatory variables. Among all the results, only one political-experience variable, membership in the Continental Congress, is ever statistically significant and only for the Virginia ratifying convention, where members of the Continental Congress were statistically less likely to vote for ratification. That the political-experience variables do not materially affect any estimated voting model strongly suggests that the variables are superfluous in determining the ratification vote in all three conventions. The logistic estimates of the alternative specifications of the voting model that include various political-experience variables reported in appendix 7 confirm this conclusion. Thus, the findings dramatically conflict with the views of nearly all constitutional and historical scholars concerning the importance of the political and officeholding experiences of those involved in the ratification process. Consequently, because the political-experience variables likely are superfluous for the three ratifying conventions, they are not included in the estimated voting models whose findings are discussed next.[23]

The Massachusetts Convention

On February 6, 1788, the Massachusetts convention ratified the Constitution 187–168, with a rather modest 52.7 percent yes vote. And the estimated model of voting indicates that the predicted probability of a yes vote is .611 for the "average" Massachusetts delegate, a reasonably accurate prediction of the actual voting outcome of 52.7 percent yes votes. The findings for the Massachusetts ratification vote reported in table 7.8 indicate there are substantial differences among ratifiers with different economic and other interests, several of which are readily apparent.[24] Recall that the incremental effect reported for each dichotomous variable is merely the difference in the predicted probability of the vote when the variable has a value of 1 and when it has a value of 0. Accordingly, the findings reported, for example, under specification 2 in table 7.8 indicate that an otherwise average delegate with merchant interests has a .270 greater predicted probability of voting in favor of ratification than does a delegate without merchant interests. It is expected that merchants in Massachusetts would have been net beneficiaries from ratification because the costs of conducting interstate and international trade were expected to decrease as a result of beneficial provisions in the Constitution concerning tariff policy, trade regulation, and national security.

The predicted probabilities of the Massachusetts ratification vote for different values of the economic and other interests, which are reported in table 7.9, differ considerably for delegates with considerably different interests. A delegate who was a merchant was almost 49 percent more

Table 7.8. Incremental and Marginal Effects of the Explanatory Variables on the Probability of a Yes Vote on Ratification at the Massachusetts Convention

Explanatory Variables	Alternative Model Specifications		
	1	2	3
Merchant	.297[a]	.270[a]	.274[a]
Western landowner	.237	.210	.214
Private creditor	.352[a]	.370[a]	.378[a]
Debtor	−.497[b]	−.457[b]	−.463[b]
Farmer	−.016	−.032	−.036
Owner public securities	.312[a]	—	—
Owner >$1,000 public securities	—	.303[b]	—
Value of public securities holdings ($)	—	—	.00003[d]
Congregational/Puritan	−.085	−.072	−.065
Baptist	−.517[a]	−.514[a]	−.506[a]
Presbyterian	−.233	−.223	−.194
English ancestry of delegate	.293[a]	.256[b]	.242[b]
Officer in Revolutionary War	.169[b]	.159[b]	.153[b]
Age of delegate	−.0014	−.0010	−.0010
Slaves per 100 whites	—	—	—
Distance to navigable water (miles)	−.0076[a]	−.0080[a]	−.0079[a]
English ancestry of citizens (percent)	.0065	.0096	.012

[a] Statistically significant at .01 level.
[b] Statistically significant at .05 level.
[c] Statistically significant at .10 level.
[d] P-value is .2012.

Note: Number of observations for each specification is 309. The dependent variable in each specification is the observed ratification vote at the Massachusetts convention, where a yes vote equals 1 and a no vote equals 0. The slave ownership variable is not used for Massachusetts because of the very limited number of slaveowning delegates. The constituent slave variable (slaves per 100 whites) is zero for all Massachusetts counties. The Episcopalian/Anglican variable is excluded because the residual "other" ancestry category is close to zero if all four of the religion variables are included. The constituent and delegate Scottish/Irish ancestry variables are excluded for Massachusetts because the residual "other" ancestry category also is close to zero for both variables. The incremental or marginal effect of each variable is calculated from the logistic estimates for the three model specifications for the Massachusetts ratification vote reported in table A7.13 in appendix 7, with all other explanatory variables at their mean values.

likely to vote for ratification than was an otherwise average delegate without merchant interests.[25] Private creditors, and public creditors with holdings in excess of $1,000, were 66 percent and 53 percent *more* likely to have supported ratification in Massachusetts than were those who were not private or public creditors, respectively. Delegates in deep personal debt were 73 percent *less* likely to have voted for the Constitution. These are quite substantial differences among creditors and debtors over the Massachusetts ratification vote. As maintained throughout this book, the clause in the Constitution mandating that the national government assume prior credit obligations of the federal government as well as other creditor-friendly provisions were likely to benefit creditors, *ceteris paribus*.

Table 7.9. Predicted Probabilities of the Ratification Vote at the Massachusetts Convention for a Delegate with Different Interests and Characteristics: Significant Variables

Economic Interests and Characteristics	Predicted Probability of a Yes Vote
The "Average" Delegate	.611
Merchant	.826
Not a merchant	.555
Owner private securities	.928
No private securities	.558
Debtor	.170
Not a debtor	.627
Owner public securities	.845
No public securities	.534
Owner more than $1,000 public securities	.872
Owner less than $1,000 public securities	.569
Public Securities Holdings (Market Value)[a]	
$ 0 (the least for any delegate)	.577
$ 500	.592
$ 1,351 (the mean)	.616
$ 2,500	.647
$ 5,000	.711
$10,000	.816
$20,000	.935
$71,073 (the most for any delegate)	.999
Baptist	.146
Not a Baptist	.660
English descendant	.650
Not an English descendant	.395
Officer	.718
Not an officer	.559
Distance from Navigable Water (Miles)	
0 (the nearest for any delegate)	.769
10	.704
21.61 (the mean)	.611
40	.465
60	.308
80	.186
90 (the farthest for any delegate)	.140

[a] Not significant at conventional levels, but the estimated effect of the variable may be precise enough to be suggestive of an influence on the ratification vote.

Note: All predicted probabilities are calculated from the estimated logistic coefficients for specification 2 reported in table A7.13 in appendix 7, except those for the ownership, and the value, of public securities are calculated from the logistic coefficients for specifications 1 and 3, respectively, in table A7.13. The predicted probability for the "average" delegate is calculated employing the mean values of all explanatory variables. For a dichotomous variable, a predicted probability is calculated when the variable has a value of 1 and when the variable has a value of 0, with all other explanatory variables at their mean values. For a continuous variable, the predicted probabilities are calculated for each value of the variable, with all other explanatory variables at their mean values. Because of rounding, the difference between the two predicted probabilities for a dichotomous variable may not be identical to its reported incremental effect. Because different specifications are used for the public securities variables, the predicted probabilities for the same securities holdings for different specifications may not equal each other.

Creditors, especially those holding public debt, expected direct benefits from the strengthened national government. In contrast, the clause in the Constitution stressing private contractual obligations and other clauses expected to be unfriendly to debtors were potentially burdensome to debtors, *ceteris paribus*.[26]

Although the political-experience variables appear superfluous, other measures of ideology—ancestry, religion, and officer status—not only matter, the magnitudes of their effects are quite large as well. For Massachusetts, Baptists were 78 percent less likely than were other religions to have ratified the Constitution, but the voting behavior of Congregational/Puritan and Presbyterian delegates was not significantly different from the behavior of those with other religious affiliations.[27] These findings partially confirm the studies of Rutland (1966), Gillespie (1989), and Lienesch (1989) that contend that dissenting sects (e.g., Baptists and Presbyterians) were ideologically opposed to the Constitution and more conservative religions (e.g., Congregational/Puritains and Episcoplian/Anglicans) were ideologically predisposed to have favored it. Otherwise average delegates who served as officers during the Revolutionary War were more than 28 percent more likely to have supported the Constitution than were those who were not officers, a result consistent with the view of Rutland (1966) that officers were ideologically inclined toward the Constitution. Delegates of English ancestry also were about 65 percent more likely to have voted for ratification than were other delegates, a result consistent with the view of Main (1961).

In terms of the influence of constituents on the ratification vote, Benjamin Randall, a Massachusetts delegate, was as transparent as possible in expressing his belief that constituents should be the paramount influence: "Everyone comes here to discharge his duty to his constituents, and I hope none will be biased by the best orators; because we are not acting for ourselves" (Elliot, 1836 [1888], vol. 2, p. 39). However, because of data limitations, there are only two measures of constituent interests for Massachusetts—the percentage of families of English ancestry and distance from navigable water in the delegate's township.[28] And, despite the positive coefficients for English ancestry, as Main's (1961) hypothesis suggests, they are never statistically significant. But Massachusetts's delegates from more commercial areas (areas nearer to navigable water) were much stronger supporters of the Constitution than were those from more isolated areas. The estimated response elasticity of distance, −.292, indicates a very small marginal influence, however. As an example of this influence, the estimated effect of distance indicates that a delegate 1 mile (or 4.5 percent) nearer to navigable water than the sample mean has a predicted probability of a yes vote only .0079 (or 1.3 percent) greater than an "average" delegate. While this magnitude obviously is very small, the effect of distance is dramatic for dramatically different distances (see table 7.9). For an otherwise average delegate zero miles from navigable water (the nearest of any Massachusetts delegate), the predicted probability of a yes vote is .769, while for a delegate 90 miles from navigable water (the farthest of any Massachusetts delegate), the predicted probability of voting for ratification is only .140. These findings offer considerable support for the already noted fears of Amos Singletary who believed that "[t]hese lawyers, and men of learning, and moneyed men" who were primarily from the more commercial, coastal areas of the state favored ratification because "they will swallow up all us little folks" who were primarily from the more isolated, less commercial areas (Elliot, 1836 [1888], vol. 2, p. 102).[29]

The overall findings for Massachusetts provide strong evidence that can be used to sort through the many competing explanations of the state's ratification process. The traditional historical literature for Massachusetts generally concludes that delegates who owned financial securities (Revolutionary War debt, bank stocks, or private debt holdings) were important players at the convention and voted for ratification (see Main, 1961; McDonald, 1958; Rutland, 1966). Yet Gillespie's (1989) more recent account of the Massachusetts convention ignores the stance taken by either private or public securities holders and downplays their importance. The results here are strongly at odds with Gillespie's account and confirm the traditional view of the ratification process in Massachusetts, especially with respect to private creditors. With respect to the impact of the amount of commercial activities in a delegate's township (as proxied by distance to navigable water), the findings here solidly contradict McDonald's (1958) claim that there was no geographical pattern in the vote at the Massachusetts ratifying convention. And, as Charles Turner indicated at the Massachusetts convention, there were reasons why delegates from more commercial areas of the state were more likely to vote yes. As Turner explained, "When . . . I consider the deplorable state of our navigation and commerce . . . the tendency of depreciating paper, and tender acts, to destroy mutual confidence, faith, and credit," he had a duty to vote for ratification (Elliot, 1836 [1888], vol. 2, pp. 170–171).[30]

The North Carolina Convention

Even though delegates to the Hillsborough convention in North Carolina voted on the Constitution on August 1, 1788, after it had already been ratified by eleven states (leaving only itself and Rhode Island out of the new government), North Carolina nevertheless resoundingly rejected the Constitution 84–184, with only 31.3 percent yes votes. The estimated model of voting indicates that the "average" delegate to the North Carolina convention has a predicated probability of a yes vote of .198, similar in magnitude to the actual voting outcome. Despite the issue of the Constitution being in a sense moot, the findings for the North Carolina ratification vote reported in table 7.10 suggest that both economic interests and ideology still significantly affected North Carolina's vote.[31] And, with substantially better data for more delegates and variables, the new esti-

Table 7.10. Incremental and Marginal Effects of the Explanatory Variables on the Probability of a Yes Vote on Ratification at the North Carolina Convention

Explanatory Variables	Alternative Model Specifications		
	1	2	3
Merchant	.672[a]	.670[a]	.663[a]
Western landowner	−.099	−.098	−.108
Private creditor	.432[b]	.440[b]	.391[b]
Debtor	−.105	−.098	−.090
Farmer	.186[c]	.186[c]	.214[b]
Slaveowner	.021	.018	—
Value of slaveholdings ($)	—	—	.00001
Owner public securities	.149	—	—
Owner >$1,000 public securities	—	.410	—
Value of public securities holdings ($)	—	—	.00009
Baptist	−.357[c]	−.365[c]	−.346[c]
Episcopalian/Anglican	—	—	—
Presbyterian	−.130	−.139	−.135
Officer in Revolutionary War	.125	.124	.116
Age of delegate	−.0032	−.0034	−.0036
Slaves per 100 whites	−.0044[a]	−.0043[a]	−.0047[a]
Distance to navigable water (miles)	−.0049[a]	−.0050[a]	−.0051[a]
English ancestry of citizens (percent)	.0090[c]	.0088[c]	.0086[d]

[a] Statistically significant at .01 level.
[b] Statistically significant at .05 level.
[c] Statistically significant at .10 level.
[d] P-value is .1130.

Note: Number of observations for each specification is 261. The dependent variable in each specification is the observed ratification vote at the North Carolina convention, where a yes vote equals 1 and a no vote equals 0. The Congregational/Puritan variable is not used because it has a value of zero for all North Carolina delegates. The Episcopalian/Anglican variable also is excluded because the residual "other" ancestry category is virtually zero if all three of the non-zero religion variables are included. The delegate English and Scottish/Irish ancestry variables are excluded because data on personal ancestry are available for only thirty-five North Carolina delegates. The incremental or marginal effect of each variable is calculated from the logistic estimates for the three model specifications for the North Carolina ratification vote reported in table A7.14 in appendix 7, with all other explanatory variables at their mean values.

mates yield several findings not found earlier in the preliminary examination of the North Carolina convention, as well as other findings quite similar to the estimates reported earlier in this chapter for the limited number of variables initially available.

Merchants and private creditors were considerably more likely to have voted yes than were other delegates. The incremental effect reported, for example, under specification 2 in table 7.10 indicates that the predicted probability of a yes vote for a merchant is .67 greater than for an otherwise average delegate who was not a merchant—an absolutely huge effect. For private creditors, the predicted probability is .44 greater than for otherwise average delegates who were not private creditors—not a small effect either. Delegates classified as farmers also were more likely to have supported ratifying the Constitution, same as the conclusions based on the pooled samples as well as the preliminary estimates for North Carolina. Farmers, to the extent their primary economic interests were in localized, less commercial activities, might have been expected to oppose the Constitution because of perceptions that trade provisions contained in the Constitution strongly favored national interests at the expense of local interests. But in North Carolina, farmers rather than merchants or plantation owners were the prominent economic interest and were involved in more than only less commercial activities. Recall that for the ratifying conventions, the measure of farming interests also is a broader measure than being strictly a "poor subsistence farmer." Consequently, North Carolina farmers might have supported the Constitution because of its expected impact on decreasing transaction costs in the economy through, among other elements, its beneficial provisions concerning tariff policy and trade regulation as well as its creation of a monetary union.[32]

The findings indicate no statistically significant impact of personal slaveholdings on the vote in North Carolina, contrary to the conclusions based on the pooled samples: However, the results do indicate that Baptist delegates, *ceteris paribus*, were not only less likely to have voted for ratification, confirming existing views on the issue, but also a lot less likely. In table 7.10, the incremental effect on the predicted probability of the vote is estimated at −.365. Moreover, while not significant at standard levels, the logistic coefficients for delegates who had served as officers in the Revolutionary War might be precise enough to be considered suggestive of a positive relationship between officer status and the ratification vote in North Carolina, as Rutland (1966) contends, with the incremental effect of being an officer estimated at .124.[33]

The predicted probabilities of voting for ratification in North Carolina for different values of the economic interests and other characteristics, which are reported in table 7.11, are substantially different for delegates with substantially different interests. While Baptists were 95 percent less likely to vote in favor of ratification, merchants were 383 percent more likely, private creditors were 242 percent more likely, and farmers were 109 percent more likely to vote yes than were otherwise average delegates who were not Baptists, merchants, private securities holders, or farmers, respectively. These are substantial effects to say the least, suggesting that economic and other interests had a substantial influence on the ratification process in North Carolina. In fact, it was substantial enough that if otherwise average delegates to the North Carolina convention were all merchants and private creditors, the Constitution almost assuredly *would* have been ratified in North Carolina. But the convention was not all merchants and private creditors. Actually, as the figures in table 7.7 show, there were hardly any at the North Carolina convention.

The effects of constituent interests are apparent in North Carolina as well. The English ancestry of constituents is statistically associated with

Table 7.11. Predicted Probabilities of the Ratification Vote at the North Carolina Convention for a Delegate with Different Interests and Characteristics: Significant Variables

Economic Interests and Characteristics	Predicted Probability of a Yes Vote
The "Average" Delegate	.198
Merchant	.845
Not a merchant	.175
Owner private securities	.622
No private securities	.182
Farmer	.357
Not a farmer	.171
Baptist	.019
Not a Bapist	.385
Officer[a]	.304
Not an officer	.180
Constituent Slaveholdings (Slaves per 100 Whites)	
6.73 (the least in any area)	.375
20	.295
39.36 (the mean)	.198
60	.123
80	.076
100	.045
123.25 (the most in any area)	.025
Distance from Navigable Water (Miles)	
0 (the nearest for any delegate)	.786
10	.728
25	.626
40	.511
65	.324
86.18 (the mean)	.198
100	.138
150	.032
255 (the farthest for any delegate)	.001
English Ancestry of Citizens (Percent English)	
70.10 (the least in any area)	.099
75	.127
77.50	.143
80	.161
84.56 (the mean)	.198
87.50	.225
91.10 (the most in any area)	.262

[a] Not significant at conventional levels, but the estimated effect of the variable may be precise enough to be suggestive of an influence on the ratification vote.

Note: All predicted probabilities are calculated from the estimated logistic coefficients for specification 2 reported in table A7.14 in appendix 7. All other details are as described in the note to table 7.9.

having voted for ratification, with a huge estimated response elasticity of 3.78. But this result may reflect the lack of personal ancestry data for North Carolina's delegates rather than the true effect of constituents' interests. Similar to the Massachusetts delegates from commercial areas, North Carolina delegates who represented more commercial areas (areas nearer to navigable water) were much more likely to have voted to ratify. The estimated response elasticity of distance is a rather large −2.16, indicating that a delegate 1 mile (or 1.16 percent) nearer to navigable water than the mean has a predicted probability of a yes vote of .0050 (or 2.53 percent) greater than the average delegate. For delegates from substantially different distances from navigable water, the predicted probabilities are substantially different, ranging from .786 to .001 (essentially zero), for the nearest to the farthest distance (see table 7.11). A delegate from the most isolated area in North Carolina had essentially a zero likelihood of voting in favor of ratification![34]

Delegates who represented areas with relatively large concentrations of slaves also were much less likely to have favored ratification, though the slave response elasticity is a modest −.858. As an example of this modest marginal effect, an increase of 1 slave per 100 whites (or 2.54 percent) more than the mean reduces the predicted probability of a yes vote by .0043 (a reduction of 2.16 percent) for an otherwise average delegate. Yet for a delegate from an area with the least slaves (6.73 per 100 whites), the predicted probability is .375, but if a delegate was from an area with the most slaves (123.25 per 100 whites), the predicted probability is .025. These estimates are consistent with the general opposition in the North Carolina convention and with a presumption that slave-owning constituents, *ceteris paribus*, expected to be net losers from ratification.[35]

The findings for the North Carolina convention help in sorting through the historical literature on the ratification process in North Carolina. For example, both Pool (1950a,b) and McDonald (1958) argue there was *no* relationship between slaveowning and voting for ratification among North Carolina delegates. At least for delegates who represented slaveowning constituents, the results here are at odds with both McDonald and Pool. Main (1961) and Risjord (1978) have suggested that slaveowning delegates and those who represented slaveowning constituents in North Carolina were more likely to have voted *for* the Constitution. The results here also are at odds with these studies. McDonald also concludes there was *no* relationship between voting and the creditor versus debtor status of North Carolina delegates. The results here are at odds with McDonald on this point as well. But Main (1961) and Risjord (1978) have suggested that there was a creditor versus debtor split on ratification of the Constitution in North Carolina. The results here provide some support for their claims. The findings also are soundly at odds with the more recent work of Lienesch (1989), who concludes that "the socioeconomic divisions were blurred" at the North Carolina convention (p. 348). The findings *are* consistent with the sentiments expressed during the ratification debates in North Carolina; as noted in chapter 6, James Galloway even thought that the framers' treatment of the slave trade in the Constitution "means to bring forward manumission" (Elliot, 1836 [1888], vol. 4, p. 101). Moreover, the strong effects found for constituent interests in North Carolina also are soundly supported by the debates. In the convention, William Lancaster even declared that he would vote against the Constitution because he was "bound by the voice of the people, whatever other gentlemen might think" and as "a great majority of the people were against it" he was too (Kenyon, 1966 [1985], p. 419).

The Virginia Convention

On June 25, 1788, the Virginia convention ratified the Constitution 89–79, with a modest 53 percent yes vote. The predicted probability for the "average" Virginia delegate is .523, a prediction virtually identical to the actual voting outcome.[36] In the Virginia convention, whose findings are reported in table 7.12, many economic interests significantly mattered, contrary to the views of most existing studies. Delegates who were debtors, slaveowners, and farmers were significantly less likely to have favored ratification than were delegates without such interests. Delegates with holdings of public securities in excess of $1,000 were significantly more likely to have supported ratification in Virginia than were those without public securities. And the estimates for the ownership of any public securities and the value of public securities holdings are both precise enough to be suggestive of a positive relationship between public securities and voting in favor of ratification as well.[37]

There are no statistically significant patterns in the vote related to merchant interests, private creditor interests, or ownership of western lands.[38] Yet once more, as Main (1961) suggsts, delegates who had served as officers in the Revolutionary War were more likely than others to have voted for ratification, although the statistical precision of the estimated effect is accurate enough only for specification 2 and still is weak. A delegate's religious affiliation, ethnic ancestry, and age do not appear to have affected voting behavior in Virginia.[39]

The predicted probabilities for the Virginia ratification vote for various values of the economic and other interests, which are reported in table 7.13, are dramatically different for delegates with dramatically different interests. For otherwise average delegates, farmers were nearly 34 percent less likely to vote for ratification, slaveowners were almost 43 percent less likely, and debtors were over 79 percent less likely than were those who were not farmers, slaveowners, or debtors, respectively. Delegates with large amounts of public securities were more than 87 percent more likely and officers were over 38 percent more likely to favor ratification than were otherwise average delegates who were not large public securities holders or officers, respectively. These magnitudes all suggest that the

Table 7.12. Incremental and Marginal Effects of the Explanatory Variables on the Probability of a Yes Vote on Ratification at the Virginia Convention

Explanatory Variables	Alternative Model Specifications		
	1	2	3
Merchant	−.253	−.280	−.250
Western landowner	.131	.082	.144
Private creditor	−.037	−.166	−.017
Debtor	−.366[c]	−.450[b]	−.335[c]
Farmer	−.205[b]	−.212[b]	−.228[b]
Slaveowner	−.334[b]	−.345[b]	—
Value of slaveholdings ($)	—	—	−.00002[c]
Owner public securities	.133	—	—
Owner >$1,000 public securities	—	.398[b]	—
Value of public securities holdings ($)	—	—	.00006
Episcopalian/Anglican	−.099	−.080	.033
Presbyterian	.346	.284	.393
English ancestry of delegate	.226	.245	.209
Scottish/Irish ancestry of delegate	.164	.196	.222
Officer in Revolutionary War	.126	.174[d]	.126
Age of delegate	.00074	.0017	.0024
Slaves per 100 whites	−.0035[a]	−.0032[b]	−.0037[a]
Distance to navigable water (miles)	−.0050[a]	−.0048[a]	−.0058[a]
English ancestry of citizens (percent)	−.011	−.0059	−.010
Scottish/Irish ancestry of citizens (percent)	−.044	−.054[c]	−.060[c]

[a] Statistically significant at .01 level.
[b] Statistically significant at .05 level.
[c] Statistically significant at .10 level.
[d] P-value is .1086.

Note: Number of observations for each specification is 165. The dependent variable in each specification is the observed ratification vote at the Virginia convention, where a yes vote equals 1 and a no vote equals 0. The Baptist and Congregational/Puritan religion variables are excluded because they have a value of zero for all delegates in Virginia. The incremental or marginal effect of each variable is calculated from the logistic estimates for the three model specifications for the Virginia ratification vote reported in table A7.15 in appendix 7, with all other explanatory variables at their mean values.

economic and other interests of the Virginia delegates made a big difference in their ratification vote.

Regarding constituent characteristics, Virginia delegates who represented areas with relatively heavy concentrations of slaveholdings were less likely than were others to have supported the Constitution, though the marginal effect is small. The estimated slave response elasticity is only −.493. As an example of the small marginal influence, a delegate from an area with 1 slave per 100 whites more than the sample mean (1.23 percent more) has a .00317 lower predicted probability of a yes vote (.606 percent lower). As in all other cases however, the predicted probabilities are dramatically different over wide ranges for the continuous variables. As indicated in table 7.13, for increasing amounts of constituent slaves for otherwise average delegates, the predicted probabilities range from .751

Table 7.13. Predicted Probabilities of the Ratification Vote at the Virginia Convention for a Delegate with Different Interests and Characteristics: Significant Variables

Economic Interests and Characteristics	Predicted Probability of a Yes Vote
The "Average" Delegate	.523
Debtor	.118
Not a debtor	.568
Farmer	.418
Not a farmer	.630
Slaveowner	.461
Not a slaveowner	.806
Owner public securities[a]	.602
No public securities	.470
Owner more than $1,000 public securities	.854
Owner less than $1,000 public securities	.456
Public Securities Holdings (Market Value)[a]	
$ 0 (the least for any delegate)	.471
$ 500	.500
$ 624.43 (the mean)	.507
$ 1,000	.529
$ 2,500	.614
$ 5,000	.740
$10,000	.901
$13,833 (the most for any delegate)	.957
Officer[a]	.625
Not an officer	.452
Constituent Slaveholdings (Slaves per 100 Whites)	
2.04 (the least in any area)	.751
10	.731
30	.679
50	.621
81.46 (the mean)	.523
100	.465
125	.387
150	.315
189.20 (the most in any area)	.218
Distance from Navigable Water (Miles)	
0 (the nearest for any delegate)	.781
10	.747
25	.689
50	.579
61.77 (the mean)	.523
80	.437
100	.346
150	.169
300	.011
500 (the farthest for any delegate)	.0003

continued

Table 7.13. continued

Economic Interests and Characteristics	Predicted Probability of a Yes Vote
Scottish/Irish Ancestry of Citizens (Percent Scottish/Irish)	
4.175 (the least in any area)	.763
5	.707
7	.636
9.17 (the mean)	.523
10	.479
11.50	.399
12.50	.349
13.74 (the most in any area)	.291

[a] Not significant at conventional levels, but the estimated effect of the variable may be precise enough to be suggestive of an influence on the ratification vote.

Note: All predicted probabilities are calculated from the estimated logistic coefficients for specification 2 reported in table A7.15 in appendix 7, except those for the ownership, and the value, of public securities are calculated from the logistic coefficients for specifications 1 and 3, respectively, in table A7.15. All other details are as described in the note to table 7.9.

to .218, a dramatically wide range, which supports the expectation that delegates who represented slave areas (or, as above, who owned slaves) were less likely to favor ratification.

Similar to the findings for Massachusetts and North Carolina, Virginia delegates who represented more commercial areas (areas nearer to navigable water) were more likely to have been ratifiers of the Constitution, though the distance response elasticity is a quite small −.562. A delegate 1 mile nearer to navigable water than the sample mean (1.62 percent nearer), accordingly, would have a predicted probability of a yes vote only .00476 greater than an otherwise average delegate (.91 percent greater).[40] Yet for a delegate nearest to navigable water, the predicted probability of voting for ratification is .781; for a delegate from the most isolated area, farthest from navigable water, the predicted probability is essentially zero; it is .0003! These findings, together with the results for Massachusetts and North Carolina, suggest that the commercial activities of constituents were most likely a very important factor in ratifying the Constitution—in fact, for Virginia, so important that had otherwise average Virginia delegates all been from the most isolated areas of the state, the Constitution most certainly would have never been ratified.

Although the estimates for the variable measuring the English ancestry of the constituents do not indicate any apparent pattern related to Virginia's ratification vote, delegates who represented counties in Virginia with heavier concentrations of individuals of Scottish/Irish ancestry were significantly less likely to have voted for ratification, consistent with the existing literature. In terms of the magnitude of the effect of the Scottish/Irish variable, its estimated response elasticity is a modest −.940. And, if counties had considerably different concentrations of Scottish/Irish descendents, the influence on the vote is quite considerable. The likelihood of voting yes ranges from only 29 percent for an otherwise average delegate from a county with the highest percentage of Scottish/Irish to more than 76 percent for a delegate from a county with the lowest percentage of Scottish/Irish (see table 7.13).[41]

The overall findings for the Virginia convention provide powerful evidence that can be used to sort through several claims about the Virginia ratification process found in the historical literature. The findings solidly conflict with the sweeping conclusion of Banning (1989), who contends that neither economic interests, nor military or political experience, nor any other private circumstance or attribute can explain the ratification vote in Virginia. However, the findings do offer some support for his claim that the ratification vote in Virginia was about navigation rights to the Mississippi, to the extent that the more commercial areas that voted for ratification wanted navigation rights and the less commercial areas that voted against the Constitution were not as concerned about those rights. The evidence is soundly at variance with the broad conclusion contained in McDonald (1958), who contends there was "no meaningful pattern whatever" between any interests and voting on ratification in Virginia (p. 268). The evidence indicates as well how wrong Rossiter (1966) is when, as noted earlier, he openly rejects an economic interpretation, suggesting "Virginia ratified the Constitution . . . because of a whole series of accidents and incidents that mock the crudely economic interpretation of the Great Happening of 1787–1788" (p. 292).

But the findings, especially for slave interests, *are* consistent with the sentiments expressed by those in Virginia that feared northern dominance of their slave-based commerce. As Richard Henry Lee, a leading Antifederalist in Virginia and a member of Congress, maintained in a December 1787 letter to Governor Edmund Randolph, one of the framers of the Constitution and a delegate to the Virginia ratifying convention, about the proposed legislature under the Constitution,

> a bare majority of votes can enact commercial laws, so that the representatives of the seven northern states, as they will have a majority, can by law create the most oppressive monopoly upon the five southern states, whose circumstances and productions are essentially different from theirs, although not a single man of these voters are the representatives of, or amendable to the people of the southern states. (Bailyn, 1993, p. 468)

The findings for the Virginia convention also are consistent with the sentiments expressed during the Virginia ratification debates that were discussed in chapter 6.

The Role of Creditors in the Three Ratifying Conventions

The role of creditor interests, especially the role of public securities holders, in the adoption of the Constitution has been a contentious issue among scholars for nearly a half-century. In Massachusetts, delegates who owned any public securities, as well as those who owned large amounts, were more likely to have favored the Constitution. But when the market value of public securities holdings is the variable, the effect is not statistically significant at conventional levels. For North Carolina, no apparent pattern in the vote related to public securities interests is indicated. This result must be interpreted with caution, however, because there were very few North Carolina delegates with public securities holdings. For the Virginia convention, the variable for public securities holdings in excess of $1,000 indicates a significantly large positive effect on the ratification vote, while the other two public securities variables are both at least suggestive of a possible positive effect on the vote.

The findings for public securities at the three ratifying conventions, along with the results that those who were private creditors also were significantly more likely than others to ratify in both Massachusetts and North Carolina, provide substantial support for the view that creditors were more likely to have favored ratification than were others. This is consistent with the negative experiences of some financial security holders during the late eighteenth century (especially during the Confederation period) because of financial and monetary conditions.[42] That creditors supported ratification also is consistent with the views of Main (1961) and McDonald (1958) concerning Massachusetts delegates but not with their conclusions concerning Virginia delegates. Main and McDonald both conclude that public securities holdings had little effect on the vote in the Virginia convention. But they certainly are referring to how the majority of the Virginia delegates with public securities voted on ratification, not to the *partial* effect of public securities per se on the likelihood of voting to ratify, as in this quantitative rexamination of the issue. Be that as it may, the estimated probabilities reported in table 7.13 indicate that delegates with public securities holdings in excess of $1,000, and average values of all other interests, were over 87 percent more likely to have favored ratification in Virginia than were otherwise average delegates. This finding certainly suggests that earlier studies misrepresented the role of public securities in the ratification vote in Virginia.[43]

The Role of Slaveowners in the Three Ratifying Conventions

Another major source of contention in the historical literature is the role of slave interests in the adoption of the Constitution. In the two southern ratifying conventions examined here, delegates who personally owned slaves were statistically less likely to have voted for ratification than were others only in Virginia. Although the value of slaveholdings is statistically significant and negative also only in Virginia, recall that when the value of slaveholdings is measured as a share of the value of total assets, or as an instrumental variable, in the overall ratification process, the estimates are negative and significant.[44] Also in both the North Carolina and Virginia conventions, the two conventions with any measurable amounts of constituent slaves in their states, delegates who represented areas with relatively large concentrations of slaves were highly less likely to have favored ratification.

The slave findings are consistent with the presumption that slaveowners, *ceteris paribus*, on net expected to lose from ratification. The findings also are at odds with historians who conclude that delegates with slaveholdings or those representing more heavily concentrated slave areas were more likely to have voted for ratification (see Main, 1961; Risjord, 1974, 1978). The findings are also at odds with other historians who argue that no pattern in the vote related to slaveholdings existed (see Pool, 1950a,b; Thomas, 1953; McDonald, 1958; Lienesch, 1989). However, these historians most certainly were drawing conclusions about how the majority of slaveowners voted on ratification, similar to inferences in the existing literature about the role of public securities, and not to the *partial* effect of slaveowning per se on the probability of voting in favor of ratification, as here.

The Role of Ideology in the Three Ratifying Conventions

With respect to another important issue found in the existing literature, the findings for the three ratifying conventions provide a degree of support for the role of personal ideology in the vote on ratification—at least as proxied with the personal attributes and experiences of the delegates. Baptists were less likely to have supported ratification in both Massachusetts and North Carolina. The findings also are at least suggestive that Episcopalian delegates might have been more likely to have supported ratification in North Carolina. Delegates of English ancestry were highly more likely to have voted for ratification in the one of the two conventions—Massachusetts—for which enough personal ancestry data exist. Delegates who were officers in the Revolutionary War were statistically more likely to have voted for ratification in Massachusetts and the estimates hint at the same relationship for the other two conventions. Yet the delegate's age, Revolutionary War experience (not as an officer), and political experience at the local, state, or national level either before or after ratification did not affect the ratification vote. The only exception is the one case in which Virginia delegates who had been members of the Continental Congress were less likely to have voted for ratification. With respect to constituent ideology, delegates who represented counties with heavier concentrations of families of English ancestry were more likely to have voted for ratification in North Carolina. The findings also indicate that delegates who represented counties with heavier concentrations of families of Scottish/Irish ancestry were less likely to have voted in favor of ratification in Virginia.

Nonnested Hypothesis Tests for the Three Ratifying Conventions

The explanatory variables employed in the empirical model may be placed into four general categories: personal economic interests, personal ideology, constituent economic interests, and constituent ideology. As discussed in appendix 2, however, the designation of a particular variable into a particular category is arbitrary in some cases. For example, distance from navigable water (or the Atlantic coast) serves to summarize various economic interests (the commercial activities) of the population of the local area in which a delegate resided, but it could also serve as a marker for geographic differences in ideology. The categorization employed to conduct the nonnested hypothesis tests, nonetheless, follows that used throughout this book, as shown, for example, in the list of variables in table 7.6. Admittedly, the choice of the "economic" or "ideology" label ultimately reflects a personal assessment of the main source of the variable's influence on voting behavior. The hypothesis tests, nevertheless, allow at the minimum a formal examination of the relative importance of the different categories of interests, even if the categories are somewhat arbitrarily chosen.

The results of the nonnested hypothesis tests, comparing ideological (nonpecuniary) and economic (pecuniary) interests, are reported in table 7.14. The results indicate that the null hypothesis that only ideology affected the vote is rejected compared to the rival hypothesis that only economic interests mattered (row 1) for all three state conventions. Likewise, the null hypothesis that only economic interests affected the vote is rejected compared to the rival hypothesis that only ideology mattered for all three conventions (row 2). The possible arbitrary designation of a particular variable into a particular category does not affect the results, as they are quite robust with respect to moving a questionable variable from one category to another. The null hypothesis is always rejected. The results

Table 7.14. Likelihood Ratios for Nonnested Hypothesis Tests of Voting on Ratification at the Massachusetts, North Carolina, and Virginia Ratifying Conventions

Null and Rival Hypotheses	Massachusetts	North Carolina	Virginia
Null: Ideology versus Rival: Economic			
H_0: $V_{ij} = f(PI_i, CI_j)$	93.18	102.57	46.63
H_A: $V_{ij} = f(PE_i, CE_j)$	(<.001)	(<.001)	(<.001)
Null: Economic versus Rival: Ideology			
H_0: $V_{ij} = f(PE_i, CE_j)$	18.27	9.45	7.74
H_A: $V_{ij} = f(PI_i, CI_j)$	(<.001)	(<.001)	(<.01)

Note: The test statistic is distributed as χ^2 with 1 degree of freedom (P-values are in parentheses). All tests are based on the set of model variables in specification 2 shown in tables 7.8, 7.10, and 7.12, respectively. The J-test results are similar when other sets of variables included in different model specifications are employed.

of the hypothesis tests imply that economic interests *and* ideology played an important role in the ratification vote in Massachusetts, North Carolina, and Virginia.

That conclusion runs counter to the views held in constitutional economics that only the beliefs or ideologies of a rational individual matter for the choice of a constitution, and that, because rational individuals are behind a veil of uncertainty or a veil of ignorance when choosing fundamental rules, partisan economic interests do not matter for constitutional choice. Recall also the conclusion in chapter 5 was that constitutional economics is unable to explain the drafting of the Constitution as well. These results provide strong support for the view that constitutional economics with its presumption of disinterested nonpartisan behavior cannot explain constitutional choices very well.

The Results for the Three Ratifying Conventions and Existing Historical Studies

As in the examination of the Philadelphia convention, the effects of the explanatory variables on the ratification votes calculated separately for delegates who owned slaves, and separately for delegates who owned public securities, could be more directly comparable to the conclusions found in the ratification literature. The historical literature nearly always discusses the influence of economic interests, especially for slave interests and public securities interests, with reference to the *overall* vote of delegates with a particular interest. Accordingly, the marginal and incremental effects for the ratification votes in Massachusetts, North Carolina, and Virginia are calculated employing the means of the variables for slaveowners and the means of the variables for public creditors, respectively. The predicted probabilities of the votes in the three conventions also are calculated employing the slave means and the public creditor means. Thus, the marginal or incremental effects of the various interests on the ratification votes and the predicted probabilities of a yes vote are estimated for the "average" slaveowner and the "average" public creditor for each convention.

The estimated effects of the explanatory variables for the "average" slaveowner for both the North Carolina and Virginia ratifying conventions, which are reported in table A7.19 in appendix 7, are qualitatively and quantitatively comparable to those reported for the "average" delegate for each convention. In fact, it is fair to say that the effects of the economic interests and characteristics on the ratification votes are nearly identical for the "average" slaveowner and "average" delegate in both conventions. And that makes perfect sense given that 80 percent of the sample of delegates for North Carolina and 84 percent for Virginia are, in fact, slaveowners.

The comparison for the Massachusetts convention, however, is problematic. The estimated specification for the Massachusetts ratifying convention does not include the slaveowner variable because of the small number of delegates who owned slaves—there are only 6 slaveowners out of 309 delegates (or 1.94 percent) in the Massachusetts sample. If the effects for the "average" slaveowner are calculated for the identical specification anyway, they also are nearly identical to those for the "average" Massachusetts delegate but not strictly comparable (see table A7.19). An alternative is to calculate the effects of the variables on the ratification vote for the "average" slaveowner for an otherwise identical model specification that includes the slaveowner variable, as in table A7.20. While still not strictly comparable to the initially estimated specification, a comparison can be made to the marginal and incremental effects of the variables for the "average" delegate employing the alternative specification, and this comparison is quite instructive.

First and foremost, the estimated effects for the "average" Massachusetts delegate for the initial and for the alternative specification are quite similar both qualitatively and quantitatively, suggesting quite robust results. The estimates for the alternative specification, moreover, indicate that the incremental effect of the now included slaveowner variable on the ratification vote in Massachusetts is significant, positive, and sizable: .367.[45] Given that a Massachusetts slaveowning delegate owned only a household slave or two, not large numbers of plantation slaves, it should not be surprising that the effect of slaveowning was to strongly increase the probability of favoring ratification. Slaveowners in Massachusetts had little in common with southern plantation slaveowners who produced export-based cash crops. The estimates for the "average" Massachusetts slaveowning delegate for the alternative specification indicate that the incremental effect of being a slaveowner is, of course, also significant, positive, and even more sizable: .494.[46] The effect of slaveholdings "swamps" the effects of nearly all other economic interests and characteristics, whose magnitudes are now relatively minor for the "average" slaveowner, except for the effects of the debtor and Baptist variables, whose negative effects on the probability of favoring ratification are still sizable. This provides additional evidence that the negative effect on the likelihood of voting for ratification for a Massachusetts delegate who was a debtor, or who was a Baptist, is especially strong.

For the "average" public creditor, whose findings are reported in table A7.21, the estimated effects for both the North Carolina and Virginia ratifying conventions are also qualitatively and quantitatively comparable to those reported for the "average" delegate for each convention. The direction and magnitude of most of the effects for the "average" public creditor are similar to those for a delegate to the North Carolina and Virginia conventions who had average values for all economic interests and characteristics. For North Carolina, in fact, the significant effects are nearly identical, except for only a few effects that are somewhat different. For Virginia, all effects are nearly identical or quite similar in magnitude. In Massachusetts, the significant effects are once again all qualitatively similar but quantitatively are sizably less in magnitude for all variables, except for debtors and Baptists, similar to the effects for the "average" slaveowner. It appears that the public securities interests of public securities owners in Massachusetts, the same as the slave interests of slave-owners, "swamp" the influence of their other interests on the ratification vote, suggesting that public creditors had especially strong interests involved in ratification. Public creditors at the Massachusetts convention apparently expected their public securities holdings to be especially affected by ratification of the Constitution.[47]

That the estimated effects of the economic and other interests on the ratification vote generally are not dramatically different whether they are calculated for the "average" delegate, the "average" slaveowner, or the "average" public creditor suggests the effects are fairly robust. And despite the fact that existing studies nearly always discuss the impact of economic interests on the vote with reference to the *overall* vote of delegates with a particular interest, the incremental and marginal effects calculated for only those delegates with a specific economic interest, even if more directly comparable to the discussions found in the existing literature, did not alter any conclusion here about the effect of any of the interests on the ratification vote.

The estimates of the predicted voting probabilities for the "average" slaveowner and the "average" public creditor, as well as for the "average" delegate, at the Massachusetts, North Carolina, and Virginia ratifying conventions are reported in table 7.15. For the "average" public creditor the predicted probability of a yes vote in each convention is substantially greater than for the "average" delegate. For Virginia, it is 21 percent greater; for Massachusetts, it is 45 percent greater; for North Carolina, it is 122 percent greater. Despite these differences, even if delegates with public securities holdings dominated each convention, the ultimate outcome most likely would not have been different. But the predicted probabilities do suggest that in Massachusetts ratification probably would have been a "done deal"; in Virginia, it would have been much easier; in North Carolina, it would have been a much closer contest.

For the "average" slaveowner, the predicted probabilities indicate that the ultimate outcome could have been different: Had slaveowners completely dominated the Virginia ratifying convention, ratification may have never taken place. The predicted probability of a yes vote for the "average" Virginia slaveowning delegate is slightly less than .45. The outcome at the North Carolina convention most certainly would have remained the same even if slaveowners had been even more dominant, as the predicted probabilities for the "average" slaveowner and "average" delegate in North Carolina are nearly identical. For Massachusetts, as already noted, the issue is problematic because the inially estimated model does not include the slaveowner variable. But relying on the predicted probability for the "average" slaveowning delegate based on the otherwise identical model specification that includes the slaveowner variable,

Table 7.15. Predicted Probabilities of a Yes Vote on Ratification for the Average Delegate, Average Public Creditor, and Average Slaveowner: Massachusetts, North Carolina, and Virginia Conventions

	Predicted Probability		
Ratifying Convention	Average Delegate	Average Public Creditor	Average Slaveowner
Massachusetts	.611	.890	.522
	n = 309	n = 63	n = 6
North Carolina	.198	.440	.212
	n = 261	n = 4	n = 210
Virginia	.523	.632	.449
	n = 165	n = 66	n = 139

Note: The predicted probabilities for the Massachusetts, North Carolina, and Virginia ratification votes are calculated from the estimated logistic coefficients for specification 2 reported in tables A7.13, A7.14, and A7.15, respectively, in appendix 7. The predicted probability for the average slaveowner at the Massachusetts convention, however, is problematic because the slaveowner variable is not included in the estimated model specification as there were only six slaveowners at the convention. An alternative predicted probability was calculated for an otherwise identical specification that includes the slaveowner variable (specification 3 in table A7.16 in appendix 7); it indicates a substantially higher probability of .936 for the average slaveowner at the Massachusetts convention. For purposes of comparison, the predicted probabilities for the alternative specification for the average delegate and average public creditor at the Massachusetts convention are .612 and .886, respectively; virtually identical to those calculated for the original specification. All predicted probabilities are calculated employing the mean values of all explanatory variables for all delegates (the "average" delegate); the mean values for the public creditor delegates only (the "average" public creditor); and the mean values for the slaveowning delegates only (the "average" slaveowner), respectively.

the slaveowning delegate was nearly certain to vote to ratify in Massachusetts (see table 7.15 note). However, I would not place that much confidence in an inference about the possible outcome in Massachusetts had slaveowners dominated, as the findings are derived from a sample of only six slaveholding delegates, who together owned a total of only eight slaves.

The Predicted Votes for the Specific Delegates to the Three Ratifying Conventions

We now know that both economic interests and ideology played an important role in the ratification votes in Massachusetts, North Carolina, and Virginia. But how well does the economic model predict the voting behavior of specific delegates? How well does a particular delegate's own interests and characteristics predict his ratification vote? The analysis so far has estimated the overall magnitude of the influence of a wide range of different values of the economic and other interests on the ratification vote. But it does not tell us how accurately the economic model predicts the vote of a specific delegate. How many of the ratification votes does the model predict correctly?

For the Massachusetts convention, how well do the economic interests and characteristics of Samuel Adams and John Hancock, for example, predict their actual ratification vote? Did they rise above their personal and constituent interests, suggesting the economic model does *not* predict their votes very well? Or did they vote their interests, suggesting the model *does* predict their ratification votes? What about the ratification votes of other delegates, for example, William R. Davie and Willie Jones in North Carolina, or Patrick Henry and James Madison in Virginia?

The predicted ratification votes for the 735 delegates to the three conventions are estimated using each delegate's own interests and characteristics in the economic model, employing the estimated logistic coefficients from the second model specification for the Massachusetts, North Carolina, and Virginia conventions contained in tables A7.13–A7.15, respectively. The predicted votes are reported in table A7.22. Relying on the same method of scoring as for the Philadelphia convention, a predicted vote is considered "correct" when an actual yes vote (equal to 1) has a predicted probability greater than .50 and when an actual no vote (equal to 0) has a predicted probability less than .50. A predicted vote of exactly .50 is *not* considered "correct" for any vote. The percentage of correct predictions for Massachusetts, as a result, is 77.0 percent; for North Carolina, 83.5 percent; and for Virginia, 72.7 percent—the economic model predicts the ratification votes quite accurately for all three ratifying conventions. The North Carolina votes are by far predicted the most accurately.

What about the votes of the more prominent members of the three ratifying conventions? Were they principled men who generally rose above their economic and other interests, voting to ratify the Constitution based on the "good of the nation"? Maybe not! The evidence is consistent with many of the more prominent delegates having voted their personal and constituent interests (see table A7.22). In the Massachusetts convention, the "distinguished" delegates Samuel Adams, John Hancock, Rufus King, and Caleb Strong, for example, each voted for ratification and their predicted probabilities of favoring ratification based on the economic model are .971, .753, .974, and .961, respectively. The economic model predicts that each would have voted in favor of ratification and, in the case of three, that they would have voted yes with near certainty, and they did! For Amos Singeltary, one of the more prominent opponents who voted against ratification in Massachusetts, the economic model predicts that he would have voted against the Constitution based on his economic interests and characteristics, with a probability of a yes vote of .330.

In the North Carolina ratifying convention, the "respected" Federalists James Iredell, Samuel Johnston, and Richard Dobbs Spaight, for example, each voted in favor of ratification, and the vote of each was consistent with a vote based on their personal and constituent interests. The estimated voting probabilities for the three delegates are .598, .962, and .695, respectively. The equally "respected" Federalist William R. Davie also voted in favor of ratification, but his predicted probability based on his specific interests and characteristics is estimated at .324, well less than 50 percent, indicating that he may have risen above his own interests to support ratification. The most prominent opponent in North Carolina, the anti-nationalist Willie Jones, voted against ratification, and his personal and constituent interests predict his behavior very well, with a predicted probability of a yes vote of .179.

In the Virginia ratifying convention, the "distinguished" Federalists James Madison, John Marshall, Edmund Randolph, and George Wythe, for example, voted for ratification, and a vote for ratification in each case is consistent with voting to satisfy their personal and constituent interests! The predicted probabilities for the four are .523, .983, .925, and .931, respectively. And only in the case of James Madison is the prediction of the economic model not overwhelmingly strong. Among the prominent opponents of the Constitution who voted against it in the Virginia convention were Benjamin Harrison, Patrick Henry, Richard Henry Lee, George Mason, and James Monroe. Interestingly, the economic model does *not* predict the ratification votes for the opponents of the Constitution nearly as well as it does for Madison, Marshall, Randolph, and Wythe. The predicted probabilities for the five opponents are .434, .513, .004, .637, and .955, respectively, indicating that, based on their personal and constituent interests, three of them should have voted *for* ratification. But they did not! And only in the case of one, Richard Henry Lee, do an opponent's interests indicate overwhelming opposition to ratification. Could it be, at least in the case of some Virginia delegates, that the "Anti-federalists" were the principled men who generally rose above their economic and other interests?

A Summary of the Findings

The estimates for the individual states indicate that delegates with the same interests voted differently in several instances in different ratifying conventions, somewhat in conflict with the implication from the pooled samples in chapter 6, but consistent with a rational choice view of the adoption of the Constitution. The differences in voting behavior are plausible given that it is likely that economic and institutional differences across states would generate differences in the impact of specific interests on voting. It is possible that some of the variables employed to measure the personal interests of the delegates, or to serve as markers for their personal ideology, act as proxies for similar but unmeasured constituent interests. It also is possible that the degree of the correlation between the observed personal-interest variables and the unobserved constituent-interest variables varies systematically across states, contributing to differences across states in the estimates for the different interest variables. Yet there is no strong reason to suspect systematic variation in the correlation between the observed and unobserved variables.

The results of the preliminary examination for the seven state ratifying conventions taken as a whole are quite similar to each other. Yet the results are based on relatively limited data for an incomplete set of delegates. For Massachusetts, North Carolina, and Virginia, the additional data allow more robust inferences about delegate voting behavior. The results for the three state conventions indicate that among the influential factors affecting the ratification vote in Massachusetts were the financial interests (private and public creditor interests, as well as debtor interests) and the merchant interests of the delegates. That these factors affected voting in Massachusetts should not be surprising given the nature of the Massachusetts economy and public policy to pay off its debt (through increased tax enforcement) during the mid 1780s—and the aftermath, Shay's Rebellion. Baptists in Massachusetts also were more likely than others were to have opposed the Constitution. Given that Baptists in Massachusetts would be very much a dissenting group, the result is quite plausible. In North Carolina, among the influential factors affecting the vote were the farming interests, and the private but not public financial securities of the delegates. Given that North Carolina may be viewed as more farming oriented than plantation oriented, and that very few of its delegates (only 1.5 percent) possessed public securities, the results also are plausible. In Virginia, among the influential factors were the slaveowning and public creditor interests of the delegates. To the extent that Virginia may be viewed as plantation oriented rather than farming oriented, and given that many of its delegates (40 percent) possessed public securities, the results are quite credible.

Although the differences in the estimates across the conventions are not all dramatic, the existence of several differences alone argues for the importance of examining each state ratifying convention separately. The results indicate there were some common patterns in the ratification vote across most of the conventions as well. Delegates from local areas with more commercial activities (as measured by proximity to navigable water) were much more likely to have voted for ratification in all but one of the conventions. Delegates who personally owned slaves or who represented local areas with greater concentrations of slaves were much more likely to have opposed ratification in two of the three southern states, as well as in Pennsylvania. The results for commercial activities and slaveholdings are consistent with the findings based on the pooled samples. The results also are consistent with the findings contained in part I on the drafting of the Constitution.

The magnitude of the influence on the ratification votes of many of the personal and constituent interests and characteristics often was very large. The incremental effects for some of the dichotomous variables were huge, in fact. The predicted probabilities of voting for ratification also were considerably different for delegates with considerably different interests and characteristics. Moreover, the estimated voting probabilities for the specific individuals who attended the Massachusetts, North Carolina, and

Virginia conventions provide strong support for the economic model of voting during the ratification process, even though some delegates were less likely to have voted their specific interests than were others. The predicted voting probabilities for the wide range of values of the explanatory variables also suggest that the ratification outcome most certainly would have been different had the interests of those who attended the ratifying conventions been different.

The findings for the personal and political data for Massachusetts, North Carolina, and Virginia, at the minimum, enhance the examination of the ratification process because the previously unobserved and omitted markers for a delegate's personal ideology are included. The lack of dramatically different estimated effects for the economic-interest variables for the three conventions from those for all seven ratifying conventions should not be interpreted as indicating that inclusion of the markers for ideology for the three conventions is unimportant. The correlation between the markers for personal ideology and the previously included economic-interest variables may be weak enough that any omitted-variable bias in the earlier results is quite small. Moreover, the findings for the previously omitted ideological-interest variables themselves, even when not significant, provide a more complete picture of the factors influencing the ratification of the Constitution. The finding that political office holding, especially local and state office holding before ratification, had *no* statistically significant influence on the ratification votes and that office holding in fact was most likely superfluous, certainly is a new and particularly important finding.

Epilogue:
The Lessons of 1787
and Ratification

The economic hypothesis of this new interpretation of the behavior of our Founding Fathers can be neatly summarized. The supporters of particular provisions in the Constitution and the supporters of ratification anticipated that the costs imposed on them by the behavior of others would have been greater under the Articles of Confederation than under the Constitution and the provisions in it. They expected collective decisions under the Constitution and the specific provisions in it to reduce these expected external costs. Consequently, they expected to benefit from the Constitution and its provisions. The opponents of particular provisions in the Constitution and the opponents of ratification anticipated that the external costs imposed on them by the behavior of others would have been greater under the Constitution and the specific provisions in it. They expected collective decisions under the Articles of Confederation to impose lower external costs on them. As a result, they expected to benefit from the Articles of Confederation and the particular provisions in it.

A compelling lesson that can be drawn from this reexamination of the design and adoption of the Constitution is that our Founding Fathers—the framers of the Constitution at Philadelphia and the delegates to the state ratifying conventions—responded rationally to the incentives they faced when determining their votes during the drafting and ratification of the Constitution. It may be debated just how strong the findings are for all the economic and ideological interests employed under every circumstance examined in this study. But that personal and constituent economic interests, influenced the Founding Fathers cannot be disputed. The founders responded to the costs and benefits they and their constituents expected as a result of their votes, suggesting a modern economic interpretation can explain the Constitution's framing and adoption.

Over the last several decades, many constitutional and historical scholars have questioned an economic interpretation of the Constitution as being too narrow or too calculating to be of much help in understanding the behavior of our Founding Fathers. It is difficult for many scholars and students of the Constitution to accept that the founders' behavior could be explained through such a "simplistic" perspective. For them, the factors that motivated our beloved founders must have been more principled, as well as more complex, than simple economic interests. Many scholars believe that in explaining the Constitution one must concentrate on the great principles and political philosophies that motivated the behavior of the founders—relegating economic interests to, at most, a minor role.

A modern economic approach is difficult for many individuals to embrace. It is nearly impossible for some. Skeptics of an economic interpretation often fail to appreciate that a modern economic approach is actually a much broader view than the simple belief that individuals are motivated by merely "selfish interests." Many individuals struggle with the notion that economics is a particular way of thinking about people; they struggle with the notion that people make rational choices. Many individuals often view economic rationality as something people merely pursue sometimes because so much of human behavior they observe surely is irrational. The application of methodological individualism and a presumption of economic rationality, in fact, can make economic reasoning on the face of it unacceptable to many scholars.

The new economic interpretation put forth in this book maintains that economic interests in the narrow pecuniary sense of the term, as well as interests in a broader nonpecuniary sense, affected the choices the founders made. This economic view of our Founding Fathers holds not only that they had preferences over material, pecuniary objects, but also that they had preferences over intangible, nonpecuniary desires, including their beliefs, ideologies, and principles; and they made choices that satisfied these broadly defined preferences given any constraints they faced.

Our Founding Fathers possessed and represented multiple interests—pecuniary as well as nonpecuniary. Some of the founders' interests coincided with each other; other interests conflicted. The founders could not have possibly satisfied all their interests with a single vote on a particular issue at the Philadelphia convention or with a single vote to either ratify or not. The framers had to decide whose interests they would support when making choices regarding which rules to include in and which to exclude from the Constitution. The delegates who attended the state ratifying conventions had to make the choice to accept or reject the set of rules as drafted by the framers. But similar to private citizens making private choices, political actors must bear costs because of their public choices. In making their choices, the founders sometimes were able to satisfy both their personal interests and their constituent interests because the interests coincided. At other times, to satisfy their constituent interests, the framers and ratifiers had to sacrifice their personal interests; and at still other times, to satisfy their personal interests, they had to sacrifice their constituent interests.

A contention often found in the literature, especially among those scholars who argue that economic interests certainly mattered, is that such interests, nonetheless, cannot account for any divisions among the supporters and opponents of the Constitution because the framers and ratifiers were like-minded men who represented similar economic interests. Yet, if the founders actually represented similar interests, there would have been few or no differences in the various measures of economic and ideological interests—the explanatory variables employed in this study. And, if that were so, the findings of the logistic regressions would have been less likely to indicate statistically significant coefficients for the explanatory variables. In the extreme, if the founders represented identical interests, if there were literally no variance in the explanatory variables, the logistic regressions could not even have been estimated. The measures of the economic interests and the markers for ideological interests could not have statistically explained the votes of the founders.

Another contention is that the supporters and opponents of the Constitution, especially during ratification, generally cannot be grouped into merchants and men of wealth as supporters and farmers and men of little wealth as opponents. McDonald (1958) long ago attempted to document the lack of such a division of interests during ratification, reporting estimates of the annual income and its source for each of the thirty delegates to the Delaware ratifying convention.[1] McDonald noted that nearly all Delaware delegates were farmers rather than merchants, that they had relatively low incomes, and that all voted for the Constitution. (Delaware unanimously ratified on December 7, 1787.) Twenty-three of the thirty delegates are classified as farmers, with their income solely from farming estimated at an average of $334. The estimated average income for all thirty Delaware delegates is $481. Yet, contrary to McDonald's view, his own income estimates indicate fairly high incomes compared to Walton and Rockoff's (1998, table 5-4, p. 109) estimates of income per free person on the eve of the Revolution in the range of $47.50 to $102.50. McDonald's estimated income for all thirty Delaware delegates is, in fact, from well over four and a half to over ten times higher than Walton and Rockoff's estimates. For the twenty-three farmers, McDonald's estimated income solely from farming is from over three to seven times higher than Walton and Rockoff's estimates. The Delaware convention, which unanimously supported the Constitution, does *not* appear to have been "primarily one of small farmers," at least in McDonald's (1958, p. 123) or other historians' sense of the term.[2]

Moreover, the statistical findings reported in this book indicate that a delegate's occupation, assets, and wealth *did* significantly influence his votes during the drafting and ratification of the Constitution. And the magnitudes of the impact on voting of many of the economic and ideological interests were quite large. Delegates who were merchants, owned private securities, owned large amounts of public securities, were officers in the Revolutionary War, or represented more commercial areas nearer to navigable water, other factors constant, generally were much more likely to vote for issues at Philadelphia when the issues were likely to materially favor those interests. They also were much more likely to vote for issues that strengthened the *national* government. At the state ratifying conventions, these delegates generally were more likely to vote for ratification of the Constitution. Conversely, delegates who were debtors, owned slaves, represented areas with heavier concentrations of slaveholdings, or represented less commercial areas farther from navigable water, other factors constant, generally were more likely to vote for issues at Philadelphia when the issues were likely to materially favor those interests. They also were much more likely to vote for issues that strengthened the *state* governments. At the state ratifying conventions, these delegates generally were more likely to vote against ratification of the Constitution.

Attention needs to be focused on what is measured by the econometric technique employed in this book. A logistic regression coefficient reported for a particular explanatory variable—for example, slaveholdings or merchant interests—measures the *partial* effect of that interest on the probability of voting in favor of the issue in question, holding all other factors constant. This means that although the estimated logistic regression equation accounts for the influences of all the measured interests on the probability of a yes vote, an estimated logistic coefficient (actually, the estimated marginal or incremental effect) for a specific variable statistically estimates the influence of a change in that variable only on the probability of a yes vote. Thus, while the *partial* effect of slaveholdings, for example, was to decrease the probability of a delegate voting in favor of the Constitution, any particular slaveholder may have actually voted *for* the Constitution because of offsetting *partial* effects of all his other interests. And, in what appears to be contrary to the prevailing views of the issue, slaveholdings did decrease the probability of supporting the Constitution, *ceteris paribus*, while in fact individual slaveowners, and individual delegates from slaveholding areas, did in fact vote for the Constitution.

As in the existing literature, a simple observation from the votes that delegates with slaveholdings, even a majority of slaveowning delegates, *supported* the Constitution does not indicate the influence of slaveholdings per se on voting on the Constitution, nor does it negate an economic interpretation of the Constitution. A simple observation from the votes that delegates with public securities holdings, even a majority of such delegates, did *not* support the Constitution does not indicate the influence of public securities holdings per se on voting on the Constitution, nor does it negate an economic interpretation of the Constitution. Because existing studies fail to account for the influence of other interests on voting when examining the votes of delegates with a specific interest, conclusions often are drawn in the existing literature that are different from those here.

What does this study suggest for the historiography of the Constitution? During the last half of the twentieth century, an economic interpretation of the Constitution has played little role in the history, law, or political science literature on the creation of the Constitution. It played no role in the economic history literature until the last decade. It was either dismissed as invalid or ignored by most scholars. While from time to time individual studies have appeared indicating the importance of economic interests in the making of the Constitution, few scholars still give much credence to economic explanations of the design and adoption of the Constitution. The modern evidence now indicates that an economic approach to explaining the creation of the Constitution deserves a much-expanded role in discussions of the issue.[3]

The findings of this study support a modern, new economic interpretation of the Constitution. As such, the findings offer support in a broad sense for a "Beardian" view of the founders—but only in the sense that broadly defined economic interests influenced the founders' behavior. The findings do *not* support a narrow "Beardian" view of the founders, that the founders can be separated into dichotomous classes, representing "personalty" and "realty" interests. Although the findings do not support the idea that "personalty" and "realty" interests per se mattered, they, nonetheless, indicate a role in the drafting and ratification of the Constitution for many of the specific economic interests of concern to Charles A. Beard in 1913.

Knowledge of the influence of economic incentives on the behavior of our founders, as well as its historical importance, contributes to a better understanding of contemporary political choices. Though the costs of monitoring and policing political representatives today are substantially less than during the drafting and ratification of the Constitution, they are still positive. While technological and political developments have lowered the costs of acquiring information about politicians, citizens still bear costs of monitoring and policing political behavior—at the minimum, it takes time to listen to the radio, watch the television, or explore the Internet. And, given the nature of representative government, political representatives can and do insulate themselves and their actions from their constituents. As a result, personally motivated behavior on the part of political actors is likely. The implication is that, if even the Founding Fathers were personally motivated, then to accurately understand contemporary political behavior, the personal economic and ideological interests of contemporary political actors, in addition to the interests of their constituents, must be taken into account.

That fundamental political institutions—the fundamental "rules of the game"—matter for understanding the performance of economies is widely acknowledged, as is the importance of the study of their historical evolution. This book contributes to the new historical, institutional economics by providing formal evidence that the economic and ideological interests of the individuals involved mattered for the choice of a fundamental political institution—the Constitution of the United States. Moreover, the evidence provided indicates the importance to the historical outcome of the specific historical actors involved in any historical process. The Constitution certainly would have been different had men with substantially different economic, financial, or personal interests been involved in its framing. And, had the men involved in its ratification had substantially different economic, financial, or personal interests, the Constitution certainly would not have been ratified, at least not as it was written.

The lesson to be learned from this book for understanding any future constitutional change in the United States, or in any country, however, is not optimistic. The evidence presented here suggests that the interests of the political actors involved in any constitutional change will influence significantly the choices they make. It has been shown not only that our original founding and constitutional choices were neither disinterested nor nonpartisan, but also that it is highly unlikely that disinterested and nonpartisan constitutional changes can take place in any society. Rational political actors with economic, personal, and political interests will always be self-interested and partisan. Constitutions are the products of the interests of the relevant players involved in the constitutional founding.

Yet perhaps the paramount lesson to be learned from our nation's constitutional founding is that, although a constitution is the product of the specific individuals involved in its creation, partisan self-interest among our founders did not generate a largely inefficient or unfair constitution, at least from the perspective of many observers. It is true, however, that the economic interests of our Founding Fathers did ensure, among other outcomes, that slavery would remain constitutionally legal until the Civil War and that holders of confederation securities would benefit from the new government. But it also is true that there are many general aspects of the Constitution that do not appear to have been overtly influenced by partisan economic interests. Thus, from the perspective of not only most Americans but also much of the world, our constitutional government is greatly admired and is not viewed as overly self-interested. The real issue then for any society involved in designing, or reforming, a constitution is, if possible, to structure its constitutional deliberations to prevent the individuals involved from personally benefiting from purely partisan self-interested behavior.

Appendixes

Documents

The Articles of Confederation

TO ALL to whom these Presents shall come, we the undersigned Delegates of the States affixed to our Names send greeting. Whereas the Delegates of the United States of American in Congress assembled did on the fifteenth day of November in the Year of our Lord One Thousand Seven Hundred and Seventy seven, and in the Second Year of the Independence of America agree to certain articles of Confederation and perpetual Union between the States of Newhampshire, Massachusetts-bay, Rhode-island and Providence Plantations, Connecticut, New York, New Jersey, Pennsylvania, Delaware, Maryland, Virginia, North-Carolina, South-Carolina and Georgia in the Words following, viz. "Articles of Confederation and perpetual Union between the states of Newhampshire, Massachusetts-bay, Rhode-island and Providence Plantations, Connecticut, New-York, New-Jersey, Pennsylvania, Delaware, Maryland, Virginia, North-Carolina, South-Carolina, and Georgia."

Art. I. The Stile of this confederacy shall be "The United States of America."

Art. II. Each state retains its sovereignty, freedom and independence, and every Power, Jurisdiction and right, which is not by this confederation expressly delegated to the United States, in Congress assembled.

Art. III. The said states hereby severally enter into a firm league of friendship with each other, for their common defence, the security of their Liberties, and their mutual and general welfare, binding themselves to assist each other, against all force offered to, or attacks made upon them, or any of them, on account of religion, sovereignty, trade, or any other pretence whatever.

Art. IV. The better to secure and perpetuate mutual friendship and inter-course among the people of the different states in this union, the free inhabitants of each of these states, paupers, vagabonds and fugitives from Justice excepted, shall be entitled to all privileges and immunities of free citizens in the several states; and the people of each state shall have free ingress and regress to and from any other state, and shall enjoy therein all the privileges of trade and commerce, subject to the same duties, impo-sitions and restrictions as the inhabitants thereof respectively, provided that such restriction shall not extend so far as to prevent the removal of property imported into any state, to any other state of which the Owner is an inhabitant; provided also that no imposition, duties or restriction shall be laid by any state, on the property of the united states, or either of them.

If any Person guilty of, or charged with treason, felony, or other high misdemeanor in any state, shall flee from Justice, and be found in any of the united states, he shall upon demand of the Governor or executive power, of the state from which he fled, be delivered up and removed to the state having jurisdiction of his offence.

Full faith and credit shall be given in each of these states to the records, acts and judicial proceedings of the courts and magistrates of every other state.

Art. V. For the more convenient management of the general interests of the united states, delegates shall be annually appointed in such manner as the legislature of each state shall direct, to meet in Congress on the first Monday in November, in every year, with a power reserved to each state, to recall its delegates, or any of them, at any time within the year, and to send others in their stead, for the remainder of the Year.

No state shall be represented in Congress by less than two, nor by more than seven Members; and no person shall be capable of being a delegate for more than three years in any term of six years; nor shall any person, being a delegate, be capable of holding any office under the united states, for which he, or another for his benefit receives any salary, fees or emolument of any kind.

Each state shall maintain its own delegates in a meeting of the states, and while they act as members of the committee of the states.

In determining questions in the united states, in Congress assembled, each state shall have one vote.

Freedom of speech and debate in Congress shall not be impeached or questioned in any Court, or place out of Congress, and the members of congress shall be protected in their persons from arrests and imprison-ments, during the time of their going to and from, and attendance on congress, except for treason, felony, or breach of the peace.

Art. VI. No state without the Consent of the united states in congress assembled, shall send any embassy to, or receive any embassy from, or enter into any conference, agreement, or alliance or treaty with any King, prince or state; nor shall any person holding any office of profit or trust under the united states, or any of them, accept of any present, emolument, office or title of any kind whatever from any king, prince or foreign state; nor shall the united states in congress assembled, or any of them, grant any title of nobility.

No two or more states shall enter into any treaty, confederation or alliance whatever between them, without the consent of the united states in congress assembled, specifying accurately the purposes for which the same is to be entered into, and how long it shall continue.

No state shall lay any imposts or duties, which may interfere with any stipulations in treaties, entered into by the united states in congress assembled, with any king, prince or state, in pursuance of any treaties already proposed by congress, to the courts of France and Spain.

No vessels of war shall be kept up in time of peace by any state, except such number only, as shall be deemed necessary by the united states in congress assembled, for the defence of such state, or its trade; nor shall any body of forces be kept up any state, in time of peace, except such number only, as in the judgment of the united states, in congress assembled, shall be deemed requisite to garrison the forts necessary for the defence of such state; but every state shall always keep up a well regulated and disciplined militia, sufficiently armed and accoutred, and shall provide and constantly have ready for use, in public stores, a due number of field pieces and tents, and a proper quantity of arms, ammunition and camp equipage.

No state shall engage in any war without the consent of the united states in congress assembled, unless such state be actually invaded by enemies, or shall have received certain advice of a resolution being formed by some nation of Indians to invade such state, and the danger is so imminent as not to admit of a delay, till the united states in congress assembled can be consulted: nor shall any state grant commissions to any ships or vessels of war, nor letters of marque or reprisal, except it be after a declaration of war by the united states in congress assembled, and then only against the kingdom or state and the subjects thereof, against which war has been so declared, and under such regulations as shall be established by the united states in congress assembled, unless such state be infested by pirates, in which case vessels of war may be fitted out for that occasion, and kept so long as the danger shall continue, or until the united states in congress assembled shall determine otherwise.

Art. VII. When land-forces are raised by any state for the common defence, all officers of or under the rank of colonel, shall be appointed by the legislature of each state respectively by whom such forces shall be raised, or in such manner as such state shall direct, and all vacancies shall be filled up by the state which first made the appointment.

Art. VIII. All charges of war, and all other expences that shall be incurred for the common defence or general welfare, and allowed by the united states in congress assembled, shall be defrayed out of a common treasury, which shall be supplied by the several states, in proportion to the value of all land within each state, granted to or surveyed for any Person, as such land and the buildings and improvements thereon shall be estimated according to such mode as the united states in congress assembled, shall from time to time direct and appoint. The taxes for paying that proportion shall be laid and levied by the authority and direction of the legislatures of the several states within the time agreed upon by the united states in congress assembled.

Art. IX. The united states in congress assembled, shall have the sole and exclusive right and power of determining on peace and war, except in the cases mentioned in the sixth article—of sending and receiving ambassadors—entering into treaties and alliances, provided that no treaty of commerce shall be made whereby the legislative power of the respective states shall be restrained from imposing such imposts and duties on foreigners, as their own people are subjected to, or from prohibiting the exportation or importation of any species of goods or commodities whatsoever—of establishing rules for deciding in all cases, what captures on land or water shall be legal, and in what manner prizes taken by land or naval forces in the service of the united states shall be divided or appropriated—of granting letters of marque and reprisal in times of peace— appointing courts for the trial of piracies and felonies committed on the high seas and establishing courts for receiving and determining finally appeals in all cases of captures, provided that no member of congress shall be appointed a judge of any of the said courts.

The united states in congress assembled shall also be the last resort on appeal in all disputes and differences now subsisting or that hereafter may arise between two or more states concerning boundary, jurisdiction or any other cause whatever; which authority shall always be exercised in the manner following. Whenever the legislative or executive authority or lawful agent of any state in controversy with another shall present a petition to congress, stating the matter in question and praying for a hearing, notice thereof shall be given by order of congress to the legislative or executive authority of the other state in controversy, and a day assigned for the appearance of the parties by their lawful agents, who shall then be directed to appoint by joint consent, commissioners or judges to constitute a court for hearing and determining the matter in question: but if they cannot agree, congress shall name three persons out of each of the united states, and from the list of such persons each party shall alternately strike out one, the petitioners beginning, until the number shall be reduced to thirteen; and from that number not less then seven, nor more than nine names as congress shall direct, shall in the presence of congress be drawn out by lot, and the persons whose names shall be so drawn or any five of them, shall be commissioners or judges, to hear and finally determine the controversy, so always as a major part of the judges who shall hear the cause shall agree in the determination: and if either party shall neglect to attend at the day appointed, without shewing reasons, which congress shall judge sufficient, or being present shall refuse to strike, the congress shall proceed to nominate three persons out of each state, and the secretary of congress shall strike in behalf of such party absent or refusing; and the judgment and sentence of the court to be appointed, in the manner before prescribed, shall be final and conclusive; and if any of the parties shall refuse to submit to the authority of such court, or to appear to defend their claim, or cause, the court shall nevertheless proceed to pronounce sentence, or judgment, which shall in like manner be final and decisive, the judgment or sentence and other proceedings being in either case transmitted to congress, and lodged among the acts of congress for the security of the parties concerned: provided that every commissioner, before he sits in judgment, shall take an oath to be administered by one of the judges of the supreme or superior court of the state, where the cause shall be tried, "well and truly to hear and determine the matter in question, according to the best of his judgment, without favour, affection or hope of reward": provided also that no state shall be deprived of territory for the benefit of the united states.

All controversies concerning the private right of soil claimed under different grants of two or more states, whose jurisdictions as they may respect such lands, and the states which passed such grants are adjusted, the said grants or either of them being at the same time claimed to have originated antecedent to such settlement of jurisdiction, shall on the petition of either party to the congress of the united states, be finally determined as near as may be in the same manner as is before prescribed for deciding disputes respecting territorial jurisdiction between different states.

The united states in congress assembled shall also have the sole and exclusive right and power of regulating the alloy and value of coin struck by their own authority, or by that of the respective states—fixing the standard of weights and measures throughout the united states—regulating the trade and managing all affairs with the Indians, not members of any of the states, provided that the legislative right of any state within its own limits be not infringed or violated—establishing and regulating post-offices from one state to another, throughout all the united states, and exacting such postage on the papers passing thro' the same as may be requisite to defray the expences of the said office—appointing all officers of the land forces, in the service of the united states, excepting regimental officers—appointing all the officers of the naval forces, and commissioning all officers whatever in the service of the united states—making rules for the government and regulation of the said land and naval forces, and directing their operations.

The united states in congress assembled shall have authority to appoint a committee, to sit in the recess of congress, to be denominated "A Committee of the States," and to consist of one delegate from each state; and to appoint such other committees and civil officers as may be necessary for managing the general affairs of the united states under their direction—

to appoint one of their number to preside, provided that no person be allowed to serve in the office of president more than one year in any term of three years; to ascertain the necessary sums of Money to be raised for the service of the united states, and to appropriate and apply the same for defraying the public expences—to borrow money, or emit bills on the credit of the united states, transmitting every half year to the respective states an account of the sums of money so borrowed or emitted—to build and equip a navy—to agree upon the number of land forces, and to make requisitions from each state for its quota, in proportion to the number of white inhabitants in such state: which requisition shall be binding, and thereupon the legislature of each state shall appoint the regimental officers, raise the men and cloath, arm and equip them in a soldier like manner, at the expence of the united states, and the officers and men so cloathed, armed and equipped shall march to the place appointed, and within the time agreed on by the united states in congress assembled: But if the united states in congress assembled shall, on con-sideration of circumstances judge proper that any state should not raise men, or should raise a smaller number than its quota, and that any other state should raise a greater number of men than the quota thereof, such extra number shall be raised, officered, cloathed, armed and equipped in the same manner as the quota of such state, unless the legislature of such state shall judge that such extra number cannot be safely spared out of the same, in which case they shall raise, officer, cloath, arm and equip as many of such extra number as they judge can be safely spared. And the officers and men so cloathed, armed and equipped, shall march to the place appointed, and within the time agreed on by the united states in congress assembled.

The united states in congress assembled shall never engage in a war, not grant letters of marque and reprisal in time of peace, nor enter into any treaties or alliances, nor coin money, nor regulate the value thereof, nor ascertain the sums and expences necessary for the defence and welfare of the united states, or any of them, nor emit bills, nor borrow money on the credit of the united states, nor appropriate money, nor agree upon the number of vessels of war, to be built or purchased, or the number of land or sea forces to be raised, nor appoint a commander in chief of the army or navy, unless nine states assent to the same: nor shall a question on any other point, except for adjourning from day to day be determined, unless by the votes of a majority of the united states in congress assembled.

The congress of the united states shall have power to adjourn to any time within the year, and to any place within the united states, so that no period of adjournment be for a longer duration than the space of six Months, and shall publish the Journal of their proceedings monthly, except such parts thereof relating to treaties, alliances or military operations as in their judgment require secresy; and the yeas and nays of the delegates of each state on any question shall be entered on the Journal, when it is desired by any delegate; and the delegates of a state, or any of them, at his or their request shall be furnished with a transcript of the said Journal, except such parts as are above excepted, to lay before the legislatures of the several states.

Art. X. The committee of the states, or any nine of them, shall be authorised to execute, in the recess of congress, such of the powers of congress as the united states in congress assembled, by the consent of nine states, shall from time to time think expedient to vest them with; provided that no power be delegated to the said committee, for the exercise of which by the articles of confederation, the voice of nine the congress of the united states assembled is requisite.

Art. XI. Canada acceding to this confederation, and joining in the measures of the united states, shall be admitted into, and entitled to all the advantages of this union: but no other colony shall be admitted into the same, unless such admission be agreed to by nine states.

Art. XII. All bills of credit emitted, monies borrowed and debts contracted by, or under the authority of congress, before the assembling of the united states, in pursuance of the present confederation, shall be deemed and considered as a charge against the united states, for payment and satisfaction whereof the said united states, and the public faith are hereby solemnly pledged.

Art. XIII. Every state shall abide by the determinations of the united states in congress assembled, on all questions which by this confederation are submitted to them. And the Articles of this confederation shall be inviolably observed by every state, and the union shall be perpetual; nor shall any alteration at any time hereafter be made in any of them; unless such alteration be agreed to in a congress of the united states, and be afterwards confirmed by the legislatures of every state.

AND WHEREAS it hath pleased the Great Governor of the World to incline the hearts of the legislatures we respectively represent in congress, to approve of, and to authorize us to ratify the said articles of confederation and perpetual union. KNOW YE that we the undersigned delegates, by virtue of the power and authority to us given for that purpose, do by these presents, in the name and in behalf of our respective constituents, fully and entirely ratify and confirm each and every of the said articles of confederation and perpetual union, and all and singular the matters and things therein contained: And we do further solemnly plight and engage the faith of our respective constituents, that they shall abide by the determinations of the united states in congress assembled, on all questions, which by the said confederation are submitted to them. And that the articles thereof shall be inviolably observed by the states we respectively represent, and that the union shall be perpetual. In Witness thereof we have hereunto set our hands in Congress. Done at Philadelphia in the state of Pennsylvania the ninth Day of July in the Year of our Lord one Thousand seven Hundred and Seventy-eight, and in the third year of the independence of America.

Josiah Bartlett
John Wentworth Junr
   August 8th 1778
On the part and behalf of the State of New Hampshire

John Hancock
Samuel Adams
Elbridge Gerry
Francis Dana
James Lovell
Samuel Holten
On the part and behalf of The State of Massachusetts Bay

William Ellery
Henry Marchant
John Collins
On the part and behalf of the State of Rhode-Island and Providence Plantations

Roger Sherman
Samuel Huntington
Oliver Wolcott
Titus Hosmer
Andrew Adams
On the part and behalf of the State of Connecticut

Ja^s Duane
Fra^s Lewis
Wm Duer
Gouv Morris
On the part and behalf of the State of New York

Jno Witherspoon
Nathl Scudder
   Novr 26, 1778.—
On the part and behalf of the State of New Jersey

Robt Morris
Daniel Roberdeau
Jon^a Bayard Smith
William Clingan
Joseph Reed
   July 22^d 1778
On the part and behalf of the State of Pennsylvania

Tho M:kean
   Feby 12 1779
John Dickinson
   May 5th 1779

Nicholas Van Dyke
On the part and behalf of the State of Delaware

John Hanson
 March 1 1781
Daniel Carroll d°
On the part and behalf of the State of Maryland

Richard Henry Lee
John Banister
Thomas Adams
Jn° Harvie
Francis Lightfoot Lee
On the part and behalf of the State of Virginia

John Penn
 July 21ˢᵗ 1778
Cornˢ Harnett
Jn° Williams
On the part and behalf of State of N° Carolina

Henry Laurens
William Henry Drayton
Jn° Mathews
Richᵈ Hutson
Thoˢ Heyward Junʳ
On the part and behalf of the State of South-Carolina

Jn° Walton
 24ᵗʰ July 1778
Edwᵈ Telfair
Edwᵈ Langworthy
On the part and behalf of the State of Georgia

The Virginia Plan, May 29, 1787

1. RESOLVED, That the articles of Confederation ought to be so corrected and enlarged as to accomplish the objects proposed by their institution; namely, common defence, security of liberty and general welfare.

2. Resolved, therefore, That the rights of suffrage, in the National Legislature ought to be proportioned to the Quotas of contribution, or to the number of free inhabitants, as the one or the other rule may seem best in different cases.

3. Resolved, That the National Legislature ought to consist of two branches.

4. Resolved, That the members of the first branch of the National Legislature ought to be elected by the people of the several States every   for the term of   ; to be the age of   years at least; to

receive liberal stipends by which they may be compensated for the devotion of their time to public service; to be ineligible to any office established by a particular State, or under the authority of the United States, except those peculiarly belonging to the functions of the first branch, during the term of service, and for the space of   after its expiration; to be incapable of re-election for the space of   after the expiration of their term of service; and to be subject to recall.

5. Resolved, That the members of the second branch of the National Legislature ought to be elected by those of the first, out of a proper number of persons nominated by the individual Legislatures; to be of the age of   years, at least; to hold their offices for a term sufficient to ensure their independency; to receive liberal stipends, by which they may be compensated for the devotion of their time to public service; and to be ineligible to any office established by a particular State, or under the authority of the United States, except those peculiarly belonging to the functions of the second branch, during the term of service, and for the space of   after the expiration thereof.

6. Resolved, That each branch ought to possess the right of originating Acts; that the National Legislature ought to be empowered to enjoy the Legislative Rights vested in Congress by the Confederation, and moreover to legislate in all cases to which the separate States are incompetent, or in which the harmony of the United States may be interrupted by the exercise of individual Legislation; to negative all laws passed by the several States, contravening in the opinion of the National Legislatrue the articles of Union; and to call forth the force of the Union against any member of the Union failing to fulfil its duty under the articles thereof.

7. Resolved, That a national executive be instituted; to be chosen by the National Legislature for the term of   years; to receive punctually at stated times, a fixed compensation for the services rendered, in which no increase or diminution shall be made so as to affect the Magistracy existing at the time of increase or diminution; and to be ineligible a second time; and that besides a general authority to execute the National laws, it ought to enjoy the Executive rights vested in Congress by the Confederation.

8. Resolved, That the executive and a convenient number of the National Judiciary, ought to compose a council of revision with authority to examine every act of the National Legislature before it shall operate, and every act of a particular Legislature before a Negative thereon shall be final; and that the dissent of the said Council shall amount to a rejection, unless the act of the National Legislature be again passed, or that of a particular Legislature be again negatived by   of the members of each branch.

9. Resolved, That a national judiciary be established to consist of one or more supreme tribunals, and of inferior tribunals to be chosen by the National Legislature, to hold their offices during good behaviour; and to receive punctually at stated times fixed compensations for their services,

in which no increase or diminution shall be made so as to affect the person actually in office at the time of such increase or diminution. That the jurisdiction of the inferior tribunals shall be to hear and determine in the first instance, and of the supreme tribunal to hear and determine, in the dernier resort, all piracies and felonies on the high seas; captures from an enemy; cases in which foreigners or citizens of other States applying to such jurisdictions may be interested, or which respect the collection of the National revenue; impeachments of any National officer; and questions which involve the national peace or harmony.

10. Resolved, That provision ought to be made for the admission of States lawfully arising within the limits of the United States, whether from a voluntary junction of Government and Territory, or otherwise, with the consent of a number of voices in the National Legislature less than the whole.

11. Resolved, That a Republican Government and the territory of each State, except in the instance of a voluntary junction of Government and territory, ought to be guaranteed by the United States to each State.

12. Resolved, That provision ought to be made for the continuance of Congress and their authorities and privileges, until a given day after the reform of the articles of Union shall be adopted, and for the completion of all their engagements.

13. Resolved, That provision ought to be made for the amendment of the articles of Union whensoever it shall seem necessary; and that the assent of the National Legislature ought not to be required thereto.

14. Resolved, That the legislative, executive, and judiciary powers within the several States, ought to be bound by oath to support the articles of union.

15. Resolved, That the amendments which shall be offered to the Confederation, by the Convention ought at a proper time, or times, after the approbation of Congress, to be submitted to an assembly or assemblies of Representatives, recommended by the several Legislatures to be expressly chosen by the people, to consider and decide thereon.

Letter from the Philadelphia Convention to Congress

IN CONVENTION, *September* 17, 1787

Sir, we have now the honor to submit to the consideration of the United States in Congress assembled, that Constitution which has appeared to us the most advisable.

The friends of our country have long seen and desired, that the power of making war, peace, and treaties, of levying money and regulating commerce, and the correspondent executive and judicial authorities should be fully and effectually vested in the general government of the Union: but the impropriety of delegating such extensive trust to one body of men is evident—Hence results the necessity of a different organization.

It is obviously impracticable in the federal government of these States, to secure all rights of independent sovereignty to each, and yet provide for the interest and safety of all—Individuals entering into society, must give up a share of liberty to preserve the rest. The magnitude of the sacrifice must depend as well on situation and circumstances as on the object to be obtained. It is at all times difficult to draw with precision the line between those rights which must be surrendered, and those which may be reserved; and on the present occasion this difficulty was increased by a difference among the several States as to their situation, extent, habits, and particular interests.

In all our deliberations on this subject we kept steadily in our view, that which appears to us the greatest interest of every true American, the consolidation of our Union, in which is involved our prosperity, felicity, safety, perhaps our national existence. This important consideration, seriously and deeply impressed on our minds, led each State in the Convention to be less rigid on points of inferior magnitude, than might have been otherwise expected; and thus the Constitution, which we now present, is the result of a spirit of amity, and of that mutual deference and concession which the peculiarity of our political situation rendered indispensable.

That it will meet the full and entire approbation of every State is not perhaps to be expected; but each will doubtless consider, that had her interest alone been consulted, the consequences might have been particularly disagreeable or injurious to others; that it is liable to as few exceptions as could reasonably have been expected, we hope and believe; that it may promote the lasting welfare of that country so dear to us all, and secure her freedom and happiness, is our most ardent wish.

With great respect, We have the honor to be
  Sir,
  Your Excellency's most Obedient and Humble Servants, George Washington, President

By Unanimous Order of the Convention
  His Excellency, The President of Congress

Resolutions of the Philadelphia Convention Concerning Ratification and Implementation

In Convention, Monday, *September* 17, 1787

Present, The States of New-Hampshire, Massachusetts, Connecticut, Mr. Hamilton from New–York, New Jersey, Pennsylvania, Delaware, Maryland, Virginia, North Carolina, South Carolina, and Georgia.

Resolved, That the preceding Constitution be laid before the United States in Congress assembled, and that it is the opinion of this convention, that it should afterwards be submitted to a convention of delegates, chosen in each State by the people thereof, under the recommendation of its legislature, for their assent and ratification; and that each convention assenting to, and ratifying the same should give notice thereof to the United States in Congress assembled.

Resolved, That it is the opinion of this convention, that as soon as the conventions of nine States shall have ratified this Constitution, the United States in Congress assembled should fix a day on which electors should be appointed by the States which shall have ratified the same, and a day on which the electors should assemble to vote for the President, and the time and place for commencing proceedings under this Constitution; that after such publication the electors should be appointed, and the senators and representatives elected; that the electors should meet on the day fixed for the election of the President, and should transmit their votes certified, signed, sealed, and directed, as the Constitution requires, to the secretary of the United States in Congress assembled; that the senators and representatives should convene at the time and place assigned; that the senators should appoint a president of the Senate, for the sole purpose of receiving, opening and counting the votes for President; and that after he shall be chosen, the Congress, together with the President, should without delay proceed to execute this Constitution.

By the unanimous order of the convention.
George Washington, President.
William Jackson, Secretary.

The Constitution of the United States

We, the People of the United States, in Order to form a more perfect Union, establish Justice, insure domestic Tranquility, provide for the common defence, promote the general Welfare, and secure the Blessings of Liberty to ourselves and our Posterity, do ordain and establish this Constitution for the United States of America.

Article I

Section 1. All legislative Powers herein granted shall be vested in a Congress of the United States, which shall consist of a Senate and House of Representatives.

Section 2. The House of Representatives shall be composed of Members chosen every second Year by the People of the several States, and the Electors in each State shall have the Qualifications requisite for Electors of the most numerous Branch of the State Legislature.

No Person shall be a Representative who shall not have attained to the age of twenty five Years, and been seven Years a Citizen of the United

States, and who shall not, when elected, be an Inhabitant of that State in which he shall be chosen.

Representatives and direct Taxes shall be apportioned among the several States which may be included within this Union, according to their respective Numbers, which shall be determined by adding to the whole Number of free Persons, including those bound to Service for a Term of Years, and excluding Indians not taxed, three fifths of all other Persons. The actual Enumeration shall be made within three Years after the first Meeting of the Congress of the United States, and within every subsequent Term of ten Years, in such Manner as they shall by Law direct. The Number of Representatives shall not exceed one for every thirty Thousand, but each State shall have at Least one Representative; and until such enumeration shall be made, the State of New Hampshire shall be entitled to chuse three, Massachusetts eight, Rhode-Island and Providence Plantations one, Connecticut five, New-York six, New Jersey four, Pennsylvania eight, Delaware one, Maryland six, Virginia ten, North Carolina five, South Carolina five, and Georgia three.

When vacancies happen in the Representation from any State, the Executive Authority thereof shall issue Writs of Election to fill such Vacancies.

The House of Representatives shall chuse their Speaker and other Officers; and shall have the sole Power of Impeachment.

Section 3. The Senate of the United States shall be composed of two Senators from each State, chosen by the Legislature thereof, for six Years; and each Senator shall have one Vote.

Immediately after they shall be assembled in Consequence of the first Election, they shall be divided as equally as may be into three Classes. The Seats of the Senators of the first Class shall be vacated at the Expiration of the second Year, of the second Class at the Expiration of the fourth Year, and of the third Class at the Expiration of the sixth Year, so that one third may be chosen every second Year; and if Vacancies happen by Resignation, or otherwise, during the Recess of the Legislature of any State, the Executive thereof may make temporary Appointments until the next Meeting of the Legislature, which shall then fill such Vacancies.

No Person shall be a Senator who shall not have attained to the Age of thirty Years, and been nine Years a Citizen of the United States, and who shall not, when elected, be an Inhabitant of that State for which he shall be chosen.

The Vice President of the United States shall be President of the Senate, but shall have no Vote, unless they be equally divided.

The Senate shall chuse their other Officers, and also a President pro tempore, in the Absence of the Vice President, or when he shall exercise the Office of President of the United States.

The Senate shall have the sole Power to try all Impeachments. When sitting for that Purpose, they shall be on Oath or Affirmation. When the

President of the United States is tried, the Chief Justice shall preside: And no Person shall be convicted without the Concurrence of two thirds of the Members present.

Judgment in Cases of Impeachment shall not extend further than to removal from Office, and disqualification to hold and enjoy any Office of Honor, Trust or Profit under the United States: but the Party convicted shall nevertheless be liable and subject to Indictment, Trial, Judgment and Punishment, according to Law.

Section 4. The Times, Places and Manner of holding Elections for Senators and Representatives, shall be prescribed in each State by the Legislature thereof; but the Congress may at any time by Law make or alter such Regulations, except as to the Places of chusing Senators.

The Congress shall assemble at least once in every Year, and such Meeting shall be on the first Monday in December, unless they shall by Law appoint a different Day.

Section 5. Each House shall be the Judge of the Elections, Returns and Qualifications of its own Members, and a Majority of each shall constitute a Quorum to do Business; but a smaller Number may adjourn from day to day, and may be authorized to compel the Attendance of absent Members, in such Manner, and under such Penalties as each House may provide.

Each House may determine the Rules of its Proceedings, punish its Members for disorderly Behaviour, and, with the Concurrence of two thirds, expel a Member.

Each House shall keep a Journal of its Proceedings, and from time to time publish the same, excepting such Parts as may in their Judgment require Secrecy; and the Yeas and Nays of the Members of either House on any question shall, at the Desire of one fifth of those Present, be entered on the Journal.

Neither House, during the Session of Congress, shall, without the Consent of the other, adjourn for more than three days, nor to any other Place than that in which the two Houses shall be sitting.

Section 6. The Senators and Representatives shall receive a Compensation for their Services, to be ascertained by Law, and paid out of the Treasury of the United States. They shall in all Cases, except Treason, Felony and Breach of the Peace, be privileged from Arrest during their Attendance at the Session of their respective Houses, and in going to and returning from the same; and for any Speech or Debate in either House, they shall not be questioned in any other Place.

No Senator or Representative shall, during the Time for which he was elected, be appointed to any civil Office under the Authority of the United States, which shall have been created, or the Emoluments whereof shall have been increased during such time: and no Person holding any Office under the United States, shall be a Member of either House during his Continuance in Office.

Section 7. All Bills for raising Revenue shall originate in the House of Representatives; but the Senate may propose or concur with Amendments as on other Bills.

Every Bill which shall have passed the House of Representatives and the Senate, shall, before it become a Law, be presented to the President of the United States; if he approve he shall sign it, but if not he shall return it, with his Objections to that House in which it shall have originated, who shall enter the Objections at large on their Journal, and proceed to reconsider it. If after such Reconsideration two thirds of that House shall agree to pass the Bill, it shall be sent, together with the Objections, to the other House, by which it shall likewise be reconsidered, and if approved by two thirds of that House, it shall become a Law. But in all such Cases the Votes of both Houses shall be determined by Yeas and Nays, and the Names of the Persons voting for and against the Bill shall be entered on the Journal of each House respectively. If any Bill shall not be returned by the President within ten Days (Sundays excepted) after it shall have been presented to him, the Same shall be a Law, in like Manner as if he had signed it, unless the Congress by their Adjournment prevent its Return, in which Case it shall not be a Law.

Every Order, Resolution, or Vote to which the Concurrence of the Senate and House of Representatives may be necessary (except on a question of Adjournment) shall be presented to the President of the United States; and before the Same shall take Effect, shall be approved by him, or being disapproved by him, shall be repassed by two thirds of the Senate and House of Representatives, according to the Rules and Limitations prescribed in the Case of a Bill.

Section 8. The Congress shall have Power To lay and collect Taxes, Duties, Imposts and Excises, to pay the Debts and provide for the common Defence and general Welfare of the United States; but all Duties, Imposts and Excises shall be uniform throughout the United States;

To borrow Money on the credit of the United States;

To regulate Commerce with foreign Nations, and among the several States, and with the Indian Tribes;

To establish an uniform Rule of Naturalization, and uniform Laws on the subject of Bankruptcies throughout the United States;

To coin Money, regulate the Value thereof, and of foreign Coin, and fix the Standard of Weights and Measures;

To provide for the Punishment of counterfeiting the Securities and current Coin of the United States;

To establish Post Offices and post Roads;

To promote the Progress of Science and useful Arts, by securing for limited Times to Authors and Inventors the exclusive Right to their respective Writings and Discoveries;

To constitute Tribunals inferior to the supreme Court;

To define and punish Piracies and Felonies committed on the high Seas, and Offences against the Law of Nations;

To declare War, grant Letters of Marque and Reprisal, and make Rules concerning Captures on Land and Water;

To raise and support Armies, but no Appropriation of Money to that Use shall be for a longer Term than two Years;

To provide and maintain a Navy;

To make Rules for the Government and Regulation of the land and naval Forces;

To provide for calling forth the Militia to execute the Laws of the Union, suppress Insurrections and repel Invasions;

To provide for organizing, arming, and disciplining, the Militia, and for governing such Part of them as may be employed in the Service of the United States, reserving to the States respectively, the Appointment of the Officers, and the Authority of training the Militia according to the discipline prescribed by Congress;

To exercise exclusive Legislation in all Cases whatsoever, over such District (not exceeding ten Miles square) as may, by Cession of particular States, and the Acceptance of Congress, become the Seat of the Government of the United States, and to exercise like Authority over all Places purchased by the Consent of the Legislature of the State in which the Same shall be, for the Erection of Forts, Magazines, Arsenals, dock-Yards, and other needful Buildings;—And

To make all Laws which shall be necessary and proper for carrying into Execution the foregoing Powers, and all other Powers vested by this Constitution in the Government of the United States, or in any Department or Officer thereof.

Section 9. The Migration or Importation of such Persons as any of the States now existing shall think proper to admit, shall not be prohibited by the Congress prior to the Year one thousand eight hundred and eight, but a Tax or duty may be imposed on such Importation, not exceeding ten dollars for each Person.

The Privilege of the Writ of Habeas Corpus shall not be suspended, unless when in Cases of Rebellion or Invasion the public Safety may require it.

No Bill of Attainder or ex post facto Law shall be passed.

No Capitation, or other direct, Tax shall be laid, unless in Proportion to the Census or Enumeration herein before directed to be taken.

No Tax or Duty shall be laid on Articles exported from any State.

No Preference shall be given by any Regulation of Commerce or Revenue to the Ports of one State over those of another: nor shall Vessels bound to, or from, one State, be obliged to enter, clear or pay Duties in another.

No Money shall be drawn from the Treasury, but in Consequence of Appropriations made by Law; and a regular Statement and Account of the Receipts and Expenditures of all public Money shall be published from time to time.

No Title of Nobility shall be granted by the United States: And no Person holding any Office of Profit or Trust under them, shall, without the Consent of the Congress, accept of any present, Emolument, Office, or Title, of any kind whatever, from any King, Prince, or foreign State.

Section 10. No State shall enter into any Treaty, Alliance, or Confederation; grant Letters of Marque and Reprisal; coin Money; emit Bills of Credit; make any Thing but gold and silver Coin a Tender in Payment of Debts; pass any Bill of Attainder, ex post facto Law, or Law impairing the Obligation of Contracts, or grant any Title of Nobility.

No State shall, without the Consent of the Congress, lay any Imposts or Duties on Imports or Exports, except what may be absolutely necessary for executing its inspection Laws: and the net Produce of all Duties and Imposts, laid by any State on Imports or Exports, shall be for the Use of the Treasury of the United States; and all such Laws shall be subject to the Revision and Controul of the Congress.

No State shall, without the Consent of Congress, lay any Duty of Tonnage, keep Troops, or Ships of War in time of Peace, enter into any Agreement or Compact with another State, or with a foreign Power, or engage in War, unless actually invaded, or in such imminent Danger as will not admit of delay.

Article II

Section 1. The executive Power shall be vested in a President of the United States of America. He shall hold his Office during the Term of four Years, and, together with the Vice President, chosen for the same Term, be elected, as follows:

Each State shall appoint, in such Manner as the Legislature thereof may direct, a Number of Electors, equal to the whole Number of Senators and Representatives to which the State may be entitled in the Congress: but no Senator or Representative, or Person holding an Office of Trust or Profit under the United States, shall be appointed an Elector.

The Electors shall meet in their respective States, and vote by Ballot for two Persons, of whom one at least shall not be an Inhabitant of the same State with themselves. And they shall make a List of all the Persons voted for, and of the Number of Votes for each; which List they shall sign and certify, and transmit sealed to the Seat of the Government of the United States, directed to the President of the Senate. The President of the Senate shall, in the Presence of the Senate and House of Representatives, open all the Certificates, and the Votes shall then be counted. The Person having the greatest Number of Votes shall be the President, if such Number be a Majority of the whole Number of Electors appointed; and if there be more than one who have such Majority, and have an equal Number of Votes, then the House of Representatives shall immediately chuse by Ballot one of them for President; and if no Person have a Majority, then from the five highest on the List the said House shall in like Manner chuse the President. But in chusing the President, the Votes shall be taken by States, the Representation from each State having one Vote; A quorum for this Purpose shall consist of a Member or Members from two thirds of the States, and a Majority of all the States shall be necessary to a Choice. In every Case, after the Choice of the President, the Person having the greatest Number of Votes of the Electors shall be the Vice President. But if there should remain two or more who have equal Votes, the Senate shall chuse from them by Ballot the Vice President.

The Congress may determine the Time of chusing the Electors, and the Day on which they shall give their Votes; which Day shall be the same throughout the United States.

No Person except a natural born Citizen, or a Citizen of the United States, at the time of the Adoption of this Constitution, shall be eligible to the Office of President; neither shall any Person be eligible to that Office who shall not have attained to the Age of thirty five Years, and been fourteen Years a Resident within the United States.

In Case of the Removal of the President from Office, or of his Death, Resignation, or Inability to discharge the Powers and Duties of the said Office, the Same shall devolve on the Vice President, and the Congress may by Law provide for the Case of Removal, Death, Resignation or Inability, both of the President and Vice President, declaring what Officer shall then act as President, and such Officer shall act accordingly, until the Disability be removed, or a President shall be elected.

The President shall, at stated Times, receive for his Services, a Compensation, which shall neither be encreased nor diminished during the Period for which he shall have been elected, and he shall not receive within that Period any other Emolument from the United States, or any of them.

Before he enter on the Execution of his Office, he shall take the following Oath or Affirmation:—"I do solemnly swear (or affirm) that I will faithfully execute the Office of President of the United States, and will to the best of my Ability, preserve, protect and defend the Constitution of the United States."

Section 2. The President shall be Commander in Chief of the Army and Navy of the United States, and of the Militia of the several States, when called into the actual Service of the United States; he may require the Opinion, in writing, of the principal Officer in each of the executive Departments, upon any Subject relating to the Duties of their respective Offices, and he shall have Power to grant Reprieves and Pardons for Offences against the United States, except in Cases of Impeachment.

He shall have Power, by and with the Advice and Consent of the Senate, to make Treaties, provided two thirds of the Senators present concur; and he shall nominate, and by and with the Advice and Consent of the Senate, shall appoint Ambassadors, other public Ministers and Consuls, Judges of the supreme Court, and all other Officers of the United States, whose Appointments are not herein otherwise provided for, and which shall be established by Law: but the Congress may by Law vest the Appointment of such inferior Officers, as they think proper, in the President alone, in the Courts of Law, or in the Heads of Departments.

The President shall have Power to fill up all Vacancies that may happen during the Recess of the Senate, by granting Commissions which shall expire at the End of their next Session.

Section 3. He shall from time to time give to the Congress Information of the State of the Union, and recommend to their Consideration such Measures as he shall judge necessary and expedient; he may, on extraordinary Occasions, convene both Houses, or either of them, and in Case of Disagreement between them, with Respect to the Time of Adjournment, he may adjourn them to such Time as he shall think proper; he shall receive Ambassadors and other public Ministers; he shall take Care that the Laws be faithfully executed, and shall Commission all the Officers of the United States.

Section 4. The President, Vice President and all civil Officers of the United States, shall be removed from Office on Impeachment for, and Conviction of, Treason, Bribery, or other high Crimes and Misdemeanors.

Article III

Section 1. The judicial Power of the United States, shall be vested in one supreme Court, and in such inferior Courts as the Congress may from time to time ordain and establish. The Judges, both of the supreme and inferior Courts, shall hold their Offices during good Behaviour, and shall, at stated Times, receive for their Services, a Compensation, which shall not be diminished during their Continuance in Office.

Section 2. The judicial Power shall extend to all Cases, in Law and Equity, arising under this Constitution, the Laws of the United States, and Treaties made, or which shall be made, under their Authority;—to all Cases affecting Ambassadors, other public Ministers and Consuls;—to all Cases of admiralty and maritime Jurisdiction;—to Controversies to which the United States shall be a Party;—to Controversies between two or more States;—between a State and Citizens of another State;—between Citizens of different States,—between Citizens of the same State claiming Lands under Grants of different States, and between a State, or the Citizens thereof, and foreign States, Citizens or Subjects.

In all Cases affecting Ambassadors, other public Ministers and Consuls, and those in which a State shall be Party, the supreme Court shall have original Jurisdiction. In all the other Cases before mentioned, the supreme Court shall have appellate Jurisdiction, both as to Law and Fact, with such Exceptions, and under such regulations as the Congress shall make.

The Trial of all Crimes, except in Cases of Impeachment, shall be by Jury; and such Trial shall be held in the State where the said Crimes shall have been committed; but when not committed within any State, the Trial shall be at such Place or Places as the Congress may by Law have directed.

Section 3. Treason against the United States, shall consist only in levying War against them, or in adhering to their Enemies, giving them Aid and Comfort. No Person shall be convicted of Treason unless on the Testimony of two Witnesses to the same overt Act, or on Confession in open Court.

The Congress shall have Power to declare the Punishment of Treason, but no Attainder of Treason shall work Corruption of Blood, or Forfeiture except during the Life of the Person attainted.

Article IV

Section 1. Full Faith and Credit shall be given in each State to the public Acts, Records, and judicial Proceedings of every other State. And the Congress may by general Laws prescribe the Manner in which such Acts, Records, and Proceedings shall be proved, and the Effect thereof.

Section 2. The Citizens of each State shall be entitled to all Privileges and Immunities of Citizens in the several States.

A Person charged in any State with Treason, Felony, or other Crime, who shall flee from Justice, and be found in another State, shall on Demand of the executive Authority of the State from which he fled, be delivered up, to be removed to the State having Jurisdiction of the Crime.

No Person held to Service or Labour in one State, under the Laws thereof, escaping into another, shall, in Consequence of any Law or Regulation therein, be discharged from such Service or Labour, but shall be delivered up on Claim of the Party to whom such Service or Labour may be due.

Section 3. New States may be admitted by the Congress into this Union; but no new States shall be formed or erected within the Jurisdiction of any other State; nor any State be formed by the Junction of two or more States, or Parts of States, without the Consent of the Legislatures of the States concerned as well as of the Congress.

The Congress shall have Power to dispose of and make all needful Rules and Regulations respecting the Territory or other Property belonging to the United States; and nothing in this Constitution shall be so construed as to Prejudice any Claims of the United States, or of any particular State.

Section 4. The United States shall guarantee to every State in this Union a Republican Form of Government, and shall protect each of them against Invasion; and on Application of the Legislature, or of the Executive (when the Legislature cannot be convened) against domestic Violence.

Article V

The Congress, whenever two thirds of both Houses shall deem it necessary, shall propose Amendments to this Constitution, or, on the Application of the Legislatures of two thirds of the several States, shall call a Convention for proposing Amendments, which, in either Case, shall be valid to all Intents and Purposes, as Part of this Constitution, when ratified by the Legislatures of three fourths of the several States, or by Conventions in three fourths thereof, as the one or the other Mode of Ratification may be proposed by the Congress; Provided that no Amendment which may be made prior to the Year One thousand eight hundred and eight shall in any Manner affect the first and fourth Clauses in the Ninth Section of the first Article; and that no State, without its Consent, shall be deprived of its equal Suffrage in the Senate.

Article VI

All Debts contracted and Engagements entered into, before the Adoption of this Constitution, shall be valid against the United States under this Constitution, as under the Confederation.

This Constitution, and the Laws of the United States which shall be made in Pursuance thereof; and all Treaties made, or which shall be made, under the Authority of the United States, shall be the supreme Law of the Land; and the Judges in every State shall be bound thereby, any Thing in the Constitution or Laws of any State to the Contrary notwith-standing.

The Senators and Representatives before mentioned, and the Members of the several State Legislatures, and all executive and judicial Officers, both of the United States and of the several States, shall be bound by Oath or Affirmation, to support this Constitution; but no religious Test shall ever be required as a Qualification to any Office or public Trust under the United States.

Article VII

The Ratification of the Conventions of nine States, shall be sufficient for the Establishment of this Constitution between the States so ratifying the Same.

Done in Convention by the Unanimous Consent of the States present the Seventeenth Day of September in the Year of our Lord one thousand seven hundred and Eighty seven and of the Independence of the United States of America the Twelfth In Witness whereof We have hereunto subscribed our Names,

George Washington—President and deputy from Virginia

Attest William Jackson *Secretary*

New Hampshire
    John Langdon Jr.
    Nicholas Gilman
Massachusetts
    Nathaniel Gorham
    Rufus King
Connecticut
    William Samuel Johnson
    Roger Sherman
New York
    Alexander Hamilton
New Jersey
    William Livingston
    David Brearley
    William Paterson
    Jonathan Dayton
Pennsylvania
    Benjamin Franklin
    Thomas Mifflin
    Robert Morris
    George Clymer
    Thomas Fitzsimons
    Jared Ingersoll
    James Wilson
    Gouverneur Morris
Delaware
    George Read
    Gunning Bedford Jr.
    John Dickinson
    Richard Bassett
    Jacob Broom
Maryland
    James McHenry
    Daniel of St. Thomas Jenifer
    Daniel Carroll
Virginia
    John Blair
    James Madison Jr.

North Carolina
    William Blount
    Richard Dobbs Spaight
    Hugh Williamson
South Carolina
    John Rutledge
    Charles Coatsworth Pinckney
    Charles Pinckney
    Pierce Butler
Georgia
    William Few
    Abraham Baldwin

APPENDIX TWO

The Data and Their Sources

The Economic and Ideological Interests at the
Philadelphia Convention

Because most of the fifty-five delegates who attended the Philadelphia convention were quite prominent, information about their economic and other interests is sufficiently available. Data on all fifty-five have been collected, though the statistical analyses of the Philadelphia convention include only the fifty-three delegates who remained after the first two weeks. The two primary sources of the data on the economic and other interests of the delegates are the detailed economic profiles contained in McDonald (1958, chap. 3) and the detailed biographical profiles contained in Rossiter (1966, chaps. 5–8). Although the ownership of many assets by the delegates in 1787 can be determined with a reasonable degree of accuracy, the monetary value of the majority of these assets cannot be determined. Consequently, many of the measures of economic interests are qualitative variables. They are dichotomous, dummy variables (measured as a 1 or a 0), indicating whether a delegate owned a particular asset or had a certain characteristic. The specific variables employed to measure the personal economic interests, PE, for each delegate are the delegate's principal occupation, ownership of private securities (primarily bank stock), the face value of the private securities owned, ownership of public securities (primarily Revolutionary War debt), the estimated market value of the public securities owned, ownership of slaves, number of slaves owned, the estimated market value of slaves owned, ownership of western lands, and whether a delegate was a net debtor. As an alternative to determining the importance of public securities holdings at the convention, a variable that measures for each delegate the estimated appreciation in the delegate's public securities holdings between 1787 and 1791, the time of the national government's assumption of the public debt, from data contained in McDonald (1958, p. 90), also is employed. The foregoing measures of economic interests represent the activities and assets in which wealth in the 1780s generally would have been concentrated, and for which data are available.

Men of much substance during the eighteenth century commonly were quite versatile and seldom would have had a single occupation as most individuals would today. The delegates to Philadelphia were no exception, making it less than completely accurate for one to refer to a delegate's primary occupation or activity. Consequently, the determination of a delegate's primary occupation or activity ultimately involves a fair amount of judgment. In fact, in several cases delegates to Philadelphia are classified as having two primary occupations or activities (see table 3.1 in chapter 3).

The delegates generally can be classified into one of five primary callings (merchant, farmer, planter, politician, and lawyer). A merchant involved in interstate and possibly international commerce, a farmer primarily involved in home or local production, and a lawyer actively engaged in the practice of law are the principal occupations employed to represent occupational economic interests. The farmer category, while one of the principal occupations, however, includes only two of the delegates at Philadelphia. Because there were only two delegates who were farmers of just modest means with a less commercial, local orientation at the convention, they either voted together or opposite each other on each of the roll-call votes. Because of this, in the statistical analysis of the individual votes at Philadelphia, the farmer variable often must be excluded from the model specification in order to obtain the maximum likelihood estimates. (The measurement of the individual votes themselves is discussed in detail in chapter 3.)

The lawyer occupation is most likely overrepresented. Many delegates who were lawyers also can be classified under another occupation. Often lawyers were politicians, planters, or merchants as well. Many college-educated men in the eighteenth century studied the law yet were not primarily practicing attorneys. Because the economic interests of the clients of delegates who were practicing attorneys are not known with any degree of certainty, a delegate's expected vote based on economic interests on any particular issue cannot be determined. Accordingly, the results for the lawyer category must be interpreted cautiously as an economic-interest category.

Because being a politician generally was not the primary economic livelihood of any of the Philadelphia delegates, the politician category, while employed in the statistical analysis of voting, is *not* considered a pecuniary economic interest per se. It may be more appropriate to interpret the results for politicians as estimating the influence of a nonpecuniary, ideological-type of interest.

The planter category is *not* employed in the statistical analysis because, being correlated with slave ownership, it would merely capture the effects of slaveowning on the part of a delegate. Delegates who were not farmers, lawyers, merchants, or slaveowners are the excluded occupational category in the statistical analysis of voting and may have been, for example, judges, ministers, physicians, or, in one case, a printer.

In addition to utilizing McDonald (1958) and Rossiter (1966), data for the economic interests and principal occupations of the Philadelphia delegates are from three other sources: Main (1960, pp. 86–110), Kelly and Harbison (1970, pp. 114–121), and Brown (1976, pp. 465–480). Brown (1976) and Main (1960) offer corrections to four of the economic interest categories listed in McDonald (1958) for a small number of delegates to the Philadelphia convention. They offer corrections to which delegates were merchants, farmers, or deeply in debt, as well as corrections to the number of slaves owned by several delegates. Brown classifies more delegates as merchants than does McDonald. (McDonald employs a more narrow definition.) Brown classifies fewer delegates as farmers because he excludes planters from the farmer classification. (McDonald tends to classify planters as farmers.) As a result, the two delegates classified as "farmer" here do not own any slaves. Main classifies fewer delegates (only three) as debtors because he includes only delegates who were both net debtors and relatively poor. (McDonald appears to include any delegate with a cash-flow problem.) The assessments of economic interests contained in Brown (1976) and Main (1960) are quite similar to the assessments contained in Rossiter (1966), who offers a detailed and documented assessment of the primary occupations and economic activities during the 1780s of the fifty-five delegates. These assessments are generally consistent with the short discussion contained in Kelly and Harbison (1970) as well. Because the classification of the economic interests and primary occupations is ultimately subjectively determined from less than perfect data, the two primary sources, with the corrections to them, are used to measure the economic interest variables that are employed in this reexamination of the drafting of the Constitution at the Philadelphia convention.

The variables that serve as the markers for the personal ideology of the delegates, PI, are each delegate's age, number of children, whether the delegate served in the military during the Revolutionary War, whether the delegate was an officer in the military, whether the delegate was a member of the Continental Congress, and whether a delegate was an English descendent. The qualitative variables are measured as dichotomous, dummy variables (measured as a 1 or a 0), indicating whether the delegate had the particular characteristic. Given the prominence of the individuals involved, this information is readily available in historical biographical dictionaries and encyclopedias. The data are from various volumes of *Biographical Directory of the American Congress, 1774–1961* (1961), *Dictionary of American Biography* (1928–1936), and *The National Cyclopaedia of American Biography* (1891).

Measures of the economic interests of the constituents of a delegate, CE, are not as readily available. The wealth status of constituents in each of the twelve states represented at the Philadelphia convention is measured employing six alternative measures of state wealth derived from the estimates of wealth per probate-type wealthholder in 1774 contained in Jones (1980, pp. 377–379). The six wealth estimates in Jones are wealth (net worth), total physical wealth, landholdings, slaves, financial claims, and financial liabilities. Average state wealth (for all six measures) for each state was estimated as a population-weighted average of the county wealth estimates for each state reported in Jones. Because no counties in New Hampshire or Georgia are included in the county wealth estimates, the estimates of average wealth in Jones for the New England region and the South are employed as estimates of average wealth in New Hampshire and Georgia, respectively. The wealth and total physical wealth estimates are substitutes for each other. As the other four wealth estimates are for particular types of assets, and in an attempt to capture the possible portfolio effects of wealth holdings in particular assets, the other four estimates (landholdings, slaves, financial claims, and financial liabilities) are calculated as a share of the wealth (net worth) estimate for each state. Each of the four wealth estimates for each state is divided by the net worth estimate for the state.

The wealth estimates in Jones are employed because contemporaneous measures of each state's wealth do not exist. To say the least, the estimates should be considered very rough approximations of the actual wealth of each state in 1787. To the extent that neither price levels nor real wealth levels in one state relative to other states changed dramatically during the 1774–1787 period, the measures of wealth derived from the estimates in Jones may serve as approximations of the *relative* wealth across states in 1787. The evidence presented in Walton and Shepherd (1979, chap. 9) suggests that it is at least approximately true that neither relative price nor wealth levels changed much across the states. In any case, the state wealth estimates are employed primarily in an attempt to control for the potential confounding influences of differences in the wealth of constituents across the twelve states. They are not employed in an attempt to estimate the influence of the actual wealth of constituents in a particular state on the votes at Philadelphia.

Another variable was constructed as a measure of constituent economic interests in an alternative attempt to capture the amount of economic or commercial activity among a delegate's constituents. Following the pioneering work of Libby (1894), historians contend that individuals from coastal areas or nearer navigable water were more likely to support issues that would strengthen the national government because they tended to be more commercially oriented than individuals from the more isolated backcountry (see Benson, 1960; Hutson, 1981; Main, 1961). Accordingly, a variable was constructed that measures the distance each delegate lived from navigable water or commercial areas. Four distance measurements were calculated as alternative measures of the amount of commercial activities in a delegate's home county: the distance from the delegate's home (1) to the nearest body of navigable water, (2) to the Atlantic coast, (3) to the nearest major city, and (4) to Philadelphia. In all four cases, distance is measured as the straight-line distance from the center of a delegate's county. With the exception of distance to Philadelphia, the distance measures produce nearly identical statistical results. The distance measurements were calculated from the historical maps contained in Cappon (1976).

Several alternative measures are employed to capture the effects of the slave interests of constituents in each of the twelve states. Three of the variables are slaves per 100 whites, slaves per slaveowning family, and the percentage of families owning slaves in each state. The data are from the 1790 census and can be found in United States Department of Commerce (1969, pp. 116–120, 135–140, 271–290). The estimate of the share (proportion) of wealth (net worth) in slaves in each state derived from the wealth estimates in Jones (1980) also serves as a fourth measure of slave interests for each state.

Given that funding the public debt (primarily Revolutionary War debt) was a major part of the debate over the Constitution, the public securities holdings of citizens might have been an important factor in explaining a delegate's vote. A proxy for the public creditor interests of constituents across the twelve states is the public funding credit per capita for each state at settlement of the national debt. The public funding credit is the amount of Revolutionary War expenditures that each state was either due from the national government, or owed to it, subsequent to funding the public debt in 1793. The data on the public credit or liability of a state at settlement in 1793 are from Ferguson (1961, pp. 331–333). The variable is at best a rough approximation to the public creditor interests of constituents. It is also employed in an attempt to control for the potential confounding influences of differences in the public securities holdings of constituents across the twelve states. It is not employed in an attempt to estimate the influence of the actual public securities holdings of constituents in a particular state on the votes at Philadelphia. The estimates of the share of wealth in financial claims and the share of wealth in financial liabilities for each state derived from the estimates in Jones (1980) serve as alternative approximate measures of the creditor and debtor interests of the constituents in each state as well. Specific measures of the holdings of public securities or the amount of debt among citizens for each state in 1787 do not exist.

Variables that serve as markers for the ideology of the constituents of a delegate, CI, are also not as readily abundant as are measures of the personal economic and other interests of the delegates to Philadelphia. Three variables that are employed as markers for constituent ideology across the states are each state's total white population, the percentage of families of English ancestry in each state, and the percentage of families of Scottish/Irish ancestry in each state. The total white population for each state is from United States Department of Commerce 1975). The ancestry data are from United States Department of Commerce (1969). The data for the three variables are from the 1790 census. The variables, while far from perfect markers for ideological differences across the states, at least capture and control for some nonpecuniary differences across the states. Many historians have argued that delegates representing more populous states were more likely to vote for issues that would strengthen the national government (see Nadelhaft, 1981; Risjord, 1978; Spaulding, 1932). Other historians have argued that delegates representing areas with a greater concentration of individuals of English ancestry, especially as opposed to Scottish or Irish ancestry, were likewise more supportive of a stronger national government (see Brown, 1976; Main, 1961).

The Economic and Ideological Interests at the State Ratifying Conventions

Data on the personal economic interests and constituent interests of 1,227 of the 1,648 delegates that attended the thirteen state ratifying conventions were initially collected. But because of missing observations for several of the primary measures of the economic interests, the data yielded a usable sample of 1,212 delegates. A primary source of the data on the personal economic interests of the ratifiers is McDonald (1958), which contains detailed economic profiles for nearly 75 percent of the ratifying delegates. McDonald includes a greater variety of assets for the ratifying delegates than for the delegates that attended the Philadelphia convention, but with less completeness. The assets owned by the state delegates that McDonald lists are the value of public securities holdings, the number of slaves owned, and in some instances acres (or value) of land owned, and the quantity of horses, livestock, ships, warehouses, mills, foundries, carriages, and a few other belongings. McDonald also includes several nonquantitative economic interests. The qualitative data are each delegate's principal occupation and a determination from the available records whether a delegate possessed private securities interests (owned bank stock, held private notes, or were otherwise private creditors), whether delegates were deeply in debt, and whether they owned western land (land on the frontier). The variables are measured as dichotomous, dummy variables (measured as a 1 or a 0), indicating whether a delegate possessed the asset or characteristic. McDonald seldom included the dollar value for private securities holdings, debts, or western landholdings. But McDonald included an estimate of the income for each delegate for one state—Delaware—that was unique in that it levied an income tax in the eighteenth century.

McDonald's (1958) data for the personal economic interests of the ratifiers, which are not in a single location but are spread over more than 200 pages (pp. 113–346), are supplemented in this study with information contained in Main (1973), Lynd (1962), and Pool (1950a,b). The additional data, with the exception of Pool's, are limited to a few variables for a small number of delegates.

The data on the personal economic interests for the North Carolina delegates, with the exception of the value of public securities holdings contained in McDonald, are from Pool (1950a,b). The data for the first North Carolina convention, which rejected the Constitution, are employed in the empirical analysis. The second convention, which ratified the Constitution, was held well after nine states ratified the Constitution and the issue of ratification was moot, so it is less likely to reflect true voting sentiments than would votes at the first North Carolina convention.

The completeness of McDonald's (1958) data varies considerably across the conventions. For all thirteen state ratifying conventions, McDonald reports the principal occupation and public securities holdings of virtually all the delegates for whom he reports any economic information, and includes his determination of the three qualitative characteristics (private creditor, debtor, and western landowner status) for many delegates. Data on the number of slaves owned, including Pool's data, are reasonably complete for all southern states except Georgia. The value or amount of nonwestern landholdings and the quantity of the other types of assets are reported more sporadically, and in fact are so sporadic that they are not directly employed in the statistical analysis of the ratification of the Constitution. Overall, the best data are for Virginia, South Carolina, and Maryland. The worst data are for Delaware and New York.

McDonald's occupational groupings for the delegates to the state ratifying conventions number about one dozen, but most delegates fall into one of four major occupations (merchant, farmer, planter, and lawyer). As in the analysis of the Philadelphia convention, merchant and farmer are employed in the statistical analysis of the ratification vote (each measured as a 1 or a 0, indicating whether a delegate was a merchant, farmer, or neither). Because McDonald did not distinguish clearly between farmer and planter, all small planters (delegates McDonald classified as planters who owned three or fewer slaves) are classified as farmers. Thus, the farmer category for the state ratifying conventions is not strictly comparable to the farmer category for the Philadelphia convention, which includes only two delegates of just modest means (with no slaves) categorized as farmers. The remaining planter category is not employed for the ratifying conventions because, as noted for Philadelphia, it would merely capture the effects of slaveowning. The lawyer occupation, again as noted for Philadelphia, is most likely overrepresented. Most delegates McDonald (1958) listed as lawyers also are classified with another occupation. Moreover, the voting expectations of the ratification delegates who were lawyers cannot be determined with much degree of certainty because accurate information about their clients is not readily available with much degree of certainty. The lawyer category accordingly is not used as an economic interest category for the analysis of the ratification vote. Delegates who were not farmers, merchants, or slaveowners are the excluded category in the logistic estimation of the ratification vote and may have been shopkeepers, frontiersmen, ministers, lawyers, politicians, or some other occupation. (Although a politician category was not initially employed in the analysis of the 1,212 delegates for the thirteen ratifying conventions, as noted below, local, state, and national politician variables were collected and ultimately, formally analyzed for 735 delegates from the Massachusetts, North Carolina, and Virginia conventions.)

Because McDonald's (1958) economic profiles for many state convention delegates contain such a great variety of assets, it is possible to obtain additional measures of the delegates' personal economic interests. It is also possible to obtain asset share measures for the slave and public securities holdings of a delegate, the only two continuous quantitative variables for which enough data are available for a large proportion of the delegates to the state ratifying conventions. The asset share measures allow the value of public securities and the value of slaveholdings of a delegate to be measured in terms of their *relative* value of the total assets of a delegate. The share measures thus allow an attempt to measure a portfolio effect of public securities holdings and slaveholdings. The share measures are based on calculating a very rough estimate of the value of a delegate's total assets and computing the share of the value of total assets held in slaves or public securities. The value of total assets of a delegate is calculated as the sum across assets of the product of the amount of a particular type of asset owned by a delegate and the value of a unit of that asset. The approximate values of various types of assets, except for slaves, for each state are obtained from Jones (1977).

McDonald reports only the number of slaves owned, not the age distribution or value of slaveholdings. The value of slaveholdings, accordingly, is calculated by multiplying the number of slaves by an estimate of the average slave price from a sample of slave prices obtained from Stanley L. Engerman (personal correspondence, 1983/1984): Slave prices for prime female and prime male for five years in the late 1780s were used to estimate the average slave price. The slave prices for prime females in Maryland pounds are £57.1 in 1786, £45.0 in 1787, £45.3 in 1788, £48.8 in 1789, and £45.7 in 1790. The slave prices for prime males are £68.5 in 1786, £58.0 in 1787, £60.4 in 1788, £56.9 in 1789, and £65.6 in 1790. The simple average of the slave prices is £55.13. At contemporaneous exchange rates between Maryland pounds and dollars, the average slave price is approximately $185.

The computation of land values is less straightforward. In some instances, McDonald (1958) reports only acres or the value of landholdings, and in a few cases both. In many cases, the location of the land is provided. From McDonald's land data and similar information in Jones (1977), very rough estimates of average prices per acre of land can be obtained for general locations. To estimate the value of landholdings, the number of acres owned is multiplied by the average price per acre for each general location. The values of other types of assets (such as livestock, horses, carriages, and the like) are estimated by calculating the average value of similar assets listed in Jones (1977) in the delegate's state. All values are converted to 1787 levels for Delaware, New Jersey, and Pennsylvania, to 1790 levels for Rhode Island, and to 1788 levels for all remaining states. Because Jones does not include data for all thirteen states, estimates of the values of assets from adjacent states are used for delegates in states Jones does not include (Jones, 1977, vol. 1, figs. 2–4).

Because not all assets are included in McDonald's (1958) profiles for each delegate, the value of a residual "other assets" is added to the total asset value. The "other assets" estimate, which is based on a delegate's principal occupation and state of residence, is obtained indirectly from Jones (1977). Estimation of the value of "other assets" is at best very rough. It is calculated in three steps. First, the values of the types of assets typically reported by McDonald in a particular state are summed for the sample of individuals contained in Jones for the same state. Second, the percentage of the total assets of each individual in Jones accounted for by the types of assets reported in McDonald are then calculated. In the final step, the average of this percentage for broad occupational classifications (e.g., farmer or merchant) is employed to estimate the value of each delegate's "other assets" in each occupational classification: $V_{OTHER} = V_{SUBTOTAL} [(100/A_{PERCENT}) - A_{PERCENT}]$, where V_{OTHER} is the value of other assets, $V_{SUBTOTAL}$ is the value of reported assets, and $A_{PERCENT}$ is the average reported assets as a percentage of total assets in the Jones sample. For delegates in states not included in the Jones sample, estimates of $A_{PERCENT}$ from adjacent states are used. The values are all converted to 1787, 1788, or 1790 levels, depending on the state, as noted above.

Obviously, the asset value measures and asset share variables contain much error. The measurement error in an explanatory variable makes any multivariate regression method an inconsistent estimation technique. In an attempt to alleviate the errors-in-variables problem, four alternative measures of specific economic interests are initially employed for the statistical examination of the overall ratification process: (1) a simple dichotomous, dummy variable (a 1 or a 0) indicating whether the delegate owned a particular asset or possessed a certain economic interest (e.g., public securities or slaves); (2) the estimated, and approximate, value of an economic interest (where applicable and available); (3) the estimated, and approximate, share of the value of the delegate's total assets held in a particular asset (again, where data permit); and (4) instrumental variables for the asset share measures. The alternative variables are employed to determine the sensitivity of the statistical results to errors in measurement.

Dichotomous (dummy) variables are less likely to be measured with error than are quantitative measurements, but they contain less information. The second alternative—the quantitative measures (continuous variables)—while containing more information (and more error), do not account for the relative value of a particular economic interest (i.e., relative to a delegate's total wealth), which might have been a more important influence on voting behavior than the absolute value of the asset. The third alternative—asset share variables—takes into account the relative value of a particular economic interest. But the variables are measured with even more error than are the other variables because very rough estimates of the value of a delegate's total wealth must be made to compute each asset share variable. The fourth alternative—instrumental variables—represents a standard statistical technique commonly employed to correct for the errors-in-variables problem (see Maddala, 1977, pp. 296–300). The technique in essence converts the share variable into a less demanding categorical variable. To construct an instrumental variable, each delegate's share measure, the slave share and public securities share, is regressed on the quartile rank of the delegate's asset share within the particular sample analyzed. The resulting regression equations are used to construct two predicted asset share variables, the slave instrument and public securities instrument, which are then employed as the instrumental variables in place of the original asset share variables.

The specific variables employed to measure the personal economic interests, PE, for each ratifying convention delegate are the delegate's principal occupation (whether a delegate was a merchant, a farmer, or neither), ownership of private securities, ownership of public securities, market value of the public securities owned, share of wealth held in public securities, the public securities instrumental variable, ownership of slaves, market value of slaves owned, share of wealth held in slaves, the slave instrumental variable, ownership of western lands, and whether a delegate was a net debtor.

To determine if there was a threshold level of public securities that affected voting on ratification, a dichotomous dummy variable (a 1 or a 0) was constructed that measures ownership of public securities among delegates with holdings greater than $1,000 in market value—an amount from nearly ten to over twenty-three times more than estimates of income per free person during the late eighteenth century. Walton and Rockoff (1998, table 5.4, p. 109) estimate income per free person on the eve of the Revolution in the range of £9.5 to £20.5 (about $47.50 to $102.50, in 1774 dollars), depending on the region considered and the capital-output ratio assumed. Their income estimates are derived from non-human physical wealth estimates in Alice Hanson Jones (1980), as presented in Walton and Rockoff (table 5.3, p. 109), which range from £38 to £62 per free person (about $190 to $310, in 1774 dollars), depending on the region considered. Schuyler (1961), noting that Charles Beard argued that individuals with "large" public securities holdings were perhaps the most important element during ratification, suggested long ago that there should be "a distinction between large and small security holders (taking, say, $1,000 in face value of securities held as the line of division between the two groups)" (p. 77). The more appropriate figure, however, is $1,000 *in market value*, as employed here.

Information on the personal and political characteristics of the delegates that can serve as markers for their personal ideology, PI, are not included in the economic profiles of the state ratifying convention delegates compiled by McDonald (1958). Because many of the delegates who attended the ratifying conventions are not nearly as prominent as those who attended the Philadelphia convention, data on the personal characteristics for many of the delegates for which economic profiles exist are not readily available. As a consequence, data on the personal and political characteristics that serve as markers for the personal ideology of the ratifying delegates, PI, are collected only for three of the state ratifying conventions—Massachusetts, North Carolina, and Virginia. The three conventions are chosen because they were among the most important and largest ratifying conventions. Massachusetts was a key New England state and Virginia was a key southern state in the contest over ratification; both were crucial to union. And North Carolina was the only state convention to explicitly reject the Constitution. The additional data collected for the Massachusetts, North Carolina, and Virginia conventions are discussed below following the discussion of the constituent variables employed in the examination of voting at the ratifying conventions.

The availability of data to measure the economic interests and ideologies of the constituents of the state convention delegates at an aggregation level below the state level are severely limited. One measure of constituent economic interests, CE, is the slaveholdings per 100 whites in a county or township of a state, which are available for each of the thirteen states. Slaveholdings per slaveowning family and percentage of families owning slaves are not available at the county or township level. The data for slaveholdings of the population for each delegate's area of representation (the county or township) are from the 1790 census in United States Department of Commerce (1969). As another measure of constituent economic interests, estimates of the distance from each delegate's home county to the nearest body of navigable water and distance from each delegate's home county to the Atlantic coast (including the Chesapeake) were complied. Substitutes for one another, the distance measures serve as proxies for the commercial activities of the constituents in the home county of each delegate. Distance is measured as the straight-line distance from the center of a delegate's home county. The distance measurements were calculated from the historical maps contained in Cappon (1976). No direct measures of the amount or value of commercial activities during the 1780s exist at the county or township level. Historical accounts of the 1780s suggest the amount of commercial activities in a local area would have been strongly correlated with direct access to navigable water, the coast, or a major city. One variable that serves as a marker for the ideology of a delegate's constituents, CI, which is available at the county or township level within each state, is the ancestry of families in each county or township. The data for ancestry of the population for each delegate's area of representation (the county or township) are from the 1790 census in United States Department of Commerce (1969).

For an analysis of the ratification vote during the overall ratification process that employs various samples of the state ratifying conventions pooled together, state-level variables can be employed as measures of constituent interests across states. Accordingly, the public funding credit per capita in each state, measured only at the state level, can be employed as a variable measuring constituent economic interests (CE) for the pooled samples of states. And population in each state, measured only at the state level, can be employed as a variable serving as a marker for constituent ideological interests (CI) for the pooled samples. But one cost of analyzing the state conventions separately is that constituent characteristics that are measurable at the state level only must be excluded because an analysis of the ratification vote at an individual convention requires the data to be measured at the county or township level, the delegate's area of representation. Thus, for an analysis of the ratification vote within individual conventions, neither the public funding credit per capita nor population can be employed for constituent interests because both are measured only at the state level. Nor can any of the various types of county wealth estimates computed by Jones (1980) be employed for an analysis of the vote within an individual state convention because the wealth estimates are available for only a limited sample of the counties in eleven of the thirteen states. This lack of data severely limits the measures of constituent economic interests and ideologies for the ratification process within individual state conventions.

The ratification votes for the delegates to the thirteen ratifying conventions for whom data were collected are from McDonald (1958) and the records of the debates at the ratifying conventions contained in Elliot (1836 [1888]) and Jensen (1976). In addition, the voting records contained in *Massachusetts Ratification Project* (1989) were used to verify the ratification votes of the Massachusetts delegates. The voting records contained in the *Journal of the Convention of North-Carolina* (1788) were used to verify the ratification votes of the North Carolina delegates.

Additional Data for the Massachusetts, North Carolina, and Virginia Ratifying Conventions

Additional data on the personal attributes and political experiences of the delegates to the Massachusetts, North Carolina, and Virginia conventions were collected. For the Massachusetts convention, data were collected for 93 more delegates (43 percent more) than initially. For the first North Carolina convention, which rejected the Constitution, data were collected for 41 more delegates (about 19 percent more) than initially. For the Virginia convention, data were collected for 11 more delegates (7 percent more) than initially. The data on the personal attributes and political experiences were collected for 309 (87 percent) of the 355 Massachusetts delegates, 261 (97 percent) of the 268 North Carolina delegates, and 165 (98 percent) of the 168 Virginia delegates. As a result, including the 1,212 ratification delegates for whom usable data were initially collected, data were collected for a total of 1,357 (or 82 percent) of the 1,648 ratification delegates. Additional data were also collected for several economic interest variables for many of the delegates at the three conventions. In particular, a greater number of delegates have been identified as merchants, private creditors, private debtors, and western landowners, especially for Massachusetts and North Carolina, where the data were initially so limited that in several cases variables could not be included in the economic model of voting without the new data.

The data on the personal characteristics that are employed as the markers for a delegate's personal ideology, PI, are the delegate's age, ancestry (ethnicity), religion, whether he was an officer in the Revolutionary War, and a large number of measures of political experience. The political-experience variables are whether the delegate held any positions in local government before or after ratification, in state government before or after ratification, whether he served in the Continental Congress before ratification or in the national government after ratification. Because the variables other than age are qualitative variables, they are measured as dichotomous dummy variables (measured as a 1 or a 0), indicating whether the delegate possessed the particular attribute or characteristic. Data for the religious affiliation, age structure, or occupations of the populations of the three states at the county or township level are not available.

The primary source of the personal characteristics of the Massachusetts delegates is an archival project that collected detailed personal biographies for all delegates (*Massachusetts Ratification Project*, 1989). One of the sources of the personal characteristics for the North Carolina delegates is the raw data from Risjord (1978), which includes the age, ancestry, religion, and political offices held for many delegates. Other sources for North Carolina are Massengill (1988), which includes political offices for nearly all delegates and age for some, and Powell (1979–1996), which includes most personal characteristics for the more prominent delegates. Revolutionary War experience for North Carolina is contained in *Rosters of Soldiers from North Carolina* (1972). The majority of data for the personal characteristics of the Virginia delegates is complied from *Appleton's Cyclopdia* (1888–1889), *Dictionary of American Biography* (1928–1936), Foote (1966), Heitman (1914), *National Cyclopedia* (1892–1950), and *Reluctant Ratifiers* (1988). Risjord's (1978) raw data also contain political experience for many Virginia delegates. For the delegates for all three state conventions, political experience in the Continental Congress prior to ratification and in the new national government after are contained in *Biographical Directory of the American Congress* (1961), Chase, Krislov, Boyom, and Clark (1976), and Sobel (1990).

The data collected on several of the personal characteristics (age, ethnicity, and religious affiliation) were not complete for all delegates in the samples for the three conventions. In an attempt to use as many of the variables as possible for all delegates in the samples, delegates with unknown age, ethnicity, and religious affiliation were assigned an imputed value for their missing observations. The imputed value for a missing observation was the average of the known values for each variable for each convention. For the Massachusetts convention, data on age were collected for 294 of the 309 delegates in the Massachusetts sample; data on ethnicity (English and Irish/Scottish ancestries) were collected for 266 delegates; data on religious affiliation were collected for 206 delegates. The averages of the known values for Massachusetts are: (1) age, 49.6 years; English ancestry, .838; Irish/Scottish ancestry, .139; Baptist, .0874; Congregational/Puritan, .699; Episcopalian/Anglican, .0194; and Presbyterian, .0583. For the North Carolina convention, data on age were collected for 86 of the 261 delegates in the North Carolina sample; data on ethnicity were collected for 35 delegates; data on religious affiliation were collected for 26 delegates. The averages of the known values for North Carolina are: (1) age, 41.76 years; English ancestry, .371; Irish/Scottish ancestry, .629; Baptist, .269; Congregational/Puritan, 0; Episcopalian/Anglican, .385; and Presbyterian, .231. For the Virginia convention, data on age were collected for 88 of the 165 delegates in the Virginia sample; data on ethnicity were collected for 80 delegates; data on religious affiliation were collected for 46 delegates. The averages of the known values for Virginia are: (1) age, 42.43 years; English ancestry, .538; Irish/Scottish ancestry, .363; Baptist, 0; Congregational/Puritan, 0; Episcopalian/Anglican, .804; and Presbyterian, .0870. Because of the small number of known values for some of the variables, however, not all are employed in the logistic estimation of the ratification votes for each of the three conventions.

In addition to the data on the economic interests of the ratifying delegates contained in McDonald (1958), *Massachusetts Ratification Project* (1989) includes data on the personal economic interests for the Massachusetts delegates. Other sources of data on the personal economic interests of the North Carolina delegates are Massengill (1988) and Powell (1979–1996), which contains data on the more prominent North Carolina delegates, including the principal occupation for all delegates for which he includes an economic biography. Risjord's (1978) raw data include information on the personal economic interests, mainly on occupations, for the Virginia delegates.

A Caveat on the Economic and Ideology Categories

A caution regarding the labeling of variables as "economic" or "ideological" is in order given the possibility that some variables might reflect both the economic interests and the ideology of a delegate. For example, public securities holdings (Revolutionary War debt) might proxy ideological preferences for the new government because holders of the public debt could have been investing in a cause—the Revolutionary War. Likewise, the distance variables might proxy a localist ideological orientation as well as capturing the lack of commercial activities in a particular location. Similarly, it is plausible to suggest that age might be at least partly an economic interest variable, because it could proxy for wealth (given life-cycle wealth accumulation). Or, officer might be partly an economic interest variable also, as well as capturing ideological orientation of a delegate, because officers and members of the Society of the Cincinnati were paid for their services in land warrants and depreciated securities. Other of the markers for ideology, however—ancestry, military service in general, or religion—would not appear to reflect obvious, *specific* economic interests. The choice of the "economic" or "ideology" label ultimately reflects a subjective assessment of the primary source of the variable's impact on voting. As a result, the distinction in this study is between primarily economic (or pecuniary) interests and primarily ideological (or nonpecuniary) interests.

Furthermore, differences in the opportunity costs of individuals associated with different personal characteristics—for example, changes in opportunity costs as individuals grow older—provide a rationale for the use of personal characteristics as markers for ideology. As North (1981) contends, "in strictly opportunity cost terms one can predict that the ideology of a young adult will be different from that of a middle-aged adult" (p. 50). While arguing for a broader view of ideology than merely an economic-based perspective, North suggests that differences in other personal characteristics—such as ethnicity—should also predict differences in ideology across individuals.

Full and Parsimonious Voting Models for the Philadelphia Convention

Table A3.1. Voting Outcomes for the Sixteen Issues at the Philadelphia Constitutional Convention of 1787

Vote[a]	Yes		No		Not Voting		Percent Yes[b]	
	Actual	Adjusted	Actual	Adjusted	Actual	Adjusted	Actual	Adjusted
1	16	20	28	33	9	0	36.4	37.7
2	19	22	24	31	10	0	44.2	41.5
3	17	19	32	34	4	0	34.7	35.8
4	10	14	31	39	12	0	24.4	26.4
5	9	15	34	38	10	0	20.9	28.3
6	10	15	33	38	10	0	23.3	28.3
7	23	28	22	25	8	0	51.1	52.8
8	32	37	10	16	11	0	76.2	69.8
9	33	41	6	12	14	0	84.6	77.4
10	29	36	10	17	14	0	74.4	67.9
11	13	20	29	33	11	0	30.9	37.7
12	15	22	27	31	11	0	35.7	41.5
13	25	30	17	23	11	0	59.5	56.6
14	12	18	30	35	11	0	28.6	34.0
15	32	38	9	15	12	0	78.0	71.7
16	3	12	33	41	17	0	8.3	22.6

[a] The actual vote is the probable vote of the delegates at the convention as determined from Farrand (1911, vol. 1, pp. 130–147, 162–173, 369–382; vol. 2, pp. 84–96, 116–128, 245–256, 352–365, 380–395, 434–440, 445–456, 457–470, 621–640). The adjusted vote is the actual vote plus the imputed vote for not voting delegates under the assumptions described in the text.

[b] Number of yes votes divided by the sum of yes and no votes.

Source: Reprinted from McGuire and Ohsfeldt (1986, table 3, p. 99), with permission.

Table A3.2a. Estimated Logistic Coefficients of the Explanatory Variables in the Full Voting Model for the Philadelphia Convention: Votes 1 through 8

Explanatory Variables	Votes							
	1	2	3	4	5	6	7	8
Constant	-6.7127 (9.1444)	-12.3918[c] (8.0329)	-2.4688 (7.4632)	-16.3802 (13.8556)	9.2605[c] (6.1954)	32.7128[b] (19.0443)	-250.7[c] (156.6)	-6.6545[c] (7.1321)
Personal Economic Interests								
Western landowner	-0.7935 (1.5174)	-1.7172 (1.5276)	2.9225 (2.4163)	2.9335[c] (2.1823)	2.8499[b] (1.6171)	-4.4363[c] (3.2378)	-7.4547[c] (5.2505)	1.1571 (1.8160)
Merchant	-1.5051 (2.4597)	-1.4026 (2.3947)	-9.3601[c] (6.2128)	-5.5739[c] (4.0232)	0.1453 (2.2037)	—	7.2982 (7.6880)	7.1945[a] (3.2208)
Farmer	3.0330 (6.7001)	U[No]	—	-1.2357 (3.9100)	—	0.6304 (137.9)	17.4136[c] (11.2448)	—
Lawyer	2.9322 (2.3336)	3.0875[c] (2.0994)	—	-1.6045 (1.8951)	0.7310 (1.6197)	—	—	2.1127 (1.4916)
Politician	3.5510[c] (2.2614)	1.6906 (1.7753)	-1.1128 (2.4733)	-2.0502 (2.4126)	2.8008[c] (2.1266)	-2.9428 (2.6562)	—	5.6411[a] (2.6951)
Debtor	4.4088 (3.5001)	-0.0270 (2.5754)	10.8558 (12.9550)	7.6227[b] (4.3424)	2.4804 (2.3000)	9.9375[c] (7.2992)	U[Yes]	-6.5335[a] (2.9044)
Number of slaves	0.0394[c] (0.0259)	-0.0242 (0.0200)	0.00894 (0.0269)	0.00144 (0.0176)	0.0129 (0.0151)	0.1159[b] (0.0647)	0.2807[c] (0.1967)	-0.0717[a] (0.0331)
Value of public securities	0.6607[b] (0.3694)	-0.0551 (0.2780)	0.4306 (0.4303)	0.3816 (0.4580)	0.2674 (0.3224)	1.8467[a] (0.8545)	-0.9897[c] (0.7328)	-0.8182[b] (0.4256)
Value of private securities	U[No]	0.1630 (0.2164)	-1.8950[c] (1.2021)	U[No]	—	-0.0885 (0.3441)	-1.7380[c] (1.3261)	0.2387 (0.2182)
Personal Ideology								
Age	0.0768 (0.0603)	-0.0261 (0.0517)	-0.1052[c] (0.0760)	-0.0249 (0.0728)	-0.0826 (0.0738)	-0.4143[b] (0.2316)	0.4167[c] (0.3184)	0.0162 (0.0517)
Continental Congress	-1.0143 (2.0385)	2.0167[c] (1.4609)	—	1.0941 (2.1612)	-1.8302 (1.7952)	—	0.0435 (3.4349)	-3.4485[c] (2.1830)

Delegate-English ancestry	-1.2462 (1.5790)	0.5530 (1.3062)	-1.1132 (1.7910)	1.8742 (2.0273)	1.2218 (1.5357)	1.1855 (2.2142)	-57.0658[c] (37.3911)	1.8831[c] (1.3744)
Officer in war	-1.2610 (1.5134)	0.5086 (1.1691)	-6.2030[b] (3.3464)	-2.0679[c] (1.5983)	-2.8054[b] (1.5530)	-5.5777[a] (2.8330)	7.3750[c] (5.3998)	0.2523 (1.1456)
Constituents' Economic Interests								
Slaves per 100 whites	-0.1736[c] (0.1215)	-0.0496 (0.0565)	-0.1272[b] (0.0773)	-0.0401 (0.0484)	0.0516[c] (0.0366)	-0.1209 (0.0945)	-0.6920[c] (0.4309)	0.0624[c] (0.0427)
Public funding credit per capita	-0.1533 (0.1802)	-0.3706[b] (0.2064)	0.5333[b] (0.2851)	-0.3672[b] (0.2178)	0.0769 (0.1497)	-0.6534[b] (0.3365)	3.1408[c] (2.0599)	-0.2177[b] (0.1282)
Wealth	0.0132 (0.0130)	0.00506[b] (0.00297)	0.00207 (0.00272)	0.00252 (0.00325)	-0.00327[c] (0.00217)	-0.00673 (0.00876)	0.1764[b] (0.1054)	0.00895[a] (0.00408)
Distance to navigable water	-0.0264 (0.0207)	-0.0383[c] (0.0249)	0.0808 (0.0657)	0.0178 (0.0240)	0.0349[b] (0.0204)	0.0679[b] (0.0385)	0.1295[c] (0.0826)	-0.0451[a] (0.0186)
Constituents' Ideology								
State population	-0.0170[a] (0.00823)	0.0308[a] (0.0121)	-0.0102 (0.00826)	-0.00964 (0.0109)	-0.0124[b] (0.00748)	-0.0246[b] (0.0141)	0.00685 (0.0129)	0.0142[b] (0.00743)
English ancestry of citizens	0.0483 (0.0737)	0.0207 (0.0690)	0.1555[c] (0.1205)	0.1967[c] (0.1416)	-0.0675 (0.0595)	-0.1443[c] (0.1069)	2.6302[c] (1.6588)	0.00237 (0.0595)
Somers' D_{yx}	.883	.839	.923	.881	.909	.961	.974	.801
R^2	.539	.499	.583	.479	.460	.575	.666	.421

[a] Statistically significant at the .05 level.
[b] Statistically significant at the .10 level.
[c] P-value is less than .20. While not considered significant at conventional levels, the coefficient may be precise enough to be treated as significant given the small sample size. See Leamer (1978, chap. 4, especially pp. 102–108, 114–117).

Note: Number of observations is 53. The asymptotic standard errors are in parentheses. Each column contains the estimates for the full voting model, described in equation 3.1, for each issue. The dependent variable for each issue is the observed vote for that issue, where a yes vote equals 1 and a no vote equals 0. Variables marked with U^{yes} or U^{no} were excluded for the vote in question because all delegates with the characteristic voted unanimously, yes or no, respectively. Other variables were excluded from a particular vote only because the logit algorithm would not converge with all nineteen variables included for that vote. The excluded variables were chosen after an analysis determined they were the specific variables preventing convergence. The minimum necessary variables were excluded to allow the logit algorithm to converge for the vote. For the interest of the reader, the estimates for votes 1 and 3 have been reported despite the errors discovered in their data. As a result of the errors however, the findings for the two votes may be questionable. Somers' D_{yx} is a measure of the degree of concordance between the predicted probability and the observed vote for each observation. It is analogous to Kendall's rank correlation coefficient. R^2 is the generalized R^2 generated for logistic regression with the RSQUARE option in the current version of SAS (version 8.0). Somers' D_{yx} and R^2 are alternative measures of the goodness of fit of the estimated model.

Table A3.2b. Estimated Logistic Coefficients of the Explanatory Variables in the Full Voting Model for the Philadelphia Convention: Votes 9 through 16

Explanatory Variables				Votes				
	9	10	11	12	13	14	15	16
Constant	-3.8199	-12.5679[c]	-6.4522[c]	11.5197[c]	-26.7514[c]	11.8140[b]	-18.4398[a]	12.5796[b]
	(5.8761)	(8.4542)	(4.9808)	(7.2376)	(17.4637)	(6.6310)	(8.6156)	(7.6440)
Personal Economic Interests								
Western landowner	-1.3161	2.7495	1.1083	2.7952[c]	5.7082	2.4727[c]	0.5694	-2.9157[c]
	(1.2354)	(2.7394)	(1.1354)	(1.8136)	(4.5770)	(1.6608)	(2.1222)	(2.2078)
Merchant	-0.1183	8.1847[b]	0.9427	-2.0076	21.5929[c]	U^{No}	5.8664[c]	-0.5713
	(1.9861)	(4.2157)	(1.5524)	(1.7851)	(14.1462)		(4.5462)	(1.9798)
Farmer	—	—	-0.1836	-3.4062	1.1718	-1.7386	4.2999	—
			(4.0835)	(4.0777)	(3.5863)	(3.0608)	(5.6527)	
Lawyer	0.9821	2.9127[c]	0.6012	—	5.3283	-0.4442	3.6142[c]	4.4724[b]
	(1.5541)	(1.9677)	(1.3929)		(4.2693)	(1.7089)	(2.4953)	(2.4629)
Politician	-0.6880	5.7636[b]	1.7124	—	13.1933[b]	-0.6231	1.2426	10.2263[b]
	(1.5992)	(3.3563)	(1.6151)		(7.1291)	(1.7677)	(2.4960)	(5.3425)
Debtor	1.4122	-7.6033[a]	U^{No}	U^{No}	-17.4319[c]	-2.2733	-5.8795[c]	—
	(2.0081)	(3.7248)			(12.4944)	(2.1935)	(3.8468)	
Number of slaves	0.0213[c]	-0.0945[a]	0.0207	0.0484[a]	-0.1978[a]	-0.0105	-0.0593[b]	-0.00334
	(0.0131)	(0.0424)	(0.0200)	(0.0246)	(0.1118)	(0.0127)	(0.0327)	(0.0304)
Value of public securities	0.5753[b]	-1.2876[b]	0.3688[c]	0.2226	-3.4408[b]	-0.1241	-1.7020[a]	0.9884[c]
	(0.3479)	(0.6761)	(0.2794)	(0.2996)	(2.0195)	(0.3884)	(0.6718)	(0.6946)
Value of private securities	U^{Yes}	0.5204[b]	-0.2977[c]	-0.4035[b]	1.0944[c]	0.00237	0.3292[c]	U^{No}
		(0.2679)	(0.2321)	(0.2138)	(0.6884)	(0.0826)	(0.2482)	
Personal Ideology								
Age	0.0586	0.00342	0.00602	-0.0458	—	-0.0324	—	0.2523[b]
	(0.0632)	(0.0601)	(0.0484)	(0.0449)		(0.0657)		(0.1311)

258

	(1)	(2)	(3)	(4)	(5)	(6)	(7)	(8)
Continental Congress	1.7126	-2.2565	-2.2015[c]	-0.3132	-4.9407[c]	-0.4796	4.1811[c]	-5.0887[c]
	(1.3781)	(2.4275)	(1.5577)	(1.4909)	(3.6460)	(1.4067)	(2.6775)	(3.2387)
Delegate-English ancestry	-1.2689	2.0773	0.8336	-0.2374	1.9967	1.2898	-2.7560	3.3179[c]
	(1.2113)	(1.6610)	(1.1702)	(1.3349)	(2.0350)	(1.4122)	(2.2925)	(2.1943)
Officer in war	1.6997[c]	2.4121	-0.3444	0.2789	9.7738[c]	-3.2632[a]	3.6812[b]	-1.1458
	(1.2454)	(1.9070)	(1.0345)	(1.0491)	(6.6873)	(1.5250)	(2.2112)	(1.8672)
Constituents' Economic Interests								
Slaves per 100 whites	-0.0685[a]	0.00860	-0.0242	-0.0116	0.0170	0.1403[a]	-0.0285	0.0439
	(0.0335)	(0.0337)	(0.0328)	(0.0444)	(0.0558)	(0.0530)	(0.0488)	(0.0570)
Public funding credit per capita	-0.0857	-0.3562[b]	-0.3375[a]	-0.2078	-0.9823[b]	0.2178	0.1414	0.2950[b]
	(0.1770)	(0.1917)	(0.1427)	(0.2015)	(0.5164)	(0.1738)	(0.2087)	(0.1643)
Wealth	0.00140	0.0139[a]	0.00368[b]	-0.0101[c]	0.00833	-0.00353[b]	0.00569	-0.00535[b]
	(0.00232)	(0.00594)	(0.00211)	(0.00721)	(0.00684)	(0.00202)	(0.00492)	(0.00299)
Distance to navigable water	-0.0172[c]	-0.0461[a]	-0.00168	0.0110	-0.1128[a]	0.0475[a]	-0.0401[b]	0.0572[b]
	(0.0125)	(0.0196)	(0.0127)	(0.0162)	(0.0555)	(0.0206)	(0.0230)	(0.0326)
Constituents' Ideology								
State population	-0.00150	0.0158[c]	-0.00419	-0.0170[a]	0.0623[b]	-0.0180[a]	0.0373[a]	-0.0400[a]
	(0.00480)	(0.0108)	(0.00504)	(0.00761)	(0.0377)	(0.00892)	(0.0173)	(0.0186)
English ancestry of citizens	0.0353	0.0506	0.0569	-0.0318	0.1138	-0.1113[c]	0.1163	-0.2322[a]
	(0.0562)	(0.0727)	(0.0496)	(0.0573)	(0.1089)	(0.0734)	(0.1018)	(0.1168)
Somers' D_{yx}	.748	.876	.820	.864	.958	.873	.919	.874
R^2	.302	.495	.453	.509	.619	.484	.531	.419

[a] Statistically significant at the .05 level.
[b] Statistically significant at the .10 level.
[c] P-value is less than .20. While not considered significant at conventional levels, the coefficient may be precise enough to be treated as significant given the small sample size. See Leamer (1978, chap. 4, especially pp. 102–108, 114–117).

Note: See the note to table A3.2a.

Table A3.3a. Estimated Logistic Coefficients of the Explanatory Variables in a More Parsimonious Voting Model for the Philadelphia Convention: Votes 1 through 8

Explanatory Variables	Votes							
	1	2	3	4	5	6	7	8
Constant	4.0170[a] (1.4299)	-2.4286[b] (1.1048)	1.6209[d] (1.1662)	2.1729[d] (1.6567)	-0.8144 (1.1889)	2.5266[c] (1.4987)	-1.4763[d] (1.0422)	-0.2552 (1.0142)
Personal Economic Interests								
Western landowner	-1.0852 (1.2252)	-0.9000 (0.9859)	0.3434 (1.1656)	1.2330 (1.2061)	3.0066[b] (1.4822)	-0.3758 (1.5398)	-0.6576 (0.9349)	0.0457 (1.0278)
Merchant	-1.4139 (1.3297)	-0.7833 (1.2192)	-1.0024 (1.4587)	-0.7668 (1.3693)	-1.1706 (1.8472)	-8.6927[b] (3.8854)	1.3054[e] (1.0979)	0.2554 (1.2245)
Number of slaves	0.0222[b] (0.0100)	-0.0101 (0.00982)	—	—	—	0.0261[b] (0.0123)	-0.00038 (0.0102)	-0.00766 (0.00788)
Slaveowner	—	—	3.9417[b] (1.7645)	3.3154[c] (1.8978)	3.1066[c] (1.7865)	—	—	—
Value of public securities	0.4018[c] (0.2385)	-0.0365 (0.1974)	0.3609[d] (0.2394)	—	0.1900 (0.2481)	1.4250[a] (0.5238)	0.0181 (0.1897)	-0.1277 (0.2066)
Owner public securities	—	—	—	1.4780[d] (0.9395)	—	—	—	—
Personal Ideology								
Delegate-English ancestry	-0.9081 (0.8954)	0.2942 (0.8153)	-0.5369 (0.9674)	0.8389 (1.0350)	0.3694 (0.9938)	1.7752[d] (1.0995)	-0.1492 (0.7854)	-0.8388 (0.8062)
Officer in War	-0.6075 (0.8444)	0.2816 (0.7717)	-2.1423[b] (0.9567)	-2.2348[b] (1.0818)	-1.5152[d] (1.0087)	-2.0930[c] (1.0977)	-0.9400[e] (0.7671)	1.2379[d] (0.8365)

Constituents' Economic Interests								
Slaves per 100 whites	-0.0498[b]	-0.00648	-0.0610[c]	-0.0800[c]	-0.0164	-0.0615[b]	0.0567[b]	0.0125
	(0.0229)	(0.0199)	(0.0319)	(0.0412)	(0.0299)	(0.0314)	(0.0222)	(0.0204)
Distance to navigable water	-0.0214	-0.0233[c]	0.0266[c]	0.0152[d]	0.0376[b]	0.0244[c]	0.00776	-0.0197[b]
	(0.0208)	(0.0141)	(0.0154)	(0.0104)	(0.0187)	(0.0133)	(0.00919)	(0.00927)
Constituents' Ideology								
State population	-0.0126[a]	0.0115[a]	-0.00760[b]	-0.0152[a]	-0.00889[c]	-0.0200[b]	0.00123	0.00655[c]
	(0.00437)	(0.00371)	(0.00386)	(0.00564)	(0.00506)	(0.00791)	(0.00338)	(0.00356)
Somers' D_{yx}	.745	.655	.703	.784	.744	.842	.673	.541
R^2	.382	.325	.346	.357	.344	.429	.309	.193

[a] Statistically significant at the .01 level.
[b] Statistically significant at the .05 level.
[c] Statistically significant at the .10 level.
[d] P-value is less than .20. While not considered significant at conventional levels, the coefficient may be precise enough to be treated as significant given the small sample size. See Leamer (1978, chap. 4, especially pp. 102–108, 114–117).
[e] P-value is between .20 and .30.

Note: Number of observations is 53. The asymptotic standard errors are in parentheses. Each column contains the estimates for a more parsimonious voting model, a subset of the full voting model described in equation 3.1, for each vote. The dependent variable for each issue is the observed vote for that issue, where a yes vote equals 1 and a no vote equals 0. For votes 3, 4, and 5 for a delegate's slave interests or public securities interests, the dichotomous variable indicating ownership of any amount of slaves or any amount of public securities was employed as a substitute variable for the amount of slaves or value of public securities owned because it produced more precise estimates for the variables for those votes. Variables for which all delegates with the characteristic voted unanimously for a particular vote were excluded from the estimation of that vote because the logit algorithm cannot converge with such variables included. Other variables were selected for exclusion because they were seldom significant in the full model, are historically more minor variables, appear to be the least likely to affect voting on the issue in question, or are variables that are likely to contain the most measurement error. For the interest of the reader, the estimates for votes 1 and 3 have been reported despite the errors discovered in their data. As a result of the errors however, not much confidence should be placed in the findings for the two votes. Somers' D_{yx} is a measure of the degree of concordance between the predicted probability and the observed vote for each observation. It is analogous to Kendall's rank correlation coefficient. R^2 is the generalized R^2 generated for logistic regression with the RSQUARE option in the current version of SAS (version 8.0). Somers' D_{yx} and R^2 are alternative measures of the goodness of fit of the estimated model.

Table A3.3b. Estimated Logistic Coefficients of the Explanatory Variables in a More Parsimonious Voting Model for the Philadelphia Convention: Votes 9 through 16

Explanatory Variables	Votes							
	9	10	11	12	13	14	15	16
Constant	3.2426[b] (1.3793)	1.2076[e] (1.1174)	0.7350 (0.9791)	2.2673[b] (1.1291)	0.0288 (1.1204)	-2.2377[c] (1.1544)	-0.0660 (1.1303)	0.5872 (1.1163)
Personal Economic Interests								
Western landowner	-1.3571[e] (1.1209)	0.7018 (1.0412)	0.6222 (0.9918)	1.7277[d] (1.1024)	0.9511 (1.1820)	1.9459[d] (1.2905)	-0.7464 (1.2187)	-1.0061 (1.4105)
Merchant	0.3207 (1.3942)	-0.0290 (1.2695)	-0.7798 (1.2127)	-2.4941[c] (1.4033)	0.0478 (1.2732)	U^{No}	2.5190[e] (2.0309)	-0.4548 (1.3973)
Number of slaves	0.0252[c] (0.0137)	-0.00298 (0.00755)	0.0113[d] (0.00805)	0.00544 (0.00821)	-0.0135[e] (0.0111)	-0.0117[d] (0.00786)	-0.00811 (0.00845)	0.00422 (0.0127)
Slaveowner								
Value of public securities	—	-0.1672 (0.1983)	0.3575[c] (0.2152)	0.0584 (0.2389)	-0.3538[c] (0.2233)	-0.2031 (0.2877)	-0.5293[c] (0.2831)	-0.0492 (0.3260)
Owner public securities	1.4865[d] (0.9275)	—	—	—	—	—	—	—
Personal Ideology								
Delegate-English ancestry	-1.1061[e] (0.9069)	-0.9219[e] (0.8346)	-0.0939 (0.7473)	0.1961 (0.7782)	-0.5718 (0.8548)	0.7376 (0.8828)	-1.2613[d] (0.9001)	0.2603 (0.8875)
Officer in War	0.8187 (0.9857)	2.1257[b] (1.0120)	-0.0312 (0.7272)	0.6609 (0.7866)	1.7875[c] (0.9323)	-1.9649[c] (1.0299)	1.2819[d] (0.9228)	0.2776 (0.8327)

Constituents' Economic Interests							
Slaves per 100 whites	-0.0649[b]	-0.0132	-0.00269	-0.0371[c]	-0.0327[d]	0.0774[a]	-0.00247	-0.0332[d]
	(0.0258)	(0.0208)	(0.0183)	(0.0213)	(0.0213)	(0.0252)	(0.0220)	(0.0257)
Distance to navigable water	-0.0217[b]	-0.0221[b]	0.0184[c]	0.0184[d]	-0.0223[b]	0.0334[b]	-0.0286[b]	0.0241[b]
	(0.0103)	(0.00961)	(0.0108)	(0.0123)	(0.0108)	(0.0137)	(0.0114)	(0.0123)
Constituents' Ideology							
State population	-0.00129	0.00214	-0.00937[a]	-0.0102[b]	0.00834[b]	-0.00530[e]	0.0121[b]	-0.00684[d]
	(0.00335)	(0.00326)	(0.00360)	(0.00401)	(0.00402)	(0.00419)	(0.00489)	(0.00422)
Somers' D_{yx}	.669	.631	.605	.674	.739	.798	.677	.620
R^2	.253	.256	.231	.325	.395	.397	.300	.223

[a] Statistically significant at the .01 level.
[b] Statistically significant at the .05 level.
[c] Statistically significant at the .10 level.
[d] P-value is less than .20. While not considered significant at conventional levels, the coefficient may be precise enough to be treated as significant given the small sample size. See Leamer (1978, chap. 4, especially pp. 102–108, 114–117).
[e] P-value is between .20 and .30.

Note: For vote 9 for a delegate's public securities interests, the dichotomous variable indicating ownership of any amount of public securities was employed as a substitute variable for the value of public securities owned because it produced a more precise estimate for the variable for the vote. All other details are as described in the note to table A3.3a.

Table A3.4. Incremental and Marginal Effects of the Explanatory Variables in the Parsimonious Voting Model on the Probability of a Yes Vote for the "Average" Public Securities Holding Delegate at the Philadelphia Convention

Explanatory Variables	Votes					
	Vote 2	Vote 7	Vote 9	Vote 11	Vote 13	Vote 14
Personal Economic Interests						
Western landowner	−.212	−.163	−.155	.143	.191	.337[d]
Merchant	−.185	.302	.026	−.159	.011	U^{No}
Farmer	U^{No}	—	—	—	—	—
Debtor	—	U^{Yes}	—	U^{No}	—	—
Number of slaves	−.0025	−.00009	.0022[c]	.0025[d]	−.0030	−.0016[d]
Value of private securities ($000s)	—	—	U^{Yes}	—	—	—
Owner public securities	—	—	.226[d]	—	—	—
Value of public securities ($000s)	−.0090	.0045	—	.079[c]	−.078[d]	−.027
Personal Ideology						
English ancestry of delegate	.072	−.037	−.092	−.021	−.123	.095
Officer	.070	−.231	.066	−.0069	.342[c]	−.222[c]
Constituents' Economic Interests						
Slaves per 100 whites	−.0016	.014[b]	−.0057[b]	−.0006	−.0072[d]	.010[a]
Distance to navigable water (miles)	−.0058[c]	.0019	−.0019[b]	.0041[c]	−.0049[b]	.0045[b]
Constituents' Ideology						
State population (000s)	.0028[a]	.00031	−.00011	−.0021[a]	.0018[b]	−.00071
Predicted Probability of a Yes Vote						
"Average" public creditor	.445	.524	.903	.331	.674	.159

[a] Statistically significant at the .01 level.
[b] Statistically significant at the .05 level.
[c] Statistically significant at the .10 level.
[d] P-value is less than .20. While not considered significant at conventional levels, the coefficient may be treated as significant given the small sample size. See Leamer (1978, chap. 4, especially pp. 102–108, 114–117).

Note: The dependent variable for each issue is the observed vote for that issue, where a yes vote equals 1 and a no vote equals 0. Variables for which all delegates with the characteristic voted unanimously for a particular vote, marked with U^{Yes} or U^{No}, were excluded from the estimation of that vote because the logit algorithm cannot converge with such variables included. Other variables were selected for exclusion because they were seldom significant in the full model, are generally considered historically minor variables, appear to be the least likely to affect voting on the issue in question, or are likely to contain the most measurement error. The incremental and marginal effects of the variables are calculated from the estimated logistic coefficients for the more parsimonious model specification of the selected votes, which are reported in table A.3.3a,b, calculated for only the twenty-nine delegates with public securities holdings, employing the mean values of the explanatory variables.

Table A3.5. Incremental and Marginal Effects of the Explanatory Variables in the Parsimonious Voting Model on the Probability of a Yes Vote for the "Average" Slaveowning Delegate at the Philadelphia Convention

Explanatory Variables	Votes					
	Vote 2	Vote 7	Vote 9	Vote 11	Vote 13	Vote 14
Personal Economic Interests						
Western landowner	−.137	−.097	−.300	.154	.192	.364[d]
Merchant	−.112	.104	.056	−.181	.0084	U[No]
Farmer	U[No]	—	—	—	—	—
Debtor	—	U[Yes]	—	U[No]	—	—
Number of slaves	−.0018	−.00005	.0048[c]	.0028[d]	−.0024	−.0028[d]
Value of private securities ($000s)	—	—	U[Yes]	—	—	—
Owner public securities	—	—	.257[d]	—	—	—
Value of public securities ($000s)	−.0066	.0023	—	.089[c]	−.062[d]	−.049
Personal Ideology						
English ancestry of delegate	.053	−.019	−.202	−.023	−.101	.177
Officer	.052	−.133	.144	−.0078	.350[c]	−.455[c]
Constituents' Economic Interests						
Slaves per 100 whites	−.0012	.0072[b]	−.012[b]	−.00067	−.0057[d]	.019[a]
Distance to navigable water (miles)	−.0042	.00098	−.0041[b]	.0046[c]	−.0039[b]	.0080[b]
Constituents' Ideology						
State population (000s)	.0021	.00016	−.00024	−.0023[a]	.0015[b]	−.0013
Predicted Probability of a Yes Vote "Average" Slaveowner	.236	.851	.746	.472	.224	.599

[a] Statistically significant at the .01 level.
[b] Statistically significant at the .05 level.
[c] Statistically significant at the .10 level.
[d] P-value is less than .20. While not considered significant at conventional levels, the coefficient may be treated as significant given the small sample size. See Leamer (1978, chap. 4, especially pp. 102–108, 114–117).

Note: The incremental and marginal effects of the variables are calculated from the estimated logistic coefficients for the more parsimonious model specification of the selected votes, which are reported in table A.3.3a,b, calculated for only the eighteen delegates with slaveholdings, employing the mean values of the explanatory variables. All other details are as described in the note to table A3.4.

Personal–Interest and Constituent–Interest Voting Models for the Philadelphia Convention

Table A4.1. Incremental and Marginal Effects of the Explanatory Variables in the Personal-Interest and the Constituent-Interest Models on the Probability of a Yes Vote at the Philadelphia Convention: Vote 2

Personal-Interest Explanatory Variables	Personal–Interest Model Specifications				
	1	2	3	4	5
Western landowner	−.034	−.045	—	.068	—
Merchant	.035	.072	—	.088	.041
Farmer	U^{No}	U^{No}	U^{No}	U^{No}	U^{No}
Debtor	−.164	−.137	—	−.165	−.174
Slaveowner	—	—	—	−.056	—
Number of slaves	−.0024[d]	−.0024[d]	−.0020	—	−.0025[d]
Value of public securities ($)	.00021[c]	.00020[c]	.00020[c]	—	—
Value of private securities ($)	.00002	.00002	.00001	—	.00001
Public or private creditor	—	—	—	.147	—
Appreciation in public securities ($)	−.00010[c]	−.00010[c]	−.00010[c]	—	—
Age	−.0058	−.0029	—	−.0049	—
Officer in war	−.043	−.057	—	−.048	−.058
English ancestry	.130	.175	—	.113	.169
Congress	.165	—	—	.144	—

Constituent-Interest Explanatory Variables	Constituent–Interest Model Specifications				
	1	2	3	4	5
Slaves per 100 whites	−.060[b]	−.0084[c]	—	−.0059	—
Slaves per slaveowning family	—	—	−.079[c]	—	—
Wealth ($)	.0017[b]	.00035	.00040	.00061[c]	.00054
Share of wealth in landholdings	4.191[b]	—	—	.946[d]	−.422
Share of wealth in financial claims	−4.716[c]	—	—	—	−3.353
Share of wealth in financial liabilities	−13.926[c]	—	—	—	.409
Share of wealth in slaves	—	—	—	—	−2.836
Public funding credit per capita ($)	—	−.035[d]	−.035[d]	−.046[c]	—
Distance from Atlantic coast (miles)	−.0030	−.0026	−.0022	—	−.0011
Distance from navigable water (miles)	—	—	—	−.0046[d]	—
State population (000s)	.0037[b]	.0032[a]	.0028[a]	.0029[b]	.0019[c]
English ancestry of citizens (percent)	−.0071	.0059	.0052	−.0059	−.018
Scottish/Irish ancestry of citizens (percent)	—	.041[d]	.050[d]	—	—

[a] Statistically significant at the .01 level.
[b] Statistically significant at the .05 level.
[c] Statistically significant at the .10 level.
[d] P-value is less than .20. While not considered significant at conventional levels, the estimated effect may be precise enough to be treated as significant given the small sample size. See Leamer (1978, chap. 4, especially pp. 102–108, 114–117).

Note: Number of observations for each specification is 53. The dependent variable in each specification is the vote on the second issue, where a yes vote equals 1 and a no vote equals 0. The farmer variable was excluded from the personal-interest model because all delegates classified as a farmer voted unanimously against Vote 2 (U^{No}).

Source: Reprinted from McGuire (1988, table 4, p. 508), with permission. Minor revisions have been made.

Table A4.2. Incremental and Marginal Effects of the Explanatory Variables in the Personal-Interest and Constituent-Interest Models on the Probability of a Yes Vote at the Philadelphia Convention: Vote 7

Personal-Interest Explanatory Variables	Personal–Interest Model Specifications				
	1	2	3	4	5
Western landowner	−.182	−.171	—	−.242	—
Merchant	.155	.135	—	.265	.180
Farmer	.143	.153	—	.178	.135
Debtor	U^{Yes}	U^{Yes}	U^{Yes}	U^{Yes}	U^{Yes}
Slaveowner	—	—	—	.530[a]	—
Number of slaves	.0058[b]	.0059[b]	.0051[b]	—	.0056[b]
Value of public securities ($)	−.00008	−.00008	−.00009	—	—
Value of private securities ($)	−.00003	−.00003	−.00002	—	−.00002
Public or private creditor	—	—	—	.052	—
Appreciation in public securities ($)	.00007[d]	.00007[d]	.00008[c]	—	—
Age	.00009	.00016	—	.0028	—
Officer in war	−.204	−.197	—	−.258[d]	−.207
English ancestry	−.131	−.147	—	−.173	−.129
Congress	.067	—	—	.099	—

Constituent-Interest Explanatory Variables	Constituent–Interest Model Specifications				
	1	2	3	4	5
Slaves per 100 whites	−.0025[d]	−.0024	—	−.0049	—
Slaves per slaveowning family	—	—	−.0092	—	—
Wealth ($)	.00015[d]	.0011[c]	.0018[d]	.0018[d]	.00007
Share of wealth in landholdings	−.220[c]	—	—	−.458	−.112[d]
Share of wealth in financial claims	−.419[c]	—	—	—	−.145
Share of wealth in financial liabilities	.00098	—	—	—	.108[c]
Share of wealth in slaves	—	—	—	—	−.128
Public funding credit per capita ($)	—	.0041	.015	.018	—
Distance from Atlantic coast (miles)	−.00004	−.00013	−.00011	—	−.00001
Distance from navigable water (miles)	—	—	—	−.00017	—
State population (000s)	.00008[b]	.00010	.00009	.00038	.00002[c]
English ancestry of citizens (percent)	.0015[b]	.0093[b]	.020[b]	.029[b]	.00040[d]
Scottish/Irish ancestry of citizens (percent)	—	−.0053	−.010	—	—

[a] Statistically significant at the .01 level.
[b] Statistically significant at the .05 level.
[c] Statistically significant at the .10 level.
[d] P-value is less than .20. While not considered significant at conventional levels, the estimated effect may be precise enough to be treated as significant given the small sample size. See Leamer (1978, chap. 4, especially pp. 102–108, 114–117).

Note: Number of observations for each specification is 53. The dependent variable in each specification is the vote on the seventh issue, where a yes vote equals 1 and a no vote equals 0. The debtor variable was excluded from the personal-interest model because all delegates classified as a debtor voted unanimously for Vote 7 (U^{Yes}).
Source: Reprinted from McGuire (1988, table 5, p. 510), with permission. Minor revisions have been made.

Table A4.3. Incremental and Marginal Effects of the Explanatory Variables in the Personal-Interest and Constituent-Interest Models on the Probability of a Yes Vote at the Philadelphia Convention: Vote 11

Personal-Interest Explanatory Variables	Personal–Interest Model Specifications				
	1	2	3	4	5
Western landowner	.0023	.107	.063	—	.053
Merchant	.0345	−.069	−.129	−.072	−.032
Farmer	.072	.103	.081	.092	.431
Debtor	U^{No}	U^{No}	U^{No}	U^{No}	U^{No}
Slaveowner	—	.107	.091	—	—
Number of slaves	.0020[c]	—	—	.0025[c]	.0028[c]
Value of public securities ($)	.00006	—	—	.00004	—
Value of private securities ($)	−.00010	—	—	−.00008	−.00007
Public or private creditor	—	−.261[c]	−.255[c]	—	—
Appreciation in public securities ($)	−.00002	—	—	—	—
Age	−.0038	−.0084	—	—	—
Officer in war	−.038	−.080	—	−.036	—
English ancestry	−.106	−.127	—	−.115	—
Congress	−.025	−.053	—	—	—

Constituent-Interest Explanatory Variables	Constituent–Interest Model Specifications				
	1	2	3	4	5
Slaves per 100 whites	—	−.0042	—	−.0057	−.00087
Slaves per slaveowning family	—	—	−.036	—	—
Wealth ($)	.0011[a]	.0011[b]	.00105[b]	.00095[b]	.00096[b]
Share of wealth in landholdings	−1.768[c]	—	—	−.057	.185
Share of wealth in financial claims	—	—	—	—	—
Share of wealth in financial liabilities	—	—	—	—	—
Share of wealth in slaves	−2.428[b]	—	—	—	—
Public funding credit per capita ($)	−.063[b]	−.069[a]	−.068[a]	−.059[b]	−.066[a]
Distance from Atlantic coast (miles)	.00045	.00005	.00016	—	−.00007
Distance from navigable water (miles)	—	—	—	.0020	—
State population (000s)	.0011	.00036	.00013	.00030	.00002
English ancestry of citizens (percent)	.041[b]	.015[d]	.015[d]	.019[c]	—
Scottish/Irish ancestry of citizens (percent)	—	−.031	−.025	—	−.049[c]

[a] Statistically significant at the .01 level.
[b] Statistically significant at the .05 level.
[c] Statistically significant at the .10 level.
[d] P-value is less than .20. While not considered significant at conventional levels, the estimated effect may be precise enough to be treated as significant given the small sample size. See Leamer (1978, chap. 4, especially pp. 102–108, 114–117).

Note: Number of observations for each specification is 53. The dependent variable in each specification is the vote on the eleventh issue, where a yes vote equals 1 and a no vote equals 0. The debtor variable was excluded from the personal-interest model because all delegates classified as a debtor voted unanimously against Vote 11 (U^{No}).

Source: Reprinted from McGuire (1988, table, 6, p. 512), with permission. Minor revisions have been made.

Table A4.4. Incremental and Marginal Effects of the Explanatory Variables in the Personal-Interest and Constituent-Interest Models on the Probability of a Yes Vote at the Philadelphia Convention: Vote 13

Personal-Interest Explanatory Variables	Personal–Interest Model Specifications				
	1	2	3	4	5
Western landowner	.304[d]	.282	—	—	—
Merchant	.325	.023	.378[d]	.386[d]	.323
Farmer	−.390	−.332	−.398	−.382	−.391
Debtor	−.530[d]	−.263	−.586[c]	−.584[c]	−.560[d]
Slaveowner	—	−.452[a]	—	—	—
Number of slaves	−.0061[a]	—	−.0055[a]	−.0053[a]	−.0055[a]
Value of public securities ($)	−.00004	—	−.00009[c]	−.00008[c]	−.00007[d]
Value of private securities ($)	.00004[d]	—	.00003[d]	.00003[d]	.00003[d]
Public or private creditor	—	−.054	—	—	—
Appreciation in public securities ($)	−.00003	—	—	—	—
Age	−.0089	−.0079	—	—	—
Officer in war	.179[d]	.271[c]	—	—	.173[d]
English ancestry	.060	.051	.075	—	.098
Congress	−.098	−.108	—	—	—

Constituent-Interest Explanatory Variables	Constituent–Interest Model Specifications				
	1	2	3	4	5
Slaves per 100 whites	—	−.013	—	−.0079	−.0097
Slaves per slaveowning family	—	—	−.112[c]	—	—
Wealth ($)	−.0021[d]	−.0023	−.0015	−.0011	−.0024
Share of wealth in landholdings	−.023	—	—	−1.215[c]	−.772
Share of wealth in financial claims	—	—	—	—	—
Share of wealth in financial liabilities	—	—	—	—	—
Share of wealth in slaves	1.283	—	—	—	—
Public funding credit per capita ($)	−.038[c]	−.034	−.039	−.063[c]	−.041
Distance from Atlantic coast (miles)	−.0034[c]	−.0051[c]	−.0047[c]	—	−.0052[b]
Distance from navigable water (miles)	—	—	—	−.0080[b]	—
State population (000s)	.00098[d]	.0032[b]	.0020[c]	.0019[c]	.0028[b]
English ancestry of citizens (percent)	−.017[c]	−.016	−.011	.0035	—
Scottish/Irish ancestry of citizens (percent)	—	.189[b]	.187[a]	—	.149[b]

[a] Statistically significant at the .01 level.
[b] Statistically significant at the .05 level.
[c] Statistically significant at the .10 level.
[d] P-value is less than .20. While not considered significant at conventional levels, the estimated effect may be precise enough to be treated as significant given the small sample size. See Leamer (1978, chap. 4, especially pp. 102–108, 114–117).

Note: Number of observations for each specification is 53. The dependent variable in each specification is the vote on the thirteenth issue, where a yes vote equals 1 and a no vote equals 0.
Source: Reprinted from McGuire (1988, table 7, p. 514), with permission. Minor revisions have been made.

Table A4.5. Incremental and Marginal Effects of the Explanatory Variables in the Personal-Interest and Constituent-Interest Models on the Probability of a Yes Vote at the Philadelphia Convention: Vote 14

Personal-Interest Explanatory Variables	Personal–Interest Model Specifications				
	1	2	3	4	5
Western landowner	.073	—	.125	.062	.104
Merchant	U^{No}	U^{No}	U^{No}	U^{No}	U^{No}
Farmer	.497	.433	.534	.452	.476
Debtor	.246	.080	.166	.115	.060
Slaveowner	—	—	$.409^a$	—	$.422^a$
Number of slaves	$.0016^d$	$.0017^d$	—	$.0021^c$	—
Value of public securities ($)	.00002	−.00002	—	—	—
Value of private securities ($)	−.00001	−.00001	—	−.00001	—
Public or private creditor	—	—	.012	—	−.028
Appreciation in public securities ($)	−.00003	—	—	—	—
Age	−.0029	—	−.0033	—	—
Officer in war	$−.266^d$	$−.242^d$	$−.267^d$	—	—
English ancestry	−.046	−.097	−.101	—	—
Congress	−.187	—	−.135	—	—

Constituent-Interest Explanatory Variables	Constituent–Interest Model Specifications				
	1	2	3	4	5
Slaves per 100 whites	—	$.013^a$	—	$.015^a$	$.011^b$
Slaves per slaveowning family	—	—	$.106^a$	—	—
Wealth ($)	−.00020	−.00022	−.00011	$−.00044^b$	−.00016
Share of wealth in landholdings	−.467	—	—	−.286	$−.514^d$
Share of wealth in financial claims	—	—	—	—	—
Share of wealth in financial liabilities	—	—	—	—	—
Share of wealth in slaves	.656	—	—	—	—
Public funding credit per capita ($)	.026	.015	.0046	.012	.0031
Distance from Atlantic coast (miles)	$.0067^b$	$.0057^a$	$.0053^a$	—	$.0038^b$
Distance from navigable water (miles)	—	—	—	$.0072^b$	—
State population (000s)	$−.0014^d$	$−.0018^b$	−.00089	$−.0011^d$	$−.0013^c$
English ancestry of citizens (percent)	.0043	−.0096	−.0097	−.0076	—
Scottish/Irish ancestry of citizens (percent)	—	$−.044^d$	$−.064^b$	—	$−.047^d$

[a] Statistically significant at the .01 level.
[b] Statistically significant at the .05 level.
[c] Statistically significant at the .10 level.
[d] P-value is less than .20. While not considered significant at conventional levels, the estimated effect may be precise enough to be treated as significant given the small sample size. See Leamer (1978, chap. 4, especially pp. 102–108, 114–117).

Note: Number of observations for each specification is 53. The dependent variable in each specification is the vote on the fourteenth issue, where a yes vote equals 1 and a no vote equals 0. The merchant variable was excluded from the personal-interest model because all delegates classified as a merchant voted unanimously against Vote 14 (U^{No}).

Source: Reprinted from McGuire (1988, table 8, p. 516), with permission. Minor revisions have been made.

Alternative Voting Model and Hypothesis Tests for Nationalism at the Philadelphia Convention

Table A5.1. Incremental and Marginal Effects of the Personal and Constituent Interests on the Probability of a Yes Vote on Nationalism at the Philadelphia Convention: Dependent Variable P^C

Explanatory Variables	Alternative Model Specifications		
	1	2	3
Personal Interests			
Western landowner	−.003 (0.28)	.044 (0.48)	—
Merchant	.080 (0.53)	.091 (0.68)	—
Farmer	−.053 (0.41)	−.042 (0.38)	—
Private securities owner	.089 (0.83)	.136 (1.30)[c]	—
Public securities owner	−.013 (0.19)	−.004 (0.05)	—
Slaveowner	−.118 (0.96)	−.094 (1.28)	—
Debtor	−.270 (1.47)[c]	−.259 (1.48)[c]	—
Age	−.0004 (1.32)[c]	−.0036 (1.10)	—
Officer in war	.163 (2.33)[a]	.169 (2.54)[a]	—
English ancestry	−.046 (0.52)	−.082 (1.16)	—
Constituents' Interests			
Slaves per 100 whites	.00006 (0.03)	—	−.0017 (1.38)[c]
Distance to navigable water	−.0023 (2.22)[a]	—	−.0024 (2.47)[a]
English ancestry of citizens	−.0038 (0.84)	—	.0070 (1.87)[b]
Population	.0003 (0.79)	—	.00008 (0.30)
Pseudo $\bar{R}^2$	.072	.071	.071

[a] Statistically significant at the .05 level.

[b] Statistically significant at the .10 level.

[c] P-value is less than .20. While not considered significant at conventional levels, the coefficient may be precise enough to be treated as significant given the small sample size. See Leamer (1978, chap. 4, especially pp. 102–108, 114–117).

Note: Number of observations is 53. The absolute values of the asymptotic t-statistics are in parentheses. The dependent variable P^C, an alternative measure of nationalism, is the proportion of a delegate's votes that was in favor of a pro-national position on six selected issues: yes votes on the second, eighth, ninth, tenth, and fifteenth issues and a no vote on the fourth issue. Pseudo $\bar{R}^2$ is calculated as $\bar{R}^2 = [(\chi^2 - 2k)/(-2L_R)]$, where χ^2 is the model χ^2 statistic, k is the number of explanatory variables in the model, and L_R is the maximum of the likelihood function restricted with only the constant in the model. It is a measure of the goodness of fit of the estimated model.

Table A5.2. Nonnested Tests of Various Rival Models of Voting on Nationalism at the Philadelphia Convention: Alternative Model Specifications

	Null Hypothesis	Alternative Hypothesis	Variables	Likelihood Ratio Test	P-Value (χ^2 with df = 1)
1a.	$P^A = f$ (PE, PI)	$P^A = f$ (CE, CI)	Full	8.62	<.01
1b.	$P^B = f$ (PE, PI)	$P^B = f$ (CE, CI)	Full	6.69	.01
1c.	$P^B = f$ (PE, PI)	$P^B = f$ (CE, CI)	Limited	4.75	.03
2a.	$P^A = f$ (CE, CI)	$P^A = f$ (PE, PI)	Full	10.27	<.01
2b.	$P^B = f$ (CE, CI)	$P^B = f$ (PE, PI)	Full	11.05	<.01
2c.	$P^B = f$ (CE, CI)	$P^B = f$ (PE, PI)	Limited	8.55	<.01
3a.	$P^A = f$ (PE, CE)	$P^A = f$ (PI, CI)	Full	7.68	<.01
3b.	$P^B = f$ (PE, CE)	$P^B = f$ (PI, CI)	Full	6.95	<.01
3c.	$P^B = f$ (PE, CE)	$P^B = f$ (PI, CI)	Limited	4.49	.04
4a.	$P^A = f$ (PI, CI)	$P^A = f$ (PE, CE)	Full	13.91	<.01
4b.	$P^B = f$ (PI, CI)	$P^B = f$ (PE, CE)	Full	12.14	<.01
4c.	$P^B = f$ (PI, CI)	$P^B = f$ (PE, CE)	Limited	10.13	<.01
5a.	$P^A = f$ (PE)	$P^A = f$ (PI), $P^A = f$ (CE), $P^A = f$ (CI)	Full	12.15	<.01
5b.	$P^B = f$ (PE)	$P^B = f$ (PI), $P^B = f$ (CE), $P^B = f$ (CI)	Full	9.82	<.01
5c.	$P^B = f$ (PE)	$P^B = f$ (PI), $P^B = f$ (CE), $P^B = f$ (CI)	Limited	9.09	<.01
6a.	$P^A = f$ (PI)	$P^A = f$ (PE), $P^A = f$ (CE), $P^A = f$ (CI)	Full	17.59	<.01
6b.	$P^B = f$ (PI)	$P^B = f$ (PE), $P^B = f$ (CE), $P^B = f$ (CI)	Full	11.40	<.01
6c.	$P^B = f$ (PI)	$P^B = f$ (PE), $P^B = f$ (CE), $P^B = f$ (CI)	Limited	9.34	<.01
7a.	$P^A = f$ (CE)	$P^A = f$ (PE), $P^A = f$ (PI), $P^A = f$ (CI)	Full	14.20	<.01
7b.	$P^B = f$ (CE)	$P^B = f$ (PE), $P^B = f$ (PI), $P^B = f$ (CI)	Full	11.10	<.01
7c.	$P^B = f$ (CE)	$P^B = f$ (PE), $P^B = f$ (PI), $P^B = f$ (CI)	Limited	9.46	<.01
8a.	$P^A = f$ (CI)	$P^A = f$ (PE), $P^A = f$ (PI), $P^A = f$ (CE)	Full	13.57	<.01
8b.	$P^B = f$ (CI)	$P^B = f$ (PE), $P^B = f$ (PI), $P^B = f$ (CE)	Full	17.07	<.01
8c.	$P^B = f$ (CI)	$P^B = f$ (PE), $P^B = f$ (PI), $P^B = f$ (CE)	Limited	38.73	<.01

Note: The null hypotheses are that the only interests that affect voting are: (1) personal interests; (2) constituents' interests; (3) economic interests; (4) ideological interests; (5) personal economic interests; (6) personal ideology; (7) constituents' economic interests; or (8) constituents' ideologies. The null hypothesis in all of the nonnested tests is rejected at the .05 level of significance or better.

Source: Reprinted from McGuire and Ohsfeldt (1997, table A.1, p. 165), with permission.

Table A5.3. Nested Tests of Exclusion Restrictions for Voting on Nationalism at the Philadelphia Convention for Different Sets of Variables in Equation 5.1: Alternative Model Specifications

Excluded Variables	Dependent Variable	Unrestricted Model	Likelihood Ratio Test	Degrees of Freedom	P-Value
(1) PE = PI = 0	P^A	5.3.1	12.50	10	.25
	P^B	5.4.1	7.48	10	.57
	P^B	5.4.4	8.72	5	.13
(2) CE = CI = 0	P^A	5.3.1	10.23	4	.04
	P^B	5.4.1	12.24	4	.02
	P^B	5.4.4	10.31	3	.02
(3) PI = CI = 0	P^A	5.3.1	8.15	5	.16
	P^B	5.4.1	7.35	5	.21
	P^B	5.4.4	8.81	2	.01
(4) PE = CE = 0	P^A	5.3.1	12.14	9	.22
	P^B	5.4.1	13.26	9	.17
	P^B	5.4.4	14.52	6	.02
(5) PE = 0	P^A	5.3.1	4.47	7	.72
	P^B	5.4.1	5.26	7	.63
	P^B	5.4.4	5.01	4	.30
(6) PI = 0	P^A	5.3.1	5.29	3	.17
	P^B	5.4.1	5.19	3	.09
	P^B	5.4.4	3.87	1	.05
(7) CE = 0	P^A	5.3.1	5.31	2	.07
	P^B	5.4.1	6.44	2	.01
	P^B	5.4.4	6.91	2	<.01
(8) CI = 0	P^A	5.3.1	2.69	2	.26
	P^B	5.4.1	2.80	2	.25
	P^B	5.4.4	1.11	1	.31
(9) PE = PI = CE = CI = 0	P^A	5.3.1	29.10	14	<.01
	P^B	5.4.1	30.47	14	<.01
	P^B	5.4.4	34.76	8	<.01

Note: The null hypothesis is that the coefficients of the excluded variables are 0 in equation 5.1 [$P_{ij} = f(PE_i, PI_i, CE_j, CI_j)$]. Unrestricted Model refers to the model specification employed in the nested tested, where 5.3.1 is the specification in table 5.3, column 1; 5.4.1, table 5.4, column 1; and 5.4.4, table 5.4, column 4.
Source: Reprinted from McGuire and Ohsfeldt (1997, table B.1, p. 166), with permission.

Voting Models for Pooled Samples of the State Ratifying Conventions

Table A6.1. Estimated Logistic Coefficients of the Explanatory Variables for Alternative Model Specifications of the Ratification Vote, 1787–1790: All Thirteen State Conventions Pooled

Explanatory Variables	Alternative Model Specifications							
	1	2	3	4	5	6	7	8
Constant	5.7039 (1.0829)	5.5958 (1.0603)	5.6447 (1.0386)	5.9353 (0.7737)	9.4487 (3.6145)	9.5150 (3.6102)	9.4496 (3.1943)	5.4128 (0.7076)
Personal Economic Interests								
Merchant	0.7575 (0.2616)	0.6711 (0.2663)	0.6238 (0.2681)	0.4662 (0.2638)	0.7691 (0.2616)	0.6838 (0.2661)	0.6369 (0.2682)	0.5659 (0.2685)
Western landowner	0.4987 (0.2264)	0.4727 (0.2264)	0.4952 (0.2263)	0.5494 (0.2221)	0.4975 (0.2271)	0.4713 (0.2270)	0.4863 (0.2272)	0.5638 (0.2238)
Private creditor	1.3072 (0.4573)	1.3123 (0.4629)	1.2319 (0.4614)	1.2909 (0.4588)	1.3135 (0.4590)	1.3213 (0.4648)	1.2351 (0.4628)	1.3602 (0.4637)
Debtor	-0.8755 (0.4354)	-0.9141 (0.4383)	-0.9300 (0.4405)	-0.8957 (0.4333)	-0.8456 (0.4367)	-0.8830 (0.4397)	-0.8956 (0.4428)	-0.8760 (0.4389)
Farmer	0.2834 (0.1673)	0.3284 (0.1680)	0.3887 (0.1697)	—	0.2630 (0.1690)	0.3087 (0.1698)	0.3606 (0.1715)	0.3542 (0.1624)
Slaveowner	-1.1628 (0.2942)	-1.1567 (0.2940)	—	-1.1391 (0.2886)	-1.1588 (0.2990)	-1.1554 (0.2991)	—	-1.1271 (0.2884)
Value of slaves ($000s)	—	—	0.00354 (0.0123)	—	—	—	0.00393 (0.0123)	—
Owner public securities	0.2367 (0.1623)	—	—	—	0.2611 (0.1639)	—	—	—
Owner >$1000 public securities	—	0.7294 (0.2180)	—	—	—	0.7529 (0.2188)	—	—
Value of public securities ($000s)	—	—	0.1030 (0.0324)	0.000094 (0.000031)	—	0.000905 (0.000576)	0.1047 (0.0327)	0.000107 (0.000033)
Constituents' Economic Interests								
Slaves per 100 whites	0.000922 (0.000564)	0.000904 (0.000569)	0.000861 (0.000587)	—	0.000919 (0.000570)	0.000905 (0.000576)	0.000817 (0.000591)	—

continued

276

Table A6.1. continued

	Alternative Model Specifications							
Explanatory Variables	1	2	3	4	5	6	7	8
Distance to navigable water (miles)	-0.0191	-0.0190	-0.0185	-0.0179	-0.0191	-0.0191	-0.0186	-0.0191
	(0.00200)	(0.00200)	(0.00200)	(0.00186)	(0.00202)	(0.00203)	(0.00202)	(0.00186)
Public funding credit per capita ($)	-0.1104	-0.1104	-0.1134	—	-0.1631	-0.1601	-0.1937	—
	(0.0393)	(0.0375)	(0.0366)		(0.1128)	(0.1131)	(0.1074)	
Constituents' Ideology								
State population (000s)	-0.00593	-0.00604	-0.00619	-0.00569	-0.0126	-0.0130	-0.0128	-0.00543
	(0.00125)	(0.00124)	(0.00121)	(0.00116)	(0.00599)	(0.00599)	(0.00527)	(0.00103)
English ancestry of citizens (percent)	0.00327	0.00474	0.00175	—	0.00683	0.00876	0.00405	—
	(0.0110)	(0.0110)	(0.0108)		(0.0116)	(0.0116)	(0.0113)	
Timing and other Factors								
Order	-0.4912	-0.5006	-0.4976	-0.5231	-1.0037	-1.0341	-1.0323	-0.4645
	(0.0964)	(0.0969)	(0.0929)	(0.0749)	(0.4883)	(0.4888)	(0.4322)	(0.0728)
Moot	1.5892	1.6624	1.7350	2.2787	4.0907	4.3186	4.0047	2.4365
	(0.5186)	(0.5155)	(0.5047)	(0.4453)	(2.1473)	(2.1477)	(1.9021)	(0.4561)
New England states	0.0325	0.0752	0.3183	—	0.0604	0.0449	0.6188	—
	(0.6575)	(0.6408)	(0.6258)		(1.0886)	(1.0895)	(1.0594)	
Southern states	1.5676	1.5896	0.7266	1.4722	2.3087	2.3370	1.5572	1.8329
	(0.5774)	(0.5653)	(0.5095)	(0.3134)	(1.0097)	(1.0048)	(0.9112)	(0.3502)
Paper money states	-0.2668	-0.2444	-0.2908	-0.4199	-0.3659	-0.3547	-0.3992	—
	(0.2967)	(0.2914)	(0.2874)	(0.1924)	(0.3094)	(0.3051)	(0.2993)	
Recommended amendments	—	—	—	—	1.6164	1.6978	1.6223	—
					(1.3494)	(1.3479)	(1.1940)	
Recommended amendments and declarations	—	—	—	—	0.7868	0.7749	1.1977	-1.0168
					(1.3858)	(1.3915)	(1.3121)	(0.3392)
Somers' D_{yx}	.616	.623	.615	.608	.617	.624	.615	.620
R^2	.256	.262	.255	.255	.257	.263	.257	.260

Note: Number of observations for each specification is 1,212. The asymptotic standard errors are in parentheses. The dependent variable in each specification is the observed vote on the ratification of the Constitution for the relevant states, where a yes vote equals 1 and a no vote equals 0. Somers' D_{yx} is a measure of the degree of concordance between the predicted probability of a yes vote and the observed vote for each observation. R^2 is the generalized R^2 generated for logistic regression with the RSQUARE option in SAS 8.0. Somers' D_{yx} and R^2 are alternative measures of the goodness of fit of the estimated model.

277

Table A6.2. Estimated Logistic Coefficients of the Explanatory Variables for the State Fixed-Effects Model of the Ratification Vote, 1787–1790: All Thirteen Ratifying Conventions Pooled

Explanatory Variables	Alternative Model Specifications			
	1	2	3	4
Merchant	0.7392[a]	0.6072[b]	0.6136[b]	0.7055[a]
	(0.2605)	(0.2677)	(0.2679)	(0.2619)
Western landowner	0.5245[b]	0.4993[b]	0.5532[b]	0.5355[b]
	(0.2256)	(0.2262)	(0.2244)	(0.2245)
Private creditor	1.3134[a]	1.2151[a]	1.2836[a]	1.2774[a]
	(0.4575)	(0.4611)	(0.4614)	(0.4583)
Debtor	−0.7950[c]	−0.8712[b]	−0.8030[c]	−0.8320[c]
	(0.4322)	(0.4401)	(0.4382)	(0.4318)
Farmer	0.2452[d]	0.3696[b]	0.2909[c]	0.2451[d]
	(0.1682)	(0.1715)	(0.1711)	(0.1680)
Slaveowner	−1.1291[a]	—	—	—
	(0.2976)			
Value of slaves	—	0.00882	—	—
		(0.0117)		
Slave share	—	—	−0.7687[d]	—
			(0.5225)	
Slave instrument	—	—	—	−0.3938[a]
				(0.1427)
Public securities owner	0.2498[d]	—	—	—
	(0.1633)			
Value of public securities	—	0.1059[a]	—	—
		(0.0327)		
Public securities share	—	—	3.2551[a]	—
			(0.7079)	
Public securities instrument	—	—	—	0.2071[b]
				(0.0905)
Distance	−0.0195[a]	−0.0187[a]	−0.0192[a]	−0.0196[a]
	(0.00200)	(0.00199)	(0.00201)	(0.00200)
Georgia	16.6155	16.4330	16.4433	16.6933
	(697.2)	(701.0)	(700.2)	(699.4)
North Carolina	1.5152[a]	0.4466[b]	0.6757[a]	1.2169[a]
	(0.3353)	(0.1986)	(0.2349)	(0.4067)
South Carolina	1.8081[a]	0.6105[a]	0.9411[a]	1.5195[a]
	(0.3627)	(0.2275)	(0.2863)	(0.4680)
Virginia	1.7196[a]	0.6406[a]	0.8572[a]	1.4686[a]
	(0.3717)	(0.2314)	(0.3033)	(0.4765)
Maryland	2.9181[a]	1.7378[a]	1.9698[a]	2.5675[a]
	(0.4690)	(0.3652)	(0.3878)	(0.5323)
Pennsylvania	2.0821[a]	1.6700[a]	1.5432[a]	2.0091[a]
	(0.3923)	(0.3614)	(0.3702)	(0.4572)
Delaware	16.0204	15.9590	15.9681	16.1915
	(599.3)	(600.1)	(598.4)	(598.8)
New Jersey	16.2158	16.1669	16.1880	16.3617
	(608.3)	(606.5)	(605.6)	(607.8)
New York	0.7133[c]	0.6317[d]	0.5643	0.8345[c]
	(0.4132)	(0.4049)	(0.4113)	(0.4751)

continued

Table A6.2. continued

Explanatory Variables	Alternative Model Specifications			
	1	2	3	4
Massachusetts	0.5650[a]	0.5137[a]	0.4801[a]	0.7271[a]
	(0.1660)	(0.1625)	(0.1650)	(0.2604)
New Hampshire	0.7672[a]	0.6883[b]	0.6990[b]	0.9396[a]
	(0.2982)	(0.2981)	(0.3008)	(0.3590)
Rhode Island	0.0749	0.1304	−0.0655	0.2183
	(0.3055)	(0.2958)	(0.3043)	(0.3741)
Connecticut	1.8016[a]	1.7949[a]	1.7026[a]	1.9427[a]
	(0.3110)	(0.3023)	(0.3056)	(0.3799)
Somers' D_{yx}	.613	.616	.621	.611
R^2	.289	.289	.298	.287

[a] Significant at .01 level.
[b] Significant at .05 level.
[c] Significant at .10 level.
[d] P-value is less than .15. While not significant given the sample size at any conventional level, the estimated effect may be suggestive of a possible influence on the ratification vote.

Note: See the note to table A6.1.

Table A6.3. Estimated Logistic Coefficients of the Explanatory Variables for the Ratification Vote: Southern States

Explanatory Variables	Alternative Model Specifications			
	1	2	3	4
Constant	7.5840	7.3757	6.8119	4.8364
	(1.6287)	(1.6172)	(1.5775)	(1.2842)
Merchant	0.4254	0.3221	0.1886	—
	(0.4435)	(0.4519)	(0.4663)	
Western landowner	0.4466	0.4224	0.4552	0.5473
	(0.2682)	(0.2671)	(0.2668)	(0.2591)
Private creditor	−0.3415	−0.3253	−0.3710	—
	(0.7145)	(0.7245)	(0.7209)	
Debtor	−1.9981	−2.1602	−2.0765	−1.9188
	(0.7433)	(0.7549)	(0.7592)	(0.7001)
Farmer	−0.1344	−0.0903	0.0979	—
	(0.2320)	(0.2329)	(0.2351)	
Slaveowner	−1.0212	−1.0179	—	−1.1155
	(0.3195)	(0.3213)		(0.3122)
Value of slaves ($000s)	—	—	0.00463	—
			(0.0126)	
Owner public securities	−0.00072	—	—	—
	(0.2398)			
Owner >$1,000 public securities	—	0.7844	—	0.6628
		(0.3179)		(0.3028)
Value of public securities ($000s)	—	—	0.1585	—
			(0.0651)	
Slaves per 100 whites	0.00113	0.00112	0.00102	—
	(0.000599)	(0.000602)	(0.000614)	
Public funding credit ($)	−0.1194	−0.1366	−0.1589	—
	(0.0459)	(0.0437)	(0.0425)	
Distance to navigable water (miles)	−0.0174	−0.0175	−0.0167	−0.0182
	(0.00250)	(0.00251)	(0.00248)	(0.00242)
Population (000s)	−0.00037	−0.00083	−0.00122	—
	(0.00131)	(0.00126)	(0.00121)	
English ancestry of citizens (percent)	−0.0260	−0.0247	−0.0259	−0.0137
	(0.0161)	(0.0160)	(0.0157)	(0.0149)
Order	−0.3419	−0.3254	−0.3445	−0.1846
	(0.0779)	(0.0775)	(0.0753)	(0.0529)
Somers' D_{yx}	.599	.608	.594	.581
R^2	.253	.261	.253	.243

Note: Number of observations for each specification is 628. All other details are as described in the note to table A6.1.

Table A6.4. Estimated Logistic Coefficients of the Explanatory Variables for the Ratification Vote: Middle Atlantic States

Explanatory Variables	Alternative Model Specifications			
	1	2	3	4
Constant	1.6462	1.3787	0.6787	1.8685
	(1.2654)	(1.2077)	(1.1411)	(1.1840)
Merchant	0.2014	0.2542	0.4256	—
	(1.0721)	(1.0403)	(1.0122)	
Western landowner	−0.5149	−0.4834	−0.6776	—
	(0.7134)	(0.7110)	(0.6799)	
Private creditor	1.8550	1.6643	0.7064	2.0758
	(1.2975)	(1.2654)	(1.1352)	(1.2524)
Debtor	0.1937	0.2291	−0.00359	—
	(1.2085)	(1.2008)	(1.2638)	
Farmer	1.4464	1.3284	1.1415	1.6223
	(0.7208)	(0.7125)	(0.6604)	(0.6661)
Slaveowner	−3.5193	−3.4715	—	−3.6744
	(1.0578)	(1.0348)		(1.0395)
Value of slaves ($000s)	—	—	−3.5745	—
			(1.6264)	
Owner public securities	−0.5743	—	—	−0.6180
	(0.6190)			(0.6134)
Owner >$1,000 public securities	—	−0.3899	—	—
		(0.6329)		
Value of public securities ($000s)	—	—	0.0695	—
			(0.0610)	
Slaves per 100 whites	0.0574	0.0530	0.0893	—
	(0.0848)	(0.0825)	(0.0893)	
Public funding credit ($)[a]	—	—	—	—
Distance to Navigable Water (miles)	−0.0287	−0.0292	−0.0263	−0.0302
	(0.00630)	(0.00630)	(0.00581)	(0.00597)
Population (000s)[a]	—	—	—	—
English ancestry of citizens (percent)	0.0547	0.0572	0.0533	0.0521
	(0.0224)	(0.0223)	(0.0215)	(0.0214)
Order	−0.4188	−0.4335	−0.3952	−0.3814
	(0.1190)	(0.1188)	(0.1149)	(0.1017)
Somers' D_{yx}	.891	.888	.873	.888
R^2	.440	.438	.413	.435

[a] The model cannot be estimated with this variable included.

Note: Number of observations for each specification is 162. All other details are as described in the note to table A6.1.

Table A6.5. Estimated Logistic Coefficients of the Explanatory Variables for the Ratification Vote: New England States

Explanatory Variables	Alternative Model Specifications			
	1	2	3	4
Constant	−9.5390	−10.5643	−9.8785	−7.7829
	(9.6127)	(9.5511)	(9.5507)	(8.5480)
Merchant	1.1129	0.9758	1.0213	0.9479
	(0.3849)	(0.3911)	(0.3860)	(0.3792)
Western landowner	2.5636	2.4217	2.3345	2.4318
	(1.0620)	(1.0557)	(1.0576)	(1.0482)
Private creditor	2.7841	2.7588	2.7491	2.7690
	(1.0621)	(1.0624)	(1.0578)	(1.0614)
Debtor	−0.7966	−0.7035	−0.8475	—
	(0.7860)	(0.7833)	(0.7841)	
Farmer	0.5451	0.6498	0.6167	0.6630
	(0.3008)	(0.2979)	(0.2957)	(0.2959)
Slaveowner[a]	—	—	—	—
Value of slaves ($000s)[a]	—	—	—	—
Owner public securities	0.8989	—	—	—
	(0.2840)			
Owner >$1,000 public securities	—	1.4246	—	1.4282
		(0.4480)		(0.4459)
Value of public securities ($000s)	—	—	0.0899	—
			(0.0492)	
Slaves per 100 whites	0.2132	0.1840	0.2060	—
	(0.1964)	(0.1924)	(0.1900)	
Public funding credit ($)	−0.2005	−0.1285	−0.1102	—
	(0.1609)	(0.1579)	(0.1563)	
Distance to navigable water (miles)	−0.0240	−0.0254	−0.0264	−0.0251
	(0.00588)	(0.00581)	(0.00580)	(0.00550)
Population (000s)	−0.00202	−0.00313	−0.00375	−0.00496
	(0.00269)	(0.00261)	(0.00258)	(0.00187)
English ancestry of citizens (percent)	0.1356	0.1509	0.1480	0.1279
	(0.0969)	(0.0961)	(0.0960)	(0.0869)
Order	−0.2505	−0.2758	−0.3026	−0.3359
	(0.1087)	(0.1069)	(0.1060)	(0.0851)
Somers' D_{yx}	.585	.585	.573	.578
R^2	.229	.233	.220	.230

[a] The model cannot be estimated with this variable included.

Note: Number of observations for each specification is 422. All other details are as described in the note to table A6.1.

Table A6.6. Estimated Logistic Coefficients of the Explanatory Variables for the Ratification Vote for the Fixed-Effects Model: Southern States

Explanatory Variables	Alternative Model Specifications			
	1	2	3	4
Merchant	0.4060	0.1646	0.1871	0.3088
	(0.4399)	(0.4667)	(0.4639)	(0.4452)
Western landowner	0.4722	0.4439	0.4998	0.4951
	(0.2675)	(0.2678)	(0.2645)	(0.2654)
Private securities owner	−0.2612	−0.3931	−0.1628	−0.1390
	(0.7143)	(0.7295)	(0.7042)	(0.7123)
Debtor	−1.8296	−2.1015	−1.8624	−1.8928
	(0.7407)	(0.7983)	(0.7501)	(0.7412)
Farmer	−0.1882	0.0736	−0.1321	−0.1619
	(0.2291)	(0.2347)	(0.2347)	(0.2278)
Slaveowner	−1.0149	—	—	—
	(0.3231)			
Value of slaves	—	0.0101	—	—
		(0.0120)		
Slave share	—	—	−0.8244	—
			(0.5421)	
Slave instrument	—	—	—	−0.2300
				(0.0914)
Public securities owner	−0.0166	—	—	—
	(0.2355)			
Value of public securities	—	0.1679	—	—
		(0.0648)		
Public securities share	—	—	3.6609	—
			(1.2325)	
Public securities instrument	—	—	—	0.00171
				(0.1232)
Distance	−0.0172	−0.0165	−0.0173	−0.0177
	(0.00231)	(0.00231)	(0.00234)	(0.00234)
Georgia	15.8397	15.7572	15.7385	15.9997
	(421.2)	(419.3)	(420.0)	(420.4)
North Carolina	1.3908	0.4036	0.6863	1.0596
	(0.3645)	(0.2120)	(0.2542)	(0.3540)
South Carolina	2.0055	0.6562	1.1034	1.7335
	(0.4137)	(0.2475)	(0.3193)	(0.4620)
Virginia	1.9167	0.7237	1.0641	1.6667
	(0.4272)	(0.2600)	(0.3470)	(0.4694)
Maryland	2.8840	1.7522	2.0298	2.4906
	(0.4880)	(0.3704)	(0.3945)	(0.4823)
Somers' D_{yx}	.595	.591	.596	.588
R^2	.252	.256	.262	.248

Note: Number of observations for each specification is 628. All other details are as described in the note to table A6.1.

Table A6.7. Estimated Logistic Coefficients of the Explanatory Variables for the Ratification Vote for the Fixed-Effects Model: Middle Atlantic States

Explanatory Variables	Alternative Model Specifications			
	1	2	3	4
Merchant	0.0665	0.2209	0.4136	0.0665
	(0.9880)	(0.9719)	(0.9642)	(0.9880)
Western landowner	−0.5005	−0.7992	−0.8921	−0.5005
	(0.6654)	(0.6377)	(0.6372)	(0.6654)
Private creditor	1.9523	1.1711	1.0231	1.9523
	(1.0671)	(1.0362)	(1.0557)	(1.0671)
Debtor	−0.1278	−0.4334	−0.3975	−0.1278
	(1.0984)	(1.1209)	(1.1071)	(1.0984)
Farmer	1.4260	1.1301	1.1104	1.4260
	(0.6744)	(0.6170)	(0.6195)	(0.6744)
Slaveowner	−2.6316	—	—	—
	(0.9251)			
Value of slaves	—	−2.3819	—	—
		(1.5653)		
Slave share	—	—	−3.6801	—
			(8.2238)	
Slave instrument	—	—	—	−2.6316
				(0.9251)
Public securities owner	−0.7789	—	—	—
	(0.5912)			
Value of public securities	—	0.0676	—	—
		(0.0643)		
Public securities share	—	—	2.1978	—
			(1.4375)	
Public securities instrument	—	—	—	−0.7789
				(0.5912)
Distance	−0.0236	−0.0217	−0.0215	−0.0236
	(0.00520)	(0.00501)	(0.00503)	(0.00520)
Pennsylvania	3.2489	2.2517	1.9185	6.6595
	(0.7791)	(0.5995)	(0.5957)	(1.7954)
Delaware	13.4551	13.4939	13.4726	16.8657
	(216.5)	(217.6)	(217.0)	(216.5)
New Jersey	14.5958	14.1329	14.1370	18.0064
	(214.8)	(221.4)	(221.3)	(214.8)
New York	1.6173	0.9698	0.9000	5.0279
	(0.6877)	(0.5484)	(0.5506)	(1.6101)
Somers' D_{yx}	.882	.870	.863	.882
R^2	.564	.547	.544	.564

Note: Number of observations for each specification is 162. All other details are as described in the note to table A6.1.

Table A6.8. Estimated Logistic Coefficients of the Explanatory Variables for the Ratification Vote for the Fixed-Effects Model: New England States

Explanatory Variables	Alternative Model Specifications			
	1	2	3	4
Merchant	1.1040	0.9956	0.9890	1.0627
	(0.3790)	(0.3779)	(0.3807)	(0.3818)
Western landowner	2.7130	2.4772	2.6638	2.7653
	(1.0636)	(1.0587)	(1.0623)	(1.0651)
Private creditor	2.8394	2.7971	2.8867	2.8714
	(1.0607)	(1.0555)	(1.0564)	(1.0609)
Debtor	−0.6932	−0.7431	−0.7484	−0.7804
	(0.7699)	(0.7737)	(0.7888)	(0.7744)
Farmer	0.5792	0.6500	0.6611	0.5857
	(0.3007)	(0.2960)	(0.2986)	(0.3006)
Public securities owner	0.9293	—	—	—
	(0.2803)			
Value of public securities	—	0.0926	—	—
		(0.0490)		
Public securities share	—	—	4.1121	—
			(1.2198)	
Public securities instrument	—	—	—	0.5923
				(0.1632)
Distance	−0.0244	−0.0267	−0.0249	−0.0240
	(0.00584)	(0.00578)	(0.00583)	(0.00583)
Massachusetts	0.3654	0.5549	0.4246	−0.2425
	(0.2267)	(0.2130)	(0.2184)	(0.3158)
New Hampshire	0.5979	0.7676	0.6156	−0.0294
	(0.4123)	(0.4048)	(0.4101)	(0.4667)
Rhode Island	−0.5753	−0.0808	−0.4002	−1.1894
	(0.3723)	(0.3262)	(0.3501)	(0.4670)
Connecticut	1.3906	1.8282	1.5828	0.7847
	(0.3866)	(0.3599)	(0.3681)	(0.4639)
Somers' D_{yx}	.585	.576	.592	.583
R^2	.285	.275	.293	.289

Note: Number of observations for each specification is 422. All other details are as described in the note to table A6.1.

Table A6.9. Estimated Logistic Coefficients of the Explanatory Variables for the Ratification Vote: States Ratifying Unconditionally

Explanatory Variables	Alternative Model Specifications			
	1	2	3	4
Constant	4.7942	4.7785	4.6787	3.5916
	(1.7926)	(1.7694)	(1.6530)	(0.5493)
Merchant	−0.1734	−0.1903	−0.1931	—
	(0.5227)	(0.5237)	(0.5248)	
Western landowner	0.6266	0.6213	0.6162	0.6875
	(0.5248)	(0.5275)	(0.5227)	(0.5188)
Private creditor	0.2822	0.3205	0.0605	—
	(0.9192)	(0.9305)	(0.8863)	
Debtor	−1.6248	−1.6162	−1.6405	−1.6627
	(0.9098)	(0.9043)	(0.8839)	(0.8871)
Farmer	1.2622	1.3617	1.2892	1.3434
	(0.5588)	(0.5621)	(0.5299)	(0.5223)
Slaveowner	−1.3455	−1.3476	—	−0.5235
	(0.6134)	(0.6156		(0.3808)
Value of slaves ($000s)	—	—	0.0164	—
			(0.0484)	
Owner public securities	0.2729	—	—	—
	(0.3927)			
Owner >$1,000 public securities	—	0.4016	—	—
		(0.4523)		
Value of public securities ($000s)	—	—	0.1034	0.000092
			(0.0679)	(0.000067)
Slaves per 100 whites	0.00165	0.00151	−0.00174	—
	(0.00941)	(0.00935)	(0.00607)	
Public funding credit ($)	−0.3575	−0.3547	−0.0698	—
	(0.2871)	(0.2853)	(0.1285)	
Distance to navigable water (miles)	−0.0102	−0.00962	−0.00869	−0.00885
	(0.00457)	(0.00454	(0.00440)	(0.00432)
Population (000s)	−0.00859	−0.00869	−0.00821	−0.00690
	(0.00320)	(0.00320)	(0.00274)	(0.00195)
English ancestry of citizens (percent)	−0.00200	−0.00154	−0.0104	—
	(0.0169)	(0.0168)	(0.01410)	
Somers' D_{yx}	.634	.643	.624	.616
R^2	.170	.171	.162	.160

Note: Number of observations for each specification is 296. All other details are as described in the note to table A6.1.

Table A6.10. Estimated Logistic Coefficients of the Explanatory Variables for the Ratification Vote: States Ratifying with Recommended Amendments Only

Explanatory Variables	Alternative Model Specifications			
	1	2	3	4
Constant	−25.6445	−26.5856	−26.7745	−25.2572
	(11.4479)	(11.3514)	(11.3492)	(11.3530)
Merchant	1.8341	1.7301	1.7253	1.7081
	(0.6049)	(0.6107)	(0.6108)	(0.6017)
Western landowner	1.4268	1.3366	1.2911	—
	(1.1589)	(1.1601)	(1.1605)	
Private creditor	2.3365	2.4230	2.4402	2.3298
	(1.0936)	(1.0945)	(1.0898)	(1.0853)
Debtor	−1.0671	−1.0679	−1.0626	—
	(2.4303)	(2.3724)	(2.3627)	
Farmer	0.4942	0.4975	0.4961	0.5846
	(0.3436)	(0.3421)	(0.3401)	(0.3376)
Slaveowner[a]	—	—	—	—
Value of slaves ($000s)	—	—	—	—
Owner public securities	0.9383	—	—	—
	(0.3879)			
Owner >$1,000 public securities	—	1.0859	—	1.0543
		(0.6152)		(0.6086)
Value of public securities ($000s)	—	—	0.0955	—
			(0.0805)	
Slaves per 100 whites[a]	—	—	—	—
Public funding credit ($)	−0.1798	−0.1727	−0.1789	—
	(0.1379)	(0.1375)	(0.1371)	
Distance to navigable water (miles)	−0.0267	−0.0283	−0.0291	−0.0265
	(0.00625)	(0.00616)	(0.00617)	(0.00571)
Population (000s)[a]	—	—	—	—
English ancestry of citizens (percent)	0.2813	0.2926	0.2954	0.2732
	(0.1218)	(0.1207)	(0.1207)	(0.1201)
Somers' D_{yx}	.586	.583	.590	.564
R^2	.246	.239	.235	.225

[a] The model cannot be estimated with this variable included because the sample consists of only the Massachusetts and New Hampshire ratifying conventions.

Note: Number of observations for each specification is 275. All other details are as described in the note to table A6.1.

Table A6.11. Estimated Logistic Coefficients of the Explanatory Variables for the Ratification Vote: States Ratifying with Amendments and Declarations

	Alternative Model Specifications			
Explanatory Variables	1	2	3	4
Constant	2.5360	1.9512	1.5893	3.2935
	(1.3004)	(1.2749)	(1.2315)	(1.2011)
Merchant	0.5019	0.3773	0.4133	—
	(0.3652)	(0.3727)	(0.3796)	
Western landowner	0.3847	0.3498	0.4145	0.3586
	(0.2610)	(0.2604)	(0.2604)	(0.2571)
Private creditor	1.0395)	0.9974	1.1021	0.9080
	(0.6332)	(0.6396)	(0.6456)	(0.6391)
Debtor	−0.6164	−0.7092	−0.5945	—
	(0.5121)	(0.5154)	(0.5201)	
Farmer	0.00229	0.0594	0.2164	—
	(0.2207)	(0.2211)	(0.2218)	
Slaveowner	−0.8959	−0.7372	—	−0.4793
	(0.2652)	(0.2541)		(0.2190)
Value of slaves ($000s)	—	—	−0.00030	—
			(0.0126)	
Owner public securities	−0.2286	—	—	—
	(0.2068)			
Owner >$1,000 public securities	—	0.6618	—	0.7599
		(0.2766)		(0.2676)
Value of public securities ($000s)	—	—	0.1022	—
			(0.0417)	
Slaves per 100 whites	0.00105	0.00103	0.000817	—
	(0.000579)	(0.000576)	(0.000586)	
Public funding credit ($)	0.0681	0.0424	0.00752	—
	(0.0362)	(0.0347)	(0.0319)	
Distance to navigable water (miles)	−0.0196	−0.0191	−0.0194	−0.0209
	(0.00249)	(0.00247)	(0.00247)	(0.00239)
Population (000s)	0.00340	0.00277	0.00120	0.00129
	(0.00128)	(0.00126)	(0.00109)	(0.000758)
English ancestry of citizens	−0.0249	−0.0192	−0.0160	−0.0293
	(0.0138)	(0.0135)	(0.0130)	(0.0132)
Somers' D_{yx}	.544	.547	.548	.537
R^2	.215	.220	.213	.208

Note: Number of observations for each specification is 641. All other details are as described in the note to table A6.1.

Table A6.12. Estimated Logistic Coefficients of the Explanatory Variables for the Ratification Vote: States Ratifying with Amendments and/or Declarations

Explanatory Variables	Alternative Model Specifications			
	1	2	3	4
Constant	2.4024	2.1552	1.1690	0.5635
	(1.2149)	(1.1913)	(1.0694)	(0.1200)
Merchant	0.9451	0.8395	0.8304	0.8250
	(0.2989)	(0.3047)	(0.3065)	(0.3013)
Western landowner	0.5562	0.5252	0.5325	0.5898
	(0.2485)	(0.2483)	(0.2500)	(0.2414)
Private creditor	1.4880	1.4693	1.5405	1.5541
	(0.5332)	(0.5394)	(0.5403)	(0.5422)
Debtor	−0.8638	−0.9188	−0.8265	−0.8672
	(0.4997)	(0.5052)	(0.5042)	(0.4972)
Farmer	0.2701	0.3028	0.3317	0.3331
	(0.1745)	(0.1751)	(0.1778)	(0.1710)
Slaveowner	−0.4474	−0.4303	—	—
	(0.1815)	(0.1820)		
Value of slaves ($000s)	—	—	−0.00073	—
			(0.0124)	
Owner public securities	0.1771	—	—	—
	(0.1686)			
Owner >$1,000 public securities	—	0.8496	—	0.9216
		(0.2461)		(0.2397)
Value of public securities ($000s)	—	—	0.1076	—
			(0.0370)	
Slaves per 100 whites	0.00131	0.00125	0.000839	—
	(0.000574)	(0.000578)	(0.000567)	
Public funding credit ($)	−0.00792	−0.0120	−0.00542	—
	(0.0244)	(0.0243)	(0.0241)	
Distance to navigable water (miles)	−0.0201	−0.0200	−0.0203	−0.0203
	(0.00231)	(0.00230)	(0.00228)	(0.00208)
Population (000s)	0.000782	0.000674	0.000612	—
	(0.000727)	(0.000732)	(0.000725)	
English ancestry of citizens (percent)	−0.0211	−0.0184	−0.00907	—
	(0.0127)	(0.0125)	(0.0114)	
Somers' D_{yx}	.538	.549	.552	.544
R^2	.204	.214	.210	.204

Note: Number of observations for each specification is 916. All other details are as described in the note to table A6.1.

Table A6.13. Estimated Logistic Coefficients of the Explanatory Variables for the Ratification Vote: First Nine States to Ratify

Explanatory Variables	Alternative Model Specifications			
	1	2	3	4
Constant	3.4530	3.7679	2.9273	2.1045
	(0.9161)	(0.8976)	(0.7698)	(0.2884)
Merchant	0.9451	0.8857	0.8012	0.6529
	(0.3364)	(0.3377)	(0.3422)	(0.3291)
Western landowner	1.4509	1.4043	1.3817	1.6847
	(0.4246)	(0.4259)	(0.4275)	(0.4147)
Private creditor	0.9256	1.0007	0.9541	1.1497
	(0.5772)	(0.5812)	(0.5783)	(0.5910)
Debtor	−1.9856	−1.9846	−1.9176	−1.8116
	(0.6194)	(0.6198)	(0.6158)	(0.6170)
Farmer	0.2037	0.2829	0.3457	—
	(0.2178)	(0.2173)	(0.2197)	
Slaveowner	−0.5164	−0.5426	—	−0.7111
	(0.2754)	(0.2741)		(0.2143)
Value of slaves ($000s)	—	—	0.00293	—
			(0.0150)	
Owner public securities	0.6259	—	—	—
	(0.1999)			
Owner >$1,000 public securities	—	0.6702	—	0.6583
		(0.2617)		(0.2542)
Value of public securities ($000s)	—	—	0.1400	—
			(0.0475)	
Slaves per 100 whites	0.00166	0.00163	0.00136	—
	(0.000637)	(0.000646)	(0.000649)	
Public funding credit ($)	−0.1698	−0.1538	−0.1814	—
	(0.0362)	(0.0352)	(0.0344)	
Distance to navigable water (miles)	−0.0187	−0.0186	−0.0184	−0.0172
	(0.00309)	(0.00313)	(0.00309)	(0.00293)
Population (000s)	−0.00272	−0.00282	−0.00205	−0.00323
	(0.00101)	(0.00101)	(0.000926)	(0.000880)
English ancestry of citizens (percent)	−0.0141	−0.0167	−0.0104	—
	(0.00856)	(0.00841)	(0.00759)	
Somers' D_{yx}	.579	.589	.594	.540
R^2	.199	.195	.201	.154

Note: Number of observations for each specification is 741. All other details are as described in the note to table A6.1.

Table A6.14. Estimated Logistic Coefficients of the Explanatory Variables for the Ratification Vote: First Nine States to Ratify Excluding Unanimous States

Explanatory Variables	Alternative Model Specifications			
	1	2	3	4
Constant	1.5758	1.9038	1.3917	0.8664
	(1.1008)	(1.0837)	(0.9048)	(0.1390)
Merchant	0.9862	0.9221	0.8279	0.8242
	(0.3378)	(0.3386)	(0.3432)	(0.3278)
Western landowner	1.4196	1.3703	1.3442	1.5114
	(0.4270)	(0.4274)	(0.4304)	(0.4122)
Private creditor	0.8503	0.9255	0.8818	0.9415
	(0.5767)	(0.5801)	(0.5808)	(0.5699)
Debtor	−2.1839	−2.1671	−2.0745	−2.0319
	(0.6755)	(0.6739)	(0.6728)	(0.6539)
Farmer	0.1813	0.2699	0.3280	—
	(0.2196)	(0.2192)	(0.2235)	
Slaveowner	−0.1914	−0.2230	—	—
	(0.2911)	(0.2892)		
Value of slaves ($000s)	—	—	0.00808	—
			(0.0150)	
Owner public securities	0.6770	—	—	—
	(0.2010)			
Owner >$1,000 public securities	—	0.7344	—	0.7059
		(0.2612)		(0.2497)
Value of public securities ($000s)	—	—	0.1477	—
			(0.0487)	
Slaves per 100 whites	0.00178	0.00175	0.00152	—
	(0.000645)	(0.000656	(0.000665)	
Public funding credit ($)	−0.1481	−0.1299	−0.1414	—
	(0.0380)	(0.0372)	(0.0367)	
Distance to navigable water (miles)	−0.0167	−0.0166	−0.0163	−0.0158
	(0.00312)	(0.00317)	(0.00313)	(0.00284)
Population (000s)	−0.00102	−0.00114	−0.00068	—
	(0.00113)	(0.00113)	(0.000999)	
English ancestry of citizens (percent)	−0.00141	−0.00410	−0.00034	—
	(0.00966)	(0.00950)	(0.00839)	
Somers' D_{yx}	.519	.532	.539	.492
R^2	.163	.158	.169	.134

Note: Number of observations for each specification is 662. All other details are as described in the note to table A6.1.

Table A6.15. Estimated Logistic Coefficients of the Explanatory Variables for the Ratification Vote: Fifth through Ninth States to Ratify

Explanatory Variables	Alternative Model Specifications			
	1	2	3	4
Constant	1.4836	1.6954	1.0479	0.8864
	(2.4953)	(2.4948)	(1.9015)	(0.1565)
Merchant	1.1564	1.0502	0.9786	0.9799
	(0.3734)	(0.3742)	(0.3779)	(0.3617)
Western landowner	3.0878	2.9258	2.9031	3.0299
	(0.8432)	(0.8293)	(0.8341)	(0.8181)
Private creditor	0.9334	0.9609	0.9436	0.8850
	(0.6685)	(0.6721)	(0.6721)	(0.6581)
Debtor	−3.9070	−3.8210	−3.6912	−3.6776
	(1.0430)	(1.0486)	(1.0432)	(1.0201)
Farmer	0.0564	0.1634	0.1810	—
	(0.2379)	(0.2368)	(0.2406)	
Slaveowner	−0.0916	−0.1535	—	—
	(0.3830)	(0.3823)		
Value of slaves ($000s)	—	—	0.000829	—
			(0.0160)	
Owner public securities	0.8601	—	—	—
	(0.2230)			
Owner >$1,000 public securities	—	1.0081	—	0.9774
		(0.3003)		(0.2880)
Value of public securities ($000s)	—	—	0.1869	—
			(0.0636)	
Slaves per 100 whites	0.00170	0.00156	0.00145	—
	(0.000683)	(0.000704)	(0.000710)	
Public funding credit ($)	−0.1499	−0.1190	−0.1201	—
	(0.0454)	(0.0441)	(0.0443)	
Distance to navigable water (miles)	−0.0187	−0.0200	−0.0194	−0.0206
	(0.00418)	(0.00416)	(0.00414)	(0.00379)
Population (000s)	−0.00101	−0.00147	−0.00138	—
	(0.00135)	(0.00133)	(0.00128)	
English ancestry of citizens (percent)	−0.00096	−0.00107	0.00527	—
	(0.0262)	(0.0262)	(0.0212)	
Somers' D_{yx}	.558	.550	.565	.515
R^2	.201	.197	.203	.178

Note: Number of observations for each specification is 600. All other details are as described in the note to table A6.1.

Table A6.16. Estimated Logistic Coefficients of the Explanatory Variables for the Ratification Vote: Tenth through Thirteenth States to Ratify

Explanatory Variables	Alternative Model Specifications			
	1	2	3	4
Constant	0.4899	0.3532	0.4359	0.0994
	(1.7141)	(1.6766)	(1.6651)	(0.2946)
Merchant	0.2729	0.2252	0.3160	—
	(0.4435)	(0.4469)	(0.4413)	
Western landowner	0.1090	0.0327	0.1067	—
	(0.2929)	(0.2946)	(0.2911)	
Private creditor	1.1973	1.1961	1.2409	1.2763
	(0.7697)	(0.7740)	(0.7826)	(0.7255)
Debtor	0.3948	0.3423	0.3847	—
	(0.6686)	(0.6758)	(0.6736)	
Farmer	0.0744	0.1400	0.1834	—
	(0.2696)	(0.2704)	(0.2714)	
Slaveowner	−0.6357	−0.3863	—	−0.6517
	(0.3152)	(0.2975)		(0.2747)
Value of slaves ($000s)	—	—	−0.00578	—
			(0.0268)	
Owner public securities	−0.2875	—	—	—
	(0.2611)			
Owner >$1,000 public securities	—	0.7873	—	0.9653
		(0.3902)		(0.3830)
Value of public securities ($000s)	—	—	0.0611	—
			(0.0463)	
Slaves per 100 whites	−0.0137	−0.0123	−0.0137	—
	(0.00348)	(0.00349)	(0.00346)	
Public funding credit ($)	0.0436	0.0253	0.0307	—
	(0.0534)	(0.0528)	(0.0520)	
Distance to navigable water (miles)	−0.0254	−0.0244	−0.0252	−0.0186
	(0.00320)	(0.00316)	(0.00315)	(0.00243)
Population (000s)	0.00737	0.00613	0.00588	0.00326
	(0.00174)	(0.00168)	(0.00156)	(0.00107)
English ancestry of citizens (percent)	−0.00619	−0.00548	−0.00704	—
	(0.0181)	(0.0177)	(0.0176)	
Somers' D_{yx}	.599	.601	.600	.560
R^2	.245	.250	.242	.223

Note: Number of observations for each specification is 471. All other details are as described in the note to table A6.1.

Table A6.17. Estimated Logistic Coefficients of the Explanatory Variables for the Ratification Vote: States with Paper Money

Explanatory Variables	Alternative Model Specifications			
	1	2	3	4
Constant	4.1912	3.2575	4.0070	1.3249
	(1.4489)	(1.3002)	(1.3031)	(0.8831)
Merchant	0.6875	0.6210	0.5209	0.3402
	(0.3931)	(0.3949)	(0.4072)	(0.3916)
Western landowner	0.2288	0.2329	0.1557	—
	(0.3049)	(0.3027)	(0.3098)	
Private creditor	0.6909	0.6535	0.6108	—
	(0.6374)	(0.6409)	(0.6513)	
Debtor	−0.4937	−0.5428	−0.4852	—
	(0.5101)	(0.5044)	(0.5092)	
Farmer	0.5011	0.5087	0.6747	0.4155
	(0.2600)	(0.2590)	(0.2640)	(0.2491)
Slaveowner	−0.6186	−0.4564	—	−0.7372
	(0.2842)	(0.2716)		(0.2156)
Value of slaves ($000s)	—	—	0.0195	—
			(0.0142)	
Owner public securities	−0.6128	—	—	—
	(0.2464)			
Owner >$1,000 public securities	—	−0.0186	—	—
		(0.2919)		
Value of public securities ($000s)	—	—	0.0653	0.000059
			(0.0346)	(0.000032)
Slaves per 100 whites	0.00163	0.00156	0.00105	—
	(0.000626)	(0.000611)	(0.000615)	
Public funding credit ($)	−0.1509	−0.1601	−0.2314	—
	(0.0662)	(0.0604)	(0.0570)	
Distance to navigable water (miles)	−0.0219	−0.0215	−0.0210	−0.0227
	(0.00278)	(0.00276)	(0.00275)	(0.00270)
Population (000s)	−0.00444	−0.00391	−0.00673	0.00178
	(0.00296)	(0.00267)	(0.00249)	(0.00114)
English ancestry of citizens (percent)	0.0229	0.0268	0.0276	0.0239
	(0.0140)	(0.0138)	(0.0140)	(0.0125)
Order	−0.3464	−0.3288	−0.3768	−0.2287
	(0.0797)	(0.0730)	(0.0729)	(0.0466)
Somers' D_{yx}	.683	.677	.683	.652
R^2	.319	.312	.317	.297

Note: Number of observations for each specification is 598. All other details are as described in the note to table A6.1.

Table A6.18. Estimated Logistic Coefficients of the Explanatory Variables for the Ratification Vote: States without Paper Money

Explanatory Variables	Alternative Model Specifications			
	1	2	3	4
Constant	9.0459	8.2542	7.5821	2.2788
	(2.6128)	(2.4882)	(2.4701)	(0.3733)
Merchant	0.8126	0.7565	0.6987	0.6621
	(0.3595)	(0.3643)	(0.3622)	(0.3523)
Western landowner	1.0386	0.9953	1.0401	1.2073
	(0.3682)	(0.3693)	(0.3624)	(0.3526)
Private creditor	1.2658	1.4254	1.4548	1.1828
	(0.6541)	(0.6638)	(0.6747)	(0.6547)
Debtor	−2.8364	−2.7369	−2.8034	−2.7662
	(1.1642)	(1.1753)	(1.1739)	(1.1894)
Farmer	0.0588	0.1600	0.1312	—
	(0.2284)	(0.2261)	(0.2243)	
Slaveowner	−1.0709	−1.0744	—	0.4109
	(0.5596)	(0.5668)		(0.2535)
Value of slaves ($000s)	—	—	−0.0252	—
			(0.0259)	
Owner public securities	0.8710	—	—	—
	(0.2198)			
Owner >$1,000 public securities	—	1.5039	—	1.5399
		(0.3645)		(0.3605)
Value of public securities ($000s)	—	—	0.1787	—
			(0.0681)	
Slaves per 100 whites	−0.00649	−0.00611	−0.00748	—
	(0.00399)	(0.00403)	(0.00395)	
Public funding credit ($)	−0.8763	−0.9219	−0.6460	—
	(0.2953)	(0.2943)	(0.2150)	
Distance to navigable water (miles)	−0.0150	−0.0152	−0.0163	−0.0123
	(0.00372)	(0.00374)	(0.00367)	(0.00318)
Population (000s)	0.00259	0.00308	0.00110	—
	(0.00224)	(0.00222)	(0.00168)	
English ancestry of citizens (percent)	−0.0334	−0.0231	−0.0239	—
	(0.0275)	(0.0259)	(0.0262)	
Order	−0.5837	−0.6073	−0.4987	−0.2395
	(0.1575)	(0.1579)	(0.1364)	(0.0579)
Somers' D_{yx}	.576	.592	.575	.511
R^2	.211	.218	.203	.170

Note: Number of observations for each specification is 614. All other details are as described in the note to table A6.1.

Table A6.19. Estimated Logistic Coefficients of the Explanatory Variables for the Ratification Vote for the Fixed-Effects Model: States with Paper Money

Explanatory Variables	Alternative Model Specifications			
	1	2	3	4
Merchant	0.6904	0.5368	0.5679	0.6863
	(0.3977)	(0.4146)	(0.4079)	(0.3995)
Western landowner	0.2641	0.1492	0.3107	0.2862
	(0.3014)	(0.3097)	(0.3004)	(0.3009)
Private creditor	1.0313	0.8180	0.9272	1.0499
	(0.6613)	(0.6612)	(0.6619)	(0.6500)
Debtor	−0.2672	−0.3995	−0.3275	−0.3195
	(0.5008)	(0.5084)	(0.5007)	(0.5062)
Farmer	0.3395	0.6667	0.4576	0.3259
	(0.2573)	(0.2656)	(0.2602)	(0.2573)
Slaveowner	−1.3234	—	—	—
	(0.3733)			
Value of slaves	—	0.0249	—	—
		(0.0140)		
Slave share	—	—	−0.4924	—
			(0.6624)	
Slave instrument	—	—	—	−0.3922
				(0.1311)
Public securities owner	−0.4812	—	—	—
	(0.2605)			
Value of public securities	—	0.0764	—	—
		(0.0367)		
Public securities share	—	—	1.9218	—
			(0.8368)	
Public securities instrument	—	—	—	−0.2112
				(0.1420)
Distance to navigable water	−0.0242	−0.0223	−0.0226	−0.0237
	(0.00280)	(0.00273)	(0.00274)	(0.00275)
Georgia	16.0020	15.7176	15.6771	16.4628
	(422.2)	(426.3)	(425.9)	(424.4)
North Carolina	1.9590	0.5835	0.8044	2.1207
	(0.4219)	(0.2236)	(0.2738)	(0.4991)
South Carolina	2.5570	0.5307	0.9826	2.7536
	(0.4729)	(0.2566)	(0.3437)	(0.6132)
Pennsylvania	2.9592	1.9729	1.9220	3.2134
	(0.4859)	(0.4063)	(0.4179)	(0.5674)
New Jersey	15.7073	15.1900	15.2762	16.2282
	(365.4)	(368.1)	(368.2)	(366.6)
New York	1.5157	0.8674	0.8550	2.0102
	(0.4784)	(0.4345)	(0.4373)	(0.5748)
Rhode Island	0.4909	0.1442	0.0325	1.0227
	(0.3373)	(0.3064)	(0.3137)	(0.4406)
Somers' D_{yx}	.685	.680	.676	.678
R^2	.330	.324	.321	.324

Note: Number of observations for each specification is 598. All other details are as described in the note to table A6.1.

Table A6.20. Estimated Logistic Coefficients of the Explanatory Variables for the Ratification Vote for the Fixed-Effects Model: States without Paper Money

Explanatory Variables	Alternative Model Specifications			
	1	2	3	4
Merchant	0.8494	0.6963	0.7148	0.7953
	(0.3592)	(0.3630)	(0.3674)	(0.3611)
Western landowner	0.9983	0.9892	0.9492	0.9610
	(0.3679)	(0.3619)	(0.3658)	(0.3684)
Private creditor	1.3013	1.5129	1.4337	1.2408
	(0.6503)	(0.6721)	(0.6509)	(0.6535)
Debtor	−2.9947	−2.9439	−2.8583	−2.9802
	(1.1647)	(1.1717)	(1.1680)	(1.1665)
Farmer	0.0438	0.0693	0.0805	0.0394
	(0.2300)	(0.2275)	(0.2316)	(0.2311)
Slaveowner	−1.1602	—	—	—
	(0.5554)			
Value of slaves	—	−0.0300	—	—
		(0.0243)		
Slave share	—	—	−0.8113	—
			(0.8764)	
Slave instrument	—	—	—	−0.5232
				(0.2534)
Public securities owner	0.8120	—	—	—
	(0.2237)			
Value of public securities	—	0.1663	—	—
		(0.0671)		
Public securities share	—	—	5.4220	—
			(1.3402)	
Public securities instrument	—	—	—	0.5274
				(0.1287)
Distance to navigable water	−0.0112	−0.0129	−0.0127	−0.0116
	(0.00326)	(0.00325)	(0.00331)	(0.00329)
Virginia	1.1188	0.5272	0.5009	0.9547
	(0.5688)	(0.2979)	(0.4352)	(0.7833)
Maryland	2.7038	1.8617	1.8283	2.4573
	(0.6602)	(0.4224)	(0.4490)	(0.8222)
Delaware	15.0760	15.1551	15.0726	15.0620
	(361.3)	(364.8)	(362.5)	(360.7)
Massachusetts	0.2852	0.4076	0.3135	0.2743
	(0.1845)	(0.1787)	(0.1833)	(0.3673)
New Hampshire	0.3772	0.4836	0.4196	0.3758
	(0.3219)	(0.3218)	(0.3276)	(0.4513)
Connecticut	1.3674	1.6779	1.5024	1.3593
	(0.3394)	(0.3288)	(0.3339)	(0.4786)
Somers' D_{yx}	.565	.561	.579	.577
R^2	.284	.278	.298	.291

Note: Number of observations for each specification is 614. All other details are as described in the note to table A6.1.

Voting Models for Massachusetts, North Carolina, and Virginia Ratifying Conventions

Table A7.1. Estimated Logistic Coefficients of the Explanatory Variables for the Ratification Vote at the Seven Ratifying Conventions, 1787–1788: Specification One

Explanatory Variables	State Ratifying Convention						
	CN	MA	NH	NC	PA	SC	VA
Constant	-62.1429	-14.3488	-58.7102[b]	2.2575	-0.2144	-4.2182	6.2756[c]
	(57.5970)	(13.5289)	(25.5730)	(2.7235)	(1.7867)	(5.1535)	(3.2092)
Merchant	1.1032	1.8003[a]	1.9627	Yes[e]	-1.3005	1.5535[c]	-1.7901[d]
	(0.8947)	(0.6884)	(1.4367)		(3.0561)	(0.8435)	(1.1814)
Western landowner	Yes[e]	—	1.0210	-0.5559	-0.1880	2.8661[b]	0.3548
			(1.2040)	(0.5290)	(1.0888)	(1.2488)	(0.4464)
Private creditor	Yes[f]	Yes[e]	-1.8955	-0.7871	3.0552[c]	-1.7849	0.7487
			(1.8321)	(1.4562)	(1.7792)	(1.6559)	(1.2352)
Debtor	No[f]	-0.3209	—	—	1.4185	-3.7081[a]	—
		(1.8316)			(1.7786)	(1.3237)	
Farmer	0.4661	0.2944	0.4122	0.7802[d]	1.9352[c]	-0.6487[d]	-0.6920[c]
	(0.9036)	(0.4039)	(0.6731)	(0.5226)	(1.0613)	(0.4431)	(0.3736)
Slaveowner	—	—	—	-0.7668	-2.4701[b]	-2.6257[b]	-1.6067[b]
				(0.5745)	(1.2036)	(1.1215)	(0.6818)
Owner public securities	1.0519[d]	1.1951[a]	0.1772	0.7289	-0.5442	-0.1799	0.2971
	(0.7166)	(0.4169)	(1.0067)	(1.3915)	(0.8229)	(0.4028)	(0.3656)
Slaves per 100 whites	—	—	—	-0.0187[b]	-2.4218[b]	0.00154[b]	-0.00975[b]
				(0.00741)	(1.1575)	(0.000767)	(0.00486)

continued

Table A7.1. continued

Explanatory Variables	State Ratifying Convention						
	CN	MA	NH	NC	PA	SC	VA
Distance to navigable water (miles)	0.0202	−0.0298[a]	−0.0260[c]	−0.0301[a]	−0.0180[b]	−0.0191[a]	−0.0151[a]
	(0.0236)	(0.00718)	(0.0137)	(0.00501)	(0.00761)	(0.00729)	(0.00567)
English ancestry of citizens (percent)	0.6500	0.1573	0.6325[b]	0.00582	0.0781[b]	0.0924[d]	−0.0338
	(0.5989)	(0.1429)	(0.2731)	(0.0298)	(0.0356)	(0.0635)	(0.0364)
Somers' D_{yx}	.474	.588	.570	.691	.811	.677	.509
R^2	.097	.238	.243	.293	.432	.297	.175
Number of Observations	92	216	59	220	62	170	154

[a] Statistically significant at the .01 level.
[b] Statistically significant at the .05 level.
[c] Statistically significant at the .10 level.
[d] P-value is less than .15.
[e] The delegates in the sample with this characteristic voted unanimously (Yes or No).
[f] The two delegates in the sample with this characteristic voted unanimously (Yes or No).

Note: The asymptotic standard errors are in parentheses. The dependent variable in each specification is the observed vote for ratification at the ratifying convention in question, where a yes vote equals 1 and a no vote equals 0. A variable excluded for any convention has insufficient variance to be included in the voting model. Somers' D_{yx} is a measure of the degree of concordance between the predicted probability of a yes vote and the observed vote for each observation. R^2 is the generalized R^2 generated for logistic regression with the RSQUARE option in SAS 8.0. Somers' D_{yx} and R^2 are alternative measures of the goodness of fit of the estimated model.

Table A7.2. Estimated Logistic Coefficients of the Explanatory Variables for the Ratification Vote at the Seven Ratifying Conventions, 1787–1788: Specification Two

Explanatory Variables	State Ratifying Convention						
	CN	MA	NH	NC	PA	SC	VA
Constant	-87.2285[d]	-15.1868	-59.3367[b]	2.3730	-0.1802	-4.7212	5.3409[c]
	(55.1146)	(13.4303)	(25.5400)	(2.7126)	(1.7692)	(5.0787)	(2.8579)
Merchant	1.1877	1.6753[b]	1.9864	Yes[e]	-1.1327	1.4335[d]	-1.4940
	(0.8723)	(0.6929)	(1.4822)		(3.2615)	(0.8752)	(1.1761)
Western landowner	Yes[e]	—	0.9893	-0.5495	0.00128	2.8981[b]	0.2466
			(1.1944)	(0.5247)	(1.1146)	(1.2239)	(0.4581)
Private creditor	Yes[f]	Yes[e]	-1.8913	-0.7870	2.7399[d]	-1.8233	1.0406
			(1.8357)	(1.4561)	(1.7433)	(1.5792)	(1.2243)
Debtor	No[f]	-0.3754	—	—	1.8551	-3.9245[a]	—
		(1.8177)			(1.8002)	(1.3606)	
Farmer	0.9331	0.2931	0.4099	0.7840[d]	1.8435[c]	-0.5857	-0.6432[c]
	(0.8366)	(0.4003)	(0.6752)	(0.5232)	(1.0831)	(0.4431)	(0.3826)
Slaveowner	—	—	—	-0.7765	-2.5215[b]	-2.6057[b]	-1.6461[b]
				(0.5705)	(1.2217)	(1.1192)	(0.6957)

continued

301

Table A7.2. continued

Explanatory Variables	State Ratifying Convention						
	CN	MA	NH	NC	PA	SC	VA
Owner >$1,000 public securities	Yes[e]	1.5168[b]	0.0673	2.4048	−0.9411	0.4377	1.4785[b]
		(0.6906)	(1.4243)	(4.4008)	(0.9333)	(0.4672)	(0.6122)
Slaves per 100 whites	—	—	—	−0.0175[b]	−2.5355[b]	0.00157[b]	−0.00874[c]
				(0.00727)	(1.1795)	(0.000767)	(0.00501)
Distance to navigable water (miles)	0.0222	−0.0318[a]	−0.0265[c]	−0.0301[a]	−0.0202[a]	−0.0188[a]	−0.0149[a]
	(0.0234)	(0.00707)	(0.0136)	(0.00499)	(0.00783)	(0.00728)	(0.00575)
English ancestry of citizens (percent)	0.9140[d]	0.1682	0.6396	0.00399	0.0815[b]	0.0954[d]	−0.0246
	(0.5724)	(0.1418)	(0.2726)	(0.0297)	(0.0365)	(0.0630)	(0.0323)
Somers' D_{yx}	.388	.581	.569	.692	.809	.663	.548
R^2	.074	.228	.242	.293	.437	.300	.208
Number of Observations	92	216	59	220	62	170	154

[a] Statistically significant at the .01 level.
[b] Statistically significant at the .05 level.
[c] Statistically significant at the .10 level.
[d] P-value is less than .15.
[e] The delegates in the sample with this characteristic voted unanimously (Yes or No).
[f] The two delegates in the sample with this characteristic voted unanimously (Yes or No).

Note: See the note to table A7.1.

Table A7.3. Estimated Logistic Coefficients of the Explanatory Variables for the Ratification Vote at the Seven Ratifying Conventions, 1787–1788: Specification Three

Explanatory Variables	State Ratifying Convention						
	CN	MA	NH	NC	PA	SC	VA
Constant	-45.1659	-16.2657	-55.2734[b]	0.9710	-0.8342	-6.1981	5.2272[c]
	(58.1180)	(13.4311)	(24.4240)	(2.5500)	(1.6560)	(4.8887)	(2.9482)
Merchant	1.0837	1.6930[b]	1.1323	Yes[e]	-0.7059	1.0809	-2.0286[c]
	(0.9389)	(0.6908)	(1.5548)		(2.5859)	(0.9757)	(1.1881)
Western landowner	Yes[e]	—	1.0163	-0.6722	-0.1476	2.9796[b]	0.3883
			(1.1858)	(0.5471)	(1.0896)	(1.2432)	(0.4440)
Private creditor	Yes[f]	Yes[e]	-4.2934	-1.6043	2.0297	-1.6409	2.2632
			(5.4303)	(1.5318)	(1.6505)	(1.5770)	(1.7831)
Debtor	No[f]	-0.4239	—	—	1.6236	-4.0338[a]	—
		(1.8333)			(1.7561)	(1.4214)	
Farmer	1.0229	0.2918	0.3838	1.2337[b]	1.6660[c]	-0.2912	-0.8461[b]
	(0.8491)	(0.3960)	(0.6692)	(0.5194)	(0.9926)	(0.4588)	(0.3997)
Value of slaveholdings ($000s)	—	—	—	0.1065[b]	-1.4192	-0.0138	-0.0904[b]
				(0.0540)	(1.9077)	(0.0187)	(0.0399)

continued

303

Table A7.3. continued

Explanatory Variables	State Ratifying Convention						
	CN	MA	NH	NC	PA	SC	VA
Value of public securities holdings ($000 s)	2.1245 (1.9347)	0.1211 (0.0876)	0.2068 (0.2625)	0.6440 (0.8369)	0.0341 (0.1018)	0.2110[b] (0.1053)	0.2355[d] (0.1497)
Slaves per 100 whites		—	—	-0.0191[b] (0.00752)	-2.9041[b] (1.2156)	0.00175[b] (0.000782)	-0.0115[b] (0.00495)
Distance to navigable water (miles)	0.0209 (0.0248)	-0.0328[a] (0.00710)	-0.0253[c] (0.0132)	-0.0279[a] (0.00473)	-0.0167[b] (0.00682)	-0.0190[a] (0.00735)	-0.0196[a] (0.00574)
English ancestry of citizens (percent)	0.4721 (0.6041)	0.1804 (0.1418)	0.5962[b] (0.2604)	0.00723 (0.0296)	0.0806[b] (0.0337)	0.0819 (0.0608)	-0.0292 (0.0338)
Somers' D_{yx}	.545	.581	.573	.688	.735	.637	.518
R^2	.149	.217	.259	.305	.385	.292	.185
Number of Observations	92	216	59	220	62	170	154

[a] Statistically significant at the .01 level.
[b] Statistically significant at the .05 level.
[c] Statistically significant at the .10 level.
[d] P-value is less than .15.
[e] The delegates in the sample with this characteristic voted unanimously (Yes or No).
[f] The two delegates in the sample with this characteristic voted unanimously (Yes or No).

Note: See the note to table A7.1.

Table A7.4. Estimated Logistic Coefficients of the Explanatory Variables for the Ratification Vote at the Massachusetts Ratifying Convention: Local, State, and National Officeholder before or after the Convention

Explanatory Variables	Alternative Model Specifications		
	1	2	3
Constant	−1.0598 (11.2954)	−2.4575 (11.1990)	−3.3469 (11.1221)
Merchant	1.4591[a] (0.5078)	1.2989[a] (0.4919)	1.3195[a] (0.4921)
Western landowner	1.2122 (0.9805)	1.0345 (0.9761)	1.0321 (0.9590)
Private creditor	2.0519[a] (0.7733)	2.2723[a] (0.7747)	2.3394[a] (0.7538)
Debtor	−2.6418[b] (1.0406)	−2.2318[b] (1.0145)	−2.2928[b] (1.1202)
Farmer	−0.0386 (0.3191)	−0.1139 (0.3141)	−0.1255 (0.3135)
Slaveowner	—	—	—
Owner public securities	1.6324[a] (0.5090)		
Owner >$1,000 public securities	—	1.6423[c] (0.8754)	—
Value of public securities holdings ($)	—	—	0.000118 (0.000094)
Congregational/Puritan	−0.2891 (0.5410)	−0.2333 (0.5283)	−0.2077 (0.5267)
Baptist	−2.3599[a] (0.8324)	−2.3558[a] (0.8270)	−2.2517[a] (0.8224)
Presbyterian	−0.8460 (0.8818)	−0.8308 (0.8712)	−0.6847 (0.8480)
Delegate-English ancestry	1.2289[a] (0.4589)	1.0373[b] (0.4400)	0.9790[b] (0.4408)
Officer in Revolutionary War	0.7583[b] (0.3176)	0.7042[b] (0.3137)	0.6777[b] (0.3113)
Delegate age	−0.00842 (0.0149)	−0.00598 (0.0146)	−0.00594 (0.0146)
Local officeholder before convention	0.3385 (0.3735)	0.1856 (0.3615)	0.2231 (0.3623)
State officeholder before convention	0.1483 (0.3210)	0.0906 (0.3190)	0.1356 (0.3180)
Continental Congress before convention	0.8663 (1.0287)	0.5495 (1.0268)	0.7004 (1.0176)
Local officeholder after convention	−0.2603 (0.4503)	−0.1930 (0.4389)	−0.1715 (0.4365)
State officeholder after convention	−0.1588 (0.3490)	−0.2057 (0.3505)	−0.1390 (0.3478)
National officeholder after convention	0.2426 (0.9264)	0.3643 (0.8964)	0.4901 (0.8866)
Slaves per 100 whites	—	—	—
Distance to navigable water (miles)	−0.0337[a] (0.00711)	−0.0344[a] (0.00697)	−0.0345[a] (0.0069)
Constituent-English ancestry (percent)	0.0112 (0.1190)	0.0289 (0.1179)	0.0382 (0.1171)
Somers' D_{yx}	.674	.657	.649
R_2	.315	.297	.293

[a] Statistically significant at .01 level.
[b] Statistically significant at .05 level.
[c] Statistically significant at .10 level.

Note: Number of observations is 309. The dependent variable in each specification is the observed ratification vote at the Massachusetts convention, where a yes vote equals 1 and a no vote equals 0. The slave ownership variable is not included because of the very limited number of Massachusetts slaveowning delegates. The variable, slaves per 100 whites, is excluded because it is zero for all Massachusetts counties. The Episcopalian/Anglican variable is excluded because the residual "other" ancestry category is close to zero when all four of the religion variables are included. The constituent and the delegate Scottish/Irish ancestry variables are excluded because the residual "other" ancestry category also is close to zero for both variables. All other details are as described in the note to table A7.1.

Table A7.5. Estimated Logistic Coefficients of the Explanatory Variables for the Ratification Vote at the North Carolina Ratifying Convention: Local, State, and National Officeholder before or after the Convention

Explanatory Variables	Alternative Model Specifications		
	1	2	3
Constant	−1.6429 (3.3760)	−1.3121 (3.3529)	−1.1947 (3.2815)
Merchant	3.2023[a] (0.9953)	3.1803[a] (0.9969)	3.1136[a] (0.9823)
Western landowner	−0.6945 (0.6330)	−0.6660 (0.6335)	−0.7489 (0.6394)
Private creditor	1.8545[b] (0.8919)	1.9127[b] (0.9047)	1.6186[c] (0.9375)
Debtor	−0.9590 (0.8952)	−0.8178 (0.8625)	−0.7700 (0.8800)
Farmer	1.1121[b] (0.5309)	1.0809[b] (0.5281)	1.2092[b] (0.5221)
Slaveowner	0.0848 (0.5261)	0.0488 (0.5238)	—
Value of slaveholdings ($)	—	—	0.000073 (0.000062)
Owner public securities	1.2454 (1.7836)	—	—
Owner >$1,000 public securities	—	1.8534 (5.3415)	—
Value of public securities holdings ($)	—	—	0.000688 (0.000917)
Baptist	−3.3363[c] (1.8801)	−3.4910[c] (1.8797)	−3.2132[c] (1.8535)
Episcopalian/Anglican	—	—	—
Presbyterian	−0.5848 (1.4708)	−0.7212 (1.4488)	−0.6605 (1.4650)
Officer in Revolutionary War	0.6782 (0.4961)	0.6611 (0.4943)	0.6255 (0.4988)
Delegate age	−0.0152 (0.0300)	−0.0172 (0.0299)	−0.0176 (0.0298)
Local officeholder before convention	−0.2676 (1.2391)	−0.2825 (1.2470)	−0.2956 (1.2396)
State officeholder before convention	0.1808 (0.4144)	0.1155 (0.4032)	0.1162 (0.4091)
Continental Congress before convention	0.6699 (1.1184)	0.6327 (1.1047)	0.3131 (1.2381)
Local officeholder after convention	—	—	—
State officeholder after convention	−0.1795 (0.3903)	−0.1461 (0.3868)	−0.2375 (0.3962)
National officeholder after convention	0.8264 (0.7588)	0.7891 (0.7549)	0.9164 (0.7717)
Slaves per 100 whites	−0.0309[a] (0.00919)	−0.0293[a] (0.00890)	−0.0310[a] (0.00917)
Distance to navigable water (miles)	−0.0317[a] (0.00512)	−0.0316[a] (0.00512)	−0.0317[a] (0.00508)
Constituent-English ancestry (percent)	0.0624[c] (0.0347)	0.0604[c] (0.0346)	0.0577[c] (0.0345)
Somers' D_{yx}	.771	.769	.772
R^2	.366	.365	.370

[a] Statistically significant at .01 level.
[b] Statistically significant at .05 level.
[c] Statistically significant at .10 level.

Note: Number of observations is 261. The dependent variable in each specification is the observed ratification vote at the North Carolina convention, where a yes vote equals 1 and a no vote equals 0. The Congregational/Puritan variable is not included because it has a value of zero for all North Carolina delegates. The Episcopalian/Anglican variable is excluded because the residual "other" ancestry category is nearly zero if all three of the non-zero religion variables are included. The delegate English and the Scottish/Irish ancestry variables are excluded because data on personal ancestry were available for only thirty-five North Carolina delegates. All other details are as described in the note to table A7.1.

Table A7.6. Estimated Logistic Coefficients of the Explanatory Variables for the Ratification Vote at the Virginia Ratifying Convention: Local, State, and National Officeholder before or after the Convention

Explanatory Variables	Alternative Model Specifications		
	1	2	3
Constant	10.5901 (6.6463)	8.8985 (6.1144)	9.8961 (6.7162)
Merchant	−1.0549 (0.8653)	−1.1468 (0.8936)	−1.1555 (0.8657)
Western landowner	0.5178 (0.5221)	0.3182 (0.5464)	0.6470 (0.5208)
Private creditor	−0.0936 (0.8389)	−0.7053 (0.8990)	0.0638 (0.9258)
Debtor	−1.7161[b] (0.8695)	−2.3069[b] (1.0034)	−1.5107[c] (0.7987)
Farmer	−1.2132[a] (0.4695)	−1.3810[a] (0.4876)	−1.3962[a] (0.4981)
Slaveowner	−1.5725[b] (0.7435)	−1.7928[b] (0.7935)	—
Value of slaveholdings ($)	—	—	−0.00008[c] (0.000043)
Owner public securities	0.4671 (0.4165)	—	—
Owner >$1,000 public securities	—	2.2009[a] (0.7439)	—
Value of public securities holdings ($)	—	—	0.000227 (0.000169)
Episcopalian/Anglican	−0.3612 (1.2068)	−0.2695 (1.3284)	0.1588 (1.2650)
Presbyterian	1.8239 (1.7291)	1.6205 (1.9687)	2.2172 (1.8344)
Delegate-English ancestry	1.2547 (1.1532)	1.4446 (1.2630)	1.2452 (1.1540)
Delegate-Scottish/Irish ancestry	0.7523 (1.1562)	0.9354 (1.2464)	1.0716 (1.1537)
Officer in Revolutionary War	0.4880 (0.4460)	0.7185 (0.4678)	0.4402 (0.4463)
Delegate age	0.00317 (0.0248)	0.00750 (0.0265)	0.0116 (0.0251)
Local officeholder before convention	0.2796 (1.4416)	0.3062 (1.4762)	0.3264 (1.4681)
State officeholder before convention	−0.1415 (0.4779)	−0.1986 (0.4957)	−0.0279 (0.4704)
Continental Congress before convention	−1.1556 (0.7603)	−1.6234[b] (0.8167)	−1.5156[c] (0.7956)
Local officeholder after convention	−14.3723 (1218.3)	−14.2107 (1218.3)	−14.6153 (1218.3)
State officeholder after convention	0.2381 (0.4082)	0.3107 (0.4223)	0.1610 (0.4056)
National officeholder after convention	−0.5345 (0.6149)	−0.7029 (0.6233)	−0.4682 (0.6142)
Slaves per 100 whites	−0.0151[a] (0.00544)	−0.0138[b] (0.00556)	−0.0155[a] (0.00553)
Distance to navigable water (miles)	−0.0209[a] (0.00628)	−0.0206[a] (0.00637)	−0.0245[a] (0.00654)
Constituent-English ancestry (percent)	−0.0639 (0.0661)	−0.0437 (0.0600)	−0.0676 (0.0663)
Constituent-Scottish/Irish ancestry (percent)	−0.1744 (0.1354)	−0.2054 (0.1389)	−0.2463[c] (0.1338)
Somers' D_{yx}	.625	.678	.661
R^2	.306	.346	.310

[a] Statistically significant at .01 level.
[b] Statistically significant at .05 level.
[c] Statistically significant at .10 level.

Note: Number of observations is 165. The dependent variable in each specification is the observed ratification vote at the Virginia convention, where a yes vote equals 1 and a no vote equals 0. The Baptist and Congregational/Puritan religion variables are excluded because they have a value of zero for all Virginia delegates. All other details are as described in the note to table A7.1.

Table A7.7. Estimated Logistic Coefficients of the Explanatory Variables for the Ratification Vote at the Massachusetts Ratifying Convention: Local, State, and National Officeholder before the Convention

Explanatory Variables	Alternative Model Specifications		
	1	2	3
Constant	−2.0448 (11.1983)	−3.3111 (11.1112)	−4.0546 (11.0465)
Merchant	1.4798[a] (0.5058)	1.3078[a] (0.4902)	1.3227[a] (0.4907)
Western landowner	1.1121 (0.9681)	0.9362 (0.9653)	0.9754 (0.9427)
Private creditor	2.0613[a] (0.7746)	2.2905[a] (0.7778)	2.3729[a] (0.7565)
Debtor	−2.6532[b] (1.0393)	−2.2218[b] (1.0014)	−2.3285[b] (1.1158)
Farmer	−0.0359 (0.3177)	−0.1172 (0.3126)	−0.1282 (0.3123)
Slaveowner	—	—	—
Owner public securities	1.6157[a] (0.5023)	—	—
Owner >$1,000 public securities	—	1.6025[c] (0.8590)	—
Value of public securities holdings ($)	—	—	0.000121 (0.000094)
Congregational/Puritan	−0.3211 (0.5334)	−0.2791 (0.5203)	−0.2459 (0.5192)
Baptist	−2.3498[a] (0.8259)	−2.3598[a] (0.8216)	−2.2668[a] (0.8171)
Presbyterian	−0.8140 (0.8798)	−0.8233 (0.8689)	−0.6844 (0.8475)
Delegate-English ancestry	1.2388[a] (0.4557)	1.0573[b] (0.4373)	0.9996[b] (0.4379)
Officer in Revolutionary War	0.7548[b] (0.3111)	0.7063[b] (0.3080)	0.6882[b] (0.3066)
Delegate age	−0.0072 (0.0146)	−0.00485 (0.0144)	−0.00552 (0.0143)
Local officeholder before convention	0.2468 (0.3113)	0.1349 (0.3033)	0.1690 (0.3030)
State officeholder before convention	0.1248 (0.3012)	0.0568 (0.2989)	0.1251 (0.2956)
Continental Congress before convention	1.0117 (0.9703)	0.7419 (0.9706)	0.9282 (0.9454)
Slaves per 100 whites	—	—	—
Distance to navigable water (miles)	−0.0335[a] (0.00705)	−0.0343[a] (0.00690)	−0.0345[a] (0.00684)
Constituent-English ancestry (percent)	0.0204 (0.1181)	0.0368 (0.1172)	0.0451 (0.1164)
Somers' D_{yx}	.672	.654	.651
R^2	.313	.296	.292

[a] Statistically significant at .01 level.
[b] Statistically significant at .05 level.
[c] Statistically significant at .10 level.

Note: See the note to table A7.4.

Table A7.8. Estimated Logistic Coefficients of the Explanatory Variables for the Ratification Vote at the North Carolina Ratifying Convention: Local, State, and National Officeholder before the Convention

Explanatory Variables	Alternative Model Specifications		
	1	2	3
Constant	−1.3111 (3.2695)	−1.0260 (3.2498)	−0.9036 (3.1622)
Merchant	3.3286[a] (0.9928)	3.3046[a] (0.9946)	3.2547[a] (0.9790)
Western landowner	−0.7386 (0.6363)	−0.7146 (0.6354)	−0.7992 (0.6425)
Private creditor	2.0222[b] (0.8951)	2.0627[b] (0.9047)	1.8601[b] (0.9242)
Debtor	−0.9165 (0.8981)	−0.7990 (0.8662)	−0.7412 (0.8835)
Farmer	1.0890[b] (0.5247)	1.0653[b] (0.5226)	1.1633[b] (0.5151)
Slaveowner	0.1062 (0.5188)	0.0777 (0.5168)	—
Value of slaveholdings ($)	—	—	0.000065 (0.000062)
Owner public securities	1.0569 (1.7762)	—	—
Owner >$1,000 public securities	—	1.8820 (5.3864)	—
Value of public securities holdings ($)	—	—	0.000645 (0.00101)
Baptist	−3.2545[c] (1.8426)	−3.3924[c] (1.8375)	−3.0803[c] (1.8149)
Episcopalian/Anglican	—	—	—
Presbyterian	−0.7599 (1.4538)	−0.8599 (1.4354)	−0.8281 (1.4526)
Officer in Revolutionary War	0.6817 (0.4890)	0.6632 (0.4872)	0.6448 (0.4898)
Delegate age	−0.0198 (0.0286)	−0.0217 (0.0285)	−0.0224 (0.0282)
Local officeholder before convention	0.000415 (1.1916)	−0.0285 (1.1951)	0.0251 (1.1898)
State officeholder before convention	0.2198 (0.3941)	0.1692 (0.3838)	0.1693 (0.3886)
Continental Congress before convention	0.9448 (1.0223)	0.9123 (1.0152)	0.6313 (1.1247)
Slaves per 100 whites	−0.0297[a] (0.00893)	−0.0284[a] (0.00872)	−0.0296[a] (0.00886)
Distance to navigable water (miles)	−0.0315[a] (0.00507)	−0.0315[a] (0.00507)	−0.0316[a] (0.00502)
Constituent-English ancestry (percent)	0.0595[c] (0.0342)	0.0579[c] (0.0342)	0.0552 (0.0341)
Somers' D_{yx}	.769	.768	.772
R^2	.363	.362	.366

[a] Statistically significant at .01 level.
[b] Statistically significant at .05 level.
[c] Statistically significant at .10 level.

Note: See the note to table A7.5.

Table A7.9. Estimated Logistic Coefficients of the Explanatory Variables for the Ratification Vote at the Virginia Ratifying Convention: Local, State, and National Officeholder before the Convention

Explanatory Variables	Alternative Model Specifications		
	1	2	3
Constant	8.6259 (5.8211)	6.7328 (5.0296)	7.7900 (5.9077)
Merchant	−1.2079 (0.8507)	−1.3810 (0.8899)	−1.2759 (0.8448)
Western landowner	0.5045 (0.5191)	0.2977 (0.5374)	0.6313 (0.5171)
Private creditor	−0.1393 (0.8288)	−0.7527 (0.8807)	−0.0119 (0.9093)
Debtor	−1.7295[c] (0.8875)	−2.3940[b] (1.0461)	−1.5446[c] (0.8219)
Farmer	−1.0656[b] (0.4423)	−1.1755[a] (0.4551)	−1.2548[a] (0.4714)
Slaveowner	−1.5280[b] (0.7214)	−1.7087[b] (0.7588)	—
Value of slaveholdings ($)	—	—	−0.00008[c] (0.000041)
Owner public securities	0.4905 (0.4160)	—	—
Owner >$1,000 public securities	—	2.1143[a] (0.7300)	—
Value of public securities holdings ($)	—	—	0.000230 (0.000161)
Episcopalian/Anglican	−0.3565 (1.2150)	−0.2554 (1.3137)	−0.1697 (1.2697)
Presbyterian	1.9732 (1.7165)	1.8083 (1.9284)	2.3874 (1.8130)
Delegate-English ancestry	1.1063 (1.1362)	1.2873 (1.2103)	1.0859 (1.1346)
Delegate-Scottish/Irish ancestry	0.6820 (1.1501)	0.8518 (1.2143)	0.9714 (1.1468)
Officer in Revolutionary War	0.5435 (0.4419)	0.7658[c] (0.4627)	0.4861 (0.4421)
Delegate age	0.0107 (0.0226)	0.0167 (0.0238)	0.0195 (0.0231)
Local officeholder before convention	−0.3923 (1.1746)	−0.3730 (1.2022)	−0.4019 (1.1894)
State officeholder before convention	−0.0656 (0.4602)	−0.1135 (0.4744)	0.0487 (0.4526)
Continental Congress before convention	−1.0969 (0.7498)	−1.5558[b] (0.7916)	−1.5128[c] (0.7814)
Slaves per 100 whites	−0.0140[a] (0.00533)	−0.0126[b] (0.00548)	−0.0148[a] (0.00540)
Distance to navigable water (miles)	−0.0209[a] (0.00629)	−0.0206[a] (0.00646)	−0.0249[a] (0.00648)
Constituent-English ancestry (percent)	−0.0468 (0.0590)	−0.0256 (0.0499)	−0.0483 (0.0593)
Constituent-Scottish/Irish ancestry (percent)	−0.1754 (0.1306)	−0.2077 (0.1325)	−0.2457[c] (0.1304)
Somers' D_{yx}	.632	.657	.642
R^2	.296	.333	.300

[a] Statistically significant at .01 level.
[b] Statistically significant at .05 level.
[c] Statistically significant at .10 level.

Note: See the note to table A7.6.

Table A7.10. Estimated Logistic Coefficients of the Explanatory Variables for the Ratification Vote at the Massachusetts Ratifying Convention: Local, State, and National Officeholder after the Convention

Explanatory Variables	Alternative Model Specifications		
	1	2	3
Constant	−1.9471 (11.3476)	−2.8581 (11.2309)	−3.8997 (11.1748)
Merchant	1.4988[a] (0.5040)	1.3225[a] (0.4899)	1.3573[a] (0.4885)
Western landowner	1.2887 (0.9718)	1.1020 (0.9653)	1.0924 (0.9553)
Private creditor	2.0834[a] (0.7682)	2.2833[a] (0.7710)	2.3806[a] (0.7497)
Debtor	−2.4266[b] (0.9812)	−2.1366[b] (0.9783)	−2.1262[b] (1.0605)
Farmer	−0.0526 (0.3176)	−0.1183 (0.3134)	−0.1338 (0.3124)
Slaveowner	—	—	—
Owner public securities	1.5586[a] (0.4996)	—	—
Owner >$1,000 public securities	—	1.6660[c] (0.8648)	—
Value of public securities holdings ($)	—	—	0.000113 (0.000092)
Congregational/Puritan	−0.3049 (0.5394)	−0.2397 (0.5282)	−0.2136 (0.5263)
Baptist	−2.3989[a] (0.8334)	−2.3845[a] (0.8279)	−2.2861[a] (0.8255)
Presbyterian	−0.9166 (0.8815)	−0.8739 (0.8712)	−0.7342 (0.8473)
Delegate-English ancestry	1.1945[a] (0.4546)	1.0264[b] (0.4375)	0.9682[b] (0.4385)
Officer in Revolutionary War	0.7281[b] (0.3148)	0.6899[b] (0.3117)	0.6559[b] (0.3089)
Delegate age	−0.00587 (0.0145)	−0.00454 (0.0143)	−0.00404 (0.0143)
Local officeholder after convention	−0.0868 (0.3768)	−0.1044 (0.3712)	−0.0690 (0.3682)
State officeholder after convention	−0.1784 (0.3240)	−0.2191 (0.3257)	−0.1440 (0.3210)
National officeholder after convention	0.5197 (0.8861)	0.5076 (0.8675)	0.7181 (0.8469)
Slaves per 100 whites	—	—	—
Distance to navigable water (miles)	−0.0324[a] (0.00692)	−0.0338[a] (0.00685)	−0.0335[a] (0.00673)
Constituent-English ancestry (percent)	0.0213 (0.1195)	0.0335 (0.1182)	0.0443 (0.1176)
Somers' D_{yx}	.669	.657	.649
R^2	.311	.296	.291

[a] Statistically significant at .01 level.
[b] Statistically significant at .05 level.
[c] Statistically significant at .10 level.

Note: See the note to table A7.4.

Table A7.11. Estimated Logistic Coefficients of the Explanatory Variables for the Ratification Vote at the North Carolina Ratifying Convention: Local, State, and National Officeholder after the Convention

Explanatory Variables	Alternative Model Specifications		
	1	2	3
Constant	−1.6651 (3.3754)	−1.3782 (3.3524)	−1.2395 (3.2715)
Merchant	3.1442[a] (0.9851)	3.1314[a] (0.9879)	3.0885[a] (0.9728)
Western landowner	−0.6791 (0.6261)	−0.6642 (0.6274)	−0.7349 (0.6313)
Private creditor	1.8151[b] (0.8854)	1.8746[b] (0.8928)	1.5871[c] (0.9229)
Debtor	−0.9005 (0.8750)	−0.7976 (0.8469)	−0.7193 (0.8614)
Farmer	1.0440[b] (0.5178)	1.0335[b] (0.5165)	1.1701[b] (0.5080)
Slaveowner	0.0799 (0.5242)	0.0474 (0.5214)	—
Value of slaveholdings ($)	—	—	0.000077 (0.000061)
Owner public securities	1.0452 (1.7258)	—	—
Owner >$1,000 public securities	—	1.8468 (5.2942)	—
Value of public securities holdings ($)	—	—	0.000657 (0.000939)
Baptist	−3.2395[c] (1.7902)	−3.3680[c] (1.7921)	−3.1021[c] (1.7723)
Episcopalian/Anglican	—	—	—
Presbyterian	−0.6845 (1.4668)	−0.7989 (1.4449)	−0.7292 (1.4612)
Officer in Revolutionary War	0.7139 (0.4899)	0.7006 (0.4880)	0.6409 (0.4952)
Delegate age	−0.0127 (0.0297)	−0.0147 (0.0296)	−0.0163 (0.0294)
Local officeholder after convention	—	—	—
State officeholder after convention	−0.1024 (0.3738)	−0.0863 (0.3727)	−0.1936 (0.3828)
National officeholder after convention	0.9811 (0.7111)	0.9283 (0.7049)	0.9778 (0.7173)
Slaves per 100 whites	−0.0296[a] (0.00891)	−0.0283[a] (0.00870)	−0.0304[a] (0.0090)
Distance to navigable water (miles)	−0.0313[a] (0.00505)	−0.0313[a] (0.00505)	−0.0315[a] (0.00501)
Constituent-English ancestry (percent)	0.0616[c] (0.0344)	0.0597[c] (0.0343)	0.0575[c] (0.0342)
Somers' D_{yx}	.768	.768	.771
R^2	.364	.364	.369

[a] Statistically significant at .01 level.
[b] Statistically significant at .05 level.
[c] Statistically significant at .10 level.

Note: See the note to table A7.5.

Table A7.12. Estimated logistic Coefficients of the Explanatory Variables for the Ratification Vote at the Virginia Ratifying Convention: Local, State, and National Officeholder after the Convention

Explanatory Variables	Alternative Model Specifications		
	1	2	3
Constant	10.4503 (6.4055)	9.0256 (5.8337)	9.6551 (6.4777)
Merchant	−0.9393 (0.8367)	−0.9724 (0.8582)	−0.9582 (0.8141)
Western landowner	0.5565 (0.5174)	0.3725 (0.5356)	0.6125 (0.5140)
Private creditor	−0.1462 (0.8055)	−0.6970 (0.8785)	−0.0526 (0.9182)
Debtor	−1.6929[c] (0.8663)	−2.2426[b] (0.9826)	−1.5357[c] (0.7928)
Farmer	−1.0347[b] (0.4355)	−1.1338[b] (0.4489)	−1.1627[b] (0.4577)
Slaveowner	−1.5191[b] (0.7213)	−1.5833[b] (0.7414)	—
Value of slaveholdings ($)	—	—	−0.00007 (0.000042)
Owner public securities	0.5058 (0.4048)	—	—
Owner >$1,000 public securities	—	2.0715[a] (0.7541)	—
Value of public securities holdings ($)	—	—	0.000242 (0.000185)
Episcopalian/Anglican	−0.4118 (1.1657)	−0.2951 (1.2447)	0.1267 (1.2149)
Presbyterian	1.4289 (1.6497)	1.0102 (1.7908)	1.6617 (1.6916)
Delegate-English ancestry	1.0884 (1.1097)	1.1521 (1.1863)	1.0453 (1.0951)
Delegate-Scottish/Irish ancestry	0.7201 (1.1224)	0.8689 (1.1927)	1.0056 (1.1109)
Officer in Revolutionary War	0.4521 (0.4338)	0.6553 (0.4479)	0.4552 (0.4323)
Delegate age	−0.00583 (0.0236)	−0.00473 (0.0247)	0.000922 (0.0238)
Local officeholder after convention	−13.8712 (1218.3)	−13.6161 (1218.3)	−14.0441 (1218.3)
State officeholder after convention	0.1282 (0.3953)	0.1690 (0.4042)	0.0977 (0.3938)
National officeholder after convention	0.6257 (0.6078)	−0.8524 (0.6133)	−0.6452 (0.6016)
Slaves per 100 whites	−0.0152[a] (0.00530)	−0.0140[a] (0.00536)	−0.0158[a] (0.00538)
Distance to navigable water (miles)	−0.0193[a] (0.00595)	−0.0185[a] (0.00588)	−0.0224[a] (0.00620)
Constituent-English ancestry (percent)	−0.0581 (0.0635)	−0.0400 (0.0571)	−0.0597 (0.0637)
Constituent-Scottish/Irish ancestry (percent)	−0.1917 (0.1294)	−0.2311[c] (0.1317)	−0.2571[b] (0.1285)
Somers' D_{yx}	.621	.648	.631
R^2	.295	.328	.294

[a] Statistically significant at .01 level.
[b] Statistically significant at .05 level.
[c] Statistically significant at .10 level.

Note: See the note to table A7.6.

Table A7.13. Estimated Logistic Coefficients of the Explanatory Variables for the Ratification Vote at the Massachusetts Ratifying Convention: All Political Variables Excluded

Explanatory Variables	Alternative Model Specifications		
	1	2	3
Constant	−2.5677 (11.2728)	−3.5543 (11.1520)	−4.4682 (11.1204)
Merchant	1.5073[a] (0.4999)	1.3339[a] (0.4870)	1.3714[a] (0.4844)
Western landowner	1.2471 (0.9672)	1.0530 (0.9621)	1.0906 (0.9436)
Private creditor	2.1312[a] (0.7635)	2.3223[a] (0.7716)	2.4702[a] (0.7525)
Debtor	−2.4026[b] (0.9659)	−2.1022[b] (0.9609)	−2.1309[b] (1.0502)
Farmer	−0.0672 (0.3149)	−0.1335 (0.3109)	−0.1522 (0.3102)
Slaveowner	—	—	—
Owner public securities	1.5635[a] (0.4927)	—	—
Owner >$1,000 public securities	—	1.6413[b] (0.8342)	—
Value of public securities holdings ($)	—	—	0.000118 (0.000092)
Congregational/Puritan	−0.3656 (0.5316)	−0.3082 (0.5187)	−0.2777 (0.5168)
Baptist	−2.4512[a] (0.8270)	−2.4283[a] (0.8216)	−2.3581[a] (0.8201)
Presbyterian	−0.9496 (0.8767)	−0.9090 (0.8665)	−0.7870 (0.8433)
Delegate-English ancestry	1.2093[a] (0.4526)	1.0483[b] (0.4348)	0.9900[b] (0.4357)
Officer in Revolutionary War	0.7432[b] (0.3089)	0.6973[b] (0.3056)	0.6723[b] (0.3039)
Delegate age	−0.00588 (0.0143)	−0.00412 (0.0142)	−0.00438 (0.0141)
Slaves per 100 whites	—	—	—
Distance to navigable water (miles)	−0.0321[a] (0.00682)	−0.0335[a] (0.00674)	−0.0333[a] (0.00664)
Constituent-English ancestry (percent)	0.0275 (0.1189)	0.0402 (0.1176)	0.0504 (0.1172)
Somers' D_{yx}	.664	.654	.647
R^2	.310	.294	.289

[a] Statistically significant at .01 level.
[b] Statistically significant at .05 level.
[c] Statistically significant at .10 level.

Note: See the note to table A7.4.

Table A7.14. Estimated Logistic Coefficients of the Explanatory Variables for the Ratification Vote at the North Carolina Ratifying Convention: All Political Variables Excluded

Explanatory Variables	Alternative Model Specifications		
	1	2	3
Constant	−0.9368 (3.2242)	−0.7445 (3.2130)	−0.6349 (3.1195)
Merchant	3.2596[a] (0.9862)	3.2460[a] (0.9882)	3.1991[a] (0.9730)
Western landowner	−0.7480 (0.6261)	−0.7383 (0.6256)	−0.8135 (0.6313)
Private creditor	1.9713[b] (0.8849)	2.0025[b] (0.8874)	1.7833[b] (0.9089)
Debtor	−0.8407 (0.8772)	−0.7670 (0.8512)	−0.6658 (0.8634)
Farmer	0.9968[c] (0.5119)	0.9920[c] (0.5112)	1.1092[b] (0.5003)
Slaveowner	0.1360 (0.5167)	0.1128 (0.5132)	—
Value of slaveholdings ($)	—	—	0.000075 (0.000059)
Owner public securities	0.7741 (1.7225)	—	—
Owner >$1,000 public securities	—	1.8443 (5.2768)	—
Value of public securities holdings ($)	—	—	0.000576 (0.00108)
Baptist	−3.3696[c] (1.7723)	−3.4483[c] (1.7691)	−3.1313[c] (1.7539)
Episcopalian/Anglican	—	—	—
Presbyterian	−0.9163 (1.4405)	−0.9791 (1.4258)	−0.9236 (1.4396)
Officer in Revolutionary War	0.6987 (0.4804)	0.6877 (0.4791)	0.6408 (0.4850)
Delegate age	−0.0200 (0.0286)	−0.0213 (0.0285)	−0.0224 (0.0282)
Slaves per 100 whites	−0.0281[a] (0.00874)	−0.0272[a] (0.00860)	−0.0288[a] (0.00877)
Distance to navigable water (miles)	−0.0313[a] (0.00499)	−0.0313[a] (0.00500)	−0.0314[a] (0.00496)
Constituent-English ancestry (percent)	0.0570[c] (0.0337)	0.0557[c] (0.0337)	0.0532 (0.0336)
Somers' D_{yx}	.767	.767	.770
R^2	.360	.359	.365

[a] Statistically significant at .01 level.
[b] Statistically significant at .05 level.
[c] Statistically significant at .10 level.

Note: See the note to table A7.5.

Table A7.15. Estimated Logistic Coefficients of the Explanatory Variables for the Ratification Vote at the Virginia Ratifying Convention: All Political Variables Excluded

Explanatory Variables	Alternative Model Specifications		
	1	2	3
Constant	8.4110 (5.5174)	6.7727 (4.7735)	7.3537 (5.5811)
Merchant	−1.0746 (0.8235)	−1.2053 (0.8540)	−1.0717 (0.7970)
Western landowner	0.5345 (0.5147)	0.3328 (0.5283)	0.5852 (0.5100)
Private creditor	−0.1462 (0.7924)	−0.6780 (0.8565)	−0.0696 (0.8987)
Debtor	−1.6777^c (0.8846)	−2.2826^b (1.0326)	−1.5218^c (0.8160)
Farmer	−0.8325^b (0.4017)	−0.8635^b (0.4084)	−0.9301^b (0.4182)
Slaveowner	−1.5181^b (0.7105)	−1.5829^b (0.7259)	—
Value of slaveholdings ($)	—	—	−0.00007^c (0.000041)
Owner public securities	0.5380 (0.4045)	—	—
Owner >$1,000 public securities	—	1.9401^a (0.7249)	—
Value of public securities holdings ($)	—	—	0.000232 (0.000172)
Episcopalian/Anglican	−0.4006 (1.1769)	−0.3216 (1.2427)	0.1323 (1.2246)
Presbyterian	1.6574 (1.6481)	1.2787 (1.7625)	1.9378 (1.6880)
Delegate-English ancestry	0.9201 (1.0966)	0.9995 (1.1493)	0.8469 (1.0729)
Delegate-Scottish/Irish ancestry	0.6657 (1.1230)	0.8010 (1.1726)	0.9083 (1.1041)
Officer in Revolutionary War	0.5076 (0.4265)	0.7061 (0.4401)	0.5070 (0.4250)
Delegate age	0.00296 (0.0218)	0.00685 (0.0226)	0.00974 (0.0222)
Slaves per 100 whites	−0.0140^a (0.00520)	−0.0127^b (0.00529)	−0.0149^a (0.00526)
Distance to navigable water (miles)	−0.0199^a (0.00605)	−0.0191^a (0.00610)	−0.0233^a (0.00620)
Constituent-English ancestry (percent)	−0.0426 (0.0556)	−0.0236 (0.0472)	−0.0407 (0.0556)
Constituent-Scottish/Irish ancestry (percent)	−0.1763 (0.1246)	−0.2152^c (0.1262)	−0.2408^c (0.1246)
Somers' D_{yx}	.623	.634	.621
R^2	.285	.315	.283

[a] Statistically significant at .01 level.
[b] Statistically significant at .05 level.
[c] Statistically significant at .10 level.

Note: See the note to table A7.6.

Table A7.16. Estimated Logistic Coefficients of the Explanatory Variables for the Ratification Vote at the Massachusetts Ratifying Convention: Model Specifications with Alternative Variables

	Alternative Model Specifications for Massachusetts			
Explanatory Variables	1	2	3	4
Constant	-3.5334 (11.0298)	-1.1248 (11.3616)	-2.6114 (11.2276)	-1.4949[b] (0.7189)
Merchant	1.4156[a] (0.4761)	1.5590[a] (0.5068)	1.3961[a] (0.4943)	1.6656[a] (0.4826)
Western landowner	1.1239 (0.9541)	0.9641 (1.0350)	0.7369 (1.0187)	—
Private creditor	2.4030[a] (0.7709)	2.3739[a] (0.8097)	2.5601[a] (0.8135)	2.2079[a] (0.7540)
Debtor	-2.0753[b] (0.9702)	-2.5981[a] (0.9585)	-2.2655[b] (0.9517)	-2.2849[b] (0.9111)
Framer	-0.2108 (0.3061)	-0.0875 (0.3185)	-0.1653 (0.3139)	-0.1547 (0.3086)
Slaveowner	—	3.1984[b] (1.5109)	2.9120[b] (1.4537)	—
Owner public securities	—	1.5226[a] (0.4984)	—	1.4142[a] (0.4755)
Owner >$1,000 public securities	1.6662[b] (0.8361)	—	1.4016 (0.8582)	—
Congregational/Puritan	-0.4093 (0.5122)	-0.3889 (0.5343)	-0.3239 (0.5212)	—
Baptist	-2.4263[a] (0.8101)	-3.0607[a] (0.9354)	-2.9855[a] (0.9263)	-2.1137[a] (0.6990)
Presbyterian	-0.8995 (0.8557)	-0.9386 (0.8767)	-0.8784 (0.8618)	—
Delegate-English ancestry	0.9786[b] (0.4288)	1.1539[b] (0.4569)	1.0007[b] (0.4392)	—
Delegate-Scottish/Irish ancestry	—	—	—	-1.2079[b] (0.4753)

continued

317

Table A7.16. continued

	Alternative Model Specifications for Massachusetts			
Explanatory Variables	1	2	3	4
Officer in Revolutionary War	0.6763[b] (0.3000)	0.7553[b] (0.3134)	0.7043[b] (0.3099)	0.7695[b] (0.3038)
Delegate age	−0.00654 (0.0139)	−0.00745 (0.0145)	−0.00558 (0.0142)	—
Slaves per 100 whites	—	—	—	—
Distance to Navigable water (miles)	—	−0.0320[a] (0.00689)	−0.0334[a] (0.00679)	—
Distance to Atlantic coast (miles)	−0.0195[a] (0.00469)	—	—	−0.0176[a] (0.00458)
Constituent-English ancestry (percent)	0.0403 (0.1163)	0.0138 (0.1198)	0.0316 (0.1183)	—
Constituent-Scottish/Irish ancestry (percent)	—	—	—	−0.2334[c] (0.1399)
Somers' D_{yx}	.624	.682	.675	.632
R^2	.272	.322	.305	.287

[a] Statistically significant at .01 level.
[b] Statistically significant at .05 level.
[c] Statistically significant at .10 level.

Note: To examine the robustness of the estimation, data on personal slave ownership are included in two of the specifications despite the small number of slaveowning delegates in Massachusetts. Both of the Scottish/Irish variables also are included in another specification despite the residual "other" ancestry category being close to zero for both variables for Massachusetts. The constituent slave variable (slaves per 100 whites), however, still is excluded from all specifications because it is zero for all Massachusetts counties. All other details are as described in the note to table A7.4.

318

Table A7.17. Estimated Logistic Coefficients of the Explanatory Variables for the Ratification Vote at the North Carolina Ratifying Convention: Model Specifications with Alternative Variables

Explanatory Variables	Alternative Model Specifications for North Carolina			
	1	2	3	4
Constant	-5.2321[c] (2.8644)	-3.0005 (3.0106)	-1.3732 (9.9465)	1.9642[c] (1.0962)
Merchant	2.8892[a] (0.8628)	3.3262[a] (0.9951)	3.2297[a] (0.9957)	2.7785[a] (0.8558)
Western landowner	-0.5368 (0.5925)	-0.7859 (0.6310)	-0.7585 (0.6237)	—
Private creditor	1.7051[b] (0.8025)	2.0639[b] (0.8960)	2.1661[b] (0.8910)	1.7835[b] (0.7688)
Debtor	-1.1629 (0.8425)	-0.8107 (0.8755)	-0.7338 (0.8535)	-1.1207 (0.8557)
Farmer	0.9753[b] (0.4752)	0.9870[c] (0.5128)	0.9779[c] (0.5123)	1.0623[b] (0.4441)
Slaveowner	-0.2143 (0.4929)	0.1522 (0.5173)	0.1302 (0.5137)	—
Owner public securities	—	—	—	—
Owner >$1,000 public securities	0.9857 (2.7975)	0.6685 (1.7748)	—	—
Congregational/Puritan	—	—	—	—
Baptist	-3.4409[b] (1.6344)	-2.1402 (1.9382)	-2.1723 (1.9580)	-1.9050 (1.7038)
Episcopalian/Anglican	—	1.7952 (1.4161)	1.8571 (1.3392)	1.6419 (1.2105)
Presbyterian	-1.0799 (1.3299)	—	—	—
English ancestry	—	—	—	—
Scottish/Irish ancestry	—	—	—	—
Officer in Revolutionary War	0.9523[b] (0.4658)	0.7474 (0.4803)	0.7286 (0.4838)	0.7555[c] (0.4437)
Delegate age	-0.0373 (0.0275)	—	—	—
Slaves per 100 whites	-0.0160[b] (0.00746)	-0.0289[a] (0.00869)	-0.0282[a] (0.00855)	-0.0128[c] (0.00697)
Distance to navigable water (miles)	—	-0.0312[a] (0.00495)	-0.0314[a] (0.00511)	—
Distance to Atlantic coast (miles)	-0.0162[a] (0.00318)	—	—	-0.0171[a] (0.00316)
Constituent-English ancestry (percent)	0.1079[a] (0.0316)	0.0562[c] (0.0334)	0.0397 (0.1003)	—
Constituent-Scottish/Irish ancestry (percent)	—	—	-0.0174 (0.1020)	-0.0926[a] (0.0332)
Somers' D_{yx}	.695	.767	.767	.674
R^2	.301	.361	.361	.287

[a] Statistically significant at .01 level.
[b] Statistically significant at .05 level.
[c] Statistically significant at .10 level.

Note: See the note to table A7.5.

Table A7.18. Estimated Logistic Coefficients of the Explanatory Variables for the Ratification Vote at the Virginia Ratifying Convention: Model Specifications with Alternative Variables

Explanatory Variables	Alternative Model Specifications for Virginia			
	1	2	3	4
Constant	7.8653 (4.7967)	6.1856 (4.0143)	4.9259 (3.6109)	4.6026[a] (1.1299)
Merchant	−1.2863 (0.8976)	−1.1391 (0.8274)	−1.2962 (0.8667)	−1.0693 (0.8475)
Western landowner	0.3418 (0.5227)	0.3153 (0.4904)	0.0663 (0.5120)	0.2239 (0.5000)
Private creditor	−0.6215 (0.8320)	0.0506 (0.7942)	−0.4243 (0.8536)	—
Debtor	−2.4818[b] (1.0487)	−1.5621[c] (0.8663)	−2.1652[b] (1.0165)	−2.1869[b] (0.9329)
Farmer	−0.8125[b] (0.4023)	−0.9802[b] (0.4196)	−1.0929[b] (0.4342)	−0.7842[c] (0.4010)
Slaveowner	−1.9650[a] (0.7418)	−1.7334[b] (0.7289)	−1.9195[b] (0.7644)	−2.1341[a] (0.7236)
Owner public securities	—	0.4817 (0.4046)	—	—
Owner >$1,000 public securities	2.1655[a] (0.7665)	—	1.9666[a] (0.7015)	1.9894[a] (0.7078)
Congregational/Puritan	—	—	—	—
Baptist	—	—	—	—
Episcopalian/Anglican	−0.6137 (1.2339)	−0.3519 (1.1794)	−0.2218 (1.2475)	—
Presbyterian	0.3676 (1.7750)	2.0600 (1.6295)	1.9353 (1.7505)	—
Delegate-English ancestry	0.6239 (1.0409)	0.5813 (0.5662)	0.6301 (0.5895)	—
Delegate-Scottish/Irish ancestry	0.1099 (1.0483)	—	—	—
Member Continental Congress	—	−1.1752 (0.7356)	−1.6606[b] (0.7769)	−0.9714 (0.7713)
Officer in Revolutionary War	0.7262[c] (0.4352)	0.5940 (0.4263)	0.8084[c] (0.4452)	0.7685[c] (0.4193)
Delegate age	0.0109 (0.0219)	0.0122 (0.0217)	0.0173 (0.0225)	—
Slaves per 100 whites	−0.0123[b] (0.00513)	−0.0138[a] (0.00528)	−0.0123[b] (0.00542)	−0.0120[b] (0.00491)
Distance to navigable water (miles)	—	−0.0225[a] (0.00632)	−0.0226[a] (0.00652)	—
Distance to Atlantic coast (miles)	−0.00984[a] (0.00289)	—	—	−0.0106[a] (0.00287)
Constituent-English ancestry (percent)	−0.0265 (0.0471)	−0.0302 (0.0420)	−0.0179 (0.0365)	—
Constituent-Scottish/Irish ancestry (percent)	−0.1749 (0.1231)	—	—	—
Somers' D_yx	.651	.613	.640	.634
R²	.303	.286	.320	.292

[a] Statistically significant at .01 level.
[b] Statistically significant at .05 level.
[c] Statistically significant at .10 level.

Note: See the note to table A7.6.

Table A7.19. Incremental and Marginal Effects of the Explanatory Variables on the Predicted Probability of a Yes Vote on Ratification for the Average Slaveowner: Massachusetts, North Carolina, and Virginia Conventions

Explanatory Variables	State Ratifying Convention		
	Massachusetts	North Carolina	Virginia
Merchant	.302[a]	.668[a]	−.259
Western landowner	.246	−.104	.083
Private creditor interest	.396[a]	.448[b]	−.158
Debtor interest	−.449[b]	−.104	−.398[b]
Farmer	−.033	.198[c]	−.211[b]
Slaveowner	—	.018	−.350[b]
Owner >$1,000 public securities	.357[b]	.417	.429[b]
Congregational/Puritan	−.077	—	—
Baptist	−.534[a]	−.383[c]	—
Episcopalian/Anglican	—	—	−.080
Presbyterian	−.217	−.146	.302
Delegate-English ancestry	.246[b]	—	.241
Delegate-Scottish/Irish ancestry	—	—	.197
Officer in Revolutionary War	.172[b]	.129[e]	.174[d]
Delegate age	−.0010	−.0036	.0017
Slaves per 100 whites	—	−.0045[a]	−.0031[b]
Distance to navigable water (miles)	−.0084[a]	−.0052[a]	−.0047[a]
Constituent-English ancestry (percent)	.010	.0093[c]	−.0058
Constituent-Scottish/Irish ancestry (percent)	—	—	−.053[c]
Predicted Probability of a Yes Vote	.522	.212	.449
Number of Observations	6	210	139

[a] Statistically significant at .01 level.
[b] Statistically significant at .05 level.
[c] Statistically significant at .10 level.
[d] P-value is .1086.
[e] P-value is .1512.

Note: The dependent variable in each column is the observed ratification vote at the respective state convention, where a yes vote equals 1 and a no vote equals 0. The incremental and marginal effects for the Massachusetts, North Carolina, and Virginia ratification votes are calculated from the logistic coefficients for specification 2 reported in tables A7.13, A7.14, and A7.15, respectively, employing the mean values of the explanatory variables calculated for the slaveowner sample only (the "average" slaveowner) for each convention.

Table A7.20. Incremental and Marginal Effects of the Explanatory Variables on the Predicted Probability of a Yes Vote on Ratification at the Massachusetts Convention for the Alternative Specification with the Slaveowner Variable: Average Delegate, Average Slaveowner, and Average Public Securities Owner

| | The Massachusetts Delegate | | |
Explanatory Variables	Average Delegate	Average Slaveowner	Average Public Securities Owner
Merchant	.280[a]	.059[a]	.122[a]
Western landowner	.156	.036	.057
Private creditor interest	.388[a]	.059[a]	.197[a]
Debtor interest	−.479[b]	−.267[b]	−.412[b]
Farmer	−.040	−.010	−.018
Slaveowner	.367[b]	.494[b]	.112[b]
Owner >$1,000 public securities	.271[d]	.059[d]	.150[d]
Congregational/Puritan	−.076	−.019	−.031
Baptist	−.578[a]	−.301[a]	−.580[a]
Presbyterian	−.216	−.077	−.118
Delegate-English ancestry	.244[b]	.091[b]	.124[b]
Officer in Revolutionary War	.160[b]	.043[b]	.061[b]
Delegate age	−.0013	−.00034	−.00056
Slaves per 100 whites	—	—	—
Distance to navigable water (miles)	−.0079[a]	−.0020[a]	−.0034[a]
Constituent-English ancestry (percent)	.0075	.0019	.0032
Predicted Probability of a Yes Vote	.612	.936	.886
Number of Observations	309	6	63

[a] Statistically significant at .01 level.
[b] Statistically significant at .05 level.
[c] Statistically significant at .10 level.
[d] P-value is .1024.

Note: The dependent variable in each column is the observed ratification vote at the Massachusetts convention, where a yes vote equals 1 and a no vote equals 0. The incremental and marginal effects for the ratification vote are calculated from the logistic coefficients for specification 3 reported in table A7.16. The effects are calculated employing the mean values of the explanatory variables calculated for all delegates (the "average" delegate), for the slaveowner sample only (the "average" slaveowner), and for the public securities owner sample only (the "average" public securities owner), respectively. The constituent slave variable (slaves per 100 whites) still is not included in the model specification because it is zero for all Massachusetts counties.

Table A7.21. Incremental and Marginal Effects of the Explanatory Variables on the Predicted Probability of a Yes Vote on Ratification for the Average Public Securities Owner: Massachusetts, North Carolina, and Virginia Conventions

Explanatory Variables	State Ratifying Convention		
	Massachusetts	North Carolina	Virginia
Merchant	.113[a]	.513[a]	−.292
Western landowner	.071	−.182	.075
Private creditor interest	.176[a]	.457[b]	−.164
Debtor interest	−.367[b]	−.187	−.504[b]
Farmer	−.014	.239[c]	−.200[b]
Slaveowner	—	.028	−.290[b]
Owner >$1,000 public securities	.173[b]	.426	.393[b]
Congregational/Puritan	−.029	—	—
Baptist	−.448[a]	−.517[c]	—
Episcopalian/Anglican	—	—	−.072
Presbyterian	−.120	−.222	.240
Delegate-English ancestry	.127[b]	—	.233
Delegate-Scottish/Irish ancestry	—	—	.178
Officer in Revolutionary War	.058[b]	.170[e]	.161[d]
Delegate age	−.00040	−.0053	.0016
Slaves per 100 whites	—	−.0067[a]	−.0030[b]
Distance to navigable water (miles)	−.0033[a]	−.0077[a]	−.0044[a]
Constituent-English ancestry (percent)	.0039	.014[c]	−.0055
Constituent-Scottish/Irish ancestry (percent)	—	—	−.050[c]
Predicted Probability of a Yes Vote	.890	.440	.632
Number of Observations	63	4	66

[a] Statistically significant at .01 level.
[b] Statistically significant at .05 level.
[c] Statistically significant at .10 level.
[d] P-value is .1086.
[e] P-value is .1512.

Note: The dependent variable in each column is the observed ratification vote at the respective state convention, where a yes vote equals 1 and a no vote equals 0. The incremental and marginal effects for the Massachusetts, North Carolina, and Virginia ratification votes are calculated from the logistic coefficients for specification 2 reported in tables A7.13, A7.14, and A7.15, respectively, employing the mean values of the explanatory variables calculated for the public securities owner sample only (the "average" public securities owner) for each convention.

Table A7.22. The Ratification Vote and the Predicted Probability of a Yes Vote on Ratification for the Delegates at the Massachusetts, North Carolina, and Virginia Ratifying Conventions

Name	County	State	Vote	Predicted Vote	Name	County
Adams Benjamin	Middlesex	MA	0	0.468	Abbott Henry	Camden
Adams Daniel	Middlesex	MA	0	0.435	Alderson Thomas	Beaufort
Adams Mark	York	MA	0	0.585	Alexander Robert	Lincoln
Adams Samuel	Suffolk	MA	1	0.971	Allen Nathaniel	Chowan
Alden Noah	Suffolk	MA	0	0.693	Allen Richard	Wilkes
Allis Josiah	Hampshire	MA	0	0.005	Allison Robert	Washington
Almy William	Bristol	MA	1	0.715	Anderson James	Chatham
Ames Fisher	Suffolk	MA	1	0.715	Anderson John	Guilford
Ames Moses	York	MA	0	0.303	Armstrong Thomas	Cumberland
Arms Consider	Hampshire	MA	0	0.177	Baker William	Gates
Ashley John Jr.	Berkshire	MA	1	0.139	Barnes Elias	Robeson
Backus Isaac	Plymouth	MA	1	0.467	Bass Andrew	Wayne
Baker Thomas M.	Worcester	MA	0	0.486	Battle Elisha	Edgecomb
Baker Samuel	Worcester	MA	1	0.294	Bell Blythel	Edgecomb
Barrell Nathaniel	York	MA	1	0.960	Benford John M.	Northampton
Bartlett Bailey	Essex	MA	1	0.920	Berringer George H.	Rowan
Bascom Moses	Hampshire	MA	0	0.095	Bethell William	Rockingham
Baxter John Jr	Suffolk	MA	1	0.827	Blair John	Washington
Baylies William	Bristol	MA	1	0.790	Bloodworth James	New Hanover
Beal Zacheus	Lincoln	MA	0	0.093	Bloodworth Timothy	New Hanover
Bean Joshua	Lincoln	MA	0	0.260	Blount Edmund	Tyrrell
Bigelow Abraham	Middlesex	MA	1	0.596	Blount John G.	Beaufort
Bigelow David	Worcester	MA	0	0.339	Bonds John	Nash
Bishop Phaneul	Bristol	MA	0	0.549	Bonner James	Beaufort
Black John	Worcester	MA	0	0.439	Boon Joseph	Johnston
Blair Timothy	Hampshire	MA	0	0.205	Borden William	Carteret
Blaney Benjamin	Middlesex	MA	1	0.584	Bostick Absalom	Surry
Bodman William	Hampshire	MA	0	0.051	Boswell James	Caswell
Bonney Benjamin	Hampshire	MA	1	0.413	Branch John	Halifax
Bourn Shearjashub	Barnstable	MA	1	0.524	Brannon James	Rowan
Bowdoin James	Suffolk	MA	1	0.765	Bridges William	Johnston
Bowdoin James Jr.	Suffolk	MA	1	0.997	Brooks Matthew	Surry
Bradbury Jacob	York	MA	1	0.851	Brown John	Wilkes
Bradley Jesse	Berkshire	MA	0	0.087	Brown Neil	Robeson
Brigham Artemus	Worcester	MA	0	0.516	Brown Thomas	Bladen
Broad Hezekiah	Middlesex	MA	0	0.471	Bryan John	Johnston
Brooks Eleazer	Middlesex	MA	1	0.944	Bryan John Hill	Jones
Brooks John	Middlesex	MA	1	0.740	Bryan Nathan	Jones
Brown David	Bristol	MA	0	0.105	Bunn Redman	Nash
Browne Benjamin	Middlesex	MA	1	0.521	Burkitt Lemuel	Hertford
Buckminster Lawson	Middlesex	MA	1	0.193	Butler Thomas	Montgomery
Bullard Jonathan	Worcester	MA	0	0.146	Cabarrus Stephen	Chowan
Burnham John	Essex	MA	1	0.986	Cade John	Robeson
Cabot Francis	Essex	MA	1	0.666	Cain Samuel	Bladen
Cabot George	Essex	MA	1	0.992	Cains John	Brunswick
Carlton Ebenezer	Essex	MA	0	0.674	Caldwell David	Guilford
Carnes John	Essex	MA	1	0.802	Campbell John A.	New Hanover
Carpenter Elisha	Berkshire	MA	1	0.071	Carrol John	Moore
Carr James	Lincoln	MA	0	0.469	Carson Thomas	Rowan
Chamberlin John	Hampshire	MA	0	0.040	Christmas Thomas	Warren
Chamberlin Staples	Middlesex	MA	0	0.666	Clinton Richard	Sampson
Choate John	Essex	MA	1	0.780	Collins Josiah	Tyrrell
Clark Adam	Hampshire	MA	0	0.184	Covington Benjamin	Richmond

State	Vote	Predicted Vote	Name	County	State	Vote	Predicted Vote
NC	1	0.163	Alexander Robert	Campbell	VA	0	0.254
NC	1	0.984	Allen John	Surry	VA	1	0.697
NC	0	0.007	Andrews Robert	Jamescity	VA	1	0.942
NC	1	0.619	Arthurs Thomas	Franklin	VA	0	0.020
NC	0	0.009	Ashton Burdet	King George	VA	1	0.585
NC	0	0.151	Bassett Burwell	James City	VA	1	0.437
NC	0	0.013	Bell David	Buckingham	VA	0	0.057
NC	0	0.056	Blair John	York	VA	1	0.520
NC	0	0.025	Bland Theodorick	Prince George	VA	0	0.820
NC	1	0.542	Blunt Benjamin	Southampton	VA	1	0.501
NC	1	0.241	Breckenridge Robert	Jefferson	VA	1	0.941
NC	0	0.268	Briggs John H.	Sussex	VA	0	0.478
NC	0	0.028	Brooke Humphrey	Fauquier	VA	1	0.919
NC	0	0.297	Brooker Edmund	Amelia	VA	0	0.274
NC	0	0.216	Buchanan Andrew	Stafford	VA	0	0.618
NC	0	0.037	Bullitt Cuthbert	Jefferson	VA	0	0.791
NC	0	0.001	Burwell Nathaniel	James City	VA	1	0.729
NC	0	0.137	Cabell Samuel	Amherst	VA	0	0.439
NC	0	0.123	Cabell William	Amherst	VA	0	0.182
NC	0	0.112	Callis W. Overton	Louisa	VA	1	0.503
NC	1	0.706	Carrington George	Halifax	VA	0	0.044
NC	1	0.992	Carrington Paul	Charlotte	VA	1	0.366
NC	0	0.135	Carter Thomas	Russell	VA	0	0.409
NC	0	0.542	Cary Richard	Warwick	VA	0	0.466
NC	0	0.215	Clay Charles	Bedford	VA	0	0.235
NC	1	0.961	Clay Green	Madison	VA	0	0.045
NC	0	0.003	Clayton William	Newkent	VA	1	0.455
NC	0	0.067	Cleindinen George	Greenbriar	VA	1	0.505
NC	0	0.067	Cocke John Hartwell	Surry	VA	1	0.707
NC	0	0.024	Coles Isaac	Halifax	VA	0	0.252
NC	1	0.398	Cooper Thomas	Henry	VA	0	0.117
NC	0	0.007	Corbin Francis	Middlesex	VA	1	0.394
NC	0	0.019	Crocket Walter	Montgomery	VA	0	0.060
NC	1	0.405	Custis Edmund	Accomac	VA	0	0.650
NC	0	0.149	Dark William	Berkeley	VA	1	0.679
NC	0	0.030	Dawson John	Spotsylvania	VA	0	0.601
NC	0	0.598	Dickenson Henry	Russell	VA	0	0.084
NC	0	0.362	Digges Cole	Warwick	VA	1	0.751
NC	0	0.475	Drew Thomas H.	Cumberland	VA	0	0.797
NC	0	0.176	Early Joel	Culpeper	VA	0	0.681
NC	0	0.067	Early John	Franklin	VA	0	0.188
NC	1	0.989	Edminson Samuel	Washington	VA	0	0.293
NC	1	0.364	Edmunds Thomas	Sussex	VA	0	0.857
NC	0	0.277	Evans John	Monongalia	VA	0	0.525
NC	0	0.297	Eyre Littleton	Northampton	VA	1	0.649
NC	0	0.020	Fisher Daniel	Greensville	VA	1	0.295
NC	0	0.187	Fleet William	King & Queen	VA	1	0.384
NC	0	0.022	Fleming William	Botetourt	VA	1	0.486
NC	0	0.014	Fowler John	Fayette	VA	0	0.761
NC	0	0.048	Gaskins Thomas	Northumber	VA	1	0.884
NC	0	0.109	Goodall Parker	Hanover	VA	0	0.230
NC	1	0.981	Gordon James	Lancaster	VA	1	0.504
NC	0	0.042	Gordon James	Orange	VA	1	0.489

continued

Table A7.22. continued

Name	County	State	Vote	Predicted Vote	Name	County
Clark Israel	Essex	MA	1	0.593	Cox John	Moore
Clark Kimball	Barnstable	MA	1	0.751	Dauge Peter	Camden
Cogswell Jonathan	Essex	MA	1	0.940	Davie William R.	Halifax
Collins Lemuel	Berkshire	MA	0	0.091	Davis Devotion	Pasquotank
Colton Elihu	Hampshire	MA	1	0.244	Dawson William	Bertie
Comstock Nathan	Suffolk	MA	0	0.758	Devane Thomas	New Hanover
Cooley Clark	Hampshire	MA	0	0.204	Dickens Robert	Caswell
Cooley Daniel	Hampshire	MA	0	0.237	Dickson William	Duplin
Cranch Richard	Suffolk	MA	1	0.991	Diggs Robert	Edgecombe
Crocker Zaccheus	Hampshire	MA	0	0.377	Dobbin William	Davidson
Curtis Caleb	Worcester	MA	0	0.307	Dodd David	Sampson
Cushing Joseph	Plymouth	MA	1	0.852	Donaldson William	Davidson
Cushing Nathan	Plymouth	MA	1	0.983	Donelson Stokely	Hawkins
Cushing William	Plymouth	MA	1	0.678	Doud Cornelius	Moore
Cutts Richard	York	MA	0	0.074	Dougan Thomas	Randolph
Cutts Thomas	York	MA	1	0.843	Douglass Joseph	Mecklenburg
Dalton Tristam	Essex	MA	1	0.916	Dunkin John	Sullivan
Dana Francis	Middlesex	MA	1	0.986	Dupree Lewis	Brunswick
Dana Stephen	Middlesex	MA	1	0.626	Dupree Sterling	Pitt
Davis Caleb	Suffolk	MA	1	0.861	Eborn John	Hyde
Davis John	Plymouth	MA	1	0.972	Elleston Goodwin	Bladen
Davis Joseph	Worcester	MA	0	0.329	Ellin Howell	Nash
Davis Moses	Lincoln	MA	1	0.763	Elliot George	Cumberland
Davis Thomas	Plymouth	MA	1	0.975	Evans Thomas	Davidson
Dawes Thomas Jr.	Suffolk	MA	1	0.988	Everegain Edward	Pasquotank
Day Jonathan	Worcester	MA	0	0.489	Farmer William	Johnston
Dench Gilbert	Middlesex	MA	0	0.380	Ferebee Joseph	Currituck
Denny Samuel	Worcester	MA	0	0.095	Ferebee William	Currituck
Dunbar Elijah	Suffolk	MA	1	0.699	Fletcher James	Wilkes
Dunham Cornelius	Dukes	MA	1	0.650	Forbes Arthur	Pitt
Dunlap John	Cumberland	MA	1	0.891	Foreman Caleb	Hyde
Durfee Thomas	Bristol	MA	1	0.401	Forster Alexious M.	Brunswick
Dwight Elijah	Berkshire	MA	1	0.085	Fort William	Edgecombe
Dwight Justus	Hampshire	MA	0	0.204	Gains James	Surry
Dyer Joshua	Cumberland	MA	1	0.616	Gallaway James	Rockingham
Eager Nahum	Hampshire	MA	1	0.412	Galloway Charles	Rockingham
Eastman Benjamin	Hampshire	MA	0	0.223	Gautier Joseph	Bladen
Eddy Samuel	Hampshire	MA	0	0.229	Gillespie Daniel	Guilford
Ely Benjamin	Hampshire	MA	0	0.332	Gillespie James	Duplin
Emerson Peter	Middlesex	MA	0	0.408	Goudy William	Guilford
Emery Jeremiah	York	MA	0	0.697	Gould Daniel	Anson
Fales David	Lincoln	MA	1	0.482	Graham Joseph	Mecklenburg
Farley Michael	Essex	MA	1	0.536	Grandy Charles	Camden
Fearing Israel	Plymouth	MA	1	0.768	Graves John	Caswell
Field Samuel	Hampshire	MA	0	0.260	Gray Etheldred	Edgecombe
Fisher Aaron	Hampshire	MA	1	0.396	Greenlee James	Burke
Fisher Jabez	Suffolk	MA	1	0.679	Gregory Isaac	Camden
Fitch Ephraim	Berkshire	MA	0	0.156	Gregory James	Gates
Fletcher Joel	Worcester	MA	0	0.102	Grove William Barry	Cumberland
Flint William	Middlesex	MA	0	0.462	Hall Durham	Franklin
Forbes Daniel	Worcester	MA	0	0.281	Hamilton John	Guilford
Fowler Silas	Hampshire	MA	0	0.377	Hanley James	Wayne
Fox John	Cumberland	MA	1	0.975	Hardiman Thomas	Davidson
Freeman Solomon	Barnstable	MA	1	0.619	Hargett Fredrick	Jones
Fuller Abraham	Middlesex	MA	1	0.607	Harrell Samuel	Hertford
Fuller John	Worcester	MA	0	0.508	Harvey Thomas	Perquimans

State	Vote	Predicted Vote	Name	County	State	Vote	Predicted Vote
NC	0	0.494	Grayson William	Prince William	VA	0	0.844
NC	1	0.775	Guerrant John	Goochland	VA	0	0.120
NC	1	0.324	Haden Joseph	Fluvanna	VA	0	0.362
NC	1	0.832	Harrison Benjamin	Charles City	VA	0	0.434
NC	1	0.927	Henry Patrick	Prince Edward	VA	0	0.513
NC	0	0.136	Hopkins Samuel	Mecklenburg	VA	0	0.606
NC	0	0.023	Humphreys Ralph	Hampshire	VA	1	0.702
NC	0	0.486	Innes James	James City	VA	1	0.639
NC	0	0.297	Jackson George	Harrison	VA	1	0.903
NC	0	0.062	Johnson James	Isle of Wright	VA	1	0.860
NC	0	0.174	Johnson Zachariah	Augusta	VA	1	0.956
NC	0	0.270	Jones Binns	Brunswick	VA	0	0.362
NC	0	0.008	Jones Gabriel	Rockingham	VA	1	0.820
NC	0	0.128	Jones John	Brunswick	VA	0	0.054
NC	0	0.050	Jones Joseph	Dinwiddie	VA	0	0.705
NC	0	0.488	Jones Walter	Northumber	VA	1	0.843
NC	0	0.117	Kello Samuel	Southampton	VA	1	0.540
NC	0	0.445	Kennon Richard	Mecklenburg	VA	0	0.586
NC	0	0.520	King Miles	Elizabeth City	VA	1	0.904
NC	1	0.613	Lawson Robert	Prince Edward	VA	0	0.238
NC	1	0.717	Lee Henry Jr.	Westmoreland	VA	1	0.788
NC	0	0.251	Lee Richard Henry	Bourbon	VA	0	0.004
NC	1	0.583	Lewis Thomas	Rockingham	VA	1	0.700
NC	0	0.062	Lewis Warner	Gloucester	VA	1	0.953
NC	1	0.647	Littlepage John Carter	Hanover	VA	0	0.262
NC	0	0.116	Logan John	Lincoln	VA	0	0.023
NC	1	0.792	Madison James Jr.	Orange	VA	1	0.523
NC	1	0.619	Marr John	Henry	VA	0	0.117
NC	0	0.058	Marshall Humphrey	Fayette	VA	1	0.606
NC	0	0.520	Marshall John	Henrico	VA	1	0.983
NC	1	0.757	Mason George	Stafford	VA	0	0.637
NC	0	0.297	Mason Stephens T.	Loudon	VA	0	0.607
NC	0	0.297	Mason William	Greensville	VA	1	0.628
NC	0	0.006	Matthews Thomas	Norfolk	VA	1	0.932
NC	0	0.004	McClerry William	Monongalia	VA	1	0.432
NC	0	0.005	McFerran Martin	Botetourt	VA	1	0.634
NC	0	0.255	McKee William	Rockbridge	VA	1	0.738
NC	0	0.024	Michaux Joshua	Cumberland	VA	0	0.111
NC	0	0.632	Miller John	Madison	VA	0	0.141
NC	0	0.056	Monroe James	Spotsylvania	VA	0	0.955
NC	0	0.042	Montgomery James	Washington	VA	0	0.498
NC	0	0.509	Moore Andrew	Rockbridge	VA	1	0.501
NC	1	0.669	Nicholas George	Albermarle	VA	1	0.446
NC	0	0.067	Nicholas Wilson C.	Albermarle	VA	1	0.431
NC	0	0.297	Pankey Stephen	Chesterfield	VA	0	0.246
NC	0	0.061	Parker George	Accomac	VA	1	0.952
NC	1	0.669	Patteson Charles	Buckingham	VA	0	0.199
NC	1	0.968	Patteson David	Chesterfield	VA	1	0.479
NC	1	0.371	Patteson Jonathan	Lunenburg	VA	0	0.270
NC	0	0.090	Pawling Henry	Lincoln	VA	0	0.001
NC	0	0.022	Peachy William	Richmond	VA	1	0.583
NC	0	0.268	Pendleton Edmund	Caroline	VA	1	0.502
NC	0	0.779	Pickett Martin	Fauquier	VA	1	0.685
NC	0	0.322	Powell Levin	Loudoun	VA	1	0.576
NC	1	0.758	Pride John	Amelia	VA	0	0.131
NC	1	0.378	Prunty John	Harrison	VA	1	0.801

continued

Table A7.22. continued

Name	County	State	Vote	Predicted Vote	Name	County
Fuller Timothy	Worcester	MA	0	0.347	Hawkins Wyatt	Warren
Fyre John	Worcester	MA	0	0.292	Haywood Egbert	Halifax
Gilmore David	Lincoln	MA	1	0.287	Herndon Joseph	Wilkes
Gleason Phine	Middlesex	MA	0	0.377	Hill Henry	Franklin
Glover John	Essex	MA	1	0.998	Hill Whitmel	Martin
Glover Jonathan	Essex	MA	1	0.999	Hines Thomas	Wake
Goldsbury John	Hampshire	MA	0	0.259	Hinton James	Wake
Goodman Noah	Hampshire	MA	1	0.365	Holmes Hardy	Sampson
Gore Christopher	Suffolk	MA	1	0.994	Holmes Lewis	Sampson
Gorham Nathaniel	Middlesex	MA	1	0.567	Hovey Seth	Hyde
Grant Samuel	Lincoln	MA	1	0.658	Humphries John	Currituck
Gray William Jr.	Essex	MA	1	0.989	Hunter Thomas	Martin
Green Jonathan	Middlesex	MA	0	0.434	Hunter Thomas	Gates
Greenleaf Benjamin	Essex	MA	1	0.983	Iredell James	Chowan
Grout Jonathan	Worcester	MA	0	0.471	Irwin Robert	Mecklenburg
Hale Moses	Worcester	MA	0	0.350	Ivey Curtis	Sampson
Hamilton John	Hampshire	MA	0	0.379	Jasper James	Hyde
Hammond Nathan	Plymouth	MA	0	0.934	Johnson Charles	Chowan
Hancock John	Suffolk	MA	1	0.753	Johnston James	Lincoln
Harnden John	Middlesex	MA	0	0.657	Johnston John	Bertie
Harrington Isaac	Worcester	MA	0	0.436	Johnston Samuel	Perquimans
Harwood David	Worcester	MA	0	0.348	Johnston Thomas	Onslow
Hastings John	Hampshire	MA	1	0.756	Jones Abraham	Hyde
Hathaway Melatiah	Bristol	MA	0	0.482	Jones John	Halifax
Heath William	Suffolk	MA	1	0.995	Jones Nathaniel	Wake
Hemmenway Moses	York	MA	1	0.911	Jones Willie	Halifax
Herrick Jacob	Essex	MA	1	0.640	Keais Nathan	Beaufort
Holden Stephen	Worcester	MA	0	0.298	Kenan James	Duplin
Holmes Abraham	Plymouth	MA	0	0.660	Kindall William	Montgomery
Hooper Hezekiah	Plymouth	MA	1	0.835	King Thomas	Hawkins
Hosmer Joseph	Middlesex	MA	1	0.662	Lancaster William	Franklin
Howard Daniel	Plymouth	MA	1	0.664	Lane Joel	Wake
Hurlbert John	Berkshire	MA	0	0.060	Lane John	Pasquotank
Hutchinson Israel	Essex	MA	0	0.326	Lanier Lewis	Anson
Ingersoll John	Hampshire	MA	1	0.470	Ledbetter George	Rutherford
Jackson Joseph	Suffolk	MA	1	0.694	Leech Joseph	Craven
James Ebenezer	Hampshire	MA	1	0.484	Lenoir William	Wilkes
Jarvis Charles	Suffolk	MA	1	0.975	Leonard Jacob	Brunswick
Jenks Nicholas	Worcester	MA	0	0.356	Lewis Howell Jr.	Granville
Jennings John	Hampshire	MA	0	0.248	Lindley Jonathan	Orange
Jones John Coffin	Suffolk	MA	1	0.976	Little William	Hertford
Jones William	Lincoln	MA	0	0.291	Locke Matthew	Rowan
Josselyn Benjamin	Worcester	MA	0	0.324	Loftin William	Montgomery
Keep Jonathan	Middlesex	MA	0	0.670	Looney David	Sullivan
King Rufus	Essex	MA	1	0.974	Lucas George	Chatham
Kinsley Martin	Worcester	MA	0	0.322	Maclaine Achibald	New Hanover
Kittridge Dr. Thomas	Essex	MA	0	0.647	Macon John	Warren
Lazell Edmund	Hampshire	MA	1	0.350	Marnes William	Nash
Learned Jeremiah	Worcester	MA	0	0.304	Marshall William	Hawkins
Leonard Nathaniel	Bristol	MA	0	0.840	Martin William	Moore
Lincoln Benjamin	Suffolk	MA	1	0.967	May John	Rockingham
Longfellow Stephen Jr.	Cumberland	MA	0	0.627	Mayo Nathan	Martin
Low John	Essex	MA	1	0.908	McAllaster Alexander	Cumberland
Low Dr. Nathaniel	York	MA	0	0.372	McAllister John	Richmond
Lurvey Benjamin	Essex	MA	1	0.693	McAnnelly Charles	Surry
Lusk Thomas	Berkshire	MA	0	0.085	McCauley William	Orange
Mann Thomas	Suffolk	MA	1	0.683	McDowall Charles	Burke

State	Vote	Predicted Vote	Name	County	State	Vote	Predicted Vote
NC	0	0.048	Randolph Edmund	Henrico	VA	1	0.925
NC	0	0.269	Read Thomas	Charlotte	VA	0	0.183
NC	0	0.002	Richardson Samuel	Fluvanna	VA	0	0.056
NC	0	0.099	Richeson Holt	King William	VA	0	0.287
NC	1	0.746	Riddick Willis	Nansemond	VA	1	0.962
NC	1	0.131	Rinker Jacob	Shen Andoah	VA	1	0.991
NC	0	0.154	Roane Thomas	King & Queen	VA	0	0.561
NC	0	0.091	Robertson Christopher	Lunenburg	VA	0	0.270
NC	0	0.174	Ronald William	Powhatan	VA	1	0.182
NC	1	0.810	Ruffin Edmund Jr.	Prince George	VA	0	0.402
NC	1	0.773	Sampson William	Goochland	VA	0	0.100
NC	0	0.613	Seymour Abel	Hardy	VA	1	0.462
NC	1	0.650	Shepherd Solomon	Nansemond	VA	1	0.884
NC	1	0.598	Simms Charles	Fairfax	VA	1	0.987
NC	1	0.284	Smith Meriwether	Essex	VA	0	0.741
NC	0	0.174	Smith Thomas	Gloucester	VA	1	0.677
NC	1	0.810	Steele John	Nelson	VA	0	0.000
NC	1	0.234	Stephen Adam	Berkeley	VA	1	0.939
NC	0	0.014	Stewart John	Greenbriar	VA	1	0.550
NC	1	0.478	Stringer John	Northampton	VA	1	0.488
NC	1	0.962	Strother French	Culpeper	VA	0	0.497
NC	0	0.691	Stuart Archibald	Augusta	VA	1	0.851
NC	1	0.431	Stuart David	Fairfax	VA	1	0.911
NC	0	0.266	Taylor James	Caroline	VA	1	0.315
NC	1	0.144	Taylor Dr. James	Norfolk	VA	1	0.863
NC	0	0.179	Temple Benjamin	King William	VA	0	0.659
NC	1	0.811	Thornton William	King George	VA	1	0.806
NC	0	0.459	Tomlim Walker	Richmond	VA	1	0.576
NC	0	0.029	Towles Henry	Lancaster	VA	1	0.471
NC	0	0.035	Trigg Abraham	Montgomery	VA	0	0.441
NC	0	0.099	Trigg John	Bedford	VA	0	0.364
NC	0	0.129	Turpin Thomas Jr.	Powhatan	VA	0	0.075
NC	1	0.832	Tyler John	Charles City	VA	0	0.566
NC	0	0.091	Upshaw James	Essex	VA	0	0.520
NC	0	0.002	Vanmeter Isaac	Hardy	VA	1	0.688
NC	1	0.639	Walke Anthony	Princess Anne	VA	1	0.802
NC	0	0.003	Walke Thomas	Princess Anne	VA	1	0.670
NC	0	0.284	Walkins William	Dinwiddie	VA	0	0.332
NC	0	0.049	Walton Matthew	Nelson	VA	0	0.000
NC	0	0.101	Washington Bushrod	Westmoreland	VA	1	0.374
NC	0	0.373	Webb James	Norfolk	VA	1	0.582
NC	0	0.032	Westwood Worlich	Elizabeth City	VA	1	0.904
NC	0	0.029	White Alexander	Frederick	VA	1	0.626
NC	0	0.085	White William	Louisa	VA	0	0.693
NC	1	0.068	Williams John	Shenandoah	VA	1	0.942
NC	1	0.709	Williams Rober	Pittsylvania	VA	0	0.215
NC	0	0.048	Wilson Benjamin	Randolph	VA	1	0.849
NC	0	0.251	Wilson John	Pittsylvania	VA	0	0.198
NC	0	0.015	Wilson John	Randolph	VA	1	0.965
NC	0	0.047	Winston Edmund	Campbell	VA	0	0.522
NC	0	0.011	Woodcock John S.	Frederick	VA	1	0.162
NC	1	0.586	Woodrow Andrew	Hampshire	VA	1	0.905
NC	0	0.139	Woods Archibald	Ohio	VA	1	0.985
NC	0	0.220	Wormley Ralph	Middlesex	VA	1	0.506
NC	0	0.003	Wythe George	York	VA	1	0.931
NC	0	0.112	Zane Ebenezer	Ohio	VA	1	0.967
NC	1	0.003	*Percent Correct for Virginia*				72.7

continued

Table A7.22. continued

Name	County	State	Vote	Predicted Vote
Manning Richard	Essex	MA	1	0.914
Mansfield Isaac	Essex	MA	1	0.661
March Ebenezer	Essex	MA	1	0.646
Marsh Nathaniel	Essex	MA	0	0.948
Mason Christopher	Bristol	MA	0	0.092
May Elisha	Bristol	MA	1	0.632
Mayhew William	Dukes	MA	1	0.877
Maynard Malachi	Hampshire	MA	0	0.263
Maynard Stephen	Worcester	MA	0	0.042
McCobb William	Lincoln	MA	1	0.527
McIntier Ezra	Worcester	MA	0	0.152
McIntosh William	Suffolk	MA	1	0.929
McLellan Joseph	Cumberland	MA	1	0.831
Merrick Aaron	Hampshire	MA	0	0.140
Merrill Samuel	Cumberland	MA	1	0.657
Mighill Thomas	Essex	MA	0	0.326
Miller Simeon	Essex	MA	1	0.719
Minot John	Middlesex	MA	0	0.401
Mitchell David	Cumberland	MA	1	0.676
Mitchell Elisha	Plymouth	MA	1	0.819
Morgan Abner	Hampshire	MA	1	0.418
Morse Benjamin	Middlesex	MA	0	0.226
Morse Jonas	Middlesex	MA	0	0.224
Murray David	Lincoln	MA	0	0.785
Nasson Samuel	York	MA	0	0.868
Niles Samuel	Plymouth	MA	1	0.690
Noyes Daniel	Essex	MA	1	0.924
Nye Thomas	Barnstable	MA	0	0.746
Nyre Samuel	Essex	MA	1	0.652
Orne Azor	Essex	MA	1	0.731
Osgood Peter Jr.	Essex	MA	0	0.295
Palmer Joseph	Barnstable	MA	1	0.945
Parker Timothy	Worcester	MA	0	0.431
Parlin Asa	Middlesex	MA	0	0.470
Parsons Theophilus	Essex	MA	1	0.919
Partridge George	Plymouth	MA	1	0.977
Patten Willis	Essex	MA	1	0.809
Payson George	Suffolk	MA	1	0.666
Payson Phillips	Suffolk	MA	1	0.821
Pearson William	Essex	MA	1	0.986
Pepper Isaac	Hampshire	MA	0	0.226
Perley Samuel	Cumberland	MA	1	0.548
Phillips William	Suffolk	MA	1	0.976
Pitts John	Middlesex	MA	1	0.463
Pomeroy Lemue	Hampshire	MA	1	0.636
Porter Elisha	Hampshire	MA	1	0.236
Pratt John	Bristol	MA	0	0.411
Preble Esaias	York	MA	0	0.775
Pulling Edward	Essex	MA	1	0.958
Putnam Daniel	Worcester	MA	0	0.355
Pynchon William	Hampshire	MA	1	0.678
Rathburn Valentine	Berkshire	MA	0	0.085
Reed Samuel	Middlesex	MA	0	0.571
Rice Thomas	Lincoln	MA	1	0.483
Richardson Moses Jr.	Suffolk	MA	0	0.662
Richmond Sylvester	Bristol	MA	1	0.418

Name	County	State	Vote	Predicted Vote
McDowall Joesph Jr.	Burke	NC	0	0.004
McDowall Joseph	Burke	NC	0	0.004
McKinnie Richard	Wayne	NC	0	0.268
McKinzie William	Martin	NC	1	0.613
Mebane Alexander	Orange	NC	0	0.010
Mebane William	Orange	NC	0	0.057
Miller Robert	Burke	NC	0	0.001
Mitchell Elijah	Granville	NC	0	0.055
Montfort Henry	Warren	NC	0	0.048
Moore George	Rutherford	NC	0	0.002
Moore John	Lincoln	NC	1	0.033
Mooring Burwell	Wayne	NC	0	0.268
Moye Richard	Pitt	NC	0	0.520
Neale Abner	Craven	NC	1	0.639
Nixon Richard	Craven	NC	0	0.639
Norwood John	Franklin	NC	0	0.099
Oliver Andrew	Bertie	NC	1	0.478
Oliver Francis	Duplin	NC	0	0.696
Owen Thomas	Bladen	NC	1	0.739
Payne James	Warren	NC	0	0.048
Payne Michael	Chowan	NC	1	0.403
Pearce Everet	Johnston	NC	0	0.215
Peebles Robert	Northampton	NC	0	0.216
Perkins David	Pitt	NC	1	0.814
Person Thomas	Granville	NC	0	0.131
Phifer Caleb	Mecklenburg	NC	0	0.159
Phillips Abraham	Rockingham	NC	0	0.011
Phillips James	Currituck	NC	1	0.773
Porter William	Rutherford	NC	0	0.006
Porterfield James	Cumberland	NC	1	0.052
Pridgen David	Nash	NC	0	0.251
Ramsey Ambrose	Chatham	NC	0	0.043
Randall William	Jones	NC	0	0.207
Rawlins Asabel	Greene	NC	0	0.137
Reading Thomas	Pasquotank	NC	1	0.647
Reddick Joseph	Gates	NC	1	0.542
Regan John	Robeson	NC	0	0.202
Relfe Enoch	Pasquotank	NC	1	0.647
Roberts George	Caswell	NC	0	0.026
Robertson Charles	Richmond	NC	0	0.087
Roddy James	Greene	NC	0	0.225
Rutherford Griffith	Rowan	NC	0	0.026
Sanders Brittain	Wake	NC	0	0.144
Sawyer Enoch	Camden	NC	1	0.669
Scott John	Sullivan	NC	0	0.134
Sharpe John	Sullivan	NC	0	0.027
Sheppard William	Carteret	NC	1	0.889
Sherrod Thomas	Franklin	NC	0	0.229
Singleton Richard	Rutherford	NC	0	0.005
Sitgreaves John	Craven	NC	1	0.916
Skinner John	Perquimans	NC	1	0.971
Skinner Joshua	Perquimans	NC	1	0.567
Slade William	Martin	NC	1	0.613
Sloane John	Lincoln	NC	1	0.013
Smith Benjamin	Brunswick	NC	1	0.794
Spaight Richard Dobbs	Craven	NC	1	0.695

continued

Table A7.22. continued

Name	County	State	Vote	Predicted Vote
Robbins Nathaniel	Suffolk	MA	1	0.687
Rodgers Daniel	Essex	MA	1	0.869
Russell Thomas	Suffolk	MA	1	0.975
Sawin Benjamin	Middlesex	MA	0	0.506
Sawtell Obadiah	Middlesex	MA	0	0.447
Sawyer Enoch	Essex	MA	1	0.370
Sedgwick Theodore	Berkshire	MA	1	0.834
Sever William Jr.	Plymouth	MA	1	0.739
Severance Moses	Hampshire	MA	0	0.227
Sewall Dummer	Lincoln	MA	1	0.689
Shaw William	Plymouth	MA	1	0.302
Sheldon Benjamin	Hampshire	MA	1	0.225
Shepard David	Hampshire	MA	1	0.375
Sheple Joseph	Middlesex	MA	0	0.271
Sherman Asaph	Worcester	MA	0	0.311
Shurtliff Francis	Plymouth	MA	0	0.813
Shute Daniel	Suffolk	MA	1	0.683
Singletary Amos	Worcester	MA	0	0.330
Skinner Thompson J.	Berkshire	MA	1	0.260
Slocum Holder	Bristol	MA	0	0.417
Smith John K.	Cumberland	MA	1	0.759
Smith Jonathan	Berkshire	MA	1	0.163
Smith Josiah	Plymouth	MA	1	0.813
Smith Thomas	Barnstable	MA	0	0.658
Snow Isaac	Cumberland	MA	1	0.943
Soule Isaac	Plymouth	MA	0	0.384
Southworth Jedidiah	Suffolk	MA	0	0.961
Spooner Walter	Bristol	MA	1	0.075
Sprague John	Worcester	MA	1	0.348
Spring Marshal	Middlesex	MA	0	0.456
Stearns David	Worcester	MA	0	0.602
Stebbins Phine	Hampshire	MA	0	0.454
Stillman Samuel	Suffolk	MA	1	0.216
Stone Joseph	Worcester	MA	0	0.365
Strong Caleb	Hampshire	MA	1	0.961
Sumner Increase	Suffolk	MA	1	0.704
Sylvester David	Lincoln	MA	1	0.859
Symmes William	Essex	MA	1	0.758
Taylor John	Worcester	MA	0	0.343
Temple Jonas	Worcester	MA	0	0.477
Thatcher David	Barnstable	MA	1	0.892
Thatcher Thomas	Suffolk	MA	1	0.713
Thomas Benjamin	Plymouth	MA	0	0.646
Thomas Joshua	Plymouth	MA	1	0.821
Thompson Isaac	Plymouth	MA	1	0.958
Thompson Samuel	Lincoln	MA	0	0.653
Thompson William	Middlesex	MA	0	0.369
Thompson William	Cumberland	MA	1	0.640
Thorndike Israel	Essex	MA	1	0.939
Thruston Daniel	Essex	MA	1	0.800
Tingley Pelatiah	York	MA	0	0.192
Tisdell Ebenezer	Bristol	MA	0	0.072
Titcomb Jonathan	Essex	MA	1	0.802
Tufts Cotton	Suffolk	MA	1	0.581
Turner Charles	Plymouth	MA	1	0.768
Turner Capt. John	Plymouth	MA	1	0.794

Name	County	State	Vote	Predicted Vote
Spencer Samuel	Anson	NC	0	0.027
Spicer John	Onslow	NC	0	0.691
Spruill Simeon	Tyrrell	NC	1	0.913
Steele John	Rowan	NC	1	0.349
Stewart Joseph	Chatham	NC	0	0.026
Stewart Thomas	Tyrrell	NC	1	0.722
Stokes William	Sumner	NC	1	0.213
Stuart James	Washington	NC	0	0.154
Styron Wallace	Carteret	NC	1	0.889
Taylor Joseph	Granville	NC	0	0.167
Taylor William	Wayne	NC	0	0.314
Tipton John	Washington	NC	0	0.062
Tipton Joseph	Washington	NC	0	0.331
Turner David	Bertie	NC	1	0.602
Tyson Thomas	Moore	NC	0	0.556
Ussory Thomas	Montgomery	NC	0	0.049
Vaughan James	Northampton	NC	0	0.216
Vestal William	Chatham	NC	0	0.122
Vinson James	Northampton	NC	0	0.216
Waddill Edmund	Randolph	NC	0	0.124
Wade Thomas	Anson	NC	0	0.042
Ward Charles	Duplin	NC	0	0.459
Whiteside James	Rutherford	NC	0	0.002
Whitty Edward	Jones	NC	0	0.596
Williams Benjamin	Craven	NC	0	0.613
Williams Edward	Richmond	NC	0	0.170
Williams John Pugh	New Hanover	NC	0	0.102
Williams Robert	Pitt	NC	0	0.633
Willis John	Robeson	NC	1	0.936
Wilson Zachias	Mecklenburg	NC	0	0.424
Winchester James	Sumner	NC	1	0.213
Winston Joseph	Surry	NC	0	0.003
Womack John	Caswell	NC	0	0.026
Wood Zebedee	Randolph	NC	0	0.112
Wootten William	Halifax	NC	0	0.131
Wynns George	Hertford	NC	1	0.400
Wynns Thomas	Hertford	NC	1	0.617
Yancey Thornton	Granville	NC	0	0.086
Yates Daniel	Onslow	NC	0	0.943

Percent Correct for North Carolina 83.5

continued

Table A7.22. continued

Name	County	State	Vote	Predicted Vote
Varnum Joseph Bradley	Middlesex	MA	1	0.645
Wales Ebenezer	Suffolk	MA	1	0.734
Washburn Israel	Bristol	MA	1	0.643
Waterman Free	Plymouth	MA	1	0.655
Webber John	Middlesex	MA	0	0.491
Wells Nathaniel	York	MA	1	0.415
West Samuel	Bristol	MA	1	0.485
Wheeler Asahel	Middlesex	MA	1	0.596
White Abraham	Bristol	MA	0	0.427
Whitman Charles	Middlesex	MA	1	0.489
Whitman Levi	Barnstable	MA	1	0.688
Whitney Daniel	Middlesex	MA	1	0.416
Wibird Anthony	Suffolk	MA	1	0.992
Widgery William	Cumberland	MA	0	0.722
Wilder Ephraim	Worcester	MA	1	0.324
Willard Jacob	Worcester	MA	0	0.313
Willard Samuel	Worcester	MA	0	0.308
Williams Ephraim	Hampshire	MA	0	0.265
Williams James	Bristol	MA	1	0.634
Williams Leonard	Middlesex	MA	1	0.454
Williston John	Hampshire	MA	0	0.204
Wilmarth Moses	Bristol	MA	1	0.625
Wilson Robert	Hampshire	MA	0	0.093
Windsor William	Bristol	MA	0	0.413
Winn Timothy	Middlesex	MA	0	0.615
Winthrop John	Suffolk	MA	1	0.901
Wood Aaron	Essex	MA	0	0.621
Wood Dr. Joseph	Worcester	MA	0	0.281
Wood Joseph	Essex	MA	1	0.640
Woods John	Worcester	MA	0	0.305
Wyman Nathan	Lincoln	MA	1	0.483

Percent Correct for Massachusetts 77.0

Note: The vote for each delegate is the observed ratification vote of the delegate at the delegate's state ratifying convention where a yes vote on ratification equals 1 and a no vote equals 0. The predicted vote for each delegate is the predicted probability of a yes vote on ratification for the delegate computed from his actual characteristics and economic interests and the estimated logistic coefficients for specification 2 of the voting model reported in tables A7.13, A7.14, and A7.15 for Massachusetts, North Carolina, and Virginia, respectively. The percent correct is the percentage of the observed yes votes (= 1) with an estimated predicted value greater than .50 plus the percentage of the observed no votes (= 0) with an estimated predicted value less than .50.

Notes

Chapter One

1. Portions of this chapter have appeared in print in McGuire and Ohsfeldt (1984, 1986, 1989a,b, 1997) and McGuire (1988), and are reprinted with permission.

2. For a representative view of the pre–Civil War historians, see Hildreth (1849).

3. The quotes are from Gladstone (1878, p. 185) and Walker (1895, pp. 28–29), respectively. For more on the position of the post–Civil War historians, see Bancroft (1882), Dawson (1871), Fiske (1888), Harding (1896), Libby (1894), and Wilson (1902).

4. For more on the acceptance of Beard's economic interpretation, see Warren (1928 [1937]).

5. See McCormick (1950), Pool (1950a, b), and Thomas (1953), respectively. None of the three studies, however, contains any systematic statistical analysis.

6. For early positive reviews of Brown (1956), see Williams (1957) and C. Page Smith (1958). For early positive reviews of McDonald (1958), see Hindle (1959) and Tate (1959).

7. For examples of economists, historians, legal scholars, and political scientists who credit Brown (1956), McDonald (1958), or both of them with proving Beard wrong, see Buchanan and Tullock (1962), Brogan (1965), Wood (1969), Riker (1979), Ackerman (1991), Klarman (1992), O'Connor and Sabato (1993), Ratner, Soltow, and Sylla (1993), and Garraty (1995).

8. For a critical review of Ferguson (1961), however, see Bruchey (1962).

9. For example, see Ferguson (1961). For an excellent discussion of the historical research in the 1960s, see Hutson (1981, pp. 349–353).

10. Some of the more prominent historical studies are Hiner and Carrell (1968), Ferguson (1969), Calhoun (1979), Diggins (1981), Hutson (1981, 1984), Goldwin and Schambra (1980, 1982), and McCorkle (1984).

11. Rakove (1996, chap. 4) holds a similar view for the ratification process. Rakove also explicitly pokes fun at the use of quantitative techniques in attempts (1) to measure roll-call voting at the Philadelphia convention and (2) to analyze

the content of the rhetoric during the ratification campaign (pp. 15, 133). Furthermore, he maintains that "*[i]deas* or *interests*—these are the classic if hackneyed antinomies upon which much of the debate over the political and intellectual history of the entire Revolutionary era has long been conducted" (p. 15, emphasis in original).

12. See the collection of Adair's essays in Colbourn (1974). Also see Corwin (1936) for the work of others in the early political science literature disbelieving an economic interpretation.

13. In later work, Diamond (1975, 1986) expands on the origins of the political theory found in *The Federalist*, among other issues comparing its politics to that found in classical antiquity. But his interpretation is less favorable than is Adair's, as Diamond suggests that the founders' politics had moved far from the pure virtue of the classical Greeks.

14. As part I of the present study will show, Riker's view of near unanimity among the framers is far from accurate. For a more comprehensive treatment of his views of the formation of the Constitution, see Riker (1987b).

15. For a more comprehensive treatment of these types of voting alignments among the state delegations, see Jillson (1988).

16. See, for examples, the studies by a number of prominent political scientists concerning the adoption of the Constitution in Grofman and Wittman (1989).

17. The "dualist" aspect of Ackerman's constitutional theory, in which he distinguishes between the "higher lawmaking" of "constitutional politics" and the lawmaking of "normal politics," bears a striking resemblance to Buchanan and Tullock's (1962) economic theory of constitutions, which distinguishes between a society's "constitutional level" and "operational level" of public decision making. But the difference is that Buchanan and Tullock develop an "economic" theory of constitutional choice, which *is* based on self-interested, rational individuals. The applicability of Buchanan and Tullock's theory to the American founding is the subject matter of chapter 5.

18. Despite his view, the analysis and evidence reported here indicate that Ackerman's praise for the scholarship of the 1950s and 1960s is "seriously" misplaced. Ackerman (1991), makes his view more than just apparent when, citing the preliminary econometric research that is the genesis of the present study, he announces, "Since I am most interested here in recovering the political meaning of the American revolution, I do not think that anything very important turns on the precise mix of economic interests at play during the ratification struggle" (p. 347, n. 4). Similar to Rakove (1996), Ackerman does not appear to understand that economic analysis and quantitative techniques can help determine the relative importance of the founders' political ideas versus their economic interests in making their constitutional choices—a point made even in my preliminary work. For his thoughts on an economic view of politics, see Ackerman (1991, p. 311). For Rakove's view on the use of quantitative techniques, see note 11 above.

19. Given that Klarman (1992, p. 784, n. 150) also acknowledges the preliminary research that is the genesis of the present study, he apparently did not consider its arguments, at least at the time of his essay, as yet convincing.

20. Kaminski (1983) contends this is the appropriate method, as the ratification contest was unique in each state because economic conditions, political institutions, and the timing of the vote differed across states, and concludes that each state should be examined individually.

21. McDonald (1958, p. 356), however, suggests that this is only superficially true about the New Hampshire convention, as there were more important factors involved in its ratification than the amount of public securities holdings.

22. Handlin and Handlin (1944) and McDonald (1958, 1963) argue there were no geographic patterns. Daniell (1970), Gillespie (1989), Hall (1972), Main (1961), and Rutland (1966) argue there were geographic patterns in one or another of the three states.

23. For more extensive discussion of late-eighteenth-century politics in Georgia, see Abbot (1957) and Coleman (1958).

24. For example, Schweitzer's (1989a,b) recent examinations of the ratification process indicate that economic interests played a role in the adoption of the Constitution—but a role different from the traditional creditor versus debtor dichotomy. Yet Schweitzer's results are limited because of the absence of any formal analysis.

25. For the discussion in American history textbooks, see Faragher, Buhle, Czitrom, and Armitage (1997), Garraty (1995), and Nash, Jeffrey, Howe, et al. (1994). For the discussion in American economic history textbooks, see Hughes and Cain (1994), Lebergott (1984), Poulson (1981), Puth (1988), Ratner, Soltow, and Sylla (1993), and Walton and Rockoff (1998). For the discussion in American government textbooks, see Burnham (1983), Burns, Peltason, Cronin, and Magleby (1998), O'Connor and Sabato (1993), Prewitt and Verba (1983), and Wilson and DiIulio (1995).

26. For a rejection of such an alignment among specific economic interests in American history textbooks, see Garraty (1995). For such a rejection in economic history textbooks, see Poulson (1981), Puth (1988), and Ratner, Soltow, and Sylla (1993). For such a rejection in American government textbooks, see O'Connor and Sabato (1993) and Wilson and DiIulio (1995).

27. For American economic history textbooks indicating most notably, if not solely, an acceptance of the findings of Brown (1956) and McDonald (1958), see Hughes and Cain (1994), Lebergott (1984), Poulson (1981), Puth (1988), Ratner, Soltow, and Sylla (1993), and Walton and Rockoff (1998). For the exception among American economic history textbooks, see Atack and Passell (1994).

28. A prominent example of the "class analysis" interpretation of Beard—and to my knowledge the only discussion of Beard in the modern economics literature—is Buchanan and Tullock (1962, pp. 25–27). The economics literature has otherwise ignored the issue of an economic interpretation of the Constitution. For an example among historians that distinguishes between a "subtle Beardian" and a "vulgar Marxist" interpretation, see Rossiter (1966). For an example contending that Beard claimed "the Framers were lining their own pockets," see Klarman (1992, p. 784, n. 150).

29. The editors further compound the problem by misrepresenting McDonald (1958), adding "Forrest McDonald's We the People provides the corrective" (Intercollegiate Review, 1999, p. 4).

30. For a discussion of the intellectual history of Beard's thesis, focusing on common misperceptions of his arguments, see McCorkle (1984, pp. 315–363). For an excellent discussion of the historiography of an economic interpretation, see Beeman (1987).

31. As noted above, a prominent example of the class analysis interpretation is Buchanan and Tullock (1962). A prominent example of an individualistic, self-interest view of Beard is Thomas (1952). For other studies by Beard that support

an individualistic, self-interest view of his *An Economic Interpretation*, see Beard (1915 [1943]) and (1922 [1934]).

Chapter Two

1. Some historians have presented the drafting of the Constitution in a manner that may appear similar. For example, Rossiter (1966) contends that the Philadelphia convention was "a notable exercise in the arts of democratic . . . politics . . . a superlative example of goal-setting and decision-making" (p. 15). According to Rossiter, the convention was about the choices the founders made. Yet he appears skeptical about referring to the framers as interested and partisan in a purely economic way. As he claims, "We know them well as everything from selfless instruments of Divine Intent to selfish agents of Economic Interests. We hardly know them at all as what they were first and foremost: skillful operators of the political machinery of constitutional democracy." As a result, the framers balanced principles and interests. But they were above all "community-minded men," like Washington, who cannot be understood, "unless we recognize his consuming belief in the existence of a common, enduring interest of the whole community that encompassed and yet rose above all private interests" (p. 69). Rossiter, as noted above, also openly rejects an economic interpretation (pp. 292–295).

2. For a good introduction to the modern economic view of political behavior, see Buchanan and Tullock (1962).

3. Delegates to the Philadelphia convention were selected to represent the delegate's state by the legislative bodies (the citizens' representatives) in each state. All states except Rhode Island selected delegates to attend the Philadelphia convention. The citizens that had the franchise did, however, elect the delegates who represented them at the state ratifying conventions.

4. See Kalt and Zupan (1984), Kau and Rubin (1979, 1982), and Peltzman (1984, 1985).

5. See Alchian and Demsetz (1972), Barro (1973), Tollison (1982), and Welch and Peters (1983).

6. Whether economic interests have more influence on political voting behavior than do ideological and political principles is debated in the economics literature. For the view that ideology is more important, see Kalt and Zupan (1984). For a study suggesting the impact of ideology has been previously overstated and that of economic interests understated, see Peltzman (1984).

7. Many delegates, however, were elected officials and had future political ambitions. Voting contrary to their constituents' interests might have adversely affected their future political ambitions and careers. And, because the completed draft of the Constitution had to be ratified by at least nine states, the document probably needed to reflect constituent interests at least in broad terms. Two states actually had second ratifying conventions. In the case of New Hampshire, its first ratifying convention adjourned without a vote and, in the case of North Carolina, its first ratifying convention voted against the Constitution. Many delegates to the ratifying conventions also were legally bound to vote as they had pledged during their election campaigns. Monitoring and policing costs, accordingly, were not so high that the delegates to Philadelphia and the state conventions could completely ignore their constituents' interests.

8. After concluding that an economic interpretation cannot account for the Constitution, McDonald (1958, pp. 415–417) proposes a "pluralistic" study to

explain the creation of the Constitution, which would take into consideration not only all economic factors but also the "countless noneconomic factors" of the geographical areas represented by the founders, as well as of the founders personally. Although McDonald's concept of a "pluralistic" study appears to resemble my economic model of the founders' behavior, because McDonald (pp. 411–414), as noted earlier, contends that a priori hypotheses about individual behavior cannot adequately explain historical events, his approach is in fact counter to the economic model developed here.

9. Higgs (1987) contains one of the more succinct conceptualizations of ideology as "a somewhat coherent, rather comprehensive belief system about social relations. . . . [S]omewhat coherent implies that its components hang together . . . rather comprehensive implies that it subsumes a wide variety of social categories. . . . [But] it tends to revolve about only a few central values. . . . [I]t tells [a person] whether what he 'sees' is good or bad or morally neutral. . . . [I]t tells him to act in accordance with his cognitions and evaluations" (p. 37).

10. Higgs (1987) suggests that "political philosophy is both broader and differently motivated" than ideology, claiming "it contains no necessary impulse toward political action" (p. 38). But the concern here is with the ideologically determined political philosophies of individuals already involved in political action; the concern is with the ideology of the men who did draft and ratify the Constitution.

11. For recent studies of contemporary political voting behavior that demonstrate the value of employing personal characteristics as markers for ideology, see Fort, Hallagan, Morong, and Stegner (1993), Gohmann and Ohsfeldt (1994), and Coates and Munger (1995). Also see the discussion in Goff and Grier (1993).

12. Many political economists contend that ideology matters when it comes to analyzing the behavior of political actors and political action, though they disagree about the relative role of a political actor's ideology versus constituent ideology. See Kau and Rubin (1982), Kalt and Zupan (1984), Higgs (1987), Grier (1993), Hinich and Munger (1994), Coates and Munger (1995), and Poole and Rosenthal (1997). Among economic historians, North (1990) argues that the role of ideology needs to be formally incorporated into models of institutional choice. And historians have long contended that a complete understanding of the making of the Constitution must take into account ideological views. See Kenyon (1955), Rossiter (1966), Bailyn (1967, 1968), Wood (1969), Diggins (1981), Hutson (1981), and McDonald (1985).

13. All states represented at Philadelphia were represented by more than one delegate. Rhode Island sent no delegates. At the state ratifying conventions, counties were represented by more than one delegate.

14. For a discussion of logistic regression and other limited dependent variable models applied to the social sciences, see Hanushek and Jackson (1977, chap. 7).

15. The assumption that the error term in the OLS regression equation has a common variance is referred to as homoskedasticity.

16. See Hanushek and Jackson (1977, p. 183). The maximization of the likelihood function for a logistic regression equation is attained with nonlinear estimation methods. See Maddala (1988, chap. 8).

17. The logistic coefficient itself measures the influence of an explanatory variable on the log of the odds ratio (the log of the predicted probability of the dependent variable divided by 1 minus the predicted probability of the dependent variable). But the coefficient can be transformed into the marginal or incremental

effect of a change in an explanatory variable on the dependent variable directly. The transformation is discussed below.

18. Another advantage of multivariate regression techniques is that they statistically explain the vote on an issue at Philadelphia or ratification employing the votes of all delegates in a sample to draw generalizations instead of relying on the specific vote of each delegate individually.

19. For continuous explanatory variables, the marginal effect is $\partial \hat{P}/\partial X_i = \beta_i \hat{P}(1 - \hat{P})$, where β_i is the estimated logit coefficient of variable X_i, $\hat{P}$ is the predicted probability of voting yes on the issue in question at the sample means $(\bar{X}_i)$ of all explanatory variables in the model specification, $\hat{P} = 1/[1 + \exp(-\alpha - \Sigma\beta_i\bar{X}_i)]$, and α is the estimated constant. For dichotomous (dummy) explanatory variables, the incremental effect is calculated as the difference in predicted values, $\hat{P}_1 - \hat{P}_0$, for the two values of X_i, where $\hat{P}_1 = 1/[1 + \exp(-\alpha - \beta_i - \Sigma\beta_j\bar{X}_j)]$ and $\hat{P}_0 = 1/[1 + \exp(-\alpha - \Sigma\beta_j\bar{X}_j)]$; and $\Sigma\beta_j\bar{X}_j$ is the sum of the products of the estimated coefficients of all other explanatory variables, X_j, at their sample means $(\bar{X}_j)$. Note that the predicted probability of a yes vote is $\hat{P}_1$ when the dummy variable equals 1 and $\hat{P}_0$ when the dummy variable equals 0. The calculations measure the marginal or incremental effect of a hypothetical "average" delegate, not the average of the estimated marginal or incremental effects over all the delegates in the sample. Train (1986, chap. 2) discusses the differences in the two measures of marginal or incremental effects.

Interestingly, there is a simple method of approximating the marginal or incremental effect of a variable on the probability of a yes vote from its logistic coefficient. The magnitude of the estimated marginal or incremental effect, as a general rule, is between one-fifth and one-fourth (20 to 25 percent) of the magnitude of the variable's coefficient.

20. The conventional R^2 statistic employed in OLS regression as a measure of the amount of variation in the dependent variable explained by the explanatory variables is problematic when the dependent variable is dichotomous, as in logistic regression. However, alternative R^2 measures, as well as other measures, of the overall goodness of fit of the estimated model for use with logistic regression have been proposed. See Maddala (1988, chap. 8).

21. Pseudo $\bar{R}^2$ is calculated as $\bar{R}^2 = [(\chi^2 - 2k)/(-2L_R)]$, where χ^2 is the model χ^2 statistic, k is the number of explanatory variables in the model, and L_R is the maximum of the likelihood function restricted with only the constant in the model.

22. Somers' D_{yx} is calculated, analogous to Kendall's rank correlation coefficient, as the correlation between the ranking of the predicted probabilities of the votes (between .00 and 1.0) and rank of the observed votes (0 or 1) for all observations.

23. The summary of the conditions during the 1780s that follows is a synthesis of the major economic studies of the period. The studies include Nettles (1962), Bjork (1963, 1964), Ferguson (1961), Shepherd and Walton (1976), Walton and Shepherd (1979), and McCusker and Menard (1985). Although the studies generally conclude that economic conditions were improving during the 1780s, none suggests that the economy was performing well.

24. A potential problem exists in claiming that delegates farther from navigable water or the coast were more likely to have opposed the Constitution because their constituents were involved in less commercial activities. Some may suggest that delegates from more isolated areas also represented constituents who favored the Constitution because of the increased protection it offered to those farther

from navigable water or coastal areas, particularly those on the frontier. Yet if "distance" from the coast or navigable water captures not only the lack of commercial activities but also a "localist" ideology, constituents on the frontier would have preferred the protection be provided with local government. In addition, the ownership of western land is expected to capture the desire for an increase in "nationally" provided protection on the frontier.

25. Farrand (1911, vol. 2, pp. 95, 220–223, 364–374, 415–416) and Elliot (1836 [1888], vol. 3, pp. 452–458, 589–590, 598–599, 621–623; vol. 4, pp. 30–32, 100–102, 176–178, 271–274).

26. Farrand (1911, vol. 2, pp. 448–451, 631) and Elliot (1836 [1888], vol. 3, p. 621; vol. 4, pp. 271–274, 298, 308–311).

27. Lynd (1967) claims that slaveowning delegates to the Philadelphia convention and members of the Confederation Congress made a vote trade in which slaveowners received three-fifths representation for their slaves in the Constitution and agreed to a prohibition on slavery in the Northwest.

28. Both economic interests and ideology in fact are expected to have influenced a founder's vote because the Constitution contained both general rules that were to be used for future collective decisions as well as bundles of more specific-interest provisions with predictable consequences for specific groups.

Chapter Three

1. The present chapter is based on the analysis contained in McGuire and Ohsfeldt (1986), and excerpts are reprinted with permission. However, all econometric findings reported in the chapter are original to this book, as they are based on updated estimations employing new data corrected for several errors discovered in the data originally employed in the published article. Thus, specific econometric findings reported in the chapter differ from those previously published in some circumstances. This chapter also presents a wealth of new econometric findings about the framers' voting behavior, based on estimations conducted specifically for this book.

2. There are two possible limitations to the approach in this chapter. First, the delegates voted as members of state delegations, not as individuals. Others have shown, nonetheless, that the delegates' votes can be determined approximately through careful use of attendance records, records of the debates including the states' votes, and James Madison's notes. Second, the use of individual roll calls may be misleading because of the existence of strategic maneuvers designed to alter the range of alternatives facing the delegates. As a result, it may be difficult to separate the influence of political maneuvering on voting behavior from the impact of personal and constituent interests. Both issues are discussed in detail in this chapter.

3. For a discussion of the movement for constitutional reform, see the excellent survey of the maneuvering that led to the Philadelphia convention in Kelly and Harbison (1970, pp. 110–113).

4. For scholarly studies of the American economy during the 1780s, see Nettles (1962), Bjork (1963, 1964), Ferguson (1961), Shepherd and Walton (1976), Walton and Shepherd (1979), and McCusker and Menard (1985).

5. For an argument of one of the framers that there was a "crisis" in government and the economy, see Paper No. 10, by James Madison, in *The Federalist* (1937 [1788]).

6. But they disagreed enough about the importance and urgency of reform that nineteen of the seventy-four delegates appointed by their states to attend Philadelphia chose not to attend. Patrick Henry, for example, did not attend because, as he has been quoted to say, "I smelt a Rat," indicating that not all of America's political leaders were convinced there was a genuine crisis in the nation (H. B. Grigsby, *History of the Virginia Federal Constitution of 1788*, I, p. 32, as cited in Farrand, 1911, vol. 3, p. 558, n. 2).

7. For a record of the debates, see Farrand (1911), reputably the best single source of information concerning what took place in Philadelphia. His three volumes contain, among other sources of information: (1) copies of the official journal of the convention; (2) James Madison's highly respected notes of the entire proceedings (including changes he made after the fact); (3) the diaries, notes, and memoranda of seven other framers (Alexander Hamilton, Rufus King, George Mason, James McHenry, William Pierce, William Paterson, and Robert Yates); (4) the Virginia and the New Jersey plans of government presented to the convention; (5) several documents recording the work of the Committee of Detail that presented the first draft of the Constitution to the convention on August 6, 1787; and (6) numerous letters and correspondence of many of the founders and their contemporaries.

8. The interested reader should compare the copy of the Articles of Confederation to the copy of the United States Constitution, both of which are contained in appendix 1.

9. Thirty-four of the fifty-five delegates were trained in the law, but it was determined that for twelve of the framers the practice of law was not a primary occupation.

10. For experience in the Continental Congress, see *Biographical Directory of the American Congress, 1774–1961* (1961). For the economic and other interests, see McDonald (1958), Main (1960), Rossiter (1966), Kelly and Harbison (1970), Brown (1976), and the sources cited therein. All data employed, including those for the occupational classifications, and the sources of the data are discussed in detail in appendix 2.

11. Information on the holdings of financial securities and slaves is contained in McDonald (1958) and Main (1960). The data, and their sources, are discussed in detail in appendix 2.

12. On the eve of the Revolution, total physical wealth per free wealth holder, based on probated estates, has been estimated to be in the range of £161 to £395 (about $800 to $2,000, in 1774 dollars), depending on the region considered. These wealth estimates are from Alice Hanson Jones (1978) as presented in Walton and Rockoff (1998, table 5-5, p. 111), which also present income estimates derived from non-human physical wealth estimates in Jones (1980). Walton and Rockoff (table 5-4, p. 109) estimate income per free person on the eve of the Revolution in the range of £9.5 to £20.5 (about $47.50 to $102.50, in 1774 dollars), depending on the region considered and the capital-output ratio assumed. The non-human physical wealth estimates in Jones (1980), as presented in Walton and Rockoff (table 5-3, p. 109), range from £38 to £62 per free person (about $190 to $310, in 1774 dollars), depending on the region considered. It is unlikely that wealth and income in the 1780s would have differed greatly from the estimates for the 1770s.

13. The Madison, Wilson, and Morris quotes are from Kelly and Harbison (1970, pp. 115–116); the Mason and Washington quotes are from Rossiter (1966, p. 118).

14. William Churchill Houston apparently played little, if any, role at the convention, as his name is never mentioned in the official journal or in the notes of any of the delegates, other than that he was present (see Farrand, 1911, vol. 1, pp. 1–75). George Wythe, however, was fairly active in the first week of the convention. He was appointed to and chaired the committee responsible for designing the rules under which the convention would operate. Several reports to the convention were delivered by Wythe during the first few days (see Farrand, 1911, vol. 1, pp. 1–17, 60).

15. Farrand (1911) contains the attendance records, including dates of known absences; the diaries, including recorded votes of individual delegates; the votes of each state; and other information.

16. Riker (1984) employs the same method to determine the votes of delegates on three issues. According to Riker, Maryland voted yes on Roll Call 11, and Daniel Carroll, Luther Martin, James McHenry, and John Mercer did not vote. The only delegate left, Daniel of St. Thomas Jenifer, must have voted yes on the motion. Riker also shows how New York voted on the Roll Call 11. Because John Lansing was not present for the vote, the state was divided, and prior sentiment would indicate a no vote for Robert Yates, Riker concludes Alexander Hamilton must have voted yes. The method of deduction is employed for the two other issues and other delegates, indicating that the procedure is a reasonable method to determine the Philadelphia votes.

17. For discussion of the motion and the issue of amending the Constitution, see Farrand (1911, vol. 2, pp. 621–622, 629–631). George Mason's quote is from James Madison's "Notes" contained in Farrand (1911, vol. 2, p. 631) and is Madison's synopsis of what was said at the convention.

18. On the importance of the form of ratification, see Kelly and Harbison (1970. chap. 5) and Jensen (1964, pp. 96–105). On the importance of the amending process, see Jenson (1964, pp. 96–105) and Rossiter (1966, chap. 11).

19. All documents contained in Farrand (1911) were examined for the content analysis.

20. In addition to the 569 recorded votes, the records of the convention indicate the existence of at least 272 other votes that were not recorded in the journal. The journal showed only whether they passed or not; 256 were affirmed and 16 failed. Neither the vote of the states nor the votes of the individual delegates are known for these motions (see Farrand, 1911).

21. Farrand (1911, vol. 2, pp. 517, 582). Farrand states that it was virtually impossible to determine numerous votes on two different occasions—between Roll Call 455 and Roll Call 472, and between Roll Call 511 and Roll Call 569. Others also argue that only a half dozen or so important votes took place during the last four days of the convention, when there were almost sixty roll-call votes. See Jensen (1964, pp. 118–121) and Rossiter (1966, chap. 11).

22. These examples of minor votes can be found in Farrand (1911): Roll Call 1 (vol. 1, pp. 29–32), Roll Call 56 (vol. 1, pp. 209–213), Roll Calls 137–139 and 141–144 (vol. 1, pp. 575–591), Roll Call 317 (vol. 2, pp. 321–324), and Roll Call 364 (vol. 2, pp. 396–399).

23. See, for examples, Kelly and Harbison (1970, chap. 5) and Rossiter (1966, chaps. 10–11).

24. Compare the first vote and the third vote in McDonald (1958, pp. 102–103) to Roll Call 30 and Roll Call 74 in Farrand (1911, vol. 1, pp. 130–147, 369–380), respectively.

25. Compare the fifth vote in McDonald (1958) to Roll Call 228 and Roll Call 230 in Farrand (1911, vol. 2, pp. 116–128).

26. McDonald was unable to determine the errors contained in his study for the two votes either (personal correspondence with Forrest McDonald, May and June 1984).

27. Tables 3.3 and 3.4 do not list all the variables, or all the alternative measures for the variables, for which data have been collected for the Philadelphia delegates. Because the estimated specifications of equation 3.1 contain both the personal-interest and the constituent-interest variables, the estimated model specifications in this chapter include fewer alternative measures and markers for each set of variables than when each set of variables is estimated separately in chapter 4. The small delegate sample size constrains the number of variables that can be included in any single specification of the voting model when the model includes both sets of variables. The findings for the other variables, as well as for the use of the various alternative substitute measures of the variables, are reported in chapter 4. The data, and their sources, for all measures of the economic and ideological interests for the Philadelphia delegates are discussed in detail in appendix 2.

28. The compromise issues possibly involved in the three votes are discussed in the next section, which reports the statistical findings for the votes.

29. See Kalt and Zupan (1984, pp. 288–289). For sophisticated discussion of the problem of strategic voting behavior, see Farquharson (1969), Enelow and Koehler (1979, pp. 157–175), and Shepsle and Weingast (1984, pp. 49–74). These studies indicate a multitude of possible voting outcomes given strategic behavior, but they offer no apparent empirical solutions to the problem of strategic voting. An attempt to empirically measure logrolling during voting is Kau and Rubin (1979, pp. 365–384), who estimate votes across issues as a function of each other. The efficacy of such an approach is dubious.

30. Because numerous votes were taken on similar issues and other votes attracted the same interests, a statistical analysis attempting to correlate all the votes at the convention with different interests would offer little help. It is not likely that such a technique applied to all possible votes could determine the existence or direction of logrolling at the convention.

31. See Farrand (1911, vol. 1, pp. 7–17). Buchanan and Tullock (1962, chaps. 9–10) also make two relevant observations about vote trading. They argue that vote trading is more likely if the vote involved leads to decisive action being taken. If the decision-making group can modify decisions through repeat voting, the vote on any issue loses economic value for a trade. Second, they argue that an individual is better off "if he accepts a decision contrary to his desire in an area where his preferences are weak in exchange for a decision in his favor in an area where his feelings are stronger" (p. 145). Strongly held interests are less likely to be traded away. Therefore, logrolling in fact might have been empirically unimportant at Philadelphia.

32. For examples of studies that mention the possible vote trade involving the fourteenth vote, see Farrand (1911), Jensen (1964), McDonald (1958, 1965), and Rossiter (1966).

33. The delegate sample size of the convention is too small for "not voting" to be considered a separate alternative in other statistical techniques that allow for more than two alternatives, such as multinomial logit or ordered probit models. Nor does the delegate sample size permit the use of statistical techniques, such as Heckman's procedure, to correct for selectivity bias (see Maddala, 1983).

34. George Read of Delaware actually signed for himself and for John Dickinson of Delaware, who was not present.

35. To determine the sensitivity of the estimates to a potential selectivity bias, equation 3.1 was first estimated for each issue employing only the votes of the framers who actually voted. It was then estimated for each issue for the actual and imputed votes under the following assumptions: (1) All framers who signed the Constitution, except three, would have voted with the majority on any particular issue on which they did not actually vote. (2) Three of the framers who signed the Constitution—Richard Bassett (Delaware), William Blount (North Carolina), and William Paterson (New Jersey)—would have voted with the minority on any missed vote because of evidence indicating they opposed the Constitution. (3) Framers who did not sign the Constitution would have voted with the majority on any missed issue if Farrand stated they favored the Constitution, and with the minority if Farrand stated they opposed it. And (4) the three nonsigning framers for whom Farrand did not determine attitudes would have voted with the minority on any missed vote. The vote under this assumption, however, was imputed for only two of the three nonsigning framers, William Houstoun (Georgia) and Alexander Martin (North Carolina). The third, William Churchill Houston (New Jersey), was excluded from all the statistical analysis because of a lack of information about his votes, as he permanently departed the convention in the first week.

A comparison of the logistic estimates obtained solely from the actual votes, with the logistic estimates employing the actual and imputed votes, produced similar results for most of the votes except for the last few, when there was a greater number of absent delegates. It should be noted that in referring to the actual vote, I am referring to the probable vote of a framer, who was determined to have voted on the issue in question, and whose vote was deduced in McDonald (1958) and from the historical records of the convention. Furthermore, because of different sizes of state delegations, a losing issue that had a majority of the states against it could have had an actual majority of individual delegates voting in favor of it. Consequently, the framers who left the Philadelphia convention because they were in the minority could not have stayed and necessarily passed the losing issues.

36. For an argument of one of the framers of the Constitution that economic interests mattered for representation in the new government, see Paper No. 35, by Alexander Hamilton, in *The Federalist* (1937 [1788]).

37. The estimated logistic coefficients, standard errors, and goodness-of-fit statistics for the logistic regressions for the sixteen votes for the full voting model are presented in table A3.2a,b in appendix 3. All nineteen explanatory variables were included in the estimated model specification for each vote unless the logit algorithm would not converge with all variables included. Variables were excluded from a particular vote only if the logistic regressions could not be estimated otherwise. Given that delegates with particular characteristics voted unanimously on some issues, variables measuring those characteristics were excluded because the voting model cannot be estimated with an explanatory variable with zero variance. Other variables were excluded from the full voting model only after an analysis determined they were the specific variables preventing convergence. The minimum number of variables necessary to allow the logit algorithm to converge for each vote was excluded. Although estimates are reported in table A3.2a for the first and third votes recall that they are votes for which uncorrectable errors were discovered. The estimates are reported merely for the interest of the reader.

As a result of the uncorrectable errors, less confidence should be placed in the findings for the two votes. Also, only fifty-three of the fifty-five delegates are included in the analysis because William Churchill Houston (New Jersey) and George Wythe (Virginia) were excluded because, as noted earlier, both left the convention within the first two weeks.

38. An alternative method of estimating the pro-national voting of the delegates is to pool the sixteen votes (or, more appropriately, the fourteen votes without known errors) from Philadelphia into a single variable measuring the proportion of all sixteen (or the fourteen) votes in favor of pro-national issues. In chapter 5, voting behavior is formally estimated employing such a single measure of a nationalist stance.

39. The estimated logistic coefficients, standard errors, and goodness-of-fit statistics for the more parsimonious model specifications for all sixteen votes are reported in table A3.3a,b in appendix 3. All estimates reported in this table are based on the adjusted votes according to the assumptions regarding delegates who did not vote and, as with the estimated full voting model, do not include data for William Churchill Houston and George Wythe. Because of the overall small sample size and the missing votes for some delegates, not all sixteen votes could be estimated unless the adjusted votes were employed. Also, as with the estimated full model, estimates are reported in table A3.3a for the first and third votes for the parsimonious model. Again, the estimates are reported merely for the interest of the reader. Because of the uncorrectable errors in the two votes, the validity of the reported findings for the votes may be dubious.

40. The calculation of the predicted probability of a yes vote is described in chapter 2.

41. The asymptotic t-statistic for the estimated coefficient of the variable measuring the number of slaves owned is 1.03 with 43 degrees of freedom, for a computed P-value of .3027 (see table A3.3a). This finding, based on estimations employing data corrected for a small number of errors found in the data in previously published research, conflicts somewhat with the finding reported in McGuire and Ohsfeldt (1986, pp. 102–104 and tables 4 and 5) that the effect of personal slaveholdings on the second vote *was* statistically significant at the .10 level. The findings here also conflict with the previously published finding that there was a statistically significant positive effect of a delegate's private securities holdings on the probability of voting for the second issue (also see pp. 102–104 and tables 4 and 5). With the corrected data here, the private securities variable did not have a statistically significant effect on voting in favor of the second issue (see table A3.2a in appendix 3).

42. The magnitude of the impact of a continuous variable on a vote can be summarized employing its response elasticity. The response elasticity is a measure of the percentage change in the predicted probability of a yes vote caused by a 1 percent change in a continuous variable and is calculated as $\varepsilon_i = \beta_i \bar{X}_i (1 - \hat{P}) = (\partial \hat{P} / \hat{P}) / (\partial \bar{X}_i / \bar{X}_i)$, where $\hat{P}$ is the predicted probability of a yes vote on a particular issue, $\bar{X}_i$ is the mean of a particular explanatory variable i, and β_i is the estimated logistic coefficient for the variable i, where the elasticity is evaluated at the means of the explanatory variables. See Hanushek and Jackson (1977, chap. 7).

43. Coalitions capable of sustaining or blocking certain special-interest legislation at the state level may have doubted their ability to create a similar coalition at the national level. Delegates who possessed or represented economic interests that had benefited from state-level special-interest legislation are expected to vote

no on the issue, while delegates who possessed or represented interests incurring costs are expected to vote yes.

44. See the records of the Philadelphia debates in Farrand (1911, vol. 2, pp. 95, 220–223, 364–374, 415–416).

45. Farrand (1911, vol. 1, p. 166). All quotations of speeches from the Philadelphia convention that follow are from James Madison's "Notes" contained in Farrand (1911) and, as noted, are Madison's synopses of what was said at the convention.

46. The asymptotic t-statistic for the estimated coefficient of the merchant variable is 1.19 with 43 degrees of freedom, for a computed P-value of .2345 (see table A3.3a).

47. The percentage effects reported for dichotomous variables in the present chapter are calculated as the difference between the predicted probabilities of a yes vote when the dichotomous variable has a value of 1 and when it has a value of 0, expressed as a percentage of the predicted probability when it has a value of 0.

48. With 43 degrees of freedom, the asymptotic t-statistic for the estimated coefficient of the public creditor variable is 1.603, for a computed P-value of .1090 (see table A3.3a).

49. Schweitzer (1989b), however, contends that support for a ban on state paper money was more complex than the traditional "creditor-debtor" story. Grubb (2000) presents evidence indicating that the states in fact were not irresponsible with the issuance of paper money during the 1780s. Consequently, the apparent indifference on the ninth issue of delegates who were in personal debt may not be that surprising even if inflationary issues of state paper money could have relieved their financial situation. For more on these views, see the discussion in chapter 6 on the ratification of the Constitution among delegates from states that did and did not issue paper money during the 1780s; especially see notes 15 and 41.

50. With 43 degrees of freedom, the asymptotic t-statistic for the estimated coefficient of the variable measuring the number of slaves owned is 1.399, for a computed P-value of .1618 (see table A3.3b).

51. With 43 degrees of freedom, the asymptotic t-statistic for the estimated coefficient of public securities is 1.585, for a computed P-value of .1130; and the t-statistic is 1.533 for the estimated coefficient of the number of slaves per 100 whites, for a computed P-value of .1251 (see table A3.3b).

52. It appears that delegates who owned western land also were more likely to vote yes on the issue. With 43 degrees of freedom, the asymptotic t-statistic for the estimated coefficient of the western land variable is 1.508, for a computed P-value of .1316. It appears as well that delegates who personally owned slaves were *less* likely to vote yes on the issue. With 43 degrees of freedom, the asymptotic t-statistic for the estimated coefficient of the personnel slaveholdings variable is 1.493, for a computed P-value of .1354 (see table A3.3b). The effect on the vote of personal slaveholdings is opposite the effect of the amount of slaves in the area the delegate represented. Perhaps these opposite effects are due to obscuring effects of a possible vote trade on the issue.

53. For studies concluding that delegates who owned slaves or represented slaveholding areas supported the Constitution, see Beard (1913 [1935], pp. 29–30), Main (1961), Risjord (1974, pp. 613–632; 1978), and Nadelhaft (1981).

54. For studies concluding that delegates who owned public securities were split over the Constitution, see McDonald (1958, 1965), Rossiter (1966), and Wood (1969).

55. Slaveowners were equally opposed to the second issue as they were to the thirteenth, and also had a much lower predicted voting probability for it than the "average" delegate (38 percent lower), but the second issue failed to pass at the convention anyway and did not become part of the Constitution. Slaveowners were strongly in favor of the seventh issue, and also had a much higher predicted voting probability for it than the "average" delegate (52 percent higher), but the issue passed at the convention regardless and became part of the Constitution.

56. Rossiter (1966, chap. 12) concludes as well that if a dozen backcountry farmers had attended the convention, there would have been no nationalist charter. While the presence of only two less commercial farmers at Philadelphia prevents the effect of this specific interest from being estimated quantitatively, Rossiter's implication that there would have been a quite different constitution had different interests been represented is supported by the findings for many other interests and characteristics.

Chapter Four

1. The analysis and findings presented in this chapter were published previously in greater detail in McGuire (1988), and are reprinted with permission.

2. As noted in chapter 1, many scholars contend that the factors motivating the delegates at the Philadelphia convention were the interests of the citizens, states, and their sections. For the contention that constituent interests were the important factors, see Benson (1960, pp. 95–174), Jensen (1964, pp. 44–45), and McDonald (1965, chap. 6).

3. The data, and their sources, for the measures of the economic and ideological interests are discussed in detail in appendix 2.

4. The entries in tables 4.3 and 4.4 summarize the direction and the significance of the estimated effects (the logistic coefficients) for all specifications estimated for each vote. For equation 4.1, the entries in table 4.3 summarize the results from up to twenty-four alternative specifications involving different combinations of the personal variables for each issue. Not all specifications were used for each vote because of unanimous voting among delegates with certain personal characteristics. (The logistic algorithm cannot converge if a variable with zero variance is included in a specification.) For equation 4.2, the entries in table 4.4 summarize the results from fifteen alternative specifications involving different combinations of the constituent variables for each issue. There was no unanimous voting among delegates with particular constituent characteristics. The entries in tables 4.3 and 4.4 indicate whether the coefficient of each characteristic was consistently significant or not across each specification, and the sign of the significant coefficients. While the results for the first and third votes are not emphasized because of the uncorrectable errors found in each, a summary of the results for the two votes is included in table 4.3 nonetheless. The findings for the first and third votes, however, may be suspect because of the known errors in both.

All results summarized in tables 4.3 and 4.4 are based on the adjusted votes according to the assumptions regarding delegates who did not vote and do not include data for the two delegates (William Churchill Houston and George Wythe) who permanently left the Philadelphia convention within the first two weeks. For the assumptions about the imputed votes for nonvoting delegates, see the discussion in chapter 3, note 35. Recall that a potential selectivity bias could be introduced by excluding delegates who did not vote on a particular issue. Estimates obtained by excluding nonvoting delegates produced similar results, with the exception of five votes (the first, seventh, twelfth, thirteenth, and sixteenth). Because the sample size is too small, the logistic routine does not converge for several specifications for the five votes without adjusting for not voting. A comparison of the results obtained from both sets of data on the votes suggests that the problem of selectivity bias does not affect most estimates.

5. That the delegates might have been more responsive to their constituents' interests than their own interests suggests the delegates might have been more concerned either with their future political ambitions or with successfully ratifying the Constitution after the convention; both are likely concerns. In either case, while the delegates would have attempted to satisfy their constituents' interests, at the same time they would not have ignored their personal interests. A formal statistical test of the difference between the estimates of the constituent-interest model and personal-interest model is problematic. The relatively large number of explanatory variables in each estimated model (depending on the specification, the minimum is between four and seven and the maximum is between eight and eleven) in combination with the relatively small sample size (fifty-three delegates when the imputed votes are included and as few as thirty-six when nonvoting delegates are excluded) yields a weak formal test of the difference between the two models.

6. The entries for the constituent interests measured by the wealth, slave, and distance variables in table 4.4 summarize their effects alternately employing the different substitute measures of each variable. For the slave variable, the entry summarizes the results for the three measures of constituent slave interests listed in table 4.2. For the wealth variable, the entry summarizes the results for all wealth measures listed in table 4.2, except the share of wealth in landholdings, which is included separately in table 4.4. For the distance variable, the entry summarizes the results for all distance measures listed in table 4.2, except distance from Philadelphia, which was never significant.

7. For the list of the sixteen votes, see table 3.2. As in chapter 3, the first and third votes are not emphasized in the present chapter either because of the uncorrectable errors found in each.

8. See Benson (1960), Hutson (1981), Libby (1894), and Main (1961).

9. All estimates reported in the tables in appendix 4 are expressed as the more intelligible marginal or incremental effect of a particular explanatory variable on the probability of a yes vote on the issue in question, with all other explanatory variables at their means. All estimates reported are also based on the adjusted votes according to the assumptions regarding delegates who did not vote and do not include data for the two delegates (William Churchill Houston and George Wythe) who left the convention within the first two weeks. Because the estimated specifications of equation 4.1 contain only the personal-interest variables and the estimated specifications of equation 4.2 contain only the constituent-interest variables, the findings reported for each of the selected votes include estimates for a greater number of the alternative measures of the economic interests and the alternative markers for ideology than in chapter 3. The sample size constrains the number of variables that can be meaningfully included in any single specification of the voting model because of the degrees of freedom in the estimation. Fewer personal-interest variables and/or fewer constituent-interest variables, accordingly,

were included when the model specified inclusion of both sets of variables, as in chapter 3.

10. The variable measuring the appreciation of public securities holdings measures the increase in the market value of a delegate's holdings between 1787 and December 1791. The data are from McDonald (1958, p. 90).

11. As for the delegates who represented constituents of English ancestry, it appears that they were more skeptical of a strong central government than Main (1961) believes.

12. Delegates from states with a larger number of Scottish and Irish descendants were marginally less likely to have voted yes.

13. Compare columns 1 and 2 to columns 3–5 in the top of table A4.5 in appendix 4.

14. For example, see Main (1960, pp. 86–110; 1961), Kelly and Harbison (1970, chap. 5), and McDonald (1965, chap. 6).

Chapter Five

1. This chapter is a revised version of McGuire and Ohsfeldt (1997), and is reprinted with permission.

2. Models of partisan voting behavior on the part of political actors are based on interest-group theories of politics—what has been referred to as political agency theory. For discussion of interest-group theories, see Stigler (1971), Peltzman (1976), and Becker (1983). For discussion of political agency theory in the context of legislative voting, see Kalt and Zupan (1984) and Peltzman (1984).

3. As discussed in chapter 3, prior to Philadelphia, the national government was quite weak relative to the state governments. States often failed to make tax payments to the national government, leaving it chronically short of funds. The national government at times was virtually impotent, as the thirteen states acted in large part as a loose federation of independent states. The Constitution substantially increased the power of the national government.

4. But partisan interests will influence the more interest-specific issues that arise during actual constitution making (Buchanan and Tullock, 1962, chap. 6).

5. A view of partisan behavior at the operational level of collective choice is consistent with the views of partisan behavior on the part of political actors presented in political agency theory and public choice economics. For discussion of this literature, see chapter 2.

6. For evidence that the distribution of wealth in late-eighteenth-century America was markedly unequal, see Jones (1980, chaps. 6–7).

7. For an extended treatment of the issue of an interest component and a theory component of constitutional preferences, see Buchanan (1991b).

8. See Buchanan (1991b, p. 57). Writing decades later about *The Calculus of Consent*, Buchanan (1991a) maintains that the "book was a mixture of positive analysis . . . and a normative defense of certain American political institutions that owe their origins to the Founding Fathers" (p. 35).

9. Holcombe (1991), however, does not analyze the actual voting behavior during the drafting of either the Articles or the Constitution.

10. The discussion of the Philadelphia convention and the delegates that follows is a synopsis of the description of the convention and delegates presented in chapter 3.

11. See the records of the Philadelphia debates in Farrand (1911).

12. During the preceding ten years, the United States had drafted and ratified a different set of rules—the Articles of Confederation—that the Philadelphia delegates all but ignored in 1787. Many of the delegates wanted another convention to consider additional rules. Several signed the Constitution only after assurances that the first Congress would amend the drafted document. For the views of delegates reluctant to sign the Constitution, see Farrand (1911, vol. 2, pp. 622–650). For the calls of delegates for another constitutional convention, see Farrand (1911, vol. 2, pp. 479, 561, 564, 631, 634; vol. 3, pp. 125, 242, 354). And, although he did not attend the Philadelphia convention, Thomas Jefferson's view on constitutional conventions is still illuminating: He believed there should be a new constitutional convention every generation (Klarman, 1992, p. 781 and n. 133).

13. See Maddala (1988, chap. 12), which argues that nonnested hypothesis tests are likely to have more power in smaller samples. A method for applying nonnested hypothesis tests to non–linear maximum likelihood estimation is presented in Smith and Maddala (1983). For formal, in-depth discussions of nonnested hypothesis tests, see Davidson and McKinnon (1981) and Mizon and Richard (1986).

14. Equations 5.3 and 5.4 are considered rivals of the empirical model of voting described in equation 5.1.

15. Specifically, nonnested hypothesis tests, or "J-tests," are conducted by selecting a null hypothesis (eq. 5.3 is the true model) and a corresponding alternative hypothesis (eq. 5.4 is the true model). The first step is to obtain the maximum likelihood estimates of the logit coefficients under the alternative hypothesis. The second step is to construct a predicted probability of a pronational vote, $\hat{P}_{ij}$, using the estimates from the alternative hypothesis. Third, the null hypothesis (eq. 5.3) is then estimated twice, once with the predicted value of $\hat{P}_{ij}$ as an additional explanatory variable (the "unrestricted" model, u) and once without the predicted value of $\hat{P}_{ij}$ (the "restricted" model, r). The likelihood ratio test statistic is $LR = -2\left[\log L(r) - \log L(u)\right]$, which has a χ^2 distribution with one degree of freedom. The estimation procedure is then repeated with equation 5.4 as the null and equation 5.3 as the alternative. The hypotheses are nonnested because the variables in one hypothesis are not a subset of the variables in the other hypothesis.

More familiar nested hypothesis tests or "N-tests" (analogous to F-tests in OLS regression) are based on comparisons of equations 5.3 and 5.4 to equation 5.1. For example, to test the null hypothesis that the coefficients of PI_i and CI_j in equation 5.1 are zero, against the alternative that they are not zero, construct the likelihood ratio test statistic using $L(u)$, the value of the likelihood function for equation 5.1, and $L(r)$, the value of the likelihood function for equation 5.3. In this case, the test statistic has a χ^2 distribution with degrees of freedom equal to the number of variables in PI_i and CI_j (i.e., the number of restrictions). As noted above, the J-tests are employed rather than the more familiar N-tests because the J-tests may have greater power in small samples than do the N-tests (Maddala, 1988, chap. 12).

16. The validity of conclusions drawn from this exercise, however, may be affected by the limited availability of data for constituent interests, and potential correlation between omitted constituent–interest variables and included personal-interest variables.

17. See chapter 3 for a detailed discussion of the nationalist implications of all votes.

18. McDonald (1958) does not include an explicit analysis of the specific content of each vote to determine a nationalist stance.

19. The empirical results are not materially affected by including or omitting the fourteenth and sixteenth votes from P^A.

20. The set of explanatory variables employed in the present chapter is limited to those shown in table 5.2 because the findings for the Philadelphia convention in chapters 3 and 4 indicate that there are few important differences in the results employing the other measures, markers, or their alternatives. The variables shown in table 5.2 are the primary measures and markers employed throughout this book. The data, and their sources, for the measures of the economic and ideological interests are discussed in detail in appendix 2.

21. For a discussion of logistic regression for grouped data, see Hanushek and Jackson (1977, chap. 7).

22. Another alternative would be to estimate the votes as "seemingly unrelated" equations. But this is not feasible computationally given the number of votes involved and the small number of delegates. To the degree that the equations truly are seemingly unrelated, estimates obtained treating each vote separately are consistent though less efficient than estimates taking nonzero error covariances across votes into account. Another alternative would be to treat the data as a "panel" and estimate a state-dependent choice model, where a delegate's vote on an issue is partially dependent on his votes on previous issues. This procedure also requires the assumption that the sequential votes are essentially the same (see Maddala, 1987). In any case, given the sample size available, this type of model is not feasible.

23. In all cases, the logistic coefficients have been transformed into the more easily interpreted marginal or incremental effects of the explanatory variables on the probability of voting in favor of a pro-national position. The marginal or incremental effect of a particular explanatory variable is calculated with all other explanatory variables at their sample means. The calculations of the incremental and marginal effects are described in chapter 2.

24. Because the perceived impact of some of the sixteen votes on the relative power of the national government probably can be considered more straightforward than for other votes, another alternative measure of nationalism actually was determined for the empirical analysis of voting on nationalism. The fifth through seventh and the eleventh through thirteenth votes were eliminated from P_{ij} in an effort to restrict the measure of a pro-national position to more purely constitutional issues, P^C. P^C is the proportion of a delegate's votes at Philadelphia that was in favor of a pro-national position on only six issues—yes votes on the second, eighth, ninth, tenth, and fifteenth issues, and a no vote on the fourth issue. The results employing P^C are qualitatively similar to those employing P^A or P^B, but in part due to the small number of votes in P^C and the correspondingly large estimated standard errors, most coefficients are not statistically significant. The pseudo $\bar{R}^2$ measures of goodness of fit for the specifications for P^C also are much lower than for the same specifications for P^A or P^B. The results for P^C are reported in appendix 5, table A5.1.

25. The nonnested hypothesis tests employ the estimates from specifications 4–6 in table 5.3 with P^A as the measure of nationalism. The findings for additional nonnested hypothesis tests that employ the larger set of variables as well as tests that employ the alternative measure of a pro-national position (P^B) with the more limited set of explanatory variables are nearly identical and are reported in table A5.2 in appendix 5.

26. The conclusion is subject to the limitations of the data measuring constituent interests. Given the absence of some constituent variables from the model, it is possible that this apparent impact of personal interests reflects omitted constituent variables.

27. For these nonnested tests, a predicted value, $\hat{P}_{ij}$, for each of the alternative hypotheses is included in the unrestricted model. The test statistic is still χ^2 with one degree of freedom. See Smith and Maddala (1983, pp. 74–76).

28. For purposes of comparison, nested test results are reported in table A5.3. Overall, the implications of the nested test results are reasonably consistent with those for the nonnested tests. The few inconsistencies may be due to the problem of estimating the comprehensive, unrestricted model with a complete set of interest variables for each type of interest (PE_i, PI_i, CE_j, CI_j), given the small sample available, as well as the incomplete and imperfect measures of each type of interest. Recall, however, that the J-test may be better than the exclusion test (N-test) at rejecting a false hypothesis in small samples. For discussion of the N-test, see note 15 above.

Chapter Six

1. Portions of the present chapter are taken from McGuire and Ohsfeldt (1989a,b), and are reprinted with permission. However, the econometric findings reported in the chapter are updated estimations of the issues originally estimated and reported in McGuire and Ohsfeldt (1989a,b), employing data corrected for a small number of errors found in the original data. Specific econometric findings reported in the chapter differ from those previously published in some circumstances. This chapter also includes many new findings based on estimations conducted specifically for this book.

2. The records of the votes analyzed from the Philadelphia convention most commonly yielded only forty-two or forty-three actual votes, and only fifty-three total votes with the imputed votes included, for each of the sixteen issues.

3. During ratification, some delegates who opposed the Constitution were persuaded to vote for ratification under the condition that the Constitution would be amended by a bill of rights. In several states, both opponents and proponents of ratification sought to alter the timing of the vote until the outcomes at other conventions were known. At Philadelphia, there were hundreds of recorded roll calls as well as hundreds of votes that were apparently never recorded. Many votes were on the same issue because repeat voting was allowed. Logrolling among the delegates certainly was possible given the very large number of votes. There were votes on compromise proposals developed throughout the convention. And strategic maneuvering concerning the agenda also was apparently common.

4. Rhode Island initially held town meetings to consider the Constitution. The Constitution was resoundingly defeated at the town meetings (237–2,798) during March 1788. Thereafter, Rhode Island did not hold a state ratifying convention until May 1790, well after the Constitution had already gone into effect.

5. The best-known single source of the arguments of the supporters of the Constitution is the collection of essays contained in *The Federalist* (1937 [1788]), written during the ratification campaign in New York by Alexander Hamilton, John Jay, and James Madison in 1787 and 1788.

6. The eminent source of the arguments of the opponents of the Constitution is the seven volumes of Herbert J. Storing's (1981) *The Complete Anti-Federalist*.

For an excellent single-volume source of the views of the opponents, see Kenyon's (1966 [1985]) *The Antifederalists*.

7. For an excellent general source of primary documents concerning the founding, see the five volumes of Kurland and Lerner (1987). On the ratification process, also see the documents in Jensen (1976).

8. A fifth state, Rhode Island, actually had the closest vote, 34–32, but it took place well after the issue of ratification was moot. See table 6.1.

9. The data on the markers for ideology have been collected for the delegates for three of the state ratifying conventions and are analyzed in chapter 7.

10. It should be noted that the formal voting model includes a delegate's ideology as an independent explanatory variable to the extent that economic interests do not determine ideology.

11. When the vote for ratification is estimated separately for a single state convention, the data measuring the interests of a delegate's constituents should be measured at the county or township level within the state because that is the delegate's level of representation at his state convention.

12. Because two of the constituent-interest variables (the public funding credit and state population) are measured at the state level only, there is no within-state variation in the variables across delegates. Consequently, neither variable can be used for the individual state convention estimation, which weakens the comparison between the influence of personal and constituent interests when examining the ratification vote at the individual state conventions in chapter 7. Both variables, however, are employed in the pooled estimations reported in the present chapter.

13. Strategic timing considerations are discussed in detail below.

14. The data, and their sources, for the measures of the economic and ideological interests for the ratifying conventions are discussed in detail in appendix 2. Recall that the influence of the wealth of constituents on the votes at Philadelphia was estimated in chapters 3 and 4 employing the alternative estimates of state wealth that were based on the county wealth estimates in Jones (1980, pp. 377–379). Yet not much importance is placed on the results for the wealth variables because of the rough estimation procedure employed to compute the variables. In fact, the results presented in chapters 3 and 4 for the wealth variables suggest they were generally unimportant. Accordingly, the alternative measures of state wealth are omitted from the statistical analysis of the overall ratification vote reported here. In any event, the results with the state wealth variables included indicate that they are somewhat superfluous for the analysis of the overall ratification vote.

15. A potential difficulty with this interpretation of the paper money dummy variable is that the experiences of the states that issued paper money during the 1780s were not identical. Schweitzer (1989b) contends that support for prohibiting state paper money during the Confederation period was more complex than the traditional "creditor-debtor" story of inflation because in several states paper money was issued during the late eighteenth century strictly as a medium of exchange. As a result, in Schweitzer's view, there is little reason to believe these states were any more irresponsible in the issue of paper money than would be a national government.

16. For a discussion of the tactics of the opponents, see Main (1961).

17. All results in table 6.4 are reported as the incremental or marginal effect of each explanatory variable on the probability of voting in favor of ratification,

holding the other explanatory variables constant. The alternative specifications reported in table 6.4 differ in terms of the variables employed to measure public securities interests and slave interests. The estimated logistic coefficients, standard errors, and goodness-of-fit statistics for the three specifications in table 6.4 are reported in specifications 5–7, respectively, of table A6.1 in appendix 6, which also reports the estimates for five additional specifications. The additional specifications differ in terms of the variables employed to measure the ownership of public securities and slaves, the absence of variables that measure the conditions of ratification, and the inclusion of only variables with significant coefficients.

It turns out that the restrictions imposed by pooling the data for all thirteen states into one sample are, in fact, formally rejected employing standard likelihood ratio tests at the 5 percent significance level. This is most likely due to differences in the nature of ratification, the chronological order of ratification, or the past issuance of paper money, across the states. Nevertheless, the findings for the overall pooled sample are still valuable for making generalizations about voting patterns during the ratification process. The results for the entire pooled sample of all thirteen conventions are qualitatively similar for many of the explanatory variables when the restrictions are relaxed in the various subsets of state conventions that are discussed later in this chapter.

18. Several historians over the years have made this very point for the ratifying conventions. See, for example, McDonald (1958) and Rossiter (1966). For detailed discussion of the determination of the farmer variables for Philadelphia and the ratifying conventions, see appendix 2.

19. The predicted probabilities are calculated for specification 1 in table 6.4, as are all other predicted probabilities and estimated effects discussed for the overall pooled sample, unless otherwise noted. The estimated logistic coefficients for specification 1 are reported in specification 5 in table A6.1.

20. For the public securities ownership variable, the asymptotic t-statistics for the estimated coefficients are 1.458 and 1.593, for computed P-values of .1447 and .1112, respectively (see specifications 1 and 5, respectively, in table A6.1).

21. The $1,000 figure is from almost ten to over twenty-three times more than estimates of income per free person on the eve of the Revolution. See the discussion in appendix 2.

22. Recall that the magnitude of the impact of a continuous variable on a vote can be summarized employing its response elasticity, which is calculated as $\varepsilon_i = \beta_i \bar{X}_i (1 - \hat{P})$. For the value of public securities, it is calculated employing the estimates presented under specification 3 in table 6.4 and is calculated at the sample means of the explanatory variables.

23. The predicted probabilities for public securities holdings in excess of $1,000 are based on the estimates presented under specification 2 in table 6.4, and those for the ownership of any public securities holdings are based on the estimates presented under specification 1.

24. For this conclusion in American history textbooks, see Garraty (1995). For the conclusion in economic history textbooks, see Poulson (1981), Puth (1988), and Ratner, Soltow, and Sylla (1993). For the conclusion in American government textbooks, see O'Connor and Sabato (1993) and Wilson and DiIulio (1995).

25. See Article VI, Clause 1, of the United States Constitution, a copy of which is in appendix 1.

26. For examples of studies concluding that slaveowners were more likely to favor ratification, see Beard (1913 [1935]), Crowl (1943, 1947), Main (1961),

Nadelhaft (1981), and Risjord (1974, 1978). For examples of studies concluding that slaveowners were divided or indifferent over the issue, see McDonald (1958), Pool (1950a,b), and Thomas (1953). Recall, however, that when these scholars refer to the effect of slaveholdings, they are referring to the *overall* vote for ratification based on how the majority of slaveowning ratifiers voted. The reference to the effect of slaveholdings here, however, is to the *partial* effect of the ownership of slaves on the probability of a yes vote, holding all other economic interests constant. The partial effect indicates whether a slaveowning ratifier was more or less likely to vote yes, taking into account the confounding effects of all other interests. The actual vote of any particular ratifier depends on the *total* of all the partial effects of all his interests on his vote, not just the partial effect of slaveholdings. As a result, a majority of slaveowning ratifiers could have voted for ratification while at the same time the *partial* effect of slaveholdings per se still *decreases* the likelihood of voting in favor of ratification.

27. The lack of statistical significance is found whether constituents' slave interests are measured as the number of slaves per 100 whites, as the percentage of families owning slaves, or as the number of slaves per slaveowning household.

28. Estimates obtained employing the distance from a delegate's home to the Atlantic coast or distance from a delegate's home to nearest major commercial city as substitutes for distance from a delegate's home to the nearest navigable water are qualitatively the same as those reported in table 6.4.

29. The computation of the total assets of a delegate as well as of the share and instrumental variables is discussed in appendix 2. Although the share and instrumental variables are based on very rough calculations of the value of a delegate's total assets, their computation and use in the voting model still are valuable in an attempt to control, if even roughly, for the wide variance in the value of total assets owned by delegates who were slaveowners or public securities owners.

30. The findings in table A6.2 are reported as the estimated logistic coefficients of the variables rather than their marginal effects. Because the state fixed-effects model is estimated as an alternative method of controlling for state-specific factors for the overall pooled vote and to determine if controlling, even roughly, for a delegate's total assets produces more precise estimates of the influence of slaveholdings and public securities holdings: The signs and significance of the logistic coefficients themselves provide sufficient information in this case. The transformation of the coefficients into the marginal or incremental effects is not necessary to determine either the direction of the impact on voting or the precision of the estimate. In any event, as noted in chapter 2, the magnitude of the marginal or incremental effect of a variable, as a general rule, can be easily approximated as between one-fifth and one-fourth of the magnitude of its logistic coefficient.

31. For the slave share variable, the asymptotic t-statistic for the estimated coefficient of the variable is 1.471, for a computed P-value of .1412 (see specification 3 in table A6.2).

32. For the public securities ownership variable, the asymptotic t-statistic for the estimated coefficient is 1.530, for a computed P-value of .1260 (see specification 1 in table A6.2).

33. The southern states are Georgia, North Carolina, South Carolina, Virginia, and Maryland. The Middle Atlantic states are Delaware, New Jersey, New York,

and Pennsylvania. The New England states are Connecticut, Massachusetts, New Hampshire, and Rhode Island.

34. The summary presented in table 6.6 for each region is based on four alternative specifications of the models that include the timing and other variables contained in TO_j and four alternative specifications of the state fixed-effects models that include the state dummy variables in place of the variables in TO_j. The alternative specifications for each model differ in terms of their inclusion of different measures of slave and public securities interests. The estimated logistic coefficients for all eight specifications summarized in table 6.6 for the three regions are reported in appendix 6, tables A6.3–A6.8.

35. The delegate slave variables are not included in the specifications for the New England region because of the very small number of slaveowners in the sample of New England delegates, which makes it difficult to meaningfully estimate the effect of slave interests in the New England ratifying conventions.

36. The findings for the state fixed-effects model for the South are reported in table A6.6; for the Middle Atlantic in table A6.7; and for New England in table A6.8.

37. The letters from the individual states to the Congress transmitting their ratification, including their interpretations or recommendations, are contained in Elliot (1836 [1888] vol. 1, pp. 318–338).

38. The summary presented in table 6.7 for each group of states is based on four alternative specifications employing different explanatory variables for slaveholdings and public securities holdings. The estimated logistic coefficients for the four specifications summarized in table 6.7 for the four samples by the nature of ratification are reported in appendix 6, tables A6.9–A6.12.

39. The summary presented in table 6.8 for each group of states is based on four alternative specifications employing different explanatory variables for slaveholdings and public securities holdings. The estimated logistic coefficients for the four specifications summarized in table 6.8 for the four samples by the chronological order of ratification are reported in appendix 6, tables A6.13–A6.16.

40. The summary presented in table 6.9 for the two groups of states is based on four alternative specifications of the models that include the timing and other variables contained in TO_j and four alternative specifications of the state fixed-effects models that include the state dummy variables in place of the variables in TO_j. The alternative specifications for each model differ in terms of their inclusion of different measures of slave and public securities interests. The estimated logistic coefficients for all eight specifications summarized in table 6.9 for the two groups of states are reported in appendix 6, tables A6.17–A6.20.

41. Recall that Schweitzer (1989b) contends that support for a ban on state paper money was more complex than the traditional "creditor-debtor" story (see note 15 above). In contrast, Grubb (2000) presents evidence that indicates support for the ban on state paper money at the Philadelphia convention was not the result of a desire for monetary stability but rather was a pursuit of national sovereignty on the part of the nationalists at the convention. Grubb's econometric evidence on early American monetary policy also indicates that states, in fact, managed their paper currencies quite well during the 1780s, which also might account for the lack of signficant findings for the states *with* paper money.

Chapter Seven

1. Kaminski (1983), for example, argues the ratification process was unique in each state because economic conditions, political institutions, and the timing of ratification differed across states.

2. See note 17 in chapter 6 for a discussion of the formal rejection of the overall pooled sample.

3. As discussed in chapter 6, in a pooled sample, the impact of institutional and other factors unique to each state can be captured only through the use of dummy variables. To the extent that any of these factors differed across states, the marginal or incremental effect of each explanatory variable thus is restricted to be constant across states. Likewise, the estimated marginal or incremental effect of each explanatory variable is restricted to be constant over time, not capturing the differential effects of strategic timing considerations across states.

4. There may be an omitted variable bias, the degree of which, if any, depends on the extent of the correlation between the previously unobserved and omitted variables (the markers for ideology) and the included economic-interest variables. If there is no correlation between the omitted and the included variables, there is no omitted variable bias.

5. Voting behavior at the first North Carolina convention, which rejected the Constitution, is estimated because the second convention in North Carolina was held well after the Constitution was ratified by the other states. Votes from the second convention would be less likely to reflect true voting sentiments than would votes from the first convention. The date, order, and tally of the ratification vote in each state are listed in table 6.1.

6. The data, and their sources, for the measures of the economic and ideological interests for the seven ratifying conventions are discussed in detail in appendix 2. The measures and markers for the seven conventions are the primary ones employed in earlier chapters.

7. As discussed above and in chapter 6, two of the constituent-interest variables (the public funding credit and population) employed in the pooled samples are measured only at the state level. Consequently, there is no within-state variation in the variables across delegates and thus neither can be used for the individual state estimation. This weakens the comparison between the influence of personal-interest and constituent-interest variables on the ratification vote within an individual state convention. Also, because of the paucity of the data on constituent interests and the absence of the markers for personal ideology, no formal tests comparing the influence of economic interests versus ideology or comparing the role of personal versus constituent interests on the ratification vote can be conducted for all seven state conventions.

8. Each table reports the results for all seven conventions but for a different model specification, differing in terms of the variables employed to measure slaveholdings and public securities holdings. The results in tables 7.3–7.5 are reported as the marginal or incremental effect of a change in each explanatory variable on the predicted probability of a yes vote on the ratification of the Constitution, holding other factors constant. The marginal or incremental effects are calculated at the sample means of the explanatory variables. The calculations of the predicted probability from the logistic estimates, of the marginal effect of a continuous variable, and of the incremental effect of a dichotomous variable are all described in chapter 2. In cases where delegates with a particular economic interest voted unanimously, the votes are indicated by "Yes" or "No" because, as noted, the marginal

or incremental effect on voting cannot be estimated for a unanimous vote. Given that the set of delegates for which data were collected for all seven conventions is less than complete, there are several cases where the number of delegates with a particular characteristic is quite small, and unanimous voting among delegates with that characteristic was not uncommon at one of the seven conventions. The logistic coefficients, stardard errors, and goodness-of-fit statistics for the model specifications reported in tables 7.3–7.5 are reported in appendix 7 in tables A7.1–A7.3.

9. With 86 degrees of freedom, the asymptotic t-statistic for the estimated coefficient of the public security ownership variable is 1.468, for a computed P-value of .1421 (see column 1, table A7.1 in appendix 7).

10. Recall that the incremental effect reported for a dichotomous variable in tables 7.3–7.5 is the difference between the predicted probability when the variable has a value of one ($\hat{P}_1$) and the predicted probability when it has a value of zero ($\hat{P}_0$). Table 7.3 reports the estimates for the model containing the dichotomous variable for ownership of any amount of public securities. Table 7.4 reports the estimates for the model containing the dichotomous variable for ownership of public securities in excess of $1,000. Table 7.5 reports the estimates for the model containing the market value of public securities owned. All predicted probabilities and other findings reported for public securities are calculated from the appropriate logistic coefficients, depending on the public securities variable in question.

11. An increase in the value of the public securities holdings of a Virginia delegate also is suggestive of a significant increase in the likelihood of voting yes. With 144 degrees of freedom, the asymptotic t-statistic for the estimated coefficient of the value of public securities is 1.573, for a computed P-value of .1158 (see column 7, table A7.3).

12. Recall that the magnitude of the impact of a continuous variable on a vote can be summarized employing its response elasticity, which is calculated as $\varepsilon_i = \beta_i \bar{X}_i (1 - \hat{P})$.

13. And in a fifth convention, Pennsylvania, the estimated coefficient of the private securities variable is statistically significant, or nearly so, and positive in two of the three specifications (see tables 7.1 and 7.2). For the specification reported in table 7.2, with 51 degrees of freedom, the asymptotic t-statistic for the estimated coefficient of the private securities variable is 1.572, for a computed P-value of .1160 (see column 5, table A7.2).

14. The variables that measure slave ownership are included only for Pennsylvania and the three southern conventions. The model specifications in tables 7.3 and 7.4 both contain the dichotomous variable for ownership of any amount of slaves. The model specification in table 7.5 contains the variable that measures the value of slaves owned. The predicted probabilities and other findings reported for slave interests are from either table 7.3 or 7.5, depending on the slave variable in question.

15. See Beard (1913 [1935]), Nadelhaft (1981), Main (1961), and Risjord (1974, 1978) for studies that conclude slaveowning delegates voted to ratify and McDonald (1958), Pool (1950a,b), and Thomas (1953) for studies that conclude there were no patterns in the vote related to slaveholdings. Recall once again that the existing ratification studies are referring to the *overall* ratification vote of the majority of slaveowners, not the *partial* effect of the ownership of slaves per se on the probability of favoring ratification, as in this book.

16. Compare table 7.5 to tables 7.3 and 7.4. Despite no significant effect on the predicted probability of voting for ratification in the North Carolina

convention of owning slaves per se, the *value* of slaveholdings for a North Carolina delegate actually had a statistically significant positive effect, a result contrary to expectations. Nonetheless, the finding should be viewed with some caution given the preliminary nature of the estimates for the seven ratifying conventions. And as argued in chapter 6 for the overall ratification, the general lack of statistical significance for the value of slaveholdings may be explained by the large variance in the value of total assets among slaveowning delegates. In an attempt to account for this, a very rough measure of the value of a delegate's total assets was estimated and an asset share variable for the value of slaveholdings and an instrumental variable as an alternative for the slave share variable were constructed. Substituting these variables for the value of slaveholdings in chapter 6 produced negative and significant coefficients: Delegates with a relatively large share of their assets in the form of slaves appear to have been less likely to have voted for the Constitution. As the asset share and instrumental variables are based on very rough estimates of a delegate's total asset values, the empirical results employing the variables are tenuous at best. The estimated results with the share and instrumental slave variables are discussed in chapter 6. Details concerning the computation of the share and instrumental slave variables are contained in appendix 2.

17. For the South Carolina convention, with 159 degrees of freedom, the asymptotic t-statistics for the estimated coefficients of the constituent English ancestry variables in the three specifications are 1.456, 1.513, and 1.347, respectively; yielding computed P-values of .1454, .1302, and .1782, respectively (see column 6, tables A7.1–A7.3).

18. The coefficient of variation, a measure of the relative dispersion in the variable, is the sample standard deviation divided by the sample mean. See the sample means and standard deviations reported in table 7.2. The specific elasticity estimates for the percentage of families of English ancestry discussed here are calculated from the model specification in table 7.3.

19. An analogous issue in a principal-agent framework is to determine the magnitude of the influence of personal interests versus constituent interests. Employing J-tests to address the issue would involve specifying two additional rival voting models: $V_{ij} = h(\text{PE}_i, \text{PI}_i)$ and $V_{ij} = h^*(\text{CE}_j, \text{CI}_j)$. The application of J-tests for these two models ideally would permit a determination of the relative importance of personal versus constituent interests. The data, however, do not permit the personal versus constituent interest issue at the three ratifying conventions to be addressed adequately because data for constituent interests at the county or township level within the individual states are too limited. Construction of the formal test statistic for the J-tests is described in chapter 5, note 15.

20. The names of all the delegates for whom data were collected for the three ratifying conventions are listed in table A7.22 in appendix 7. The table also lists for each delegate his actual vote on ratification and the estimated predicted probability of a yes vote based on the delegate's specific economic and other interests. The findings for the predicted voting probabilities are discussed later in this chapter.

21. The data, and their sources, for the measures of the economic and ideological interests for the three ratifying conventions are discussed in detail in appendix 2.

22. Admittedly, this may be a rather poor measure of ambitions for future public office. Actual public offices or appointments held after a delegate's convention cannot possibly capture the ambitions of any delegate that attempted to

seek office but failed to win election or appointment. However, there is no other measure of the delegates' ambitions for future public offices that is quantifiable and can be employed in a statistical analysis.

23. The estimated logistic coefficients, standard errors, and goodness-of-fit statistics for the model specifications that contain the various combinations of the prior and future political-experience variables are reported in tables A7.4–A7.12 in appendix 7. Tables A7.4–A7.6 contain the logistic estimates for model specifications that include, for the political variables, the six political-experience variables that measure whether a delegate was a local, state, or national officeholder *before* his ratifying convention, or a local, state, or national officeholder (or appointee) *after* his ratifying convention. Tables A7.7–A7.9 contain the logistic estimates for model specifications that include the three variables that measure whether a delegate was a local, state, or national officeholder *before* his ratifying convention. Tables A7.10–A7.12 contain the logistic estimates for model specifications that include the three variables that measure whether a delegate was a local, state, or national officeholder (or appointee) *after* his ratifying convention. (For the estimates for membership in the Continental Congress for the Virginia convention, see specifications 2 and 3 in tables A7.6 and A7.9, respectively.) The estimates contained in tables A7.4–A7.12 should be compared to those in tables A7.13–A7.15, which contain the logistic coefficients, standard errors, and goodness-of-fit statistics for the model specifications that *exclude* all political-experience variables—the model specifications for which the incremental and marginal effects are reported in tables 7.8, 7.10, and 7.12 in the text. The alternative model specifications reported in each table of tables A7.4–A7.15 differ in terms of the measure of each delegate's slaveholdings and public securities holdings employed in the voting model.

24. The specific estimates and predicted probabilities discussed in the text for Massachusetts are calculated from specification 2 in table 7.8, unless otherwise noted. The estimated effects of the explanatory variables generally are similar in magnitude for all model specifications. The alternative specifications reported in table 7.8 differ in terms of the measure employed in the model of the slave and public securities holdings of each delegate. As noted above, the estimated logistic coefficients for the model specifications reported in table 7.8 are contained in table A7.13. The preliminary estimates reported earlier in this chapter for the variables initially available for Massachusetts, based on an incomplete voting model with fewer data, are strikingly similar to the present estimates for Massachusetts, which are based on the complete voting model with substantially better data for 43 percent more delegates. This suggests that the findings for Massachusetts are fairly robust.

25. The percentage effects reported in the text for the dichotomous variables are calculated as the difference between the predicted probabilities of a yes vote reported in table 7.9 when the dichotomous variable has a value of 1 and when it has a value of 0, expressed as a percentage of the predicted probability when it has a value of 0.

26. Because there are only six slaveowners in the Massachusetts delegate sample, the estimated specifications reported in table 7.8 (and, as a result, the predicted probabilities reported in table 7.9) do not include the variable that measures whether a delegate was a slaveowner. Findings for alternative specifications that include the slaveowner variable, however, indicate that owning any amount of slaves *increased* the likelihood of voting for ratification in Massachusetts.

The alternative specifications of the voting model for Massachusetts, with the slaveowner variable included, are reported in table A7.16 in appendix 7 (see specifications 2 and 3).

27. In estimated alternative model specifications not reported, the coefficient of the Episcopalian/Anglican variable was never significant either.

28. See the discussion of the data for the Massachusetts convention in appendix 2.

29. Substituting distance from the Atlantic coast for distance to navigable water yields essentially the same results for the ratification vote in Massachusetts. The results employing distance from the Atlantic coast for two alternative specifications of the voting model for Massachusetts are reported in table A7.16 (see specifications 1 and 4).

30. Several studies in the literature also conclude that Massachusetts delegates from areas closer to navigable water or the coast were more likely to have favored the Constitution. See Gillespie (1989), Hall (1972), Main (1961), and Rutland (1966).

31. The specific estimates and predicted probabilities discussed in the text for North Carolina are calculated from specification 2 in table 7.10, unless otherwise noted. The alternative model specifications reported in table 7.10, whose findings are similar, differ in terms of the measure employed in the model of the slave and public securities holdings of each delegate. As noted above, the estimated logistic coefficients for the model specifications reported in table 7.10 are contained in table A7.14.

32. For a discussion of the monetary environment in the United States prior to 1787 and the benefits of the monetary union created by the Constitution, see Rolnick, Smith, and Weber (1994).

33. The asymptotic t-statistics for the estimated coefficients of the officer variable in the three model specifications reported in table A7.14 are 1.455 (P-value = .1458), 1.435 (P-value = .1512), and 1.321 (P-value = .1864) (see specifications 1–3, respectively).

34. Substituting distance from the Atlantic coast for distance to navigable water yields essentially the same results for the ratification vote in North Carolina. The results employing distance from the Atlantic coast for two alternative specifications of the voting model are reported in table A7.17 in appendix 7 (see specifications 1 and 4).

35. The expectations of slaveowners about the effects of ratification on slavery refer to the expected effects of the Constitution on owning slaves per se, taking into account and controlling for the effects of the Constitution on all other economic interests of slaveowners. Because of the expected effects of the Constitution on other assets and interests, any specific delegate who represented slaveowners or who personally owned slaves may have actually favored ratification. Regardless, during ratification, the fears on the part of the slaveowning delegates, and those who represented slave areas, about potential future negative restrictions on slavery and the use of slaves are unambiguous. See Elliot (1836 [1888], vol. 3, pp. 452–458, 589–590, 598–599, 621–623; vol. 4, pp. 30–32, 100–102, 176–178, 271–274). For their fears about the expected negative effects of potential future navigation acts, see Elliot (1836 [1888], vol. 3, p. 621; vol. 4, pp. 271–274, 298, 308–311).

36. The specific estimates and predicted probabilities discussed in the text for Virginia are calculated for specification 2 in table 7.12, unless otherwise noted. The alternative model specifications reported in table 7.12 differ in terms of the

measure of the slave and public securities holdings of each delegate employed in the model. The estimated effects are generally similar for all model specifications. As noted above, the estimated logistic coefficients for the model specifications reported in table 7.12 are contained in table A7.15.

37. The asymptotic t-statistic for the estimated coefficient of the variable measuring ownership of public securities is 1.330 (P-value = .1835); it is 1.352 (P-value = .1762) for the estimated coefficient of the variable measuring the value of public securities holdings. See specifications 1 and 3, respectively, in table A7.15.

38. The estimated coefficients for the merchant variable, however, hint at a possible negative relationship between the variable and the ratification vote. For the three model specifications reported in table A7.15, the asymptotic t-statistics for the estimated merchant coefficients are 1.305 (P-value = .1919), 1.413 (P-value = .1582), and 1.345 (P-value = .1787). See specifications 1–3, respectively, in table A7.15.

39. The results for two alternative specifications of the voting model that include the variable measuring membership in the Continental Congress and delete the variable measuring personal Scottish/Irish ancestry are nearly identical, except that the Continental Congress variable, as noted above, is significant, or nearly so, and negative in the two specifications. These results are reported in table A7.18 in appendix 7 (see specifications 2 and 3).

40. Substituting distance from the Atlantic coast for distance to navigable water yields very similar results for the ratification vote in Virginia. The results employing distance from the Atlantic coast for two alternative specifications of the voting model are reported in table A7.18 (see specifications 1 and 4).

41. Similar to the findings for Massachusetts and North Carolina, the estimates reported above for the variables initially available for Virginia, based on an incomplete voting model with fewer data, are strikingly similar to the new estimates for Virginia, which are based on the complete voting model with substantially better data for 7 percent more delegates. This suggests that the findings for Virginia also are fairly robust.

42. For the financial and monetary environment in the nation overall during the 1770s and 1780s, see Ferguson (1961) and Riesman (1989). For Massachusetts, see Ferguson (1961) and McCusker (1978). For North Carolina, see Morrill (1969). For Virginia, see Ernst (1973), Brock (1975), and Schweitzer (1989a).

43. It is worth noting that the preliminary estimates reported above for Virginia that were based on the incomplete voting model with fewer data indicate a very similar effect for large public securities holdings. The earlier estimate that public securities holdings in excess of $1,000 increased the predicted probability of voting for ratification from .512 to .822 (a 60.5 percent increase) compares favorably to the present estimate of an increase in the predicted probability of a yes vote from .456 to .854 (an 87 percent increase).

44. See the discussion of the findings for the share and the instrumental variables in chapter 6.

45. Compare the estimated effects for the "average" Massachusetts delegate under specification 2 in table 7.8 with those reported in the first column of table A7.20.

46. See the second column of table A7.20. The estimated effects for the "average" slaveowner reported in the second column can be compared directly to the effects for the "average" delegate reported in the first column.

47. For purposes of comparison, the estimated effects for the "average"

Massachusetts public securities owner for the alternative specification that includes the slaveowner variable are reported in the third column of table A7.20. A comparison with the effects reported in the first column of table A7.21 suggests that the findings for the "average" Massachusetts public securities owner are quite robust, as both sets of estimates are nearly indentical.

Epilogue

1. McDonald's (1958, pp. 121–123) income estimates are based on income tax assessments in Delaware, which were unusual for the 1780s. Delaware in fact is the only state ratifying convention for which McDonald includes estimates of the delegates' income.

2. At the time of McDonald's (1958) study, the modern estimates of income on the eve of the Revolution, of course, did not exist.

3. Most general discussions of the subject give little credence to economic explanations of the founders' behavior (see, e.g., the textbooks cited in chapter 2). The major exceptions are Atack and Passel (1994) and Wilson and DiIulio (1995).

References

Abbot, William W. (1957), "The Structure of Politics in Georgia: 1782–1789," *William and Mary Quarterly* 14: 47–65.

Ackerman, Bruce (1991), *We the People: Foundations*, Vol. 1, Cambridge: The Belknap Press of Harvard University Press.

Alchian, Armen, and Harold Demsetz (1972), "Production, Information Costs, and Economic Organization," *American Economic Review* 62: 777–795.

Appleton's Cyclopdia of American Biography (1888–1889), New York: D. Appleton and Company.

Atack, Jeremy, and Peter Passell (1994), *A New Economic View of American History* (2nd edition), New York: W. W. Norton and Company.

Bailyn, Bernard (1967), *The Ideological Origins of the American Revolution*, Cambridge: Harvard University Press.

Bailyn, Bernard (1968), *The Origins of American Politics*, New York: Alfred A. Knopf.

Bailyn, Bernard (1993), *Debate on the Constitution*, New York: The Library of America.

Bancroft, George (1882), *History of the Formation of the Constitution of the United States*, Boston: Little, Brown and Company.

Banning, Lance (1989), "Virginia: Sectionalism and the General Good," in Michael Allen Gillespie and Michael Lienesch, editors, *Ratifying the Constitution*, Lawrence: University of Kansas Press: 261–299.

Barro, Robert J. (1973), "The Control of Politicians: An Economic Model," *Public Choice* 14: 19–42.

Beard, Charles A. (1913 [1935]), *An Economic Interpretation of the Constitution of the United States*, New York: Macmillan Publishing Company.

Beard, Charles A. (1915 [1943]), *The Economic Origins of Jeffersonian Democracy*, New York: The Free Press.

Beard, Charles A. (1922 [1934]), *The Economic Basis of Politics*, New York: Alfred A. Knopf.

Becker, Gary S. (1983), "A Theory of Competition among Pressure Groups for Political Influence," *Quarterly Journal of Economics* 98: 371–400.

Beeman, Richard (1987), "Introduction," in Richard Beeman, Stephen Botein, and Edward C. Carter II, editors, *Beyond Confederation: Origins of the Constitution and American National Identity*, Chapel Hill: University of North Carolina Press: 3–19.

Benson, Lee (1960), *Turner and Beard: American Historical Writing Reconsidered*, Glencoe, IL: The Free Press.

Biographical Directory of the American Congress, 1774–1961 (1961), Washington, DC: United States Government Printing Office.

Bishop, Hillman M. (1949), "Why Rhode Island Opposed the Federal Constitution: Paper Money and the Constitution," *Rhode Island History* 8: 1–10, 33–44, 85–95, 115–126.

Bjork, Gordon Carl (1963), "Stagnation and Growth in the American Economy, 1784–1792," Ph.D. dissertation, University of Washington.

Bjork, Gordon Carl (1964), "The Weaning of the American Economy: Independence, Market Changes, and Economic Development," *Journal of Economic History* 24: 541–560.

Blinkoff, Maurice (1936), "The Influence of Charles A. Beard upon American Historiography," *The University of Buffalo Studies* 12: 1–84.

Brennan, Geoffrey, and James M. Buchanan (1985), *The Reason of Rules. Constitutional Political Economy*, Cambridge: Cambridge University Press.

Brock, Leslie V. (1975), *The Currency of the American Colonies, 1700–1764: A Study in Colonial Finance and Imperial Relations*, New York: Arno Press.

Brogan, Denis W. (1965), "The Quarrel over Charles Austin Beard and the American Constitution," *Economic History Review* 18: 199–223.

Brown, Richard D. (1976), "The Founding Fathers of 1776 and 1787: A Collective View," *William and Mary Quarterly* 33: 465–480.

Brown, Robert E. (1956), *Charles Beard and the Constitution: A Critical Analysis of an Economic Interpretation of the Constitution*, Princeton, NJ: Princeton University Press.

Bruchey, Stuart (1962), "The Forces Behind the Constitution: A Critical Review of the Framework of E. James Ferguson's *The Power of the Purse*," *William and Mary Quarterly* 19: 429–438.

Brunhouse, Robert L. (1942), *The Counter-Revolution in Pennsylvania, 1776–1790*, Harrisburg: Pennsylvania Historical Commission.

Buchanan, James M. (1975), *The Limits of Liberty: Between Anarchy and Leviathan*, Chicago: University of Chicago Press.

Buchanan, James M. (1990), "The Domain of Constitutional Economics," *Constitutional Political Economy* 1: 1–18.

Buchanan, James M. (1991a), "From Private Preferences to Public Philosophy: The Development of Public Choice," Chap. 3 in James M. Buchanan, editor, *Constitutional Economics*, Oxford: Blackwell.

Buchanan, James M. (1991b), "Interests and Theories in Constitutional Choice," Chap. 5 in James M. Buchanan, editor, *The Economics and Ethics of Constitutional Order*, Ann Arbor: University of Michigan Press.

Buchanan, James M., and Gordon Tullock (1962), *The Calculus of Consent: Logical Foundations of Constitutional Democracy*, Ann Arbor: University of Michigan Press.

Buchanan, James M., and Viktor Vanberg (1989), "A Theory of Leadership and Deference in Constitutional Construction," *Public Choice* 61: 15–27.

Burnham, Walter Dean (1983), *Democracy in the Making: American Government and Politics*, Englewood Cliffs, NJ: Prentice-Hall.

Burns, James MacGregor (1963), *The Deadlock of Democracy: Four-Party Politics in America*, Englewood Cliffs, NJ: Prentice-Hall.

Burns, James MacGregor, J. W. Peltason, Thomas E. Cronin, and David B. Magleby (1998), *Government by the People* (17th edition), Upper Saddle River, NJ: Prentice-Hall.

Butler, Nicholas Murray (1939), *Building the American Nation*, New York: Charles Scribner and Sons.

Calhoun, Daniel (1979), "Continual Vision and Cosmopolitan Orthodoxy," *History and Theory* 18: 257–286.

Cappon, Lester (1976), editor, *Atlas of Early American History: The Revolutionary Era, 1760–1790*, Princeton, NJ: Princeton University Press.

Chase, Harold, Samuel Krislov, Keith O. Boyum, and Jerry N. Clark (1976), editors, *Biographical Dictionary of the Federal Judiciary*, Detroit: Gale Research Company.

Coates, Dennis, and Michael Munger (1995), "Legislative Voting and the Economic Theory of Politics," *Southern Economic Journal* 61: 861–872.

Cochran, Thomas C. (1932), *New York in the Confederation: An Economic Study*, Philadelphia: University of Pennsylvania Press.

Colbourn, Trevor (1974), editor, *Fame and the Founding Fathers: Essays by Douglass Adair*, New York: W. W. Norton and Company.

Coleman, Kenneth (1958), *The American Revolution in Georgia, 1763–1789*, Athens: University of Georgia Press.

Commager, Henry Steele (1958), "The Constitution: Was It an Economic Document?" *American Heritage* 10: 58–61, 100–103.

Corwin, Edward S. (1914), "Review of Beard's *An Economic Interpretation of the Constitution*," *History Teachers Magazine* 5: 65–66.

Corwin, Edward S. (1920), *The Constitution and What It Means Today*, Princeton, NJ: Princeton University Press.

Corwin, Edward S. (1936), "The Constitution as Instrument and as Symbol," *American Political Science Review* 30: 1071–1085.

Crowl, Philip (1943), *Maryland During and After the Revolution: A Political and Economic Study*, Baltimore: Johns Hopkins University Press.

Crowl, Philip (1947), "Anti-Federalism in Maryland, 1787–1788," *William and Mary Quarterly* 4: 446–469.

Dahl, Robert A. (1956), *A Preface to Democratic Theory*, Chicago: University of Chicago Press.

Daniell, Jere R. (1970), *Experiment in Republicanism: New Hampshire Politics and the American Revolution, 1741–1794*, Cambridge: Harvard University Press.

Davidson, Russell, and James G. McKinnon (1981), "Several Tests for Model Specification in the Presence of Alternative Hypotheses," *Econometrica* 49: 781–793.

Dawson, Henry B. (1871), "The Motley Letter," Historical Magazine. 9: 157–201.

Diamond, Martin (1959), "Democracy and *The Federalist*: A Reconsideration of the Framers' Intent," *American Political Science Review* 53: 52–68.

Diamond, Martin (1975), "The Revolution of Sober Expectations," in Irving Kristol, Martin Diamond, and G. Warren Nutter, editors, *The American Revolution: Three Views*, New York: American Brands: 57–85.

Diamond, Martin (1986), "Ethics and Politics: The American Way," in Robert H. Horowitz, editor, *The Moral Foundations of the American Republic*, Charlottesville: University Press of Virginia: 75–91.

Dictionary of American Biography (1928–1936), New York: Charles Scribner and Sons.

Diggins, John P. (1981), "Power and Authority in American History: The Case of Charles A. Beard and His Critics," *American Historical Review* 86: 701–730.

Dodd, William E. (1913), "Review of Beard's *An Economic Interpretation of the Constitution*," *American Historical Review* 19: 162–163.

Dodd, William E. (1916), "Economic Interpretation of American History," *Journal of Political Economy* 24: 489–495.

Dorn, James A. (1991), "Madison's Constitutional Political Economy: Principles for a Liberal Order," *Constitutional Political Economy* 2: 163–186.

Eavey, Cheryl L., and Gary J. Miller (1989), "Constitutional Conflict in State and Nation," Chap. 13 in Bernard Grofman and Donald Wittman, editors, *The Federalist Papers and the New Institutionalism*, New York: Agathon Press.

Elkins, Stanley, and Eric McKitrick (1961), "The Founding Fathers: Young Men of the Revolution," *Political Science Quarterly* 76: 181–216.

Elliot, Jonathan (1836 [1888]), editor, *The Debates in the Several State Conventions on the Adoption of the Federal Constitution as Recommended by the General Convention at Philadelphia, in 1787*, 5 vols. Philadelphia J. B. Lippincott.

Enelow, James M., and David H. Koehler (1979), "Vote Trading in a Legislative Context: An Analysis of Cooperative and Noncooperative Strategic Voting," *Public Choice* 34: 157–175.

Ernst, Joseph A. (1973), *Money and Politics in America: 1755–1775*, Chapel Hill: University of North Carolina Press.

Faragher, John Mack, Mari Jo Buhle, Daniel Czitrom, and Susan H. Armitage (1997), *Out of Many: A History of the American People* (2nd edition), Upper Saddle River, NJ: Prentice-Hall.

Farquharson, Robin (1969), *Theory of Voting*, New Haven: Yale University Press.

Farrand, Max (1911), editor, *The Records of the Federal Convention of 1787*, 3 vols., New Haven: Yale University Press.

Faulkner, Harold Underwood (1924 [1960]), *American Economic History*, New York: Harper and Row.

The Federalist: A Commentary on the Constitution of the United States, Being a Collection of Essays Written in Support of the Constitution Agreed Upon September 17, 1787, by the Federal Convention (1937 [1788]), New York: The Modern Library.

Ferguson, James E. (1961), *The Power of the Purse: A History of American Public Finance, 1776–1790*, Chapel Hill: University of North Carolina Press.

Ferguson, James E. (1969), "The Nationalists of 1781–83 and the Economic Interpretation of the Constitution," *Journal of American History* 56: 241–261.

Fink, Evelyn C., and William H. Riker (1989), "The Strategy of Ratification," Chap. 14 in Bernard Grofman and Donald Wittman, editors, *The Federalist Papers and the New Institutionalism*, New York: Agathon Press.

Fiske, John (1888), *The Critical Period of American History*: 1783–1789, Boston: Houghton, Mifflin and Sons.

Foote, William Henry (1966), *Sketches of Virginia, Historical and Biographical*, Richmond: John Knox Press.

Fort, Rodney, William Hallagan, Cyril Morong, and T. Stegner (1993), "The Ideological Component of Senate Voting: Different Principles or Different Principals?" *Public Choice* 76: 39–58.

Garraty, John A. (1995), *The American Nation: A History of the United States* (8th edition), New York: HarperCollins College Publishers.

Gillespie, Michael Allen (1989), "Massachusetts: Creating Consensus," in Michael Allen Gillespie and Michael Lienesch, editors, *Ratifying the Constitution*, Lawrence: University of Kansas Press: 138–167.

Gladstone, William Ewart (1878), "Kin beyond the Sea," *North American Review* 127: 179–212.

Goff, Brian L., and Kevin B. Grier (1993), "On the (Mis)Measurement of Legislator Ideology," *Public Choice* 76: 5–20.

Gohmann, Stephan F., and Robert L. Ohsfeldt (1994), "U.S. Senate Voting on Abortion Legislation: A More Direct Test for Ideological Shirking," *Research in Law and Economics* 16: 175–196.

Goldwin, Robert A., and William A. Schambra (1980), editors, *How Democratic Is the Constitution*? Washington, DC: American Enterprise Institute.

Goldwin, Robert A., and William A. Schambra (1982), editors, *How Capitalistic Is the Constitution*? Washington, DC: American Enterprise Institute.

Grier, Kevin B. (1993), "Introduction: Ideology and Representation in American Politics," *Public Choice* 76: 1–4.

Grofman, Bernard, and Donald Wittman (1989), editors, *The Federalist Papers and the New Institutionalism*, New York: Agathon Press.

Grubb, Farley (2000) "Creating the U.S. Dollar Currency Union, 1761–1811: A Quest for Monetary Stability or a Grab for Sovereignty?" Department of Economics, University of Delaware, unpublished paper (April).

Hall, Arnold B. (1913), "Review of Beard's *An Economic Interpretation of the Constitution*," *American Journal of Sociology* 19: 405–408.

Hall, Van Beck (1972), *Politics without Parties: Massachusetts, 1780–1791*, Pittsburgh: University of Pittsburgh Press.

Handlin, Oscar, and Mary Handlin (1944), "Radicals and Conservatives in Massachusetts after Independence," *New England Quarterly* 17: 343–355.

Hanushek, Eric, and John E. Jackson (1977), *Statistical Methods for Social Scientists*, New York: Academic Press.

Harding, Samuel (1896), *The Contest over the Ratification of the Federal Constitution in the State of Massachusetts*, New York: DaCapo Press.

Heitman, Francis B. (1914), *Historical Register of Officers of the Continental Army during the War of the Revolution, April 1775, to December 1983*, Washington, DC: The Rare Book Shop Publishing Company.

Higgs, Robert (1987), *Crisis and Leviathan: Critical Episodes in the Growth of American Government*, New York: Oxford University Press.

Hildreth, Richard (1849), *The History of the United State of America*, 6 vols, New York: Harper and Brothers.

Hindle, Brooke (1959), "Review of McDonald's *We the People*," *Journal of Economic History* 19: 139–140.

Hiner, Ray, and William Carrell (1968), "The Constitution of 1787: A Review of Changing Interpretations," *Social Education* 32: 13–24.

Hinich, Melvin, and Michael C. Munger (1994), *Ideology and the Theory of Political Choice*, Ann Arbor: University of Michigan Press.

Hofstader, Richard (1968), *The Progressive Historians: Turner, Beard, Parrington*, New York: Alfred A. Knopf.

Holcombe, Randall G. (1991), "Constitutions as Constraints: A Case Study of Three American Constitutions," *Constitutional Political Economy* 2: 303–328.

Holcombe, Randall G. (1992), "The Distributive Model of Government: Evidence from the Confederate Constitution," *Southern Economic Journal* 58:762–769.

Hughes, Jonathan (1983), *American Economic History*, Glenview, IL: Scott, Foresman.

Hughes, Jonathan, and Louis P. Cain (1994), *American Economic History* (4th edition), New York: HarperCollins College Publishers.

Hutson, James H. (1981), "Country, Court, and Constitution: Anti-federalism and the Historians," *William and Mary Quarterly* 38: 337–368.

Hutson, James H. (1984), "The Creation of the Constitution: Scholarship at a Standstill," *Reviews in American History* 12: 463–477.

Intercollegiate Review (1999), "The Fifty Worst (and Best) Books of the Century," 35: 3–13.

Jensen, Merrill (1964), *The Making of the American Constitution*, Princeton, NJ: Van Nostrand.

Jensen, Merrill (1976), editor, *The Documentary History of the Ratification of the Constitution*, Madison: State Historical Society of Wisconsin.

Jillson, Calvin C. (1981), "Constitution Making: Alignment and Realignment in the Federal Convention of 1787," *American Political Science Review* 75: 598–612.

Jillson, Calvin C. (1988), *Constitution Making: Conflict and Consensus in the Federal Convention of 1787*, New York: Agathon Press.

Jillson, Calvin C., and Cecil L. Eubanks (1984), "The Political Structure of Constitution Making: The Federal Convention of 1787," *American Journal of Political Science* 28: 435–458.

Jones, Alice Hanson (1977), *American Colonial Wealth: Documents and Methods*, 3 vols., New York: Arno Press.

Jones, Alice Hanson (1980), *Wealth of a Nation to Be: The American Colonies on the Eve of the Revolution*, New York: Columbia University Press.

Journal of the Convention of North-Carolina (1788), Hillsborough: North Carolina Constitutional Convention, 1788.

Kahn, Paul W. (1992), *Legitimacy and History: Self-Government in American Constitutional Theory*, New Haven: Yale University Press.

Kalt, Joseph P., and Mark A. Zupan (1984), "Capture and Ideology in the Economic Theory of Politics," *American Economic Review* 74: 279–300.

Kaminski, John P. (1983), "Antifederalism and the Perils of Homogenized History: A Review Essay," *Rhode Island History* 42: 30–37.

Kau, James B., and Paul H. Rubin (1979), "Self-Interest, Ideology, and Logrolling in Congressional Voting," *Journal of Law and Economics*, 22: 365–384.

Kau, James B., and Paul H. Rubin (1982), *Congressmen, Constituents, and Contributors: Determinants of Roll Call Voting in the House of Representatives*, Boston: Nijhoff.

Kelly, Alfred H., and Winfred A. Harbison (1970), *The American Constitution: Its Origins and Development* (4th edition), New York: W. W. Norton and Company.

Kenyon, Cecelia M. (1955), "Men of Little Faith: The Anti-Federalists on the Nature of Representative Government," *William and Mary Quarterly* 12: 3–43.

Kenyon, Cecelia M. (1966 [1985]), *The Antifederalists*, Boston: Northeastern University Press.

Klarman, Michael J. (1992), "Constitutional Fact/Constitutional Fiction: A Critique of Bruce Ackerman's Theory of Constitutional Moments," *Stanford Law Review* 44: 759–797.

Kurland, Philip B., and Ralph Lerner (1987), editors, *The Founders' Constitution*, 5 vols., Chicago: University of Chicago Press.

Latané, John H. (1913), "Review of Beard's *An Economic Interpretation of the Constitution*," *American Political Science Review* 19: 697–700.

Leamer, Edward E. (1978), *Specification Searches: Ad Hoc Inference with Nonexperimental Data*, New York: John Wiley and Sons.

Lebergott, Stanley (1984), *The Americans: An Economic Record*, New York: W. W. Norton and Company.

Levermore, Charles H. (1914), "Review of Beard's *An Economic Interpretation of the Constitution*," *American Economic Review* 4: 117–119.

Libby, Orin G. (1894), *The Geographical Distribution of the Vote of the Thirteen States on the Federal Constitution*, Madison: University of Wisconsin Press.

Lienesch, Michael (1989), "North Carolina: Preserving Rights," in Michael Allen Gillespie and Michael Lienesch, editors, *Ratifying the Constitution*, Lawrence: University of Kansas Press: 343–367.

Lowenberg, Anton D., and Ben T. Yu (1992), "Efficient Constitution Formation and Maintenance: The Role of 'Exit,'" *Constitutional Political Economy* 3: 51–72.

Lynd, Staughton (1962), *Anti-federalism in Dutchess County, New York: A Study of Democracy and Class Conflict in the Revolutionary Era*, Chicago: Loyola University Press.

Lynd, Staughton (1967), *Class Conflict, Slavery, and the United States Constitution*, New York: Bobbs-Merrill.

Maddala, G. S. (1977), *Econometrics*, New York: McGraw-Hill.

Maddala, G. S. (1983), *Limited Dependent and Qualitative Variables in Econometrics*, New York: Cambridge University Press.

Maddala, G. S. (1987), "Limited Dependent Variable Models Using Panel Data," *Journal of Human Resources* 22: 305–338.

Maddala, G. S. (1988), *Introduction to Econometrics*, New York: Macmillan Publishing Company.

Main, Jackson Turner (1960), "Charles A. Beard and the Constitution: A Critical Review of Forrest McDonald's *We the People*," *William and Mary Quarterly* 17: 86–110.

Main, Jackson Turner (1961), *The Antifederalists: Critics of the Constitution, 1781–1788*, Chapel Hill: University of North Carolina Press.

Main, Jackson Turner (1973), *Political Parties before the Constitution*, Chapel Hill: University of North Carolina Press.

Massachusetts Ratification Project: "The Great Debate of '88" (1989), Boston: Massachusetts State Archives.

Massengill, Stephen E. (1988), *North Carolina Votes on the Constitution: A Roster of Delegates to the State Ratification Conventions of 1788 and 1789*, Raleigh: Division of Archives and History, North Carolina Department of Cultural Resources.

McCorkle, Pope (1984), "The Historian as Intellectual: Charles Beard and the Constitution Reconsidered, "*American Journal of Legal History* 28: 314–363.

McCormick, Richard (1950), *Experiment in Independence: New Jersey in the Critical Period*, Brunswick, NJ: Rutgers University Press.

McCusker, John J. (1978), *Money and Exchange in Europe and America, 1600–1775: A Handbook*, Chapel Hill: University of North Carolina Press.

McCusker, John J., and Russell R. Menard (1985), *The Economy of British America*, Chapel Hill: University of North Carolina Press.

McDonald, Forrest (1958), *We the People: The Economic Origins of the Constitution*, Chicago: University of Chicago Press.

McDonald, Forrest (1963), "The Anti-Federalists, 1781–1789," *Wisconsin Magazine of History* 46: 206–214.

McDonald, Forrest (1965), *E Pluribus Unum: The Formulation of the American Republic, 1776–1790*, Boston: Houghton-Mifflin.

McDonald, Forrest (1985), *Novus Ordo Seclorum: The Intellectual Origins of the Constitution*, Lawrence: University of Kansas Press.

McGuire, Robert A. (1988), "Constitution Making: A Rational Choice Model of the Federal Convention of 1787," *American Journal of Political Science* 32: 483–522.

McGuire, Robert A., and Robert L. Ohsfeldt (1984), "Economic Interests and the American Constitution: A Quantitative Rehabilitation of Charles A. Beard," *Journal of Economic History* 44: 509–519.

McGuire, Robert A., and Robert L. Ohsfeldt (1986), "An Economic Model of Voting Behavior over Specific Issues at the Constitutional Convention of 1787," *Journal of Economic History* 46: 79-111.

McGuire, Robert A., and Robert L. Ohsfeldt (1989a), "Self-Interest, Agency Theory, and Political Voting Behavior: The Ratification of the United States Constitution," *American Economic Review* 79: 219-234.

McGuire, Robert A., and Robert L. Ohsfeldt (1989b), "Public Choice Analysis and the Ratification of the Constitution," Chap. 12 in Bernard Grofman and Donald Wittman, editors, *The Federalist Papers and the New Institutionalism*, New York: Agathon Press.

McGuire, Robert A., and Robert L. Ohsfeldt (1997), "Constitutional Economics and the American Founding," *Research in Law and Economics* 18: 143–171.

Mizon, Grayham E., and Jean-Francois Richard (1986), "The Encompassing Principle and Its Application to Testing Non-nested Hypotheses," *Econometrica* 54: 657–678.

Morrill, James R. (1969), *The Practice and Politics of Fiat Finance: North Carolina in the Confederation*, Chapel Hill: University of North Carolina Press.

Mueller, Dennis C. (1989), *Public Choice II*, New York: Cambridge University Press.

Nadelhaft, Jerome J. (1981), *The Disorders of War: The Revolution in South Carolina*, Orono: University of Maine at Orono Press.

Nash, Gary B., Julie Roy Jeffrey, John R. Howe, Peter J. Frederick, Allen F. Davis, and Allan M. Winkler (1994), *The American People: Creating a Nation and a Society* (3rd edition), New York: HarperCollins College Publishers.

National Cyclopedia of American Biography (1891–1950), New York: James T. White and Company.

Nettles, Curtis P. (1962), *The Emergence of a National Economy, 1775–1815*, New York: Holt, Rinehart, and Winston.

North, Douglass C. (1981), *Structure and Change in Economic History*, New York: Norton.

North, Douglass C. (1990), *Institutions, Institutional Change and Economic Performance*, New York: Cambridge University Press.

O'Connor, Karen, and Larry J. Sabato (1993), *American Government: Roots and Reform*, New York: Macmillan Publishing Company.

Peltzman, Sam (1976), "Toward a More General Theory of Regulation," *Journal of Law and Economics* 19: 211–240.

Peltzman, Sam (1984), "Constituent Interest and Congressional Voting," *Journal of Law and Economics* 27: 181–210.

Peltzman, Sam (1985), "An Economic Interpretation of the History of Congressional Voting in the Twentieth Century," *American Economic Review* 75: 656–675.

Polishook, Irwin H. (1961), *Rhode Island and the Union 1774–1795*, Evanston, IL: Northwestern University.

Pool, William C. (1950a), "An Economic Interpretation of the Ratification of the Federal Constitution in North Carolina, Part I," *North Carolina Historical Review* 27: 119–141.

Pool, William C. (1950b), "An Economic Interpretation of the Ratification of the Federal Constitution in North Carolina, Part II," *North Carolina Historical Review* 27: 289–313.

Poole, Keith T., and Howard Rosenthal (1997), *Congress: A Political-Economic History of Roll Call Voting*, New York: Oxford University Press.

Poulson, Barry W. (1981), *Economic History of the United States*, New York: Macmillan Publishing Company.

Powell, William S. (1979–1996), editor, *Dictionary of North Carolina Biography*, Vols. 1–6, Chapel Hill: University of North Carolina Press.

Prewitt, Kenneth, and Sidney Verba (1983), *An Introduction to American Government* (4th edition), New York: Harper and Row.

Puth, Robert C. (1988), *American Economic History* (2nd edition), New York: The Dryden Press.

Rakove, Jack N. (1996), *Original Meanings: Politics and Ideas in the Making of the Constitution*, New York: Alfred A. Knopf.

Ratner, Sidney, James H. Soltow, and Richard Sylla (1993), *The Evolution of the American Economy: Growth, Welfare, and Decision Making* (2nd edition), New York: Macmillan Publishing Company.

Rawls, John A. (1971), *A Theory of Justice*, Cambridge: Harvard University Press.

Reluctant Ratifiers: Virginia Considers the Federal Constitution (1988), Richmond: Virginia Historical Society.

Riesman, Janet A. (1987), "Money, Credit, and Federalist Political Economy," in Richard Beeman, Stephen Botein, and Edward C. Carter II, editors, *Beyond Confederation: Origins of the Constitution and American National Identity*, Chapel Hill: University of North Carolina Press: 128–161.

Riker, William H. (1979), "The Verification of Scientific Generalizations by Historical Case Studies: The Genesis of the American Constitution." Presented at the annual meeting of the Social Science History Association, Cambridge, MA.

Riker, William H. (1984), "The Heresthetics of Constitution-Making: The Presidency in 1787, with Comments on Determinism and Rational Choice," *American Political Science Review* 78: 1–16.

Riker, William H. (1987a), "The Lessons of 1787," *Public Choice* 55: 5–34.

Riker, William H. (1987b), *The Development of American Federalism*, Boston: Kluwer Academic Publisher.

Riker, William H. (1991), "Why Negative Campaigning Is Rational: The Rhetoric of the Ratification Campaign of 1787–1788," *Studies in American Political Development* 5: 224–283.

Risjord, Norman K. (1974), "Virginians and the Constitution: A Multivariant Analysis," *William and Mary Quarterly* 31: 613–632.

Risjord, Norman K. (1978), *Chesapeake Politics 1781–1800*, New York: Columbia University Press.

Roche, John P. (1961), "The Founding Fathers: A Reform Caucus in Action," *American Political Science Review* 55: 799–816.

Rolnick, Arthur J., Bruce D. Smith, and Warren E. Weber (1994), "The Origins of the Monetary Union in the United States," in Pierre L. Siklos, editor, *Varieties of Monetary Reforms: Lessons and Experiences on the Road to Monetary Union*, Dordrecht: Kluwer Academic: 323–349.

Rossiter, Clinton (1966), *1787: The Grand Convention*, New York: Macmillan Publishing Company.

Rosters of Soldiers from North Carolina in the American Revolution (1972), Baltimore, MD: Genealogical Publishing Company.

Rutland, Robert Allen (1966), *The Ordeal of the Constitution: The Antifederalists and the Ratification Struggle of 1787–1788*, Norman: University of Oklahoma Press.

Schuyler, Robert Livingston (1961), "Forrest McDonald's Critique of the Beard Thesis," *Journal of Southern History* 27: 73–80.

Schweitzer, Mary M. (1989a), "A New Look at Economic Causes of the Constitution: Monetary and Trade Policy in Maryland, Pennsylvania, and Virginia," *The Social Science Journal* 26: 15–26.

Schweitzer, Mary M. (1989b), "State-Issued Currency and the Ratification of the U.S. Constitution," *Journal of Economic History* 49: 311–322.

Shepherd, James F., and Gary M. Walton (1976), "Economic Change after the American Revolution: Pre- and Post-war Comparisons of Maritime Shipping and Trade," *Explorations in Economic History* 13: 397–422.

Shepsle, Kenneth A., and Barry R. Weingast (1984), "Uncovered Sets and Sophisticated Voting Outcomes with Implications for Agenda Institutions," *American Journal of Political Science* 28: 49–74.

Smith, C. Page (1958), "Review of McDonald's *We the People*," *Mississippi Valley Historical Review* 45: 493–495.

Smith, J. Allen (1907), *The Spirit of American Government*, New York: Macmillan Publishing Company.

Smith, Marlene A., and G. S. Maddala (1983), "Multiple Model Testing for Nonnested Heteroskedastic Censored Regression Models," *Journal of Econometrics* 21: 71–82.

Sobel, Robert (1990), editor, *Biographical Directory of the United States Executive Branch, 1774–1989*, New York: Greenwood Press.

Spaulding, E. Wilder (1932), *New York in the Critical Period: 1783–1789*, New York: Columbia University Press.

Stigler, George J. (1971), "The Theory of Economic Regulation," *Bell Journal of Economics* 2: 3–21.

Storing, Herbert J. (1981), *The Complete Anti-Federalist*, Vols. 1–7, Chicago: University of Chicago Press.

Sunstein, Cass R. (1984), "Naked Preferences and the Constitution," *Columbia Law Review* 84: 1689–1732.

Sunstein, Cass R. (1985), "Interests Groups in American Public Law," *Stanford Law Review* 29: 29–87.

Sunstein, Cass R. (1988–1989), "Beyond the Republican Revival," *Yale Law Journal* 97: 1539–1590.

Taft, William Howard (1913), *Popular Government*, New Haven: Yale University Press.

Tate, Thaddeus (1959), "Review of McDonald's *We the People*," *William and Mary Quarterly* 16: 418–420.

Thomas, Robert E. (1952), "A Re-appraisal of Charles A. Beard's *An Economic Interpretation of the Constitution of the United States*,'" *American Historical Review* 57: 370–375.

Thomas, Robert E. (1953), "The Virginia Convention of 1788," *Journal of Southern History* 19: 63–72.

Tollison, Robert (1982), "Rent Seeking: A Survey," *Kyklos* 35: 575–602.

Train, Kenneth (1986), *Qualitative Choice Analysis*, Cambridge: The MIT Press.

United States Department of Commerce, Bureau of Census (1969), *A Century of Population Growth*, New York: Reprinted by Geneological Publishing Company.

United States Department of Commerce, Bureau of Census (1975), *Historical Statistics of the United States: Colonial Times to 1970*, Washington, DC: Government Printing Office.

Walker, Francis A. (1895), *The Making of the Nation, 1783–1817*, New York: Charles Scribner and Sons.

Walton, Gary M., and Hugh Rockoff (1998), *History of the American Economy* (8th edition), New York: The Dryden Press.

Walton, Gary M., and James F. Shepherd (1979), *The Economic Rise of Early America*, New York: Cambridge University Press.

Warren, Charles (1928 [1937]), *The Making of the Constitution*, Boston: Little Brown.

Welch, Susan, and John G. Peters (1983), "Private Interests and Public Interests: An Analysis of the Impact of Personal Finance on Congressional Voting on Agricultural Issues," *Journal of Politics* 45: 378–396.

Williams, William (1957), "Review of Brown's *Charles Beard and the Constitution*," *William and Mary Quarterly* 14: 442–448.

Wilson, James Q., and John J. DiIulio, Jr. (1995), *American Government* (interactive edition), New York: D. C. Heath and Company.

Wilson, Woodrow (1902), *A History of the American People*, Vols. 1–5, New York: Harper and Brothers.

Wood, Gordon S. (1969), *The Creation of the American Republic 1776–1787*, Chapel Hill: University of North Carolina Press.

Wood, Gordon S. (1980), "Democracy and the Constitution," in Robert A. Goldwin and William A. Schambra, editors, *How Democratic Is the Constitution?* Washington, DC: American Enterprise Institute: 1–17.

Wood, Gordon S. (1987), "Interests and Disinterestedness in the Making of the Constitution," in Richard Beeman, Stephen Botein, and Edward C. Carter II, editors, *Beyond Confederation: Origins of the Constitution and American National Identity*, Chapel Hill: University of North Carolina Press: 69–109.

Index